*American Indian Sovereignty
and the U.S. Supreme Court*

American Indian Sovereignty and the U.S. Supreme Court

THE
MASKING
OF JUSTICE

DAVID E. WILKINS

UNIVERSITY OF TEXAS PRESS
Austin

Parts of this book that were published in earlier versions are listed in the
Acknowledgments.

Requests for permission to reproduce material from this work should be sent to
Permissions, University of Texas Press, Box 7819, Austin, TX 78713-7819.

∞ The paper used in this publication meets the minimum requirements of
American National Standard for Information Sciences—Permanence of Paper for
Printed Library Materials, ANSI Z39.48-1984.

LIBRARY OF CONGRESS CATALOGING-IN-PUBLICATION DATA

Wilkins, David E. (David Eugene), 1954–
    American Indian sovereignty and the U.S. Supreme Court : the
masking of justice / David E. Wilkins.
        p.   cm.
    Includes bibliographical references and index.
    ISBN 0-292-79108-9 (cl : alk. paper). — ISBN 0-292-79109-7 (paper :
alk. paper)
        1. Indians of North America—Legal status, laws, etc.   2. United
States. Supreme Court.   3. Justice, Administration of—United
States.   I. Title.
KF8205.W527
342.73'0872—dc21   97-1988

Contents

Preface

> There is nothing in the whole compass of our laws so anomalous, so hard to bring within any precise definition, or any logical and scientific arrangement of principles, as the relation in which the Indians stand toward this [United States] government and those of the states.
>
> —U.S. Attorney General Hugh Swinton Legare [1]

> It is argued, because the Indians seek the courts of Kansas for the preservation of rights and the redress of wrongs, sometimes voluntarily, and in certain specified cases by direction of the Secretary of the Interior, that they submit themselves to all the laws of the State. *But the conduct of Indians is not to be measured by the same standard which we apply to the conduct of other people.* (emphasis mine)
>
> —*The Kansas Indians* [2]

In the fall of 1993, I attended a conference at the National Science Foundation in Washington, D.C. On Saturday, following the conference doings, my friends Rudy Coronado Jr. and John Archuleta and I set out to visit as many of the massive and inspiring architectural structures as possible.

Leaving the National Archives Building, we walked by the Department of Justice. On its west side, high above the street, was inscribed the following passage: "Justice is the great interest of man on earth; wherever her temples stand there is a foundation for social security, general happiness, and the improvement and progress of our race." I was bemused by this statement, particularly the reference to "our race."

When I returned to Boulder, I immediately began making inquiries about the Justice Department's quote. I soon found that the quotation is an abridged version of an eloquent testimonial given by Daniel Webster in honor of Joseph Story, a justice of the Supreme Court who died December 12, 1851. This is Webster's complete statement:

Justice, sir, is the great interest of man on earth. It is the ligament which holds civilized beings and civilized nations together. Wherever her temple stands, and so long as it is duly honored, there is a foundation for social security, general happiness, and the improvement and progress of *our race*.[3] (emphasis mine)

This unabridged version is certainly more grammatically correct, and knowing its date of origin, 1851, enabled me to better comprehend the meaning behind the phrase "our race." Although Webster would probably have excused himself by saying he was referring to the "human race," the dictionary definition of *race* emphasizes narrowing and classifying, and there is no getting around the fact that his choice of words was unfortunate at best. I pondered why the Justice Department insisted on perpetuating this exclusionary phrase over the many years after it had first been used. Surely the more appropriate language to be used by the Justice Department would have been "the improvement and progress of humanity," since the scales of justice are considered to be color-blind. It is important to ponder the reality of why such an exclusive phrase remains inscribed on the walls of the Department of Justice. I believe every vestige of America's exclusionary past must be stricken from every corridor of government, particularly the department which is about the administration and enforcement of justice for all.

In the study that follows, details are presented in which the United States government and, in particular, the Supreme Court have been unable and, in some cases, almost unwilling to cast away a battery of disparaging and debilitating phrases that have limited or terminated the rights of indigenous peoples as distinctive groups. This is not a comforting thought because of the Supreme Court's unique role as the preeminent institution vested with the authority of deciding the "finality of rational principles."[4] This is so, said Thurmond Arnold, because law concerns the "spiritual welfare of the people" and is preserved in their form of government. And, in spiritual things, said Arnold, "it is essential that men do right according to some final authority."[5] Arnold believed it was faith in a higher law that enabled the Supreme Court to function effectively as the branch of government most responsible for maintaining social stability.[6]

But, as this study reveals, "the law" as developed, articulated, and manipulated by the High Court has actually contributed to the diminution of the sovereign status of tribes and has placed tribes and their citizens/members in a virtually destabilized state. Beginning, most intensely, with

Johnson v. McIntosh in 1823, we will consider fifteen important Indian law decisions, concluding with the 1992 decision, *County of Yakima v. Confederated Tribes and Bands of the Yakima Nation.*

While this book covers a wide span of time, it is not a history per se. The book's already inordinate length precludes an in-depth historical analysis of the nearly two hundred years this study examines. Thus, readers looking for significant historical detail of the many important policies and personalities of the eras these cases arose in are encouraged to consult other accounts which expand on these matters. Several worthwhile books, all of which are given in my reference section, trace the ambivalent attitudes and policies of the U.S. government toward tribal nations—see, for example, Roy Harvey Pearce, *Savagism and Civilization: A Study of the Indian and the American Mind* (1953); Wilcomb E. Washburn, ed., *The American Indian and the United States: A Documentary History*, 4 vols. (1973); Angie Debo, *A History of the Indians of the United States* (1970); Robert Berkhofer Jr., *The White Man's Indian: Images of the American Indian from Columbus to the Present* (1978); Francis P. Prucha, *The Great Father: The United States Government and the American Indian*, 2 vols. (1984); Calvin Martin, ed., *The American Indian and the Problem of History* (1987); Robert A. Williams Jr., *The American Indian in Western Legal Thought* (1990); and Albert Hurtado and Peter Iverson, eds., *Major Problems in American Indian History: Documents and Essays* (1994).

Readers interested in specific Indian policy periods have a plethora of quality studies to choose from. For the Indian removal era (early 1800s to 1840s), consult Grant Foreman's two classic studies, *Indian Removal: The Emigration of the Five Civilized Tribes of Indians* (1932) and *The Last Trek of the Indians* (1946), and see Jill Norgren's *The Cherokee Cases: The Confrontation of Law and Politics* (1996).

There are a number of solid treatments of the allotment and assimilation eras (1860s–1920s)—see, for example, Frederick E. Hoxie, *A Final Promise: The Campaign to Assimilate the Indian, 1880–1920* (1984); and Janet McDonnell, *The Dispossession of the American Indian: 1887–1934* (1934).

The critically important New Deal era of the 1930s is covered thoroughly in Lawrence C. Kelly's *The Assault on Assimilation: John Collier and the Origins of Indian Policy Reform* (1983); Vine Deloria Jr. and Clifford M. Lytle, *The Nations Within: The Past and Future of American Indian Sovereignty* (1984); and Thomas Biolsi, *Organizing the Lakota: The Political Economy of the New Deal on the Pine Ridge and Rosebud Reservations* (1992).

The 1950s entailed the disastrous termination policy in which the federal government systematically attempted to sever the unique political relationship between itself and various indigenous groups. This policy has been ably examined by Larry W. Burt, *Tribalism in Crisis: Federal Indian Policy, 1953–1961* (1982); and see Nicholas C. Peroff, *Menominee Drums: Tribal Termination and Restoration, 1954–1974* (1982) for a case study of the effects of the policy on a tribal community.

The 1960s to the present have received the focus of a variety of scholars intent on explaining the federal government's shift from termination to self-determination and the eruption of indigenous activism. See Alvin M. Josephy Jr., ed., *Red Power: The American Indians' Fight for Freedom* (1971); D'Arcy McNickle, *Native American Tribalism* (1973); Stephen Cornell, *The Return of the Native: American Indian Political Resurgence* (1988); Joane Nagel, *American Indian Ethnic Renewal: Red Power and the Resurgence of Identity and Culture* (1996); and see the collective works of Vine Deloria Jr., who has written extensively on this period. Among his contributions are *Custer Died for Your Sins: An Indian Manifesto* (1969, repr. 1988); *Behind the Trail of Broken Treaties: An Indian Declaration of Independence* (1974, repr. 1985); and *American Indian Policy in the Twentieth Century* (1985).

A comment about terminology. Throughout the book several terms are used interchangeably in referring to indigenous peoples in a collective sense—tribal nations, tribes, Alaskan Natives, indigenous nations, and indigenous peoples. But I use only one when I am referring to individual indigenous persons—Indian or American Indian. Of all the terms I've mentioned, "Indian" is easily the most problematic (though some argue that the term "tribe" is also pejorative and hints strongly of colonialism), and I use it with some hesitation for two reasons: first, because of its obvious geographical inaccuracy and second, because it erroneously generalizes and completely ignores the cultural diversity evident in the hundreds of distinctive indigenous nations present in North America, each with their own name for themselves. One could thus argue that continued usage of the term attests to surviving vestiges of colonialism. Nevertheless, the term *Indian* or *American Indian* is the most common appellation used by many indigenous and nonindigenous persons and by institutions, and so it will be used in the text when no tribe is specified. (Specified tribes will be referred to with the singular collective favored by *Merriam Webster's Collegiate Dictionary* [10th ed.] for tribes as, for example, "the Cherokee.")

I have, moreover, intentionally avoided using the phrase "Native

American" because, as Matthew Snipp notes in *American Indians: The First of This Land* (1991), it "creates even greater confusion than the term it was once proposed to replace—namely, American Indian. American Indians are easily distinguished from Asian Indians by a single locational adjective, but 'Native Americans' include Hawaiian natives and the descendants of immigrants from all nations, along with American Indians, Eskimos, and Aleuts." The expressions "Native Peoples" and "Native Nations" may be less confusing, but these terms and the intriguing phrase "First Nations" are used almost exclusively by Canadian and Alaskan indigenous groups.

Finally, some readers may walk away from this book with a sense that the author is decidedly pro-Indian and anti-Supreme Court. It is certainly true that I am a firm believer in indigenous collective and individual rights; however, I am also well aware that tribal nations are not pristine or idyllic communities. Tribal nations, like all other communities, have produced their share of individuals who sometimes violate laws—both tribal and nontribal. Indian criminality, as one element of the indigenous experience, has, unfortunately, been neglected in the literature, although a few studies are available on the subject.[7]

This study, however, is focused on the U.S. Supreme Court, and while it paints a portrait of the High Court that is far from positive, it is not my intention to depict the court as an evil institution bent on the destruction of indigenous rights. On balance, when one weighs the historical and policy record, the Supreme Court, compared with the Presidency or the Congress, has the better track record of acknowledging tribal sovereignty, upholding Indian treaty rights, and construing the distinctive nature of Indian rights. But, as will be shown, when the Court has chosen to disavow indigenous rights, as it has done in most of the cases examined in this book, it has done so in a manner that has left tribal nations wondering about the actual meaning of democracy, justice, and consent.

In the first chapter and in the conclusion I note that the Court has the potential—which has sometimes been fulfilled—of being the branch of American government most likely to respect the rights of tribal nations because of its power of interpretation, its relative independence from an often-fickle electorate and the electoral process, and its status as a deliberative body. It is my hope that this study will inspire a reexamination of these particularly egregious decisions. It is in that spirit that I write.

DAVID E. WILKINS
September 1996

Acknowledgments

This study has evolved over a number of years during which, thankfully, many positive forces have contributed to its development and have directly influenced both the product and the producer. I have many to thank for their generous support, constructive criticism, and unabashed encouragement, and I hope I succeed in crediting most of these.

I am deeply indebted to the following sources for the extraordinary funding support I have received over the past several years: the Graduate College at the University of North Carolina/Chapel Hill; the Ford Foundation for two fellowships—a dissertation and a postdoctoral award; and summer support from the University of Arizona's associate vice-president for research.

The finishing touches were applied to this project during my fellowship at the Center for Advanced Study in the Behavioral Sciences at Stanford, California. Thanks to Professors Neil Smelser and Robert Scott, other colleagues, and the warm, knowledgeable, and efficient staff for providing an ideal institutional and collegial atmosphere most conducive to scholarly endeavor.

A special note of appreciation is extended to two individuals who helped me secure the funds and the time that enabled me to complete this study: Christine M. O'Brien, program supervisor of the Ford Minority Fellowship Program; and Charles A. Geoffrion, vice-president for research at the University of Arizona.

I have also been considerably aided by the professional and courteous library staffs at the Native American Rights Fund Library, the University of Colorado/Boulder's Norlin Library and Law School, and the University of Arizona's Main and Law libraries.

Special thanks to Denise Allyn, administrative associate for my home department of Political Science at the University of Arizona, and Gladys Bloedow, her counterpart at the Department of History, University of Colorado/Boulder, which hosted my sabbatical.

I owe an immeasurable debt to Patricia (Trish) Morris, my home department's word-processing specialist. She skillfully transcribed the entire dictated text of this manuscript and then, even more magically, interpreted my hopelessly unintelligible hand-written edits. She performed her tasks with talented grace and with nary a complaint.

I advance a heartfelt sense of gratitude to Theresa J. May of the University of Texas Press. She had faith in the original topic, was encouraging throughout the long publication process, and granted me several extensions to complete the book. I must also thank Jane H. Chamberlain, my editor, for a meticulous reading and critical analysis of the manuscript. Jane and the Press's assistant managing editor, Lois Rankin, worked closely with me during the critical months of the prepublication process. I am deeply grateful to Dr. James Anaya for his thoughtful critical appraisal of the manuscript in its rudimentary stages. Finally, Ms. Vivian Arviso read the entire manuscript and provided constructive criticism and many helpful suggestions.

This book also owes much to several academic colleagues: Tsianina Lomawaima (Creek), David Gibbs, Jim and Jeanne Clark, Richard Cortner, John Garcia, Tom Holm, and, especially, Clifford M. Lytle.

I would like to thank the students who have participated in my course called American Indians and the Supreme Court. Their insightful readings, thoughtful and often biting critiques of the cases, and our sometimes heated but always civil discussions on many of the Court's opinions, helped me to refine my own understanding of these pivotal cases.

Franke Wilmer, who teaches political science at Montana State University, also deserves a special thanks. Our numerous verbal, written, and cyberspace conversations over the past two years bettered important parts of this study.

I also wish to thank the following close friends (and their families) for their prayers and unflagging friendship: George Whitewolf (Monacan/Lakota), David Marshall (Cherokee/Creek), Rudolph (Rudy) Coronado Jr. (Mexican/Lumbee), and Brenda St. Germaine (Ojibwa). George Whitewolf, in particular, deserves my most sincere thanks. As my principal spiritual teacher for nearly two decades, he has helped me weather difficult episodes that might otherwise have left me listless.

I also extend my admiration to my extended family—my parents, Daniel Webster Wilkins and Thedis Ray Wilkins, and to my siblings Senowskey Wilkins, Roger Wilkins, Deborah Wilkins, Webster Wilkins, Mike Wilkins, Craig Wilkins, Leon Strickland, and Arnold Locklear. Similarly, I want to thank the family of my wife, Evelyn, who belongs to the Diné (Navajo Nation). I pay special tribute to her grandmother, Nellie Fowler, who intuitively understood this complex topic; she lived life and experienced death as a sovereign Diné person.

Finally, I thank the two personal forces who are most responsible for guiding me in this study (and beyond). First, my family, which consists of my wife, Evelyn, and our three children—Sion, Niłtooli, and Nazhone. My wife froze her own teaching career in order to devote her undivided attention to rearing and home-educating our children, sustaining our home, meeting the requests and responsibilities of her family and my own, and continuing to provide me with all the spiritual, intellectual, and emotional support that I have needed in this undertaking. I respectfully codedicate this book to the four of them.

The second force is that of my intellectual patron, Vine Deloria Jr. (Lakota), and his wife, Barbara. Vine somehow was able and, more importantly for me, was willing to read the entire manuscript. His critical and constructive comments and editing skills helped clarify the focus of this book and reduce its inordinate length. Aside from this, his unwavering support for me and my family (and my tribe, the Lumbee) over the years has enabled me to reach academic heights that would have been otherwise unattainable.

Thanks, Vine and Barbara. This book is respectfully codedicated to the two of you.

Parts of this book appeared in preliminary form elsewhere. A portion of Chapter 2 appeared as "The Cloaking of Justice: The Supreme Court's Role in the Application of Western Law to America's Indigenous People," *Wicazo Sa Review*, vol. 10, no. 1 (Spring 1994): pp. 1–13; "Who's in Charge of U.S. Indian Policy? Congress and the Supreme Court at Loggerheads over American Indian Religious Freedom," *Wicazo Sa Review*, vol. 8, no. 1 (Spring 1992): pp. 40–64; and "*Johnson v. McIntosh* Revisited: Through the Eyes of *Mitchel v. United States*," *American Indian Law Review*, vol. 19, no. 1 (July 1994). A segment of Chapter 3 appeared in "Indian Treaty Rights: Sacred Entitlements or 'Temporary Privileges'?" *American Indian Culture and Research Journal*, vol. 20, no. 1 (March 1996). Portions of Chapter 4 appeared as "Judicial 'Masks': Their Role in Defining and Redefining the Tribal-Congressional Relationship—1870–1924," in Michael K. Green, ed., *Issues in Native American Identity* (New York: Peter Lang, 1995), pp. 81–165.

I am grateful to the editors and publishers involved for permission to reprint their material.

*American Indian Sovereignty
and the U.S. Supreme Court*

Legal Masks, Legal Consciousness

Vine Deloria Jr. has vigorously insisted for years that it is impossible to understand how the coordinate branches of the United States government arrive at policy decisions regarding the constitutional and treaty rights of American Indian tribes, and individuals constituting these tribes, without total immersion in a historical context. He argues[1] that legal scholars, jurists, politicians, and bureaucrats have reduced what is inappropriately known as "federal Indian law" to such a point that "legal theories are tested not by comparison with reality, but by comparison with abstractions which idealize human rationality in order to give to events and incidents a sense of meaning which they would not otherwise enjoy."[2] The process, Deloria says, represents what Alfred N. Whitehead once termed, in a different context, "the fallacy of misplaced concreteness." This fallacy entails the assumption that familiar abstractions represent absolute reality and is linked with the belief that it is only when certain methodologies are used that truth can be discerned. Deloria argues that "federal Indian law" is the epitome of this sort of intellectual activity. "It conveys," says Deloria, "almost no significant meaning, it rarely is tangent to the world of human affairs, and it covers a multitude of historical sins with the shellac of legality."[3]

If the tribal nations of North America had been organized into a monolithic unit, as the inaccurate but persistent term "Indian" implies, it might have been possible for the federal government to develop a coherent body of legal principles and relevant doctrines to deal with them. Such was not the case then, nor is such a code even remotely possible as we come to the end of the twentieth century. Today, there are over 550 "federally acknowledged tribal entities," each of which has a unique history of cultural and political relations with the United States. (The term *federally acknowledged tribal entity* is used by the Bureau of Indian Affairs to identify the various indigenous groups which are recognized as having a political relationship with the federal government—it includes tribal nations, bands, villages, communities, and pueblos, as well as Alaskan

Inuits and Aleuts.) The quoted figure does not include state-recognized tribes, nor does it include the more than one hundred nonrecognized groups which are in the process of petitioning the federal government in the hope of securing federal recognition.

We see, then, that "federal Indian law" as a discipline having coherent and interconnected premises is wholly a myth; however, the United States Supreme Court, the institution responsible for producing much of the data cumulatively referred to as "federal Indian law," is certainly a real institution, operating with a distinctive collective consciousness unique to American governmental institutions. It is this particular institution and fifteen of its policy products—Supreme Court decisions— that will occupy my attention throughout this study.

Supreme Court cases are the epitome—the most succinct enunciation—of what is termed "the law." This phrase conveys a multitude of views, ideas, constructs, and interests. "The law" is alleged to be neutral, free of bias, and rational; in reality, of course, it is none of these. Nevertheless, the "legal scientist," Thurman Arnold's term for individuals who make their living articulating the law, "is compelled by the climate of opinion in which he finds himself to prove that an essentially irrational world is constantly approaching rationality; that a cruel world is constantly approaching kindliness; and that a changing world is really stable and enduring."[4]

In Arnold's powerful work *The Symbols of Government*, he describes the law as the "most mysterious and most occult" of the disciplines of learning[5] because the student, as well as the average person, is led to believe that "the law" entails something more than legal texts and institutional habits. Arnold describes how, despite irrefutable evidence to the contrary, people persist in believing that there are basic "principles of law" which exist independent of particular cases or specific human activity. Law exists, he says, rather because "humanity cannot find comfort without it."[6] The fundamental principles of law, according to Arnold, "do not represent what we do, but what we ought to do. The science of law is not the method which judges actually use, but the method which they ought to use."[7] The major function of these vaunted principles is to comfort us through control of society because belief in the sanctity of law is essential to the perpetuation of the dream that the United States is a perfectible society.

I intend to demythologize "the law," as expressed through the language of fifteen Supreme Court opinions that have affected Indian law, by focusing upon the broad institutional, societal, and, most important, historical effects of the Court's very political activities. These decisions have not only had a tremendous, often devastating, impact on tribal sovereign status and aboriginal land title, but they have also contributed significantly to the confusion surrounding relationships between tribal governments and the U.S. government. They have elevated congressional authority vis-à-vis tribal nations, and they have alternately reaffirmed and ignored the principle of judicial deference to the political branches. In addition, they have dismantled treaty rights, adversely affected the status of individual Indians, constricted—and in some cases eclipsed—tribal criminal jurisdiction, and seriously jeopardized the practice, nay, the very existence of Indian spiritual ways.

I have selected fifteen cases (see Appendix A), beginning with the 1823 *Johnson v. McIntosh* decision, in which the court grappled directly with the issue of indigenous property rights, and concluding with the 1992 *County of Yakima v. Yakima* decision in which the Supreme Court revived a voided federal statute to allow a county government to impose a tax on Indian lands. These cases are the most egregious examples of precedent in which the Court has applied linguistic semantics, rhetorical strategies, and other devices to disempower tribal governments and to disenfranchise individual Indians.

The Supreme Court has also handed down a host of equally powerful opinions which have affirmed the sovereign or semisovereign status of tribes and recognized their inherent rights as governments, independent and separate nations not beholden to the United States Constitution for their existence. These positive outcomes for American Indians have received attention by a number of worthy scholars, and I encourage readers to consult their works.[8] My project here is, rather, an in-depth analysis of exceptions to this affirmative judicature to show how indeterminately "the law" has been applied to tribal groups.

David Kairys commented in *With Liberty and Justice for Some* that "the legal system's emphasis on principles, ideals, and consistency and the tradition of offering at least some explanation for the results of decisions affects some outcomes and is preferable to naked or wholly unaccountable force . . . [L]aw is driven and determined by *people* rather than disinterested or neutral logic, reasoning, or methodology. . . ."[9] Through the data and analysis presented here, I demonstrate beyond a reasonable doubt that on many occasions the Supreme Court's rulings have had little to do with logic, reasoning, or legal ideals. This is an important issue, because within the field of Indian policy and law, many people—especially lay individuals (both tribal and nontribal) and many political and legal commentators as well—have made "the law" into something that people are expected to prostrate themselves before. Many believe that if a policy is laid out in "the law," and particularly if it is a Supreme Court decision, that pronouncement is somehow unassailable. The notion that Supreme Court justices are infallible has certainly been damaged by the revelations of the Bork and Thomas confirmation hearings, but the High Court's decisions, pluralistic as many of them now are, continue to resonate with authority and legitimacy even when their legitimacy and authority can be questioned, especially from an indigenous perspective.

The air of sanctity that Supreme Court cases exude was especially pronounced in the initial 170 years of the Court's history, when preexisting tribal political and property rights were first addressed by the Supreme Court, almost always without any direct tribal or Indian involvement in the litigation. The extraconstitutional[10] status of tribal nations, affirmed by hundreds of Indian treaties, and the placement of tribes in the Commerce Clause of the U.S. Constitution as distinctive polities, continues to form the broad but still largely tenuous parameters of the tribal-federal relationship. This unique political relationship became even more complex in 1924 when the United States unilaterally imposed federal citizenship on all Indians who were not yet citizens. The result was that while Indian individuals were now recognized as federal and state citizens they nevertheless retained their tribal citizenship. This meant, as the Supreme Court later determined, that whereas Indians were indeed entitled to federal benefits and privileges of citizenship, the federal government still enjoyed virtually unlimited political authority over their lives, property, and rights due to their status as "Indians by race." States, by contrast, have been hobbled in their efforts to deal directly with tribes because of the Indian Commerce Clause in the Constitution, which federalized the tribal-federal relationship. Interestingly, even with federal and state citizenship, individual Indians enrolled in recognized tribes still are not guaranteed the most basic constitutional protections enjoyed by nonindigenous Americans.

Throughout these selected fifteen cases, the actions of the Supreme Court, characterized by self-interest, political expediency, and cultural arrogance, have generated and reified a number of novel extralegal and extraconstitutional doctrines (e.g., doctrine of discovery, domestic-dependent nationhood, wardship/dependency status, plenary power, geographic incorporation, implicit divestiture) which have often been used to mask questionable federal and administrative activities against tribes and individual Indians.

This study analyzes the genesis, evolution, and transformation of these legal constructs and the ramifications they have had and continue to have on tribal sovereignty and Indian rights. In effect, the "rule of law" has been utilized by the Supreme Court to make political actions of the United States appear legitimate and lawful, although tribal nations are not afforded constitutional protection because they were not created pursuant to, and are not beholden to, the U.S. Constitution.

The political independence of the Court, vacillations in federal Indian policy—from the assimilation of Indians to a recognition of tribal political separatism—and conflicts over federal and state jurisdiction regarding tribes enable the Court to exercise a tremendous amount of discretionary authority when it comes to handling Indian issues. As a coordinate branch of the federal government, the Court has generally chosen to act in one of two ways. First, it tends to defer to the Congress by presuming that the political branches always have acted in "good faith" toward tribes. At other times, it has felt compelled to create a fictitious congressional intent to legitimate what Congress has done, regardless of whether the legislation originally had anything to do with Indians or not. Arnold has noted that the Supreme Court "should be the concrete dramatization of the ideal that there is a power which prevents government action which is arbitrary, capricious, and based on prejudice."[11] However, the fifteen cases I will be discussing in these chapters depict a Court that often acts arbitrarily, capriciously, and prejudicially.

Critical legal and historical analysis of these fifteen cases, review of other historical and political materials, and appropriate discussion of the social context and individual backgrounds of some of the justices should go far toward explaining why and how the Court arrived at these important Indian law decisions. More importantly, this discussion leads to a larger issue of why the core democratic concepts of fairness, justice, and consent of the governed have not yet been fully realized for tribal nations and their citizens despite clearly pronounced treaty rights, federal policies of Indian self-determination and tribal self-governance, positive judicial precedents, and a triple citizenship.

THEORETICAL FRAMEWORK:
CRITICAL LEGAL THEORY AND MASKS OF THE LAW

The political struggles that have plagued the tribal-federal relationship beg for clear, preferably simple, explanations; however, the complexity of this relationship prevents such simplistic answers. In analyzing the fifteen cases, a broad, dual-theoretical framework is needed to provide plausible explanations for the Court's major Indian law decisions. Critical Legal Theory[12] with the creative approach developed by John T. Noonan Jr. was chosen to provide theoretical guideposts for this study of the Supreme Court.[13]

Advocates of Critical Legal Theory (Crits) posit that the Supreme Court operates with a distinctive "legal consciousness," which serves a critical role as a perceptual filter, as well as a perceptual pool, that binds even apparently disparate decisions together.[14] This consciousness is not easily measured and so is unquantifiable.

Duncan Kennedy suggests, however, that legal consciousness is an entity "with a measure of autonomy."[15] He defines it as "the particular form of consciousness that characterizes the legal profession as a social group at a particular moment. The main peculiarity of this consciousness is that it contains a vast number of legal rules, arguments, and theories, a great deal of information about the institutional workings of the legal process, and the constellation of ideals and goals current in the profession at a given moment."[16] It is, moreover, a combination of intellectual operations and terms that develop according to a unique pattern. Critical legal theorists stress that legal consciousness can influence results that are distinguishable from those of economic interest and political power. According to Kennedy:

> The notion behind the concept of legal consciousness is that people can have in common something more influential than a checklist of facts, techniques, and opinions. They can share premises about the salient aspects of the legal order that are so basic that actors rarely if ever bring them consciously to mind.
>
> Yet everyone, including actors who think they disagree profoundly about the substantive issues that matter, would dismiss without a second thought (perhaps as not a legal argument or as simply missing the point) an approach appearing to deny them.
>
> These underlying premises concern the historical background of the legal process, the institutions involved in it, and the nature of the

intellectual constructs which lawyers, judges, and commentators ma-
nipulate as they attempt to convince their audiences.[17]

Critical legal theorists argue that during the late nineteenth and early
twentieth centuries, a common ideological consciousness arose among
leading academics, practicing lawyers, and jurists that cut across divi-
sions in practice specialty and political orientation.[18] This new form of
legal thought amounted to a rationalistic restructuring of the legal uni-
verse that Mensch calls "classical legal thought."[19] As American economic and social life was being transformed, the legal elite, including
the Supreme Court, joined forces with treatise writers and leaders of the
bar to share a view of the "law" that allied the legal profession with science "against both philosophical speculation and the crudities of democratic politics."[20]

During this classical period, the legal elite transformed its attitude
about the set of legal relationships that make up the American legal system—private citizen to private citizen, private citizen to state, legislature
to judiciary, and federal to state government. Previously these relationships had been seen as qualitatively distinct; during the period in question they came to be regarded as four distinctive instances of a single
general relationship. The role of the judiciary, then, "was the application
of a single, distinctively legal, analytic apparatus to the job of policing
the boundaries of these spheres."[21]

The fact that tribal nations were outside this legal matrix meant that
the Supreme Court either deferred to the political branches or drew
from the limited bank of information about tribes, with all its cultural bi-
ases, that had accrued within the Court's own institutional memory and
judicial consciousness, which rarely afforded a realistic picture of tribes
or their own indigenous institutions of governance. Evidence of this
ideological consensus can be found in the fact that of the ninety Supreme Court cases involving tribal sovereignty during this historical era,
there was written dissent in only five: *The Cherokee Tobacco* (1871);
Leavenworth Railroad Company v. United States (1876); *Elk v. Wilkins*
(1884); *Choctaw Nation v. United States* (1886); and *Donnelly v. United
States* (1912).

Advocates of Critical Legal Theory argue that conflicting decisions
are made because they are based on different and often controversial
moral and political ideas. Neither lawyers nor jurists can provide simple
answers to complex political and legal questions because the legal system, like society at large, is unable to reconcile the contradictory in-

stincts that arise when people confront social problems. Rather than deciding which of these conflicting instincts to follow, "the law" seeks to
embrace them all. Critical Legal Theory argues that "law" is really politics clothed differently and that it obscures the nature of judicial decision
making when courts and legal commentators present legal issues as if
they were objective or even relatively objective matters of legal reasoning rather than political choices. A significant strength of this intellectual approach to understanding law is that it seeks a theoretical and practical understanding that places juridical institutions and individual actors
in their social and historical contexts.

THE "MASKING" OF JUSTICE: LAW AS MAGIC

John T. Noonan Jr., in his telling study *Persons and Masks of the Law*,[22]
offers incisive observations about the place of "persons" or—for my
purposes—tribes and tribal citizens in the law. His thesis is that people
involved in cases in the American legal tradition are often given "masks"
that conceal their true character. These masks, as Noonan defines them,
are "legal constructs which suppress the humanity of a participant in the
process."[23] Noonan's primary example is the case of African Americans
and the institution of slavery. The humanity of blacks was shielded,
"masked," in American law behind various descriptions normally reserved for property of one sort or another (real, personal, etc.). Once
"the law" had characterized blacks as "property," they could then be
sold, bartered, or even killed without the legal system's actually confronting the fact that African Americans were human beings entitled to
basic human rights and liberties.

Noonan explains how "enlightened" individuals like Thomas Jef-
ferson and George Wythe, "though supporting liberty and advocating
emancipation of slaves, actually did nothing, even when vested with
political power, to end slavery." He points out that they accepted the
entrenched legal framework that had codified the institution of slavery.
As a result, they ignored the humanity of African Americans by placing
"masks" or legal constructs on both their own feelings and those of the
slaves, thus magically removing humanity from the legal process.

For Noonan, there are two basic kinds of masks—those that are imposed on others (as "property" for slaves), and those that are put on one-
self (as the "Court" in the mouths of judges and "the law" according to
judges, law professors, and attorneys).[24] These masks are socially fash-

ioned and are dangerous because they "have been stamped with approval by society's official representatives of reason."

The Supreme Court's Indian decisions are also pocked with such masks. Tribes have, at various times, been defined by the Court as a "culturally deficient" set of individuals who were "in need of cultural improvement"; as "domestic-dependent nations" which were alleged to be dependent upon the federal government at a time when they were legitimate independent sovereigns subject to no other political power; and as "dependent wards," who were (and in some cases still are) subject to virtually omnipotent paternalistic federal guardians. The Supreme Court has manufactured or refined other "masks" to justify intrusions on tribal sovereignty at the federal, state, and, recently, the county level: the doctrine, later appropriated by federal officials, that the "discovery" of America by the European countries vested an absolute property title to the discovering nation, thereby reducing tribal claims to aboriginal lands to those of a mere tenant; the political question doctrine which for nearly a century and a half denied tribes a legal forum for the adjudication of their rights of lands, treaty enforcement, etc.; the theory of congressional and even federal plenary power over tribes; and the so-called trust doctrine.[25]

Although crediting the Marxist argument that "masks are often employed by the ruling class to protect their own interests above those of the lower classes," Noonan notes that legal constructs are not simply tools of power, nor are they acts of "violence." The legal process "aims at compromise, avoidance of conflict, peaceful direction of conduct."[26] Masks cannot be treated "as armament." Instead, they are more aptly conceived as a "set of communications," as "magical ways by which persons are removed from the legal process."[27]

A synthesis of Critical Legal Theory and Noonan's approach will go far toward providing a conceptual framework to explain the fifteen Supreme Court cases that will be examined in these chapters. Both emphasize a concept of the law as "masks." Both agree that "law" must be placed in the larger historical and social context. A significant difference, however, is that while Critical Legal Theorists speak of "law" as primarily a legitimating device utilized by elites situated at the top of the social, political, and economic hierarchy, Noonan asserts that "law" affects not only those it is used against but those who wield it as well.[28] In other words, while the justices may seem to be masters of the law, there are also times when the law masters them.

The conjunction, therefore, between the basic premises and legal constructs offered by Critical Legal Theory and Noonan's characterization of legal "masks" operating with reciprocal effects on both sides of the legal equation supports and gives additional convincing argument as to why the Court treats tribes and their members the way it does. Further evidence that the Court operates with a distinctive consciousness is seen in the fact that the judiciary has never voided a single congressional act that diminished or abrogated any inherent or aboriginal tribal rights. And while the Rehnquist Court is willing to challenge congressional authority in other areas of law (e.g., interstate commerce), and has occasionally rendered decisions which seem to conflict with current congressional Indian policy, which in recent years has emphasized a measure of tribal self-determination,[29] the Court and the Congress still adhere to the historically and constitutionally inaccurate idea that places tribes in a subservient political/legal position to the federal and sometimes even the state governments.[30]

From the beginning of its relations with the Indians, the Supreme Court's legal consciousness has stressed tribes' allegedly inferior cultural, political, technological, social, and spiritual status in relation to the prevailing lifestyle of Euro-America. This judicial predisposition can be divided into three types, constitutional/treaty, civilizing/paternalistic, and nationalist/federalist,[31] each wielding a distinctive set of "masks" that have been fashioned to symbolize the legal process and conceal or disfigure the humanity of all of the actors in the legal drama. In the analysis that follows, each type of consciousness is accompanied by one or more sets of legal masks which are examined with specific comments relating to the parties, the law, and the Court.

CONSTITUTIONAL / TREATY

The basic assumption of this legal consciousness is that constitutional or treaty considerations (i.e., ratified treaties or agreements) are the only relevant instruments for the adjudication of a legal dispute between tribes and federal/state governments. This consciousness is evident in Supreme Court opinions dealing with tribal sovereignty which generally acknowledge the inherent sovereignty of tribal nations and their pre- and extraconstitutional aboriginal rights of self-government. These decisions have generally left tribal nations free of the constitutional constraints applicable to the states and the federal government.

This consciousness has usually employed the following masks: for the parties, one party (the Congress) is understood as being within the Constitution's purview, while the other (tribes), is understood to be outside its parameters. The two parties are politically connected by ratified treaties or the treaty-type of agreements that are recognized under the Constitution as being the "supreme law of the land," and by tribal tradition and custom as being "sacred covenants."

In a mask for the legal process, the Court is seen primarily as a legitimator of policies developed by the political branches. This is an orthodox version of the Court as a body that represents self-restraint and functions primarily as an interpreter of the Constitution, not as a policy-making entity. In this "model of law" approach,[32] the Court is seen as an agent for interpreting and applying preexisting laws: it is bound, although not absolutely, by the doctrine of stare decisis (past precedent). In most of the Supreme Court cases utilizing this legal consciousness tribes have been victorious. Such victories included *Worcester v. Georgia* (1832), which affirmed the sanctity of Indian treaties; *The Kansas Indians* (1866), which acknowledged the distinctive political standing of tribes and their freedom from state interference; *Ex parte Crow Dog* (1883), which recognized the inherent sovereignty of tribes; and *Talton v. Mayes* (1896), which discussed the extraconstitutional basis of Cherokee sovereignty and many other historical and contemporary cases.

Of the fifteen cases examined herein, only one, *United States v. Sioux Nation* (1980), can be classed under the constitutional/treaty category. But even this pro-Indian decision was not a complete tribal victory, because the Court perpetuated several masks that have diminished the sovereignty of tribal nations without tribal consent. The writings of the legal commentators who argue that the Supreme Court is the tribes' most articulate and best friend focus almost exclusively on constitutional/treaty cases and choose to ignore or downplay the significance of the other two types of judicial consciousness and the decisions they evoke. I choose to reverse this order and focus, with the exception of *Sioux Nation*, exclusively on those cases that demonstrate the latter two types of judicial masking.

CIVILIZING/PATERNALISTIC

The basic assumption of this type of legal consciousness is that "the law" is the most effective instrument for civilizing indigenous (read: primitive) peoples who are considered culturally inferior. An excellent example of this view can found in a federal district court case, *United States v. Clapox* (1888). This decision involved a determination of the status of the federally created Courts of Indian Offenses (referred to by the acronym COF for the Code of Federal Regulations from which they sprang) that had been developed by the Bureau of Indian Affairs in 1883. These courts, manned by agent-appointed Indian judges, were charged with enforcing a Code of Federal Regulations designed to "civilize" and assimilate Indians by punishing tribal members who engaged in tribal dances, polygamy, traditional healing ceremonies, or any activity deemed "heathenish" by the local agent and the commissioner of Indian affairs.

Commissioner of Indian Affairs Hiram Price stated in his annual report of 1883: "There is no good reason why an Indian should be permitted to indulge in practices which are alike repugnant to common decency and morality; and the preservation of good order on the reservations demands that some active measures should be taken to discourage and, if possible, put a stop to the demoralizing influence of heathenish rules."[33]

Five years later, an Umatilla woman (identified as "Minnie") was arrested, tried by the COF, and charged with adultery. She was subsequently freed from jail by several friends who later were caught and charged with her jail break. When the case reached the federal court, the main issue to be addressed involved the status of the COF—as to whether they were constitutional courts organized pursuant to section 1, article 3, of the Constitution or had been developed under some other authority. In explaining its decision, the court explicitly capsulized the general view of the federal policymakers of the time regarding Indian cultures. The court held that the offenses courts were not constitutional courts but "mere educational and disciplinary instrumentalities, by which the government of the United States is endeavoring to improve and elevate the condition of these dependent tribes to whom it sustains the relation of guardian." "In fact," said the court, "the reservation itself is in the nature of a school, and the Indians are gathered there, under the charge of an agent, for the purpose of acquiring the habits, ideas, and aspirations, which distinguish the civilized from the uncivilized man."[34] Continuing this reasoning, the individuals who were responsible for Minnie's futile rescue were convicted and charged with "flagrant opposition to the authority of the United States on this reservation," and their actions were deemed "directly subversive of this laudable effort to accustom and advocate these Indians in the habit and knowledge of self government."[35]

For most federal policymakers and many Euro-Americans in that era, the allegation of tribal cultural "inferiority" was justified in a number of ways. Tribes were viewed as technologically primitive. Federal lawmakers and early social scientists invariably classified all tribal-based cultures as hunter/gatherer societies, perceived as inferior to an agriculturalist-based society that had pride in its domestic industries. Finally, indigenous peoples were purportedly "pagans" or "savages," perceived as being without legitimate religious beliefs since they had little or no knowledge of Jesus Christ or the Christian church.[36]

Some tribes, notably the Cherokee, Choctaw, Chickasaw, Creek, and Seminole (often referred to as the "Five Civilized Tribes"), and the various Pueblo groups, were, at least for the first century or more of U.S./tribal interaction, perceived as being less savage[37] or pagan than other tribes, although Pueblo status actually changed from a perceived "civilized" state in 1877 to a more "primitive" state in 1913. These tribes, therefore, were for a significant period treated with more leniency both by the Supreme Court and by the political branches. Nevertheless, for both the allegedly "wild" tribes and the so-called civilized tribes, a fundamental belief prevailed among most of the federal policymakers, including the Court, that all Indians could and should be culturally "elevated" with proper education, training, and spiritual (read: Christian) guidance. Hence, paternalistic policies (e.g., Christian missionaries funded by the federal government, boarding schools, reservations, and the individualization of tribal lands and funds) were developed by the Congress and sanctioned by the Supreme Court to impose this cultural transformation.

Civilizing/paternalistic consciousness generally employed three types of masks for the parties involved and the legal process. Two sets of masks were applied to tribal nations. The first caricatured certain tribes as "wild," "heathenish," or "savage" (tribes of the Great Plains, the Midwest, the Pacific Northwest, and the Desert Southwest—especially Navajo, Apache groups, Tohono O'odham, Ute, etc.). The second set portrayed the "Five Civilized Tribes" and others as "civilized," "peaceful," and "hardworking." Gradations of "savagery" were applied to the various tribes, and the Court vacillated in the manner in which it employed these masks. The masks for the Supreme Court, on the other hand, portray it, and by extension the federal government, as deeply moralistic, Christian, and nearly always above reproach.

The Law is masked as an absolutely essential element in moving Indian persons and tribes from an uncivilized to a civilized state. The focus here was never on whether or not such a cultural transformation was justifiable; rather it was on whether it would take place gradually or rapidly. The paternalism that characterized federal Indian policy during this era, also known, in a legal error, as the "guardian/ward" relationship, had two faces—it could be benevolent (viewing Indians as helpless children or incompetent wards), or it could be malevolent (viewing Indian lands, resources, and political rights as commodities to be unilaterally and forcefully taken or abrogated).[8]

NATIONALISM/FEDERALISM

This third type of judicial consciousness holds at its core the assumption that law was conceived as a prime mechanism for furthering the political development of the United States as a nation-state. The process of political development is a topic of great interest for those attempting to shape their society, as well as for those attempting to understand the political world. Accordingly, one perspective holds that political development occurs "primarily in response to the development of the economic and social systems. Because of increases in the elements of modernization, such as greater economic development, urbanization, and social mobilization, there is a need for a more complex and more efficient political system."[39]

Barrington Moore, for example, in his classic study *Social Origins of Dictatorship and Democracy* (1966),[40] compared the three major roads taken by nation-states from the preindustrial to the modern world.[41] He treated in detail the struggles of Great Britain, the United States, France, Japan, China, and India to achieve modernity. According to Moore, all the major capitalist democracies passed through a civil war or a period of revolutionary violence in which certain aspects of the old order were destroyed; he cites slavery and the Civil War (1861–1865) in the case of the United States. This transformation was necessary, Moore said, because slavery was incompatible with political development along democratic lines. In effect, the destruction of the institution of slavery made it possible for the social, political, and economic struggle to continue within a democratic framework.[42]

After the Civil War, industrial capitalism advanced significantly. Important political changes included developments that involved the role of the federal government and "big property." A good example is the railroads, which received massive grants of land (in many cases tribally owned and inhabited), financial support, and property in the public domain. Similar developments occurred for timber and mining interests.

As the country's political structure struggled to mature in the last quarter of the nineteenth century, several key concepts emerged that would influence the shape and direction of nationalism. These included political democracy, political stability, political culture, political institutions, political participation, and political integration.[43] While each of these is an important concept, it is integration that bears special significance for the status of tribal nations in the United States. Political integration generally refers to the holding together of a political system; specifically, the two types relevant to this study are national integration and territorial integration. National integration is the "process of bringing together culturally and socially discrete groups into a single territorial unit and of establishing a national identity. This also involves plural societies, with distinct ethnic, religious, linguistic, or other groups and strata."[44] Territorial integration, on the other hand, is the establishment of "national central authority over subordinate political units or regions. [It] means objective territorial control."[45]

The United States has historically had an assimilative political culture in a hierarchical structure (white in relation to blacks, Indians, and Asian Americans), within which there have also been parallel ethnic relations (WASP, Irish, Italian, Jewish, etc.). Political development has generated various responses to the problem of the national integration of indigenous groups: social engineering, assimilation, cultural genocide, partition (segregation), and expulsion.[46] Of these, assimilation, or the effort to induce the merger of a politically subordinate cultural group into the politically dominant cultural group, has been the most persistent response. And the Supreme Court has occupied a central role in this assimilation campaign.

The Supreme Court's utilization of "the law" served not only as an instrument of "civilization," but also as the federal government's most vital and effective "instrument of empire building."[47] Hence, some of the cases that came before the Court involved questions relating to the diminished status of tribes, a status that often was denied any existence whatsoever. Related to this is a theory of federalism in which the Supreme Court, acting as a coordinate branch of the federal government, clearly identifies Congress as the only constitutional source entitled to deal with tribes. This policy development is in direct contrast to what African Americans have experienced. There, at least historically, the states were granted virtually free reign to assert their dominance over blacks. Tribal nations, on the other hand, were generally shielded from the states, though the shielding device used by the federal government was effective congressional omnipotence over Indian sovereignty and Indian civil, political, and property rights.

This legal consciousness used two different kinds of masks for the parties involved. The mask worn by federalizing agents viewed the United States as the core unit such that nonfederal entities must either be absorbed or vanquished. The masks applied by the Court to the tribes divided them according to degree of "savagery," as described above, into the assimilable and unassimilable, tribal nations that were deemed capable of being Americanized (from a Euro-American perspective) and joining the United States as separate, though integrated, political entities[48] versus those mostly western tribes that were caricatured as "wild" and "uncivilized." In masking the legal process, *Law* was clearly an agent of national unity. During the late 1800s and well into the twentieth century, the Court rendered a number of decisions indicating a clear intent to dilute the extraconstitutional status of tribes by unilaterally declaring them "wards" of the government and disavowing their separate, independent status. The assertion of congressional power over tribal lands, resources, and rights is evidence of this nationalizing effort.

The three types of legal consciousness I have described are hypothetical, ideal concepts which rest on facts and assumptions that come directly from observation. They reflect the broadness of the continuum on which the Supreme Court operates. It should be pointed out that some cases will exhibit more than one form of judicial consciousness, and many will employ more than one set of masks.

By identifying the prevailing judicial consciousness and the attendant masks utilized by the Court which have served to deny or constrain the inherent sovereignty of tribal nations, I hope to establish a sense of the moral basis of law, the critical element that has seemingly been abandoned in American jurisprudence but is still fundamentally recognized by tribal nations in their understanding of treaties and federal statutes.[49] In basic moral terms, tribal nations understand that their governmental powers, in the words of Milner Ball, "cannot simply evanesce and reappear in the hands of another nation's government."[50] Nevertheless, during the course of the past two centuries, indigenous nations have often seen the Supreme Court's decisions work grave injustices against them, their lands, their political powers, and their cultural systems.

Tribal nations, we shall see, are fundamentally different from their neighboring sovereigns: ". . . different, not less developed: 806 different languages, a different spirituality, different aesthetics, different ways of living on and with the earth, different ways than capitalism and Marxism for putting people to work."[51] The Supreme Court, however, often chose to deny or alter indigenous reality by legitimating federal and, in some cases, state, political goals which aimed at the eradication or transformation of indigenous differentness through the indeterminate language of the law.

This study is divided into seven chapters. Chapter 2 analyzes three cases, *Johnson v. McIntosh*, *United States v. Rogers*, and *The Cherokee Tobacco* case. Thematically, these three opinions dealt with aboriginal land title, defined the political status of tribes, provided justification for the notion of manifest destiny, and established the historic precedent that Indian treaties could be unilaterally overridden despite objections by any tribal nation.

Chapter 3 also focuses on three cases: *United States v. Kagama*, *Ward v. Race Horse*, and *Lone Wolf v. Hitchcock*. These cases established and reaffirmed the doctrine of congressional plenary power over tribes and their resources, sanctioned state authority over tribes, and articulated the precedent that treaties were merely "temporary privileges" that could be disallowed by the federal government.

In Chapter 4, three crucial cases are reviewed—*United States v. Nice*, *Northwestern Bands of Shoshone Indians v. United States*, and *Tee-Hit-Ton Indians v. United States*. *Nice* dealt with the status of Indian allottees, while *Shoshone* and *Tee-Hit-Ton* involved unsuccessful tribal efforts to protect aboriginal land holdings.

Chapter 5 scrutinizes *Oliphant v. Suquamish Indian Tribe* and *United States v. Sioux Nation of Indians*. *Oliphant* involved the question of a tribe's power of criminal jurisdiction over non-Indians, while *Sioux Nation*, the one case among my selections that has been interpreted as a "victory" for the tribal party by some commentators, involved land title and treaty rights.

Chapter 6 entails the three most recent cases: *Lyng v. Northwest Indian Cemetery Protective Association*, *Employment Division, Dept. of Human Resources v. Smith*, and *County of Yakima v. Confederated Tribes and Bands of the Yakima Indian Nation*. These cases are powerful and traumatic examples of judicial decision-making involving tribes and individual Indians who are seen as lacking constitutional or statutory rights to freedom of religion. The growing issue of state/county jurisdiction over Indian-owned land is evident as these cases dictate a look into the future.

In a concluding chapter, I will bring this study to closure by highlighting the major themes and premises discerned and by taking a serious look at the short- and long-term implications of these historic Supreme Court decisions for tribes who persist in arguing that they retain an extraconstitutional standing as distinctive polities. In a modern democracy struggling to deal with issues of pluralism and multiculturalism, the issue is relevant. As Ball notes, "The very basic differentness of Indians is itself a source of instruction, a particularly important one for a powerful nation like the United States that finds itself needing to learn survival in a world composed of many nations whose unlikenesses are more and greater than their likenesses. Non-Indians have much to receive from Indians across the distance of their difference." [52]

The Era of
Defining Tribes,
Their Lands, and
Their Sovereignty

CHAPTER 2

Indigenous nations are often classed alongside African Americans, Asian Americans, and Hispanic Americans as among the more vulnerable racial and ethnic minorities in the United States. American Indian peoples make up less than one percent of the nation's population, slightly fewer than two million. Like the other groups mentioned, most tribal nations are severely disadvantaged economically and have astounding levels of unemployment and poverty.[1] But although tribal nations share some socioeconomic characteristics with other minority groups,[2] the differences distinguishing tribes from the other groups profoundly exceed any parallels that might be drawn.

Tribes enjoy cultural traits and practices which differ from predominant Euro-American cultural characteristics and those common to other ethnic and minority groups. Because of the tremendous level of cultural and political differentiation, tribal nations have had difficulty developing long-term political alliances with each other or with other racial, ethnic, or special interest groups.[3] Indigenous nations, in short, fall easily within the purview of the Court as "discrete and insular" groups which sometimes require special protection from discrimination.

To define their status, it is important to identify certain characteristics of tribal nations. First, and most obvious, tribal nations are indigenous to the United States, while all other individuals and groups are immigrants. Second, "tribalism" or "tribal status" is a unique concept emphasizing collective or group rights and affirming the sovereign status of the group, unlike liberalism which celebrates individualism and individual rights.[4] Third, the concept of "expatriation" is uniquely relevant to tribes and their members as a result of the political dimension of their identity and their multiple-citizenship status.[5] In *Standing Bear v. Crook* (1879), for example, a federal court held that Indians had the right to withdraw from their tribe—to expatriate from their nation and live apart—if they so desired.

In sum, the coupling element for the above characteristics is that tribal nations still have and exercise a measure of *inherent sovereignty*. There is, of course, a bewildering array of interpretations of the nature and extent of tribal sovereignty. But, as Chaudhuri notes, "This question like so many others is affected by cultural presuppositions without the benefit of clear formulations of comparative law. As in other culturally defined questions of Indian policy, the dominant influence is that of Anglo-American legal culture rather than aboriginal perspectives on authority."[6] And although Chaudhuri characterizes the body of case law on Indian sovereignty as a "middle-eastern bazaar where practically anything is available to those who are eager and earnest and have the resources for persisting in the adversary system of justice,"[7] this text accepts as a foundational postulate that tribal sovereignty does exist and that it has been recognized, even if sporadically and across time, in many of the basic political acts of the federal government.

From an indigenous perspective, then, tribal sovereignty has several manifestations. First, from both an internal and intergovernmental perspective, it entails a political/legal dimension—including, but not limited to, the power to adopt its own form of government; to define the conditions of citizenship/membership in the nation; to regulate the domestic relations of the nation's citizens/members; to prescribe rules of inheritance with respect to all personal property and all interests in real property; to levy dues, fees, or taxes upon citizen/members and noncitizen/nonmembers; to remove or to exclude nonmembers of the tribe; to administer justice; and to prescribe the duties and regulate the conduct of federal employees.[8]

Second, and more broadly, tribal sovereignty entails a cultural/spiritual dimension. Sovereignty "can be said to consist more of continued cultural integrity than of political powers and to the degree that a nation loses its sense of cultural identity, to that degree it suffers a loss of sovereignty."[9] Corroborating this culturally and spiritually based perspective is the recent work of Gerald Alfred, a Mohawk political scientist who asserts that for the Kahnawake Mohawk the Euro-American conception of "sovereignty" has been abandoned "in favour of an indigenous reformulation. It is based instead upon a mutual respect among communities for the political and cultural imperatives of nationhood—a flexible sharing of resources and responsibilities in the act of maintaining the distinctiveness of each community."[10] In its simplest terms, says Alfred, Kahnawake Mohawk express their sovereignty through the Mohawk word *tewatatowie*, 'we help ourselves.' Mohawk sovereignty, then, is seen as much more than interests and boundaries; it has to do with the balance and harmony between the various human communities, between the Mohawk people and the land, and between the Mohawk and other communities.

This tribal sovereign status was not delegated to the tribes by the courts, the federal government, or the states. It is original and inherent, though it has been directly impacted by various federal and state laws, policies, and regulations. Tribal sovereignty has been recognized by several European nations; the federal government through hundreds of treaties, nearly 400 of which were ratified by the Senate and proclaimed by the President; and by the states, who were forced to concede that as a result of the Commerce Clause of the Constitution they lacked authority to deal with tribal nations. Thus, fundamentally, the tribal relationship to the United States is a political one, although it is a relationship affected by tribal culture. One noted legal scholar puts it this way: the tribes' legal status "is not a matter of race or birth but is a matter of contract or consent."[11] Therefore, the legal status of tribal nations derives from their recognized cultural and political citizenship in a tribal nation, which is wholly unlike the status of other minority groups in the U.S.

TRIBES AS EXTRACONSTITUTIONAL ENTITIES

Chief Justice John Marshall said in 1831 that "the relation of the Indians to the United States [was] marked by peculiar and cardinal distinctions which exist no where else" (*Cherokee Nation v. Georgia*, 1831). In penning this striking passage Marshall was attempting to define, for the federal government, the novel political relationship of the tribal nations with the United States. This case and Marshall's inventive passage are frequently cited today by policymakers, commentators, and scholars who wrestle with the existence of racially based tribal nations, the majority of which are completely landlocked by both state and federal jurisdictions. Most tribal nations operate under their own constitutions and exercise a multitude of governmental powers, some of which legally conflict with the Federal Constitution.[12]

Marshall's phraseology compels one to seek the parameters within which tribal-federal relationships exist in this modern democracy. Succeeding generations of scholars, politicians, administrators, and jurists have confirmed that "peculiar and cardinal distinctions" do indeed mark the tribal-federal relationship. Among the numerous peculiarities to be explored are the racial dimension; the distinctive governmental dimension of tribal life and the pre- and extraconstitutional connection tribes have to the federal government, evidenced by the bilateral treaty process; and the sheer numbers of separate tribal groups and nations.

These peculiarities and distinctions have combined to create an exotic juridical potage seasoned by the Court's innovative development of legal doctrines justifying, on the one hand, the imposition of federal authority over tribal lands and Indian citizens and, on the other, creating a set of legal (some say moral, e.g., "trust doctrine") barriers designed to protect tribes from federal agencies, states, and private parties. For example, the trust doctrine has been used to justify racial discrimination against Euro-American employees of the Bureau of Indian Affairs (*Morton v. Mancari*, 1974).

Marshall, of course, because of his enormous intellectual gifts, his belief in federal supremacy over states' rights, his compassion for tribes, and his position in time, appears to bear primary responsibility for the current confused state of tribal-federal relations. A number of scholars have critically analyzed Marshall's comments in *Cherokee Nation* and his other important Indian law decisions.[13] Though differing, sometimes vehemently, in their interpretations of Marshall's doctrines, they concur, generally, in the opinion that he blended his federalist convictions and his sense of moral obligation to Indians with a pragmatic need to reconcile tribal status within the constitutional framework of the United States. He was not, however, particularly successful in his efforts to fit tribal nations into the American political framework, as this study will show.

While scholars and policymakers will continue to debate the meaning of tribal sovereignty as it emerged from the Marshall court era, one could credibly argue that tribal nations, in the words of Justice Smith Thompson, who dissented in the *Cherokee* case, were indeed "foreign" to the United States in their political relationship. Thompson said: "It is their political condition that constitutes their *foreign* character, and in that sense must the term *foreign* be understood as used in the Constitution. It can have no relation to local, geographical, or territorial position. It cannot mean a country beyond sea. Mexico or Canada is certainly to be considered a foreign country, in reference to the United States. It is the political relation in which one government or country stands to another, which constitutes it [as] foreign to the other" (emphasis original).[14] Thompson's dissent played a pivotal role in Marshall's *Worcester* (1832) opinion, which recognized the political distinctiveness of the Cherokee Nation and the supremacy of Indian treaties over state laws.

The description of tribes as "governments" stems from their status as the original sovereigns of America with whom various European states and, later, the United States, engaged in binding treaties and agreements. Clearly, the tribes' sovereign status continued throughout the colonial period and under the Articles of Confederation, the Northwest Ordinance, and the earliest draft of the U.S. Constitution.

The Constitution mentions Indians three times. In two specific instances Indians are excluded from official population enumerations for determining congressional representatives (Article I, section 2, clause 3 ". . . excluding Indians not taxed . . ." and the Fourteenth Amendment, section 2, which also refers to "Indians not taxed"). In the third instance, Indians are expressly referenced in the Commerce Clause (Article I, section 8, clause 3), which empowers Congress to "regulate commerce with foreign nations . . . states . . . and with the Indian tribes." This Commerce Clause is the only source of explicit power delegated to the Congress. Theoretically, the clause should not have extended to Congress any greater power over tribes than a legislature exercises over states, though in historical and contemporary practice such has not been the case.[15]

The Constitution specifies two other important sources of federal authority to deal with tribes—the power to make treaties and the power to make war and peace. The Commerce Clause provision as originally interpreted was narrowly construed by Congress. An 1834 House report states: "The right of self-government in the Indian tribes does not exclude the right of the United States to make laws for the regulation of trade with the Indian tribes, so far as our citizens are concerned. This right is by the Constitution of the United States vested in Congress, and cannot be surrendered."[16] The intent here was twofold. First, Congress, not the states, was recognized to be the primary agent to regulate trade with tribes. Second, Congress was involved in a laborious, almost futile, effort to prevent white traders from defrauding tribes. Congress saw both functions as essential to maintaining a positive tribal-federal relationship. The combined effect of these distinctive constitutional clauses and tribal extraconstitutional features is illustrated by the statement from *Elk v. Wilkins* that general congressional laws are inapplicable to Indian tribes "if their application would affect the Indians adversely, unless congressional intent to include them is clear."[17]

There is solid historical and constitutional support for the doctrine that "Congress has no constitutional power over Indians except what is conferred by the Commerce Clause and other clauses of the Constitution."[18] More importantly, it must be remembered that the constitutional clauses already mentioned—commerce, enumeration, and treaty making, plus the power of making war and peace—did not explicitly grant the federal government the power to regulate Indians or Indian affairs. The Commerce Clause, the only explicit power, merely states that Congress will be the branch to treat with Indian tribes. A corollary to the principle of congressional enumeration, identified by Felix S. Cohen, involved the power of the commissioner of Indian affairs, who was authorized to oversee "the management of all Indian affairs [of the federal government]" but whose office over time came to be read as having the power of "the management of all the affairs of Indians."[19]

Notwithstanding the extensive historical, political, and legal data that support the extraconstitutional standing of tribal nations vis-à-vis the federal government, tribes, as this study will show, have often found that the Supreme Court has failed to restrict federal powers that have operated to diminish the inherent rights of tribal nations. Using such concepts as plenary power, the "political question" principle, and the trust doctrine, the federal government has often made "choices about the rights and resources of Indian people that were not bound by external standards or subject to judicial review."[20]

Keeping in mind the extraconstitutional status of tribes, we must now direct our attention to individual Indian status; for it is in part this unique conjunction of rights—individual and collective—that further distinguishes Indians from the rest of the American populace. Before 1924 nearly two-thirds of all Indians had received federal citizenship via treaty provisions or individual allotments of land. Following World War I, the federal government unilaterally extended the franchise to all other Indians,[21] though Commissioner Leupp asserted as late as 1905 that there was no "authority of law to naturalize Indians."[22] This extension of citizenship did not, however, enfranchise tribes, and it did not impair preexisting tribal rights. Hence, Indians became the only people in the United States with dual, later triple citizenship (when individual states extended the franchise to Indians).

As federal citizens, Indians were ostensibly accorded the same constitutional safeguards and rights as other Americans. But national citizenship has not always proven an adequate shield for Indian political, civil, and, especially, property rights. To understand this anomaly we will analyze the Supreme Court case which addressed and, in fact, formalized the issue of multiple tribal citizenship. In this major case, *United States v. Nice* (1916), the Court held that an enfranchised Indian allottee was still subject to congressional power (covered in Chapter 4). Congress's power, as interpreted by Chief Justice Willis Van Devanter, had both a constitutional (Commerce) and an extraconstitutional (tribal "dependency") base. Van Devanter said that "citizenship is not incompatible with tribal existence or continued guardianship, and so may be conferred without completely emancipating the Indians or placing them beyond the reach of congressional regulations adopted for their protection." [23]

In essence, and ironically, *Nice* served to seal the status of tribal Indians in perpetual legal and political limbo during an era in which the federal government's primary Indian policy goal remained detribalization, individualization, and assimilation. Henceforth, tribal members who had been enfranchised were simultaneously recognized as federal citizens *and* as members of dependent groups subject to overriding congressional authority. With this fascinating dichotomous status—Indians as citizens and subjects—enshrined in federal law, it is questionable exactly what benefits federal citizenship did bestow upon the tribal citizen. Ostensibly, citizenship should have meant that the federal government retained no more power to legislate Indian lives and property than it does in regard to the lives and property of any other citizens. In fact, as this study shows, the U.S. asserted, at its discretion, plenary authority over the political affairs as well as the civil and property rights of not only tribes but individual Indians as well. [24]

CONGRESSIONAL PLENARY POWER

Plenary power is one of the most intriguing doctrines in political science, constitutional law, and federal Indian policy. This concept entails the soul of what is deemed a constitutional impasse with, on the one hand, the federal government acknowledging the sovereignty of American Indian tribal governments, and, on the other hand, extending its self-described politically superior position over tribes.

There is considerable disagreement among scholars and federal lawmakers on the nature of plenary power. Those who define it as exclusive and preemptive say that it is a power which only Congress may exercise, free of typical constitutional constraints due to the extraconstitutional status of tribal rights. [25] Those who define it as unlimited and absolute regard it as an aberrant and nondemocratic doctrine which Congress arbitrarily uses to oppress or even eradicate tribal or individual political, civil, or property rights. [26]

First cited by the Supreme Court in the seminal case *Gibbons v. Ogden* in 1824, plenary power has often been used by the federal courts in cases dealing with the extent of federal powers. It is a concept which has fostered confusion, because, as Engdahl says, "it conceals several issues which, for purposes of constitutional analysis, must be kept clear and distinct."[27] Engdahl incorrectly states that "no federal power is plenary in the full sense of the term, because as to all of them at least the prohibitions of the Bill of Rights apply."[28] He chooses to ignore the fact that the federal Bill of Rights is problematic as applied to tribal nations because tribal governments were not created under the auspices of the Constitution. While the 1968 Indian Civil Rights Act[29] applied certain portions of the Constitutional Bill of Rights to tribal governments in regard to their plenary activities affecting tribal citizens and other reservation residents, the Bill of Rights does not protect tribes or their members from congressional actions aimed at reducing tribal sovereignty, political rights, or aboriginal Indian lands.

A more important factor promoting scholarly and public confusion over the term "plenary" is that the concept conflates several very different questions.[30] First, *plenary* is sometimes defined as *exclusive;* this definition is used most frequently when Congress enacts Indian-specific legislation like the Indian Reorganization Act[31] or when it enacts Indian preference laws which withstand reverse discrimination suits.[32] This is an exclusively legislative power which the Congress may exercise in keeping with its policy of treating tribes in a distinctively political manner or, when deemed appropriate, in recognizing rights that Indians have been deprived of because of their extraconstitutional standing.

Second, plenary is often defined as an exercise of federal power which may *preempt* state law. Again, the Congress's commerce power serves as a prime example, as does the treaty-making process, both of which preclude involvement of the states. The constitutional disclaimers that a majority of western states had to include in their organic documents before they were considered eligible for admission as states give further evidence of federal preemption.[33] Typically, these disclaimers consisted of provisions in which the state declared that it would never attempt to tax Indian lands or property without both tribal and federal consent and without having first amended its own constitution.

A third definition of plenary is "unlimited or absolute."[34] This definition includes two subcategories: a) power which is not limited by other textual constitutional provisions; and b) power which is unlimited regarding congressional objectives. There is ample evidence in Indian law and policy of all three applications of plenary power to tribes by the federal government.[35] For instance, when Congress is exercising plenary power as the *exclusive* voice of the federal government in its relations with tribes, and is acting with the consent of indigenous people, then it is exercising authority in a legitimate manner. Also, when Congress is acting in a plenary way to *preempt* state intrusion into Indian Country, absent tribal consent, then it is properly exercising an enumerated constitutional power. However, when Congress is informed by a federal court that it has "full, entire, complete, absolute, perfect, and unqualified"[36] authority over tribes and individual Indian citizens, a fundamental and unconstitutional authority has been created.

Canfield, writing in 1881, long before most individual Indians were naturalized as American citizens, observed that congressional power over tribes was absolute because tribes were distinct and independent—if "inferior"—peoples, "strangers to our laws, our customs, and our privileges." He went on to say that "[t]o suppose that the framers of the Constitution intended to secure to the Indians the rights and privileges which they valued as Englishmen is to misconceive the spirit of their age. . . ."[37] By the time *Mashunkashey* was decided in 1942, all Indians had been enfranchised; yet they were informed by the court that absolute federal power was a reality confronting them.

In a constitutional democracy, defined as a system of governance that places formal limits on what government can do, even exclusive authority has some limits. Tribes, however, because of their extraconstitutional status, cannot rely upon express constitutional provisions, particularly those found in the Bill of Rights, to limit the federal government or its constituent branches. Unfortunately, due to several Supreme Court decisions, even individual Indians, who should be entitled to constitutional protection as citizens of the United States, find that in a number of areas they remain without adequate protection from state or federal authority.

Johnson v. McIntosh (1823)

A "PECULIAR" POLITICAL RELATIONSHIP: THE MASKING BEGINS

The cardinal distinguishing features of tribal nations are their reserved and inherent sovereign rights based on their separate, if unequal, political status. This was affirmed in hundreds of treaties and agreements, acknowledged in the Constitution's Commerce Clause, recognized in thousands of pieces of federal legislation, and expounded upon in hundreds of federal court opinions. The bilateral political relations that ensued between the various Indian tribes and the colonizing European nations, and later the fledgling United States, were considered essential by each of the European and European-derived nations in their quest for one or more of the following: trade goods, unconverted tribal souls, and geographical and political hegemony. Tribes, of course, also experienced important social, cultural, and economic transformations as a consequence of these cross-cultural and cross-political interactions. This study does not need to reiterate the enormity of the tribal destruction resulting from these close encounters of the European kind.[38]

By the time the United States had established itself as the dominant European-derived player, the principal political tool used by the United States to relate to tribal nations was well known: the treaty process. These presidentially directed and Senate-ratified documents, combined with Congress's oversight of commercial relations between tribal nations and the U.S. based on the Commerce Clause, meant that the federal government had exclusive authority to deal with tribal nations. In 1789, the First Congress passed the first thirteen statutes, of which four dealt primarily with Indian affairs and reflected this doctrine of exclusive congressional authority in the development of Indian policy; however, it would rest with the Supreme Court to define the political status of tribes from a federal standpoint.

John Marshall, the third chief justice, and his colleagues were largely responsible for developing, in several cases[39] during the early 1800s, the legal underpinning for the tribal-federal-state relationship. These cases involved (1) tribal property rights, (2) tribal political status in relation to the states, (3) tribal status in relation to the federal government, and (4) the international standing of tribal treaty rights. The details of these cases are generally well known, with the exception of the *Mitchel* decision.[40] However, it is *Johnson* that warrants concentrated attention, and we will consider it first because of the stunning and convoluted details that emerged from the decision, and because it was the earliest effort by the Supreme Court to tackle Indian issues in a comprehensive fashion.

According to most legal commentators, *Johnson* is the foundational case addressing aboriginal possessory rights. The principal question to be resolved by the Court was whether the Indian title which had been ceded by the Illinois and Piankeshaw tribes to plaintiffs Joshua Johnson and Thomas J. Graham under two separate land transactions in 1773 and 1775 could be "recognized in the courts of the United States" or whether the title purchased from the United States in 1818 by the defendant, William McIntosh, to land that was part of Johnson's original purchase from the Indians could be considered valid. "The inquiry," stated Chief Justice Marshall, "therefore, is, in a great measure, confined to the power of Indians to give, and of private individuals to receive, a title, which can be sustained in the courts of this country."[41] As will be shown, it was much more than this.

The Illinois and Piankeshaw tribes had actually sold the same land to both the plaintiff and the defendant, although Johnson's and Graham's deeds predated McIntosh's by over forty-five years. The prerevolutionary land transactions between the plaintiffs, Johnson et al., and the tribes had been conducted—as was the custom in land sales—in an open sale at a British military post in full view of both military and civil officers. The completed deeds were then attested to by these same officers. Furthermore, the Indian chiefs who ceded the land to the plaintiff's predecessors were the duly authorized leaders of their nations.

The title, therefore, should have been guaranteed by Great Britain since it was clearly a legitimate land transaction. In fact, the general land policy of Great Britain, the United States, and Spain was that once land was sold by an Indian tribe to duly authorized individuals or nations, as it was in a number of territories and states—Michigan, Wisconsin, Arkansas, Ohio, Tennessee, Louisiana, Missouri, and Mississippi—it was regarded as having been thereafter excluded from all subsequent sales which might have overlapped the same territory.

Evidence abounds of other pre- and postrevolutionary individual/tribal land transactions which were recognized as valid by the federal government.[42] For example, in 1800 a House Committee dealt with the petition of Isaac Zane, who sought to have his Indian-derived tract of land validated by Congress. The committee's report indicated that Congress took such petitions seriously and was more than willing to confirm Indian grants to individuals provided that a strong case was made

> . . . That the petitioner state that he was made a prisoner by the Wyandot Indians . . . that his attachments to the white people [have] subjected him to numberless inconveniencies and dangers during the almost continual wars which existed between the United States and the Indians, until the peace of Greenville, in 1795. That, previous to that period, a tract of land [four miles square] on which he now lives, had been assigned to him by the Wyandot Indians, and that no idea was entertained, when that treaty was made, that the land which had been given him would fall within the boundary of the United States (which now appears to be the case) and, of consequence, that no provision was

made in that treaty in his favor. All of which the committee have reason to believe is perfectly true . . . Having taken these circumstances
into consideration . . . the committee have concluded that the petitioner ought to have confirmed to him a tract of land equal, in some
degree, to the intentions of the Indians, and to the services rendered
by the petitioner to the United States; they therefore recommend to
the House the adoption of the following resolution. . . .[43]

The committee then moved to introduce a bill authorizing the President
to convey, in fee-simple title, the 2,560 acres Zane had received from the
Wyandot.

As pointed out in *Johnson*, the eruption of the American Revolution
had made it impossible for Johnson et al. to validate their title and take
possession of the land since the purchasers ran afoul of the American
colonists. However, Johnson and Graham had been petitioning Congress since 1781 seeking relief for their unfulfilled land title.[44]

Marshall did not address the question as to how these prerevolutionary land purchases were different from previous purchases made by
English/American colonists in the thirteen colonies before the Revolutionary War, since Great Britain was the settled and dominant European
sovereign and this procedure—individuals purchasing land under British auspices—was commonly used to purchase Indian lands.

Instead, the Marshall Court raised and then proceeded to answer an
entirely different and far more troubling question—especially since the
Indian tribes were not parties in the suit—as to whether tribes had a title
that could be conveyed to whomever they chose. By generating this
question and then answering it negatively, Marshall's court, in the process of this unanimous opinion, both created and recreated a set of legal
rationalizations to justify the reduction of Indian rights without allowing any room for listening to the Indian voice. More importantly, Marshall arrived at the conclusion that Indian tribes did not have full title,
they had merely an "impaired" and therefore incomplete title that could
not be conveyed to whomever they wished.

This is evidently his purpose in the second paragraph of his opinion
where he states:

As the right of society to prescribe those rules by which property may
be acquired and preserved is not, and cannot, be drawn into question;
as the title to lands, especially, is, and must be admitted to depend
entirely on the law of the nation in which they lie; it will be necessary,
in pursing this inquiry, to examine, not simply those principles of ab-

stract justice . . . which are admitted to regulate, in a great degree the rights of civilized nations . . . but those principles also which our own government has adopted in the particular case, and given us as the rule for our decision.[45]

Here Marshall was asserting that if the rule of law or "abstract justice" was in conflict with the national government's right to generate rules favorable to its own property and political needs then it was the Court's duty to construct principles or amend existing principles which would sanction those new standards. In other words, the rule of law, which should have led to a decision in favor of the plaintiffs (Johnson et al.) because of their preexisting and lawfully executed property rights, was circumvented in this case by what amounted to a political decision cloaked in judicial doctrines and strengthened by the politically expedient compromise agreed to by the founders of the American Republic which "provided for the cession of frontier claims by the 'landed' states to a federal sovereign claiming exclusive rights to extinguish Indian title claimed by purchase or conquest . . . [and] settled the legal status and rights of the American Indian in United States law."[46]

The bulk of Marshall's opinion served to lay out and transform the "doctrine of discovery."[47] This doctrine has been vilified by a number of writers,[48] and one scholar has argued that the discovery principle is actually a limitation on the rights of the "discovering" states and has little directly to do with indigenous rights.[49] Notwithstanding the substantial arguments of the minority, the reality for tribes over the years has been that the major principles emanating from *Johnson*—the discovery doctrine, the inferior status of Indian property rights, the notion of conquest, the allegedly inferior cultural standing of tribes, the impaired ability of tribes to sell their "incomplete" title, and the "so-called" diminished political status of tribes—have had lasting implications for indigenous-nonindigenous relations.[50]

Marshall's retrospective vision of "discovery"—the definitive principle in the case—created a "landlord-tenant" relationship between the federal government and the Indian tribes. "The federal government, as the ultimate landlord, not only possessed the power to terminate the 'tenancy' of its occupants but also could materially affect the lives of Indians through its control and regulation of land use."[51] Several well-worn quotes from the opinion give clear evidence of this unilateral transmutation of Indian property and political rights, based solely on the Court's own self-generated notions. In this case, the Court was willing to violate even Euro-American individual property rights to place itself in a superior political position relative to tribal nations who were not even parties to the dispute.

On the "Discovery" Principle: Masking the Discovery Doctrine

On the discovery of this immense continent, the great nations of Europe were eager to appropriate to themselves so much of it as they could respectively acquire . . . But as they were all in pursuit of nearly the same object, it was necessary, in order to avoid conflicting settlements . . . to establish a principle, which all should acknowledge as the law by which the right of acquisition, which they all asserted, should be regulated, as between themselves. This principle was, that discovery gave title to the government by whose subjects, or by whose authority, it was made, against all other European governments, which title might be consummated by possession. The exclusion of all other Europeans necessarily gave to the nation making the discovery the sole right of acquiring the soil from the natives, and establishing settlements upon it. It was a right with which no European could interfere. . . .[52]

The United States, then, have unequivocally acceded to that great and broad rule by which its civilized inhabitants now hold this country. They hold, and assert in themselves, the title by which it was acquired. They maintain, as all others have maintained, that discovery gave an exclusive right to extinguish the Indian title of occupancy, either by purchase or by conquest; and gave also a right to such a degree of sovereignty, as the circumstances of the people would allow them to exercise.[53]

On the Tribes' Impaired Rights to both Soil and Sovereignty

In the establishment of these relations, the rights of the original inhabitants were, in no instance, entirely disregarded; but were, necessarily, to a considerable extent, impaired. They were admitted to be the rightful occupants of the soil, with a legal as well as just claim to retain possession of it, and to use it according to their own discretion; but their rights to complete sovereignty, as independent nations, were necessarily diminished, and their power to dispose of the soil, at their own will, to whomever they pleased, was denied by the original fundamental principle, that discovery gave exclusive title to those who made it.[54]

An absolute title to lands cannot exist, at the same time, in different persons, or in different governments. An absolute [title] must be an exclusive title, or at least a title which excludes all others not compatible with it. All our institutions recognise the absolute title of the crown, subject only to the Indian right of occupancy, and recognize the absolute title of the crown to extinguish that right. This is incompatible with an absolute and complete title in the Indians.[55]

So too, with respect to the concomitant principle, that the Indian inhabitants are to be considered merely as occupants, to be protected, indeed, while in peace, in the possession of their lands, but to be deemed incapable of transferring the absolute title to others. However this restriction may be opposed to natural right, and to the usages of civilized nations, yet, if it be indispensable to that system under which the country has been settled, and be adapted to the actual condition of the two people, it may, perhaps, be supported by reason, and certainly cannot be rejected by courts of justice.[56]

It has never been contended that the Indian title amounted to nothing. Their right of possession has never been questioned. The claim of government extends to the complete ultimate title, charged with this right of possession, and to the exclusive power of acquiring that right.[57]

The thrust of the Court's message in *Johnson* was that indigenous peoples do not have the natural right exercised by citizens of "civilized" nations to sell their property to whomever they wish. Basically, Marshall had acknowledged that tribal nations possessed certain rights and a form of title that could be disposed of under certain situations. To legitimate the denial of full tribal territorial sovereignty and complete political sovereignty, Marshall pulled together a conflicting and confusing potpourri of arguments. First, he couched his argument against recognition of full tribal property rights on the basis of their allegedly inferior, non-Christian cultural status, though he tried to downplay this cultural ethnocentrism by saying, "We will not enter into the controversy, whether agriculturalists, merchants and manufacturers have a right, on abstract principles, to expel hunters from the territory they possess, or to contract their limits."[58] Marshall believed that leaving the Indians alone in sole possession of their territory was tantamount to "leaving the country a wilderness."[59]

Marshall made several equivocal statements about the doctrine of "conquest" and how this alleged domination had affected the relationship between tribes and European and Euro-American nations. After a long discussion about the limitations placed upon conquered peoples by the conquering nation, Marshall rechanneled and redirected his thoughts, stating that the "law which regulates, and ought to regulate in general, the relations between the conqueror and the conquered, was incapable of application to a people [tribes] under such circumstances."[60] The result was that the Court created a "new and different rule, better adapted to the actual state of things. . . ."[61] That "rule" was Marshall's innovative deployment of the historically fictitious doctrines of discovery and conquest to legitimize the United States' power over tribes.[62]

In a remarkable admission Marshall said, "However extravagant the pretension of converting the discovery of an inhabited country into conquest may appear; if the principle has been asserted in the first instance, and afterwards, sustained; if a country has been acquired and held under it; if the property of the great mass of the community originates in it, it becomes the law of the land, and cannot be questioned."[63] This is an amazing confession. The Chief Justice was candidly admitting that the doctrines of discovery and of conquest were nothing more than extravagant pretenses without any basis in fact. Nevertheless, the Supreme Court had decided for purely political and economic reasons to transform these legal fictions into legal concepts.

Marshall went on to argue that Johnson and Graham, as successors to the original purchasers of Indian title in the two prerevolutionary land transactions, had, in buying land within Indian Country, incorporated themselves within that tribal territory and therefore held their acquired title under tribal protection and were subject to tribal law.[64] The United States, by contrast, in concluding postrevolutionary treaties with the tribes for the same territory, had secured recognizable title to the lands in dispute partly because the tribes had been at war with the United States and retained the right to annul any previous land grant they had made to American citizens.[65] In short, the Chief Justice was saying that the plaintiffs' claims were defeated because the tribes themselves had extinguished their interests by selling the land again, this time to the United States.

In his conclusion, Marshall had cleverly reached a political/legal compromise that avoided two contrasting visions of Indian title: 1) that the doctrine of discovery completely vanquished Indian title in toto or 2) that tribes held a title equal to the fee-simple title that was wholly unaffected by the claims of the European and U.S. "discoverers."[66] The former would have left the tribes with no enforceable interests whatsoever; the latter would have nullified state and federal grants derived from Indians. The end result, of course, was the enshrinement, the institutionalization of a theory of tribal subordination to the federal government.[67] Put more pithily, "*Johnson*'s acceptance of the Doctrine of Discovery into U.S. law preserved the legacy of 1,000 years of European racism and colonialism directed against nonwestern peoples. White society's exercise of power over Indian tribes received the sanction of the Rule of Law in *Johnson v. McIntosh.*"[68]

A solid argument can be made[69] that *Johnson* was implicitly overruled by two later cases, *Worcester v. Georgia* (1832) and especially *Mitchel v. U.S.* (1835). The fact remains, however, that this decision is still regularly cited by commentators and, more importantly, relied upon as "good" precedent by the Supreme Court, as will become evident in the discussion of later cases involving jurisdiction and land claims.

THE FORCED PIERCING OF
TRIBAL SOVEREIGNTY BY FEDERAL LAW

The period of twenty-three years between *Johnson* and *United States v. Rogers* (1846) was a wildly tumultuous era in both indigenous and American history. If there is no such viable entity as "federal Indian law," with a clear and well-delineated set of principles and precepts that are generally followed, then it is also true that there is not and has never been—with a brief exception of the first few years of the American Republic—any such creature as federal Indian policy operating with a distinctive conceptual framework and with explicit terms and constructs forming an overarching paradigm. What Commissioner of Indian Affairs William Dole said in 1864 has from the early 1800s been as true as it is today: "From a glance at the history of our relations with the Indian, it will appear that we have been governed by the course of *events*, rather than by the adoption of a well-settled *policy.*"[70]

In the mid-to-late nineteenth century this dichotomy of Indian policy and law appeared under another set of somewhat less dichotomous terms: Removal versus Civilization. The removal position, expressed in the Indian Removal Act of 1830[71] and numerous treaties, many of which tribes were coerced into signing, advocated the voluntary and, "when necessary," the forced dispossession of Indians from their aboriginal homelands. As Commissioner of Indian Affairs Elbert Herry noted in his annual report for 1831: "Gradually diminishing in numbers and deteriorating in condition; incapable of coping with the superior intelligence of the white man, ready to fall into the vices, but inapt to appropriate the benefits of the social state; the increasing tide of white population threatened soon to engulf them, and finally to cause their extinction."[72] A majority of federal officials would not accept this allegedly inevitable situation. The federal government responded by developing the Indian Removal program which, it was thought, would save the tribes from obliteration since they would be "under the protection of the United States. . . ."[73]

The phrase "under the protection of the United States" is, of course, intrinsically connected to the option of "civilizing" the Indian tribes. The idea of "civilization" for indigenous peoples had been a major impetus animating much of the federal policymakers' agenda since the formation of the American Republic. In fact, in 1818, a House committee report noted, "in the present state of our country, one of two things seems to be necessary, either that those sons of the great forest should be *moralized* or *exterminated:* humanity would rejoice at the former, but shrink with horror from the latter."[74]

Both positions are grounded in the assumption that indigenous peoples were different—politically, culturally, socially, spiritually—in ways that could not and should not be tolerated. And while the two positions sparked ample and often vigorous debate in congressional, judicial, and executive chambers, "they functioned to exclude from discourse a third ideological point of view, that of cultural relativism. The idea that Indians in America should be allowed to perpetuate a radically different cultural heritage from that of white settlers . . . was not seriously entertained throughout much of American history.[75]

Still, the tension between these two opposite yet interrelated concepts—removal and civilization—fueled both knowingly and unknowingly a chain of events that would culminate in Chief Justice Roger Taney's perplexing decision in *United States v. Rogers.* In the last half of the nineteenth century, political relations between tribes and the U.S. were largely determined either by treaties or by Indian trade and intercourse acts. These acts, the first passed in 1790, the final and enduring one in 1834,[76] were established to systematize the regulation of Indian trade, restrict liquor in Indian territory, and protect the disposition of tribal lands. The 1834 codification was also important in that it incorporated the germane provisions of an 1817 law which extended federal criminal jurisdiction over interracial (Indian and non-Indian) crimes in Indian Country.[77]

During this era, Indian-on-Indian crimes were not affected by these laws, because to adjudicate such matters would have been a direct violation of tribal sovereignty. Efforts continued, however, on the part of some federal lawmakers to control even solely domestic tribal matters. For example, the internal schism among the Cherokee Indians in the 1840s prompted President James K. Polk on April 13, 1846, to suggest

> the propriety of making such amendments of the laws regulating intercourse with the Indian tribes as will submit to trial and punishment in the courts of the United States all Indians guilty of murder, and such other felonies as may be designated, when committed on other Indians within the jurisdiction of the United States. Such a modification of the existing laws is supported, because if offenders against the laws of humanity in the Indian Country are left to be punished by Indian law, they will generally, if not always, be permitted to escape with impunity. This has been the case in repeated instances among the Cherokees.[78]

Three months later, a bill was introduced that would have extended the criminal laws of the United States over Indian Country. The Committee on the Judiciary, which recommended the bill, noted that they had arrived at that conclusion because it would "be the best calculated of anything to put an end to the frequent murders in the Indian Country."[79]

The Cherokee Nation, astutely aware of their treaty-recognized sovereign rights, quickly and forcefully responded to President Polk's statement and the vigorous congressional sentiment to have federal law intrude into Cherokee territory. On May 4, 1846, Principal Chief John Ross and others memorialized the Senate on the difficulties within their nations and their relations to the United States. Ross began by saying that the Indian nations had always been recognized as separate sovereignties. He described their treaty rights and said the Cherokees "have always had their own legislatures" and have "without interference, made such laws they considered best suited to the peculiar circumstances of their country and people."[80] Ross and his colleagues presciently noted that "so, also, if the laws of the U.S. may be extended over the Indian Country in specialized cases, why may it may not be done in all cases? And surely, if the U.S. may enact laws, they have the right to administer and execute them . . . What is the limitation of this power, but the unrestricted discretion of the American government upon any given case arising upon any supposed necessity?"[81]

The Cherokee delegation concluded their memorial by stating that the United States' "monstrous pretension" in mandating its criminal laws over Cherokee country was without precedent and without legal basis. Enactment of the laws of criminal jurisdiction would have represented the demise of an essential attribute of sovereignty. "If this may be done," said the Cherokee, "surely all the residue of less important powers may be in the same manner arrogated and the right to prescribe all the laws, and to appoint judges to administer, and officers to execute them."[82]

While the Cherokee Nation was, for the moment, successful in fending off the federal intrusion of criminal jurisdiction over purely domestic criminal offenses, the Court's handling of white-on-white crime—even if the offending white had been adopted by Indians—committed in Indian Country would initiate a chain of events that was to unilaterally redefine the legal and political standing of tribal nations.

United States v. Rogers

THE ENSHRINEMENT OF RACE-BASED LAW AND THE GENESIS OF THE "POLITICAL QUESTION" DOCTRINE MASK

This case arose in 1845 in the Cherokee Nation, a portion of which was geographically situated in the State of Arkansas. Importantly, as in *Johnson*, the Cherokee Nation was not a party in the suit; nevertheless, the judicial language generated by Chief Justice Taney in this case—language which is without historical or legal foundation—was to have, as John Ross predicted at the time of the decision, a debilitating and long-lasting effect not only on the Cherokee Nation but on all tribal nations.[83]

Based on prior treaties, the United States had limited jurisdiction over Indian territory. Article 5 of the 1835 treaty with the Cherokee stated that the federal government would "secure to the Cherokee Nation the right by their national council to make and carry into effect all such laws as they may deem necessary for the government and protection of the *persons* and *property* within their own country belonging to their people or *such persons as have connected themselves with them:* provided always that they shall not be inconsistent with the Constitution of the United States and such acts of Congress as have been or may be passed regulating trade and intercourse with the Indians. . . ."[84] (emphasis mine).

HISTORICAL BACKDROP

William S. Rogers, a white man, had voluntarily emigrated into the Cherokee Nation sometime during 1836. In November of that year he married a Cherokee woman in a traditional tribal ceremony. Their marriage lasted until her death in 1843. During the course of their marriage they had several children who continued to reside within the boundaries of their Cherokee homeland. And Rogers, having incorporated himself in Cherokee territory, was treated, recognized, and had been adopted as a Cherokee by the "proper authorities thereof, and exercised and exercises all the rights and privileges of a Cherokee Indian in said tribe. . . ."[85]

Rogers, a yeoman, got into a deadly scuffle in September 1844 with Jacob Nicholson, who, like Rogers, was Euro-American by race, had married into the Cherokee Nation, and was, by Cherokee law, a citizen of their nation. Rogers killed Nicholson by stabbing him in the side with a five-dollar knife.[86] Rogers was arrested, then indicted by the grand jury in the district court of Arkansas in April 1845. When he was brought into federal court to hear the indictment, Rogers, representing himself, argued that the district court lacked jurisdiction to try him because both he and the deceased were regarded legally as *Indians* by the Cherokee Nation and under the 1834 trade and intercourse act the United States lacked jurisdiction in such cases.

U.S. District Attorney Samuel H. Hempstead responded by arguing that an American citizen could not expatriate himself, particularly to an Indian tribe, without some positive federal law authorizing him to do so. He went on to say that whites could not join tribes by marriage, emigration, or adoption unless the federal law allowed it. Hempstead conveniently overlooked the far-from-uncommon occurrence of American citizens renouncing their citizenship and applying for citizenship in another nation (subject to a decision by the receiving country whether to receive or repatriate the individual's application).

The district attorney's assertion that whites could not be adopted into Indian tribes without federal consent was also inaccurate. For years, a small but steady stream of whites had left American soil and settled with Indian tribes. Such an individual, as Marshall noted in *Johnson*, whether purchasing land or otherwise settling in Indian territory, "incorporates himself with them, so far as respects the property purchased; holds their title under their protection, and [is] subject to their laws."[87]

On the contrary, Hempstead's argument was that the act of Congress relating to Indian-on-Indian crimes did not encompass whites who had intermarried and/or who resided in Indian territory. The district attorney's argument, and this would prove crucial, was that a decision in favor of Rogers "would encourage worthless Americans to take refuge on the frontier."[88]

The district court, with Supreme Court Justice Peter Daniel sitting as a circuit judge alongside District Judge Benjamin Johnson, took the issue under advisement, no doubt comprehending the importance of the question involved. As they pondered whether to resolve the decision between them or to send it up to the Supreme Court by way of certificate of division,[89] the local newspaper, *The Arkansas Gazette*, on April 22, 1845, suggested in an article that if Rogers's argument proved the superior one, then Congress should step forth with legislation to give the federal courts jurisdiction—notwithstanding that there was no basis in law for such an action—that would intrude into the jurisdictional heart of Indian territory. The paper excitedly noted that "the peace of the frontier and the enforcement of law and justice require this."[90]

After due consideration, Daniel and Johnson decided that the issues warranted Supreme Court review. Justice Daniel left Little Rock on April 28 for the long ride back to Washington, D.C., under the assumption that Rogers would remain in jail until the forwarded questions could be answered by himself and his colleagues on the Supreme Court during the following term. Less than a month later, on May 13, and long before the Court would hear the case, Rogers and his cellmate, an escaped slave, attacked their jailer and escaped. In a spirited effort to return to Indian Country, Rogers attempted to ford a river but drowned. Several days later his body was recovered.[91] The case should therefore have been rendered moot since Rogers's death suspended justiciable controversy. But the Supreme Court never learned of Rogers's death.[92] When the case came up in the January term of 1846, the federal government was represented by Attorney General Mason. No counsel appeared for Rogers, which during that era was not unusual since not all defendants could afford lawyers and since defendants were not required to appear on their own behalf.

THE CERTIFIED QUESTIONS

The district court had certified six questions to the Supreme Court. While Justice Taney, writing for a unanimous court, "abstain[ed] from giving a specific answer to each question,"[93] the sparsely worded opinion, only slightly more than three pages long, dramatically revised the actual history of the tribal-federal relationship, unilaterally redefined the legal and political standing of tribes—especially over questions related to tribal citizenship and membership—and mischaracterized the property rights of Indians. Although the Court chose not to address the six questions, they are analyzed herein because they give testimony to the astonishing arrogance on the part of federal officials over what should have been an easily decided opinion.

The first question centered on whether American citizens could voluntarily cede their allegiance to the United States without the federal government's prescribing the conditions of such a severance. This question ignored the fact that Rogers had long since disavowed his political rights as an American when he entered Cherokee country in 1836 and was adopted by that tribe. The lower court argued as if he carried U.S. citizenship, when all evidence pointed out that he had not done so for nearly a decade. It does not appear that the district court or the Supreme Court made any effort to contact the Cherokee Nation's national office in Tahlequa, Oklahoma, to determine whether he was, indeed, an adopted member of the tribe, as he maintained all along.

Second, the lower court queried whether a "federal" citizen could "transfer" his political allegiance to another government. The justices, more specifically, asked whether a citizen had the right or the power vested in him "as a free moral and political agent, or derived to him from the law of nature or from the law of nations" to abandon his allegiance and carry it over to another government.[94]

The third question reflected extraordinary paternalistic and ethnocentric innuendo, particularly when placed alongside the prior knowledge of Indian nations and their sovereign status. Was a tribe "a separate and distinct government or nation, possessing political rights and power such as authorize them to receive and adopt, as members of their state, the subjects or citizens of other states or governments . . . and to naturalize such subjects or citizens, and make them exclusively or effectually members, subjects, or citizens of the said Indian tribe, with regard to civil and political rights and obligations?"[95] This question began innocently enough with a characterization of tribes that has been a persistent thorn in the federal government's efforts to understand tribal standing in relation to the United States: tribes that had not been created under the federal Constitution and yet existed as nonincorporated parties outside that framework while geographically residing within the boundaries of the United States and being territorially surrounded by the United

States. The question began thus: "Could the tribe of Indians residing without the limits of any one of the States, but within the territory of the United States" be recognized as a distinctive polity?

This notion of *geographic* incorporation as compared to *political-legal* incorporation is crucial and reappears, particularly in contemporary case law,[96] as a divisive element that works to preclude a smooth return to justice for tribes because the courts vacillate dramatically over its interpretation. In *Cherokee Nation v. Georgia* (1831), for instance, Marshall noted that while Indians had an undoubted right of occupancy, their lands were still *within* the territory to which the United States asserted a title independent of the Indians' assertions. Marshall synthesized the Cherokee's political and geographical existence and generated a novel status in law—a "domestic-dependent" national status. By contrast, the same Court a year later in *Worcester v. Georgia* emphatically stressed the tribes' "foreign" political status to the United States notwithstanding their geographical or territorial position vis-à-vis the United States.

The fourth certified question was whether a white person, by his own actions combined with those of the tribe, could become in his "social, civil, and political relations and condition a Cherokee Indian." Fifth, the Court asked, did the twenty-fifth section of the 1834 Trade and Intercourse Act, which exempted from federal jurisdiction crimes committed by Indians against other Indians, apply only to what were termed "full-blood Indians," or did it also apply to adopted persons and others residing in Indian territory? Here we see the introduction into federal Indian law of race as a definitive variable. The last question centered on whether, based on Rogers's plea, the Supreme Court even had jurisdiction to hear the case.

MASKING WITHIN THE DECISION: THE OPINION

Taney quickly moved to cast off most of the questions his colleague Justice Daniel and the district judge had sent up, saying that some were not "material in the decision of the case."[97] One of the most important powers of the Court is the right to be selective not only in the cases heard, but in the questions to be answered. "The power to decide what to decide," says David O'Brien, "also enables the court to set its own agenda."[98]

Having discarded most of the questions, Taney moved swiftly and rendered a decision that was every bit as traumatic for tribes as his infamous *Dred Scott* decision,[99] to be discussed later in this chapter, would be for African Americans. Taney's decision in *United States v. Rogers* began:

The country in which the crime is charged to have been committed is a *part of the territory* of the United States, and not within the limits of any particular State. It is true that it is occupied by the tribe of Cherokee Indians. But it has been *assigned to them* by the United States, as a place of domicile for the tribe, and they hold and occupy it with the *assent of the United States*, and under their authority. The native tribes who were found on this continent at the time of its discovery have *never been acknowledged or treated as independent nations* by the European governments, nor regarded as the owners of the territories they respectively occupied. On the contrary, the *whole continent was divided and parcelled out*, and granted by the governments of Europe as if it had been vacant and unoccupied land, and the Indians continually held to be, and treated as, *subject to their dominion and control*.[100] (emphasis mine)

The italics flag erroneous statements illustrating the Court's unanimous fabrication of a new history which would justify deeper federal encroachments into tribal sovereignty. The most inaccurate statements are as follows. First was the presumption that Cherokee land was actually territory belonging to the United States and that their territory had been "assigned" to them. As the Cherokee had been relocated from the Southeast to the West, these lands had been exchanged for the Cherokee's ancestral homes in "fee simple." In other words, the Cherokee merely transferred their aboriginal land rights from their eastern territory to territory in the west. The land clearly belonged to the tribe and was not "part of the territory" of the United States in the sense of property. It was patented to the Cherokee Nation by the President of the United States under the terms of the 1830 Removal Act and prior agreements. Article Five, for instance, of the 1835 treaty described earlier, began with this statement: "The United States hereby covenant and agree that the lands ceded to the Cherokee Nation in the foregoing article shall, in no future time without their consent, be included within the territorial limits or jurisdiction of any state or territory."[101] The United States retained only the Fort Gibson military reservation (and even that would revert back to the Cherokee Nation if the U.S. abandoned it) and the right to establish other posts and military roads "for the interest and protection" of the Cherokee. The individual property rights of Cherokee citizens were to be respected and in the event they were interfered with, the federal government was bound to provide just compensation.[102]

The second inaccuracy was the idea that the Cherokee held title to their lands only with the "assent of the United States and under their authority." The only *authority* retained by the United States, besides control and ownership of the military fort and construction of certain structures, involved the federal government's pledge to "protect the Cherokee Nation from domestic strife and foreign enemies and against intestine wars between the several tribes," and the promise to protect the Cherokee against "interruptions and intrusions from citizens of the United States, who may attempt to settle in the country without their consent. . . ."[103] The President of the United States had the "authority" and, more importantly, the duty to remove such interlopers.

Third, Taney's most brazen fabrication was that tribes had "never been acknowledged or treated as independent nations" or regarded as "the owners of the territories they respectively occupied." This double assault on tribes as legitimately recognized nations and as property owners ignored the evidence of several hundred preexisting treaties which European nations and later the United States had negotiated with Indian nations. Further, ample evidence through Supreme Court case law— particularly the Marshall Court's Indian law decisions in *Worcester v. Georgia* (1832), which affirmed the sanctity of Indian treaties and the independence of tribal nations, and *Mitchel v. United States* (1835), which emphasized the fact that tribes were the possessors of a property title that was as "sacred as fee-simple"—documented the existence of a title that could be sold by the tribes to whomever they chose. This right is also evidenced by the distinctive placement of tribes in the Commerce Clause as separate polities.

Finally, Taney inaccurately stated that the lands of the United States had been effectively "divided and parcelled out" as if there had been no prior human presence and the tribes thereafter were dealt with as "subjects" of the discovering European nations.

The pivotal notion in Taney's historically and politically inaccurate characterization of indigenous/western relations is the term "consent" as defined in the Northwest Ordinance of 1787, which stated that the federal government would never violate the rights or properties of tribes without their consent. One of the tribal policies wielded by Europeans and Euro-Americans has been to view the tribes as "primitive cultures," indigenous groups not entitled to the same degree of respect as Western nations. Ignoring the precedent of consent, this attitude could pretentiously proclaim that by "discovery," Europeans, and later Americans, could lay claim to the Americas in disregard of actual Indian presence. Had consent not been a viable doctrine, there would have been no need for the hundreds of treaties that were entered into with tribal nations. Had consent not been a viable doctrine, there would have been no call for such presidential pronouncements as George Washington's Third Annual Message in 1791, in which he proposed to ensure the "happiness" of the Indians by seeing that they received the benefits of an "impartial dispensation of justice." And had consent not been a viable doctrine, the United States, from its inception, would have been enacting laws that subjected tribes to federal domination, rarely the case up to this historical point, as demonstrated by Taney's own Court.

Continuing his discussion, Taney, in language which served as a precursor to the plenary power notion[104] that would be definitively unleashed in *United States v. Kagama* (1886; see Chapter 3), said that "from the very moment the general government came into existence to this time, it has exercised its power over this unfortunate race in the spirit of humanity and justice, and has endeavored by every means in its power to enlighten their minds and increase their comforts, and to save them if possible from the consequences of their own vices."[105] The Chief Justice had not only reinvented history—wrongly asserting that the federal government had *always* wielded unlimited power over tribes—but had also belittled the Indians with the language of cultural stereotype.

Taney then interjected what would later become one of the Supreme Court's most effective doctrines not only to deny tribal nations justice but, perhaps more accurately, to prevent their even having a forum for the airing of tribal or individual Indian grievances against federal, state, corporate, or private interest in judicial corridors. Taney articulated the "political question" doctrine as follows:

> But had it been otherwise, and were the right and the propriety of exercising this power now open to question, yet it is a question for the *law-making* and *political departments* of the government, and *not for the judicial*. It is our duty to expound and execute the law as we find it. . . .[106] (emphasis mine)

With this somewhat inarticulate but nonetheless effective pronouncement, the federal government had bestowed upon itself virtually unconstrained power to do what it wanted to anyone in Indian territory. Taney was now saying that even if Rogers or other parties had a case, the political question doctrine precluded the Court from even hearing the claims. Taney's disclaimer of judicial initiative effectively masked his own actions. He was not merely expounding or executing the law; he and the rest of the Court had vigorously stepped outside that purely interpretive role and had dramatically redefined tribal political and property status.

The political question doctrine warrants immediate analysis because it ranks alongside the plenary power concept as one of the most effective judicial strategies utilized by the Supreme Court to diminish and in some cases to eradicate tribal rights. But while plenary power may be defined in a constructive way—as exclusive or preemptive—to protect Indian rights from state advances, the political question construct has no such redeeming definitional value from a tribal standpoint. It has received ample scholarly attention,[107] and rightfully so, because it was a favorite judicial tactic from the time of this case until its demise in 1980 with *United States v. Sioux Nation*.[108]

To restate, the commerce and treaty-making clauses of the Constitution extended to the political branches of the federal government precise and exclusive authority to regulate the federal government's affairs with Indian tribes. Because of this constitutional allocation of authority, the Supreme Court generally deferred to the legislative and executive branches in the area of Indian affairs.[109] In fact, the power of judicial review over the substantive content of federal Indian policy was limited to the same extent as was judicial power to review foreign affairs decisions. "In analogy to legal concepts governing foreign relations, the federal government's power to make treaties with the Indians was considered a political question, beyond judicial examination."[110] In other words, the Court's only legitimate concern is whether the political branches of government, federal or state, have exceeded constitutional limitations. And as long as the political branches act within their constitutional powers, "whether they have done wisely or well is a 'political question' which is not for the courts to consider."[111]

Prior to its negation in 1980, the political question rule had been used frequently by the Supreme Court as a rationale to exclude from review the following issues of critical importance to American Indian tribes: the status of Indian nations, the validity and operation of Indian treaties under international law and foreign constitutional law, the power of Congress to legislate over Indian people and their territory, the historical claims of tribes against the United States, and the title to Indian lands.[112]

Although the political question doctrine is now defunct, there is nothing in the current canon of "Indian law" to prevent its resuscitation. Moreover, the Court still maintains—though on a more selective basis today because of the Rehnquist Court's willingness to act in a powerful policymaking capacity—a deferential position to Congress in the field of Indian affairs. While this deference may have been understandable so long as tribes were dealt with as foreign nations and so long as challengers—states or individuals—were often confronting federal authority, it is unclear why the Court is presently unable to "define the extent of Congress's power over Indian affairs."[113] The result of this failure to restrain Congress has only encouraged further unrelenting assertions of congressional power over tribal nations.

In the last section of his opinion, Chief Justice Taney introduced and elaborated what "the law" mythically denies—an explicit racial standard and classification system in a political context. The question of Rogers's status as a Cherokee was the key. If he was a recognized Cherokee, then under the 1834 non-Indian Intercourse statute, the Cherokee Nation had jurisdiction. If he was white, however, then federal law applied. Taney, of course, had already vested in Congress what it had never before possessed—a virtually absolute power over Indians, their territory, and Indian Country's residents—completely unconnected to treaty or constitutional law. And in so doing, he cleared the way for the next step, which was to proclaim "that the Indian tribes residing within the territorial limits of the United States are subject to their [U.S.] authority, and where the country occupied by them is not within the limits of one of the States, Congress may by law punish any offence committed there, no matter whether the offender be a white man or an Indian."[114]

But Taney did not stop even there. He proceeded to involve the Supreme Court in a pseudoscientific anthropological exercise to determine who could be recognized as a Cherokee Indian:

> Consequently, the fact that Rogers had become a member of the tribe of Cherokees is no objection to the jurisdiction of the court, and no defence to the indictment, provided the case is embraced by the provisions of the act of Congress [1834]. . . . And we think it very clear, that a white man who at mature age is adopted in an Indian tribe does not thereby become an Indian, and was not intended to be embraced in the exception [1834 Indian-on-Indian Crimes] above mentioned. He may by such adoption become entitled to certain privileges in the tribe, and make himself amenable to their laws and usages. Yet he is not an Indian; and the exception is confined to those who by the usages and customs of the Indians are regarded to belonging to their race. It does not speak of members of a tribe, but of the race generally,

of the family of Indians; and it intended to leave them both, as regarded their own tribe, and other tribes also, to be governed by Indian usages and customs.[115]

This definition of the Indian "race" has little to do with "law." Mere pseudoanthropology in legal raiment, it does, however, have much to do with a convoluted theory of race. Of equal importance is the basis on which the Supreme Court denied Rogers's status as an Indian, especially in light of the Court's failure to contact the Cherokee Nation's office, who could have verified or denied Rogers's citizenship in the tribe. Without jurisdiction, the court acted to deny the political status of tribes, a status long recognized in treaty, historical, and constitutional circles.

In a subsequent passage, Taney said it would "perhaps be found difficult to preserve peace among them, if white men of every description might at pleasure settle among them, and, by procuring an adoption by one of the tribes, throw off all responsibility to the laws of the United States, and claim to be treated by the government and its officers as if they were Indians born."[116] This is probably the most substantive issue behind the Court's ruling. Taney was worried, and understandably so, that whites would use Indian territory as a refuge to which they could return after committing their crimes. But neither the government nor the Court made an effort to consult with the Cherokee Nation's officials although the crime had occurred on their land. The territorial sovereignty of the Cherokee Nation was thus denied. Rogers, according to Taney, was purportedly one of a class of men "who are most likely to become Indians by adoption, and who will generally be found the most mischievous and dangerous inhabitants of the Indian Country."[117] But Rogers had lived in Cherokee country for nearly a decade, had married into the nation, and was in the process of raising a family. Taney had no objective basis for predicting that members of this ambiguous class would all be "mischievous and dangerous" persons. This fabricated argument, passed off as a legal fact, was added to the body of legal fictions that gained respectability as legal concepts.

Taney concluded the decision by evoking the 1835 Cherokee Treaty of New Echota from which he cited a portion of article 5 recognizing Cherokee self-government, but he maintained that the treaty provision was not in conflict with his interpretation of the 1834 Intercourse law. Taney insisted, however, that there was a conflict between a portion of article 5 of the Cherokee treaty and that section of the provision which said that Cherokee authority could not be "inconsistent with the U.S. Constitution" or other federal laws. There was no conflict, however, between the treaty provision and the 1834 statute as to the question of whether Rogers was a Cherokee citizen. If he was, as the evidence strongly suggested, then the treaty provision should have held. Justice Taney would not be dissuaded by Cherokee sovereignty, treaty law, or historical facts. He insisted that regardless of Rogers's having assumed responsibilities as a Cherokee, "his responsibility to the laws of the United States remained unchanged and undiminished. He was still a white man, of the white race, and therefore not within the exception in the act of Congress."[118]

WILL THE REAL TANEY PLEASE STAND UP!

Four short years later, the Supreme Court once again had an opportunity to comment on the political status of the Cherokee Nation. *Parks v. Ross*[119] involved an action brought by George Parks, the administrator for Samuel Parks, against John Ross, principal chief and superintending agent of the Cherokee Nation, for services (namely the provision of wagons and teams for relocating Cherokees) rendered by Samuel Parks (a Cherokee citizen) to Ross and the Cherokee Nation, who had been forced to remove from Georgia between 1838 and 1839. The facts of this case are less important than the following passage, written by Justice Robert Grier, who delivered the opinion for the unanimous court. Grier said:

> The Cherokees are in many respects a *foreign and independent nation. They are governed by their own laws and officers, chosen by themselves.* And though in a state of pupilage, and under the guardianship of the United States, this government has delegated no power to the courts of this district to arrest the public representatives or agents of Indian Nations who may be casually within their local jurisdiction, and compel them to pay the debts of their nation, either to an individual of their own nation, or a citizen of the United States.[120] (emphasis mine)

Still more revealing would be the language used by Chief Justice Taney in the crushing *Dred Scott v. Sandford* (1857).[121] That case had held that blacks had no rights which whites had to respect; they could not be citizens; and slavery could not be banned in unsettled territories. The following passage not only provides a much more accurate appraisal of tribal standing than did his opinion in *Rogers*, it also documents Taney's awareness of the facts that were masked in *Rogers* and his disingenuousness in employing them only when it suited his purpose to do so.

> The situation of this population [African-American] was altogether unlike that of the Indian race. The latter, it is true, formed no part of the colonial communities, and never amalgamated with them in social connections or in government. But although they were uncivilized, they were yet a *free and independent people*, associated together in nations or tribes, and *governed by their own laws*. Many of these political communities were situated in territories to which the white race claimed the ultimate right of dominion. But that claim was acknowledged to be subject to the right of the Indians to occupy it as long as they thought proper, and neither the English nor colonial Governments claimed or exercised any dominion over the tribe or nation by whom it was occupied, nor claimed the right to the possession of the territory, until the tribe or nation consented to cede it. *These Indian Governments were regarded and treated as foreign Governments*, as much so as if an ocean had separated the red man from the white; and their freedom has constantly been acknowledged, from the time of the first emigration to the English colonies to the present day, by the different Governments which succeeded each other. Treaties have been negotiated with them, and their alliance sought for in war; and the people who compose these Indian political communities have *always been treated as foreigners not living under our Government*.[122] (emphasis mine)

These comments, like many of Taney's remarks in *Rogers*, are dicta—that is, expressions which do not embody the determination of the Court. They were Taney's individual views and were not binding in subsequent cases; however, they do succinctly demonstrate Taney's dramatic vacillations from one case to the next. For example, in *Rogers*, tribes are not and have never been regarded as independent nations. Yet, in *Ross* and *Dred Scott* tribes are regarded as essentially the political equals of foreign governments. What is important is that it is the *Rogers* decision that has been the precedent cited in a multitude of cases which have adversely affected tribes by evoking a diminished, inferior tribal sovereignty, by the persistent use of the political question doctrine, and by the construction of a racial dimension to federal Indian policy and law.

In the summer of 1846, shortly after the *Rogers* pronouncement, the Senate Committee on the Judiciary convened and inquired into the "expediency," not the constitutionality, of extending federal criminal laws over the Indian territory.[123] The committee said the subject was one of "great interest and importance" because the 1834 law had been ineffective in controlling "crimes of the most shocking character. . . ."[124] The committee instructed Commissioner of Indian Affairs William Medill, T. Hartley Crawford, and William Armstrong for their opinions on the matter. Commissioner Medill responded for the group and, drawing expressly upon *Rogers*, said the federal government had the "original power . . . to subject the Indian tribes within the limits of their sovereignty to any system of laws having for their object the prevention or punishment of crimes, or the melioration of the condition and improvement of the red race. . . ."[125] "The correct doctrine on this point" was laid out, continued Medill, in the "views of the highest judicial tribunal of the land [and] must be deemed to be conclusive."[126]

Medill went further and said that this federal power of guardianship was essential to Indian "civilization" and the "improvement of their moral and intellectual condition."[127] While acknowledging that the United States historically had not interfered with internal tribal matters, "as the guardian of the Indians, and responsible for their welfare and happiness, . . . the United States [has] not, in any case, wholly divested itself of the power to *interfere*, when the laws of a tribe have been oppressive and unjust, or have been so enforced as to excite domestic strife and bloodshed."[128]

POST–CIVIL WAR INDIAN REFORM, 1866–1871:
THE PRECURSOR TO *CHEROKEE TOBACCO*

Frederick Jackson Turner once remarked that by the end of the Civil War "the West would claim the President, Vice-President, Chief Justice, Speaker of the House, Secretary of the Treasury, Post-master General, Attorney-General, General of the Army, and Admiral of the Navy."[129] Turner hypothesized that this was because the West was the "region of action, and in the crisis it took the reins."[130] He described how the "free lands are gone, the continent is crossed, and all this push and energy is turning into channels of agitation."[131]

The focus of much of this "agitated" behavior was tribal lands, tribal souls, and tribal culture. Within a spectacularly brief period, 1866–1871, there occurred several critical shifts, as well as continuations, in federal Indian policy and law. First, those tribes who had sided with the Confederacy in the Civil War were compelled to negotiate new treaties by which they surrendered vast areas of land.[132] Second, Congress authorized an Indian Peace Commission to negotiate peace treaties to end the growing hostilities between western tribes and Americans.[133] Third, in 1869 a ten-member Board of Indian Commissioners was authorized. Composed of prominent philanthropists, this unpaid group of influential eastern citizens was to work closely with the secretary of the interior in administering the political relationship between tribes and the United States.[134]

Fourth, President Grant, in an effort to eliminate abuses in the Indian office, and as part of the larger plan to assimilate the tribes, laid out his famous "Peace Policy." This policy assigned the Indian agencies scattered throughout the country to various Christian denominations. According to Grant, "No matter what ought to be the relations between such settlements and the aborigines, the fact is they do not harmonize well, and one or the other has to give way in the end."[135]

According to Grant, "a system which looks to the extinction of a race is too horrible for a nation to adopt without entailing upon itself the wrath of all Christendom and engendering in the citizens a disregard for human life and the rights of others, dangerous to society."[136] It was not, however, merely the wrath of other "civilized nations" that propelled the Grant administration to seek alternatives to warfare with the tribes. Economics and the railroads also played a key role in his decisions.

In the report issued by the Senate's Committee on the Pacific Railroad, Senator William Stewart (R., Nevada) wrote that tribes "can only be permanently conquered by railroads. The locomotive is the sole solution of the Indian question, unless the government changes its system of warfare and fights the savages the winter through as well as in summer."[137] Furthermore, Senator Stewart noted that the past thirty-seven years of wars with tribes had cost the United States twenty thousand lives and more than $750,000,000. In fact, urged Stewart, "the chairman of the House Committee on Indian Affairs estimated recently that the present current [expense] of our warfare with the Indians was $1,000,000 a week—$144,000 dollars a day."[138] Grant's "Peace Policy," it was believed, could do no worse and would undoubtedly be far less expensive and more morally defensible.

The fifth and most important modification in Indian policy centered on the subject of whether or not to continue the treaty process with tribal nations.[139] The rapidity and comprehensiveness of western expansion had forced federal officials to rethink their Indian policy. Treaty-making thus came under fire. Commissioner of Indian Affairs D. N.

Cooley in his 1866 *Annual Report* noted that peace could best be maintained with tribes by "treaty arrangements" and he urged "the continuance of the policy which has met with such gratifying success during the present and last year. . . ."[140]

In his *Annual Report* for 1869, Commissioner Ely S. Parker, a Seneca Indian, rekindled the treaty debate. He believed that the treaty process with tribes should be closed, though he agreed that treaties already in force should be faithfully executed.[141] On February 11, 1871, Representative William Armstrong (R., Pennsylvania) introduced the following joint resolution:

> That hereafter no Indian nation or tribe within the territory of the United States shall be acknowledged or recognized as an independent nation, tribe, or power, with whom the United States may contract by treaty; *and all treaties or agreements hereafter made by and between them, or any of them, and the United States shall be subject to the approval of Congress:* Provided, That nothing herein contained shall be considered to invalidate or impair the obligation of any treaty heretofore lawfully made and ratified with any such Indian nation or tribe.[142] (emphasis mine)

This House resolution, except for the important underscored passage, which was later deleted, was attached as an amendment to the Interior Department's 1872 appropriation bill. The deleted sentence was an acknowledgment that although the ratification process was changing, the essence of the treaty relationship itself was to be preserved. The amendment underwent intense bipartisan scrutiny but was eventually approved. Representative Sargent (R., California) proudly noted that the adoption of this measure had three beneficial results: (1) it would end what he called an "improvident system"; (2) it would save the federal government millions of dollars; and (3) it would give the House a voice in the process of negotiations with tribes.[143]

Although the substance of treatymaking continued in the form of agreements, this transformation in diplomatic relations presaged major problems for tribes and the tribal-federal relationship. Commissioner Francis A. Walker in his 1872 Indian Affairs *Annual Report* posed several interesting questions: What of tribal rights to lands which not been covered by treaty? What about tribes who had not yet been treated with, but who had the same political standing as treated tribes? How was the federal government legally going to secure title to tribal lands it desired?[144]

The answer, of course, was negotiated agreements. Although negotiations continued, however, the 1871 amendment represented a novel and dangerous way of perceiving the political relationship between tribes and the federal government. And although Congress continued to authorize commissions to negotiate agreements, it could, when it so desired, simply enact statutes which did not require tribal consent.[145]

This grave modification in the political relations between tribes and the federal government created a "feeling of betrayal among the Indians and vested dictatorial powers in the Indian agents, who were no longer seen as advocates for the tribes but as antagonists who sought to force immediate change and destroy tribal customs and practices."[146]

The Cherokee Tobacco

THE GENESIS OF REPUDIATION BY THE MASK OF "IMPLIED REPEAL"

Before moving into an analysis of this case, it is important to consider the prominent role the Cherokee Nation played in the Court's development of legal principles and legal masks which both enervated and devastated tribal sovereignty. The two most famous cases, of course, are *Cherokee Nation v. Georgia* (1831) and *Worcester v. Georgia* (1832). *The Cherokee Tobacco*, while not directly involving the Cherokee Nation as a party, originated in their territory, and Swayne's opinion had clear ramifications on the Cherokee Nation's status. The case actually involved two Cherokee individuals, but the legal principles emerging from the decision affected not only the Cherokee Nation but all other tribes with treaty rights. In Chapter 3 I will discuss yet another case involving the Cherokee Nation, *Cherokee Nation v. Southern Kansas Railway* (1890), a powerful case which further reduced the sovereign rights of the Cherokee Nation.

In the *United States Reports*, the volumes which contain the official versions of each Supreme Court decision, the case under discussion is entitled simply *The Cherokee Tobacco*. But in both the *Lawyer's Edition* and the *Supreme Court Report*, which are privately published editions containing information not available in the official edition, the full title of the case does more than raise interest: *Two Hundred and Seven Half-Pound Papers of Smoking Tobacco, etc.,*[147] *Elias C. Boudinot et al., Claimant Plaintiffs in error v. United States.* The "et cetera" amounts to what must have been a nearly complete inventory of the holdings of the defendant; and this intriguing title reveals the law's priorities in elevating such items as tobacco, tobacco products, and other items of property over the human players.

While each of the post–Civil War policy developments discussed earlier was crucial in recasting tribal-federal political relations, in general, the two most pertinent shifts for a discussion of *The Cherokee Tobacco* were the Cherokee Treaty of 1866 and the treaty termination law of 1871. Article 10 of the Cherokee Treaty stated that Cherokee citizens had the right to sell any product or merchandise without having to pay "any tax thereon which is now or may be levied by the United States."

Two years later, on July 20, 1868, Congress enacted a general revenue law. Section 107 of this law said that the internal revenue laws imposing taxes on liquor and tobacco products were to be "construed to extend to such articles produced anywhere within the exterior boundaries of the United States, whether the same shall be within a collection district or not." Justice Noah Swayne wrote the decision in this case for a deeply fractured Court (three justices concurred with Swayne, two dissented, and three did not participate). Swayne indicated the legal direction he was heading by noting at the outset of the opinion that the case involved "first, the question of the intention of Congress, and second, *assuming the intention to exist*, the question of its [Congress's] power to tax certain tobacco in the territory of the Cherokee nation, in the face of a prior treaty between that nation and the United States, that such tobacco should be exempt from taxation"[148] (emphasis mine). Swayne's assumption of Congress's intent, the crucial variable in the decision, yields one of the most problematic and ambiguous doctrines in Indian law— whether tribes, as preexisting and extraconstitutional entities, may be *included* or *excluded* under the scope of general laws enacted by Congress. The documentary evidence—including the preexisting political status of tribes (a status not created by or subject to the United States Constitution), prior Supreme Court precedent, the treaty relationship, and the constitutional clauses acknowledging the distinctive status of tribal polities—clearly supports exclusion. Indian territories, in other words, were not regarded as included in congressional enactments unless the tribe had given its explicit consent and unless they were expressly included in the law. Out of *The Cherokee Tobacco*, however, would emerge a new interpretation—that general congressional acts do apply to tribes unless Congress explicitly *excludes* them. This so-called inclusion theory is only one of several bizarre rules that flowed from this case.

HISTORICAL BACKGROUND

The defendant, Elias C. Boudinot, was a mixed-blood Cherokee who, with his uncle, negotiated a business deal with tobacco-factory owners in Missouri and then moved the operation into Cherokee Nation territory because of its tax-exempt status. This case, although not argued or decided until *after* the treaty termination rider had already become law on March 3, 1871, actually originated early in 1870, well before the cessation of treatymaking. And while there is nothing to indicate that Swayne's decision was directly correlated with the ending of treaties, one can speculate fairly securely that the legislative and judicial branches each had some awareness of what the other was doing on the subject. This is crucial to remember because as a result of this decision, and in conjunction with the treaty-ending law, tribes were rendered completely susceptible to federal congressional power.

MASKING WITHIN THE DECISION: THE OPINION

Swayne stated, "the only question argued in this court . . . is the effect to be given respectively to the 107th section of the act of 1868, and the 10th Article of the treaty of 1866, between the United States and the Cherokee Nation of Indians."[149] Swayne briskly summarized Boudinot's and his attorney's arguments and those of the U.S. attorneys and said, "considering the narrowness of the questions to be decided, . . . the case seems to us not difficult to be determined, and to require no very extended line of remarks to vindicate the soundness of the conclusions at which we have arrived."[150] His cavalier attitude is surprising considering what was at stake: the power of the federal government to extinguish, by an intent implied by the Court, a section of a ratified treaty with the Cherokee Nation without the consent of the Cherokee people; the power of the government to tax tribal members who were not American citizens and who thus had no political representation in Congress; and the power of the United States to violate the self-imposed protective trust relationship it had established with the Cherokee people long before.

Selectively drawing from the precedents established in *Cherokee Nation v. Georgia*, *U.S. v. Rogers*, *Johnson v. McIntosh*, and *Mackey v. Coxe*, Swayne relied on the unsupported argument that tribes inhabited territory considered to be a "part of the United States" and that Congress had undeniable authority over such territory. These notions of tribal territorial incorporation and an ill-defined presumption that the United States was inherently superior to the Cherokee Nation (discussed fully within the *Johnson* decision) had become reified by this time. Thus, Swayne could comfortably say that "both these propositions are so well settled in our jurisprudence that it would be a waste of time to discuss them or to refer to further authorities in their support."[151] Swayne declared, inaccurately, that there was an ample base of law which supported both propositions.[152] In fact, both theories, geographical incorporation and congressional authority over tribes, are flatly contradicted by the Court's rulings in *Worcester, Mitchel,* and *Kansas Indians,* and the resilient doctrine of tribal sovereignty.

In a passage similar to one enunciated in *Rogers* that has little to do with law and much to do with economics and reality, Swayne stated that the 1868 Revenue Act applied only to the sales of liquor and tobacco. This was considered by the Court to be essential because "nowhere would frauds to an enormous extent as to these articles be more likely to be perpetrated if this proposition were withdrawn. Crowds, it is believed, would be lured thither by the prospect of illicit gain."[153] Swayne, like Taney, had manufactured a fictitious scenario of potentially immoral individuals who would be tempted to take advantage of the tax break afforded the Boudinot smokeshop by the 1866 treaty provision. One scholar has suggested this as a possible scenario:

> Although it is not a matter of "official" record, one cannot ignore the probable attitude of U.S. government personnel toward non-payment of Federal taxes by recently surrendered enemies, taxes which weighed heavily on Union manufacturers in New York, Louisville, and St. Louis.[154] While westering whites were invading Indian preserves in defiance of treaty provisions, the Cherokee tobacco factories were invading adjacent commercial markets to the east under conditions which probably would be characterized today as "unfair trade practices." Had this continued, the laws of supply and demand could, in time, have forced a concentration of the nation's tobacco manufacturing industry within the borders of Indian Territory as a means of escaping Federal excises.[155]

Plausible as this scenario may be, it had nothing to do with the treaty rights guaranteed to the Cherokee by the federal government. Moreover, on what legitimate basis does the Supreme Court act when it interferes with or stifles the internal affairs of tribal nations without tribal consent in the form of some type of contractual agreement? Reading in a congressional intent that was nowhere evident in any of the accompanying political or legal documents, Swayne said:

> This consideration [of "illicit gain"] doubtless had great weight with those by whom the law was framed. The language of the section is as clear and explicit as could be employed. It embraces *indisputably the Indian territories*. Congress not having thought proper to *exclude them* it is not to this court to make the exception. If the exemption had been intended it would doubtless have been expressed. There being no ambiguity, there is no room for construction. It would be out of place. The section must be held to mean what the language imports. When a statute is clear and imperative, reasoning *ab inconvenienti* is of no avail. It is the duty of the courts to execute it. Further discussion of the subject is unnecessary. We think it would be like trying to prove a self-evident truth. The effort may confuse and obscure but cannot enlighten. It never strengthens the pre-existing conviction.[156] (emphasis mine)

Swayne was using semantics to cover his own policy interjection. Simply stated, had Congress meant to include Indian Territory in the Indian Revenue law, an inclusion that would have violated the 1866 treaty, it would have said so. Congress chose not to. Swayne and his colleagues, however, decided to do what Congress had refused to do. Furthermore, because tribes are not an integral part of the federal constitutional framework, as their treaty rights attest, the basis that Swayne assumed is that Congress *meant* to include them barring a fundamental change in either the Constitution (to incorporate tribes) or in the mutually agreed-upon 1866 treaty provision which guarantees the right of the tribal members to sell any product or merchandise "without any taxing restraint."

While there was no evidence that Congress in enacting the 1868 revenue law intended to abrogate article 10 of the 1866 treaty, Justice Swayne had devised a scenario in which the treaty provision and the municipal law were placed in direct conflict. "Undoubtedly," said Swayne, "one or the other must yield. The repugnancy is clear and they cannot stand together."[157] This is a typical and extremely effective judicial ploy wherein the Court creates a hypothesized chain of events in which two statutes, or in this case, a statute and a treaty provision, are in alleged conflict even though the two laws had separate origins and separate purposes. Having crafted such a semantic impasse, a justice is then able to "choose" the law that will meet the end goals of the Court. In this case, a compact between two sovereign nations was arbitrarily pitted against a mere domestic revenue law. The compact lost.

Swayne began his opinion with the obligatory statement that the Constitution, the laws of the United States, and treaties are the supreme law of the land. And after correctly noting that a treaty was incapable of altering the federal Constitution, he said that the Constitution had not settled the issue of what happens when treaties and congressional enactments were "in conflict." Having abstractly set up the parameters of the discussion in this way, Swayne then said: "A treaty may supersede a prior act of Congress, and an act of Congress may supersede a prior treaty. In the cases referred to these principles were applied to treaties with foreign nations. Treaties with Indian nations within the jurisdiction of the United States, whatever considerations of humanity and good faith may be involved and requiring their faithful observance, cannot be more obligatory." [158]

Over time, this section has been shortened to the following rule, popularly known as the "last-in-time" rule. In effect, whichever is latest in time, be it a treaty or a statute, stands. This was and remains a catastrophic precedent for tribes because the treaty termination law enacted two months earlier had effectively frozen tribes in political limbo and left them completely at the mercy of Congress. Theoretically and practically, any law enacted after March 3, 1871, could override any prior treaty. Tribal nations, moreover, were no longer recognized as polities capable of treating with the United States, yet they remained separate if wholly unequal sovereigns, outside the pale of the American Constitution. Swayne's effort to equate Indian treaties with foreign-nation treaties was a smoke screen, for obviously, foreign nations may continue to negotiate treaties with the United States and are not subject to federal domestic legislation.

Swayne attempted to soften this bludgeoning precedent by saying that the revenue law extended over the Indian territories "only as to liquors and tobacco. In all other respects the Indians in those territories are exempt." If tribes are exempt from all other revenue laws, then why not those applying to liquor and tobacco? Swayne rationalized it this way: "Revenue is indispensable to meet the public necessities. Is it unreasonable that this small portion of it shall rest upon these Indians? The [fraud] that might otherwise be perpetrated there by others, under the guise of Indian names and simulated Indian ownership, is also a consideration not to be overlooked."[159] Tribes, however, were not a part of the public. They did not then receive services or benefits as part of that population, receiving instead only what they were entitled to under treaties and the political relationship.

Finally, Swayne, who seemed to be personally acquainted with Boudinot, concluded his opinion by stating that while the two had acted under a "misapprehension of their legal rights," there was nothing impugning their "integrity or good faith."[160] While this statement appears somewhat trivial, it is actually quite important. Swayne and the Court had conflated the individual rights of Boudinot with the collective rights of tribes. All tribes have suffered as a result of this misperception, notwithstanding the high-sounding comments made about the individual claimants.

THE DISSENT OF JUSTICES BRADLEY AND DAVIS

Felix S. Cohen, an authority in the area of Indian policy and law, suggested in his classic work, *Handbook of Federal Indian Law*, that the precedent in *The Cherokee Tobacco* was implicitly overruled in the 1912 case *Choate v. Trapp*, which involved the state of Oklahoma's futile attempt to tax individual Indian lands. He based his observation on the fact that the *Choate* opinion was unanimous, while *The Cherokee Tobacco* was a four-to-two decision with three justices not involved in the decision.[161] This is still unresolved, but it is obvious that the dissent by Justice Joseph P. Bradley, concurred with by his brother David Davis, contained a vastly different interpretation of the doctrine of congressional intent and what was necessary to abrogate Indian treaty provisions.

Bradley began the dissent by emphatically noting:

> In my judgment it was not the intention of Congress to extend the internal revenue law to the Indian territory. That territory is an exempt jurisdiction. Whilst the United States has not relinquished its power to make such regulations as it may deem necessary in relation to that territory, and whilst Congress has occasionally passed laws affecting it, yet by repeated treaties the government has in effect stipulated that in all ordinary cases the Indian populations shall be autonomies, invested with the power to make and execute all laws for their domestic government. Such being the case, all laws of a general character passed by Congress will be considered as not applying to the Indian territory, unless expressly mentioned.[162]

Bradley's statement acknowledges that nothing in the federal Constitution or in any law or treaty vests in Congress power over Indian Territory, though he insinuates that the legislature may act if it so desires. Bradley's reliance on and deference to the treaty-established rights of the tribe sanctioned by the Senate and the President is an important reminder that organic tribal law is derived from an entirely different source than that of the United States or the individual states. He and Justice Davis accepted the argument raised by Boudinot and A. H. Garland (Boudinot's attorney) that "the United States have never asserted a right to levy taxes upon the property of Indians, within the Indian Country. No treaty has ever stipulated such a right. No one ever imagined that any such right existed, or anticipated that it would ever be presented." [163]

Bradley's second principal disagreement with the majority, one that would be utilized on many occasions in future Indian law cases, centered on the "implied" nature of the abrogation of an expressed treaty provision. As he said: "An express law creating certain special rights and privileges is held never to be repealed by implication by any subsequent law couched in general terms, nor by any express repeal of all laws inconsistent with such general law, unless the language be such as clearly to indicate the intention of the legislature to effect such appeal." [164] Briefly put, Bradley was saying that specific legal rights could not be overridden by general statutory laws.

After having closely examined all the evidence, Bradley concluded that the case involved much more than the mere alleged conflict between two comparable laws:

> The case before us is, besides, a peculiar one. The exempt jurisdiction here depends on a solemn treaty entered into between the United States government and the Cherokee Nation, in which the good faith of the government is involved, and not on a mere municipal law. It is conceded that the law in question cannot be extended to Indian territory without an implied abrogation of the treaty *pro-tanto*. And the opinion of the court goes upon the principle that Congress has the power to supersede the provisions of a treaty. In such a case there are peculiar reasons for applying with great strictness the rule that the exempt jurisdiction must be expressly mentioned to be affected. [165]

Here again we see the phrase "peculiar" being applied to the indigenous-federal relationship. In this situation Bradley seems keenly aware of the extreme political disadvantage tribes were being placed in by this decision, and he was concerned about what it said about the moral character of the United States, which was violating its own laws. This is more eloquently stated by Albert Pike and Robert W. Johnson in their brief for Boudinot:

On National Character

The United States is a great nation, able to dictate its own terms to a feeble people, under its protection, with which it was treating; and by a law of natural justice which can never be abrogated, it cannot demand that doubts as to the meaning of the language used by itself shall be resolved in its own favor. It was within its power to express itself to clearly . . . restrict them in the exercise of any of the rights before enjoyed by them, or impose new burdens on them. . . .[166]

On Treaty Abrogation

Certainly, as to treaties with foreign powers, the proposition that we have supposed above is true. The parties there are equal. There is no arbiter between them, and no tribunal before which one of them can enforce the contracts of the other. There are no antecedent relations of trust and confidence between them that qualify the treaty, and make it inviolable. . . . But an Indian treaty is one made with a small people that has accepted the *protection* of the United States. It is less a treaty than a compact . . . between guardian and ward. It is even more sacred than a formal compact made by the government with its own citizens; . . . To them [the Indians] the United States are pledged, by every tie of honor and good faith that human ingenuity can invest, not to violate the treaties and agreements made with them . . . It is not a question, therefore, of repealing one law by another law. It is a question of repealing a contract lawfully made, by the protector with those under its protection. . . .[167] (emphasis original)

Lastly, Bradley observed that other territories, such as Alaska, were exempted from the 1868 internal revenue law. Since Alaska was exempt, and there was nothing in the act that specifically excluded that territory, he wondered how tribes, who were also excluded and who, in addition, had explicit treaty provisions, could be held subject to the revenue law.

CONCLUSION

Elias Boudinot eventually secured some financial relief from Congress and the Court of Claims for the material losses he endured.[168] However, the political and legal losses sustained by tribes as a result of this decision have yet to be rectified. Since tribal rights were defined by treaties and not by the Constitution, and since treaty rights—frozen in 1871—could now be eradicated by "later" and implicit congressional laws, tribal political standing and treaty-based rights have remained tenuous at best.

CHAPTER 3

The Era of
Congressional Ascendancy
over Tribes: 1886–1903

The four cases under examination in this chapter—*United States v. Kagama, Cherokee Nation v. Southern Kansas Railway Company, Ward v. Race Horse*, and *Lone Wolf v. Hitchcock*—were considered during the period from 1886 to the early 1900s, which encompassed the most onerous and vicious years of federal Indian policy. It was a policy era bent on the destruction of tribes as identifiable cultural, sociological, and religious bodies. In the years from 1871 to *Kagama*, and in the two decades after the *Kagama* decision, "Congress exercised powers over Indians which, if asserted against State citizens, would not have survived constitutional challenge. Confiscation of property, restrictions on the Indians' use of their property, and supervision of tribes' political affairs violated even the somewhat looser First and Fifth Amendment standards applicable to the territories. . . ."[1]

The congressional acts and policies responsible for most of these vast reductions of tribal sovereignty, property, and civil and political rights included the assignment of Indian agencies to religious societies; the establishment of the Courts of Indian Offenses; the Major Crimes Act of 1885;[2] the General Allotment Act of 1887;[3] the 1891 amendment to the General Allotment Act;[4] the Curtis Act of 1898;[5] and the Burke Act of 1906.[6] It will become evident after studying these cases that the Court, as a partner alongside the political branches, maintained an extremely deferential position to the legislative branches, which adopted policies and laws focused on the detribalization and assimilation of Indians into American society, treaties and tribal extraconstitutional rights notwithstanding.

These cases exemplify the brand of legal consciousness earlier described as nationalist/federalist. In this type of consciousness, the concepts of political development, nation-state, nation-building, nationalism, and national integration are defined by the Court in such a way that there is no room for, sometimes not even any acknowledgment of, any other sovereign than that which is the sole expression of national unity (i.e., the federal government and the constituent states). Thus, the stark denial followed by the virtual elimination (usually by cultural and structural assimilation) of tribes as distinctive polities was considered an essential element in the nation-building process occurring in the United States after the Civil War. The goal was the assimilation of tribal members, followed by the imposition of a single view of political democracy that everyone in the nation was subjected to, both the dominant and the subordinate groups.

In an article written in 1934, W. G. Rice attempted to explain the anomalous legal position of American Indians. He noted: "The law has long been uncertain and its future is uncertain chiefly because the fundamental question of whether destruction of tribal life is to be encouraged is undecided."[7] There was at that time, said Rice, "no sure aim either to preserve tribal culture or, on the contrary, to melt it down in the great cauldron of American life."[8] Rice's depiction is not only simplistic, it is also deeply ethnocentric. Nevertheless, the "either-or" scenario he drew was nonchalantly accepted at the time and, unfortunately, still pervades the thinking of many federal officials.

Scholars and government officials alike have argued that it was perfectly permissible for Congress to act without regard for the Constitution in its dealings with tribes precisely because tribes were extraconstitutional. As expressed by Canfield: "The Constitution was an instrument framed for a nation of independent freemen, who had religious convictions worth protecting . . . To suppose that the framers of the Constitution intended to secure to the Indians the rights and privileges which they valued as Englishmen is to misconceive the spirit of their age, and to impute to it an expansive benevolence which it did not possess."[9]

The legal consciousness known as nationalist/federalist led to a major assault on the sovereignty and property of the previously favored "Five Civilized Tribes." The Five Tribes, and several others, were originally excluded from the provisions of the 1887 Dawes Severalty Act (a.k.a. the General Allotment Act). This act entailed the individualized distribution of tribal lands into private tracts in various amounts (heads of household received 160 acres, single persons were entitled to 80 acres, and all others received 40-acre allotments). This privatization of Indian land was considered essential for the rapid assimilation of Indians into Euro-American culture; but it also served the interest of the burgeoning Euro-American population, who could purchase the "surplus" (Indian land left after allotment) land for settlement purposes.

The Five Tribes were excluded from the Dawes Act's provisions because they held fee-simple titles to their communal lands. The first major threat to the autonomy of the Five Tribes came in the form of a special commission, authorized by Congress in 1893 and headed by Henry Dawes, the sponsor of the allotment act.[10] The commission's purpose was to force the Five Tribes to negotiate agreements with the federal government that called for the allotment of their lands. Not surprisingly, the tribal leaders fought against allotment and refused voluntarily to surrender their lands for individualization, despite the commission's persistence.

In March 1898, as the patience of certain powerful congressmen and bureaucrats ran low, the House Committee on Indian Affairs issued its findings and legislative recommendations in a report indicating the government's frustration in the face of the political savvy and the determination of the tribes to resist efforts to abrogate their treaties, destroy their tribal governments, and radically reduce their land holdings. It stated:

> It appears that the title to lands in the Indian Territory has been conveyed by patents to the tribes, and cannot be taken from them without their consent. There are about 20,000,000 acres of land thus owned. It is rich in mineral deposits, and contains a large area of splendid farming and grazing lands. . . . For the last few years the Dawes Commission has been endeavoring to secure agreements with the various tribes, but so far there has been little accomplished. Agreements were made with the commissioners of several tribes—all, in fact, except the Cherokees—but the Creek agreement was rejected by the tribes when the vote was taken upon it. The Chickasaws rejected the joint agreement with the Choctaws and Chickasaws. . . . In view of the fact that it is now impossible to secure agreements with the tribes, and the fact that the title is in the tribes, your committee has provided for the allotment of the exclusive use and occupancy of the surface of the lands of each of the nations. . . .[11]

What the committee "provided for" was a bill, which would become law three months later, entitled The Curtis Act.[12] With this act, Congress unilaterally and in direct violation of treaty and statutory law, terminated the legal existence of the Five Civilized Tribes. This detailed measure provided for the establishment and regulation of townsites; for the management of leases of Indian mineral rights; authorized the Dawes Commission to create enrollment lists which would serve as the basis for deciding who received land allotments; prohibited the expansion of lands; and also abolished the court systems of the tribal governments in Indian territory. The United States also assumed gradual control over tribal revenues and the Indians lost control of their elaborate educational systems. These and other developments transformed the once independent and wealthy nations of the Five Tribes to a poverty status that would take decades for them to rise above. In the words of the most articulate chronicler of the woes of the Five Civilized Tribes, Angie Debo:

> At the beginning of the present century about seventy thousand of these Indians owned the eastern half of the area that now constitutes the state of Oklahoma, a territory immensely wealthy in farmland and forest and coal mines, and with untapped oil pools of incalculable value. They ruled themselves and controlled this tribal property under constitutional governments of their own choosing, and they had attained a degree of civilization that made them at once the boast of the Indian Office and living examples of the benefits of travelling the white man's road. Their political and economic tenure was guaranteed by treaties and patents from the Federal Government, and warned by the tragic fate of all Indians who had lost their homes, they insisted upon the observance of these conditions. But white people began to settle among them, and by 1890 these immigrants were overwhelmingly in the majority. Congress therefore abrogated the treaties, and the Indians received their land under individual tenure and became citizens of Oklahoma when it was admitted to the Union in 1907. The orgy of exploitation that resulted is almost beyond belief. Within a generation these Indians, who had owned and governed a region greater in area and potential wealth than many an American state, were almost stripped of their holdings, and were rescued from starvation only through public charity.[13]

United States v. Kagama

THE MASKS OF PLENARY POWER, WARDSHIP, AND PROPERTY

Criminal law was a major arena for this conflict on whether to respect or obliterate tribal autonomy. Before the 1880s, relations between tribes and the United States were largely determined either by treaties or by the so-called Indian trade and intercourse acts. These intercourse acts, discussed in the previous chapter, were designed to regulate the general and commercial relations between tribes and Americans. Importantly, the Intercourse acts extended minimal federal jurisdiction over Indians and only in their affairs with whites. Internal tribal sovereignty, especially offenses committed by Indians against Indians, was not touched by the laws. According to Prucha, until the mid-1800s there were no federal treaty or statutory constraints on the internal affairs of tribes.[14]

The idea of imposing federal criminal jurisdiction over purely internal tribal disputes slowly gained momentum as western expansion inexorably led to the encirclement of tribal lands with the concomitant rise of a "reservation policy." In fact, Commissioner of Indian Affairs George Manypenny bluntly stated in 1856 that "the conviction and execution, under our criminal laws, of all Indians guilty of the murder of Indians, would, it is believed, put a stop to the war parties." Such a policy, the commissioner further observed, would be "an act of humanity," with "a most salutary influence" on tribal behavior.[15]

By 1866 the arguments favoring federal jurisdiction were both refined and broadened. It was no longer simply a desire to "make an example" of one Indian for another's benefit. The goal was the inevitable civilization of the Indians whether they wanted it or not. Commissioner D. N. Cooley resurrected Manypenny's idea for the imposition of a federal criminal law code applicable to reservation Indians. Cooley alleged the following: "Retaliation is the law of the Indian; and if, in his early approaches to civilization, he is compelled to abandon that law, he looks for a substitute in the white man's law."[16] The Board of Indian Commissioners declared in 1871 that until Indians were brought under "the domination of law, so far as regards crimes committed against each other," the government's best efforts to civilize the Indians would be handicapped.[17]

The issue of Indian-on-Indian crimes eventually arrived at the Supreme Court in 1883 with the case of a Sioux leader, Crow Dog, who had been sentenced to death by the First District Court of South Dakota for the murder of Chief Spotted Tail. In this landmark case, *Ex parte Crow Dog*, the Supreme Court held that the United States lacked jurisdiction over crimes committed by one Indian against another. This decision was an important, if stilted, statement on tribal sovereignty and served as the final catalyst necessary to propel the jurisdictional changes viewed as essential by the melange of groups that desired to have federal law replace tribal law.

On March 3, 1885, a short year and a half after *Crow Dog*, these groups received their wish when Congress, by a rider attached to the general appropriations act, extended federal criminal jurisdiction over "all" Indians for seven major crimes—murder, manslaughter, rape, assault with intent to kill, arson, burglary, and larceny.[18] In reality, however, several tribes, most notably the Five Civilized Tribes, were excluded from this act's provisions. In fact, the Supreme Court would continue to recognize the Five Tribes as sovereigns capable of handing down judgments on major crimes over individuals within their jurisdiction. Although this attack on tribal sovereignty was not fatal, enactment of the appropriation act rider set precedence for actions by Congress and indicated the future direction of much federal Indian legislation. There was, however, some initial doubt as to the constitutionality of this profound federal intrusion on tribal sovereignty, and this became the central issue in *Kagama*.

THE ATTORNEYS' WAR OF PERSPECTIVES

The facts in *Kagama* are simple enough. Two Indians from the Hoopa Valley Reservation in Humboldt County, California, Kagama (alias "Pactah Billy") and Mahawaha (alias "Ben"), had been indicted for the murder of another Indian, Iyouse (alias "Ike"). The murder occurred on June 24, 1885, on the Hoopa Reservation, some three months after the Major Crimes Act had been passed. The reservation had been established in 1864 along the Trinity River northeast of Eureka, California. Kagama and Mahawaha's attorney, Joseph Redding, argued in his brief to the Supreme Court that the Major Crimes Act was unconstitutional and should be voided because (1) Congress's power to regulate commerce with Indian tribes was not an authorization for that body to enact criminal laws regulating Indian-on-Indian crimes committed within an Indian reservation; (2) until the Major Crimes Act, Congress had always "recognized and held inviolate tribal rights and the social system of the Indian tribes on their reservation"; and (3) in nearly all the congressional legislation enacted before the Major Crimes Act, and in virtually every treaty with Indians, a clause had been inserted in which the United States disclaimed jurisdiction over crimes committed by one Indian against another.[19]

Redding said: "The very idea of the reservation system is predicated upon the theory that the Indians are not citizens, are not foreign subjects, are not subject to the jurisdiction of the United States, except where a question of commercial intercourse is an element in the offense committed."[20] Redding stated that he could not discover any legal justification for Congress's imposition of its criminal laws over domestic Indian matters. "If an Indian sees fit to burn his neighbor's wigwam, what question of commercial intercourse there arises? None whatsoever. If Congress has authority to make them amenable for the offenses defined in this act, it can include all of the offenses in the calendar. . . . But if an Indian kills an Indian on a reservation there is no such connecting link between the Government and the Indian in such an act which, under the Constitution of the United States as it now stands, would give the Federal Courts jurisdiction."[21]

Conversely, the brief for the United States by Attorney General A. H. Garland[22] and Solicitor General John Goode relied on several novel arguments to support what they contended was the constitutionality of the Crimes Act. They began by reminding the justices of the "magnitude and importance" of the Court's exercising judicial review of a political act. More importantly, and not surprisingly, they advocated a much broader interpretation of the Indian Commerce Clause. Acknowledging that Indian-on-Indian crimes were historically exempted, though only because it "would have been impossible to enforce such a provision at that time,"[23] Garland and Goode asserted that the 1871 treaty rider that had terminated the treaty process between tribal nations and the federal government effected a "revolution in the policy of the government respecting Indian affairs."[24] This provision, they claimed, signaled that the Hoopa Reservation Indians no longer constituted a sovereign nation. And because the Indians had already "receded before the progress of the white man's civilization," it was imperative for the government to step forth to protect the remaining Indians.[25] Such protection, they alleged, necessarily had to include a policy which would subject the Indians to federal jurisdiction. Interestingly, Garland and Goode emphasized that tribes in the Indian territory (especially the Five Civilized Tribes, whom Garland had earlier represented) that had "an organized government," should be exempted from the Act's provisions. Their perception was that the Five Tribes were "civilized enough" because of their institutionalized forms of governance modeled loosely after those of the United States.

Finally, and in an incredible passage, the government's attorneys laid out what was for them the definitive argument:

> If we are asked in what respect the commission of a crime by an Indian upon an Indian can relate to the questions of intercourse with an Indian tribe, we deem it an efficient answer to say that if we have to maintain intercourse with the Indians, it is necessary and proper that

they shall not be permitted to destroy each other. If they are permitted to murder each other, it is certainly an interference with intercourse; because the number with whom intercourse will be held is thereby diminished.[26]

This was a fascinating rationale for intruding upon the inherent sovereignty of tribes suggested by the highest-level legal minds in the government—that Indians would exterminate themselves if Congress was not allowed to step in and assert control over internal tribal criminal matters. This statement suggests that Indian reservations—except the Five "Civilized" Tribes—were absolutely lawless and anarchic. In closing, Garland and Goode described both the *Rogers* and *Cherokee Tobacco* precedents as having invested in Congress all the authority necessary to enact the Major Crimes Act. "Because Congress has not heretofore gone [this] far," said the attorneys, "is no reason it could not do so. It is purely a question of policy, of which Congress is the judge. . . ."[27]

MASKING WITHIN THE DECISION: THE OPINION

The case was heard in the District Court of the United States for the District of California and San Francisco. After Kagama and Mahawaha's indictment, the case was certified to the Circuit Court of the United States for the District of California. However, the importance of the issues involved led a circuit judge and a district judge to certify several questions to the United States Supreme Court. The case was argued on March 2, 1886, and decided on May 10, 1886. Of the six questions sent forth, Justice Samuel Miller, for the Court, chose to focus on two: Whether section 9 of the Major Crimes Act which made it a federal offense for an Indian to kill another Indian was a constitutional act and within the power of Congress to enact; and whether the federal courts had the jurisdictional authority to "try and punish an Indian belonging to an Indian tribe for committing the crime of murder upon another Indian belonging to the same Indian tribe, both sustaining the usual tribal relations, said crime having been committed upon an Indian reservation made and set apart for the use of the Indian tribe to which said Indians both belong."[28]

The importance of section 9 of the Indian Appropriation Act, the section in dispute, justifies its full recitation:

That immediately upon and after the date of the passage of this act all Indians committing against the person or property of another Indian or other person any of the following crimes, namely, murder, man-slaughter, rape, assault with intent to kill, arson, burglary, and larceny within any Territory of the United States, and either within or without the Indian reservation, shall be subject therefor to the laws of said Territory relating to said crimes, and shall be tried therefor in the same courts and in the same manner, and shall be subject to the same penalties as are all other persons charged with the commission of said crimes, respectively; and the said courts are hereby given jurisdiction in all such cases; and all such Indians committing any of the above crimes against the person or property of another Indian or other person, within the boundaries of any State of the United States, and within the limits of any Indian reservation, shall be subject to the same laws, tried in the same courts and in the same manner, and subject to the same penalties as are all other persons committing any of the above crimes within the exclusive jurisdiction of the United States.[29]

However, despite the inclusiveness of the language of this measure, even this apparently national law exempted the Five Civilized Tribes. Representative John Rogers (D., Arkansas) stated during debate on the proposed measure in 1885: "Now, in the Indian Territory they have no laws except the Indian laws, and of course Congress does not intend, I imagine, to confer jurisdiction upon the federal courts."[30]

Justice Miller said that the act was "separable into two distinct definitions of the conditions under which Indians may be punished for the same crimes as defined by the common law." This application of U.S. common law to Indian communities is puzzling. Treaty law and the Commerce Clause are the source of U.S. authority to deal with tribes. Conversely, common law is that system of laws which originated in England, based on court decisions and the doctrines implicit in those cases, and on customs and usages rather than on codified written laws. Miller appears to have relied on a common-law understanding of section 9 for two reasons. First, it was the particular legal system that he was most familiar with. Second, a reliance on treaty law and the Commerce Clause would have denied federal jurisdiction. In effect, Miller unilaterally selected a different well from which to draw the law—using resources that would prove compatible with his extraconstitutional actions.

The two distinct definitions that Miller gleaned from the appropriation act were as follows: first, where the Indian-on-Indian crime was committed in a *territorial jurisdiction*, whether on or off an Indian reservation; and second, where the offense occurred within the boundaries of a state but within an Indian reservation. In the first case, Miller said the territory would have jurisdiction; in the second, the United States would have jurisdiction.[31] Here we see that the Court was completely ignoring the distinctive status of Indian homelands. First, Indian reservations are not *territories* of the United States. Miller conceded as much when he noted that "this proposition [Indian-on-Indian crimes being subject to territorial jurisdiction] itself is new in legislation of Congress. . . ."[32] It certainly was, and the Court did not even seek to determine if there was, in fact, a constitutional basis for such an action. This lack of action indicated that the Court had already determined that it was going to defer to Congress on this matter. Even though Congress's crime measure action was clearly unconstitutional, the Court was intent on finding a way to rationalize the act.

Next, Miller asserted the second distinction enunciated in the act— that the United States would have jurisdiction over Indian-on-Indian matters even arising within state boundaries—was a further intrusion that challenged and displaced state jurisdiction. Miller was proceeding to develop a false scenario that would allow him to set up the United States as the only legitimate political power with criminal jurisdiction, thus flouting the long-established treaty relationship between tribes and the United States under which neither federal territories nor states, nor the federal government itself, had jurisdiction over internal tribal affairs.

Federal Power Despite Constitutional Silence

Miller, continuing his analysis without any consideration of the separate and historically independent status of the Indians of the Hoopa Reservation, said, "Although the offence charged in this indictment was committed within a State and not within a Territory, the considerations which are necessary to a solution of the problem in regard to the one must in a large degree affect the other."[33] Plainly, in the nationalist/ federalist consciousness which now had saturated the Supreme Court, Miller could discuss the events of the case and not even mention the Hoopa Reservation as having an actual political existence apart from the United States, territories, or states.

Continuing his disregard of a century of federal legislation, the treaty process, and early Supreme Court precedents, Miller noted that the Constitution itself said little about the tribal-federal relationship. "The Constitution," said Miller, "is almost silent in regard to the relations of the government which was established by it to the numerous tribes of

Indians within its borders."[34] Miller then proceeded to describe the Enumerative and Commerce Clauses, which are the only clauses that expressly mention the Indians. The Court accurately stated that neither these clauses nor any other language in the Constitution provided the United States with any legal power "to enact a code of criminal law for the punishment of the worst class of crimes known to civilized life when committed by Indians."[35]

The Commerce Clause, in particular, which had been heavily relied upon by government attorneys in their bizarre "extermination theory," was analyzed by Miller and found to be insufficient as a basis on which to justify federal jurisdiction over Indians in Indian country. In Miller's words:

> [W]e think it would be a very strained construction of this clause, that a system of criminal laws for Indians living peaceably in their reservation, which left out the entire code of trade and intercourse laws justly enacted under that provision, and established punishments for the common-law crimes of murder, manslaughter . . . and the like, without any reference to their relation to any kind of commerce, was authorized by the grant of power to regulate commerce with the Indian tribes.[36]

If Congress lacked constitutional authorization under the Commerce and Taxation clauses, and had not secured it via the treaty process, then Congress had no basis for exerting such power. Likewise, there was no enumerated power, nor had tribes given their consent. At this point, Miller and the Court should have declared the law unconstitutional and released Kagama and Mahawaha.

In an earlier case, *United States v. Bailey*,[37] under a similar circumstance, a federal circuit court had been called upon to test the constitutionality of an 1817 law which purported to give the federal government jurisdiction over crimes committed by Indians against whites on Indian lands. *Bailey*, however, held that by this law "Congress [had] transcended their Constitutional powers" and declared the act null and void.[38] The Court said: "The Cherokee country can in no sense be considered a territory of the United States, over which the federal government may exercise exclusive jurisdiction; nor has there been any cession of jurisdiction by the state of Tennessee; . . . if the state has no jurisdiction, or has failed to exercise it, it does not follow that the federal government has a general and unlimited jurisdiction over the territory; for its powers are delegated, and cannot be assumed to supply any defect of power on the part of the state."[39]

Expanding its statement on the delegated and limited nature of the federal government's authority, the Court said that this was "a principle so obvious as not to admit of controversy; though the extent of those powers has given rise to much discussion and wide differences of opinion."[40] Thus, when the validity of a congressional act is in question, said the Court, "we must look to the constitution for the power to pass such an act."[41] Unlike Miller, who would discard the Commerce Clause and the Constitution itself in his effort to legitimize the Major Crimes Act, *Bailey* more soundly observed that the United States had to rely on the Commerce Clause—as it had in enacting the Intercourse laws—for "there is no other clause of the constitution which can have any bearing upon the point under consideration; and if the power is not given by this article, it is given nowhere."[42]

And while acknowledging that Congress clearly had the authority to regulate commerce with Indian tribes, the Court refused to concede that this clause somehow authorized Congress to "assume a general jurisdiction and prescribe for the punishment of all offences."[43] The Court said "the power of congress is limited to the regulation of a commercial intercourse, with such tribes of Indians that exist, as a distinct community, governed by their own laws, and resting for their protection on the faith of treaties and laws of the Union. Beyond this, the power of the federal government in any of its departments cannot be extended."[44]

The circuit court was aware that Congress had enacted a law without constitutional mooring and concisely observed the danger in such an action: "It is argued that unless the defendant can be tried under the act of congress, there is no law by which he can be punished. If on this ground the federal government may exercise jurisdiction, where shall its powers be limited? The constitution is no longer the guide, when the government acts from the law of necessity. This law always affords a pretext for usurpation. It exists only in the minds of those who exercise the power, and if followed must lead to despotism."[45]

The question, then, is: what had changed from the *Bailey* decision in 1834 to *Kagama* in 1886 that would justify Miller's shunning of the very constitutional principles the Supreme Court is charged with interpreting? The Constitution had not been amended to allow the federal government greater authority over tribes. The Indians of the Hoopa Reservation had not negotiated a treaty or series of treaties in which they had invited or been forced to allow federal authority over their internal criminal matters. What had changed was the Court's perception of the status of tribes and its perception of Congress's power in relation to those tribes.

The Mask of Denied Tribal Sovereignty

In this radical opinion, which in effect would culminate in a startling precedent—the sustaining and judicial embellishment of federal legislative authority over tribes without a constitutional basis—Miller noted: "While we are not able to see, in either of these clauses of the Constitution and its amendments, any delegation of power to enact a code of criminal law for the punishment of the worst class of crimes known to civilized life when committed by Indians, there is a suggestion in the manner in which the Indian tribes are introduced into that clause, which may have a bearing on the subject before us."[46] Since Miller had discarded the Constitution as his guide, he had, as the *Bailey* Court predicted, effectively unleashed himself and the government from the restraint of democratic principles and the rule of law and instead fell upon the "law of necessity," which only "affords a pretext for the usurpation" of legitimately derived rights.[47]

Miller could now freely roam the linguistic landscape and suggest any language as justification for federal criminal jurisdiction over Indians. The constitutional void was displaced by the manufacture of several legal masks held together by a consciousness that was grounded in nationalism/federalism and steeped in ethnocentrism. The masks included geographical incorporation, Indian wardship/dependency/helplessness which necessitated federal guardianship, plenary power, and the discovery doctrine. Before launching into his theory of unlimited federal authority over limited tribal polities, Miller prefaced his most-cited passage of alleged Indian wardship, dependency, etc., by semantically reducing the constitutionally recognized political standing of tribes. This is the same rhetorical tactic John Marshall employed in the *Cherokee Nation* case to deny the Cherokee's legal standing to sue in the Supreme Court by declaring them "domestic-dependent nations." Miller couched his diminishment of tribal sovereignty thus:

> The commerce with foreign nations is distinctly stated as submitted to the control of Congress. Were the Indian tribes foreign nations? If so, they came within the first of the three classes of commerce mentioned, and did not need to be repeated as Indian tribes. Were they nations, in the minds of the framers of the Constitution? If so, the natural phrase

would have been "foreign nations and Indian nations," or, in the terseness of language uniformly used by the framers of the instrument, it would naturally have been "foreign and Indian nations."[48]

The Court completely denied the territorial sovereignty of the Hoopa Reservation by drawing upon the geographical incorporation argument of *U.S. v. Rogers,* and the decision synthesized with the spirit of nationalism that was surging in Washington, D.C., and throughout the nation. The Court stated: "But these Indians are within the geographical limits of the United States. The soil and the people within these limits are under the political control of the Government of the United States, or of the States of the Union. There exist within the broad domain of sovereignty but these two."[49]

Clearly this is a false argument—that either the United States or the individual states have sovereignty over tribes—entirely ruling out tribal sovereignty; however, it was a principal ploy used by the Court. Miller expanded the position of the Court by noting that Congress's power to organize territorial governments—he was treating tribes, at least for the moment, as territories—and make laws for territorial inhabitants, was derived not from the Commerce Clause or the Property Clause but arose "from the ownership of the country in which the Territories are, and the right of exclusive sovereignty which must exist in the National Government, and can be found nowhere else."[50]

In other words, Miller was saying that, based on the mere ownership of land, an ownership based on the problematic doctrine of discovery announced in *Johnson* and refurbished in *Rogers,* the federal government had secured virtually an unlimited—since it was bound by no constitutional constraints—power over tribes and their sovereign political and civil rights. Standing alone, this is an astonishing declaration: that land ownership generates unfettered power. Miller then restated the relevant doctrines advanced in *Rogers*—the discovery doctrine, the political question doctrine, and the rudimentary idea of federal plenary power that Taney had crafted. He combined these with the idea that the Hoopa Reservation was land "owned" by the United States since it was geographically located in the state of California which had been purchased from Mexico by the United States.

In the final section of his opinion, Miller revisited and dramatically restated John Marshall's analogy in the *Cherokee Nation* case that the Indian's relations to the United States "resemble those of a ward to his guardian." In his drive to rationalize his judicial and nonconstitutional construction denying tribal sovereignty and supporting federal rather than state sovereignty over Indian tribes, Miller claimed that this power had to be in the "competency of Congress" because "these Indian tribes *are* the wards of the nation. They are communities *dependent* on the United States. Dependent largely for their daily food. Dependent for their political rights"[51] (emphasis original). This plenary "dependency" necessarily mandated, in Miller's ideology, a plenary congressional authority to protect and defend the tribes.

In one of the Court's most-quoted statements, often used, ironically, by Indians or Indian advocates in support of tribal independence from states, Miller said: "They [the Indian tribes] owe no allegiance to the States, and receive from them no protection. Because of the local ill feeling, the people of the States where they are found are often their deadliest enemies. From their very weakness and helplessness, so largely due to the course of dealing of the Federal Government with them and the treaties in which it has been promised, there arises the duty of protection, and with it the power. This has always been recognized by the Executive and by Congress, and by this court, whenever the question has arisen."[52] The crux of the case was this: Miller had elevated the Congress to a position as a plenary paternal entity over allegedly plenary "dependent" tribes. Such an action was possible because the Court had abandoned the idea of the existence of tribal political or territorial sovereignty, and because the central government felt compelled to reassert its preeminent position vis-à-vis tribes. The Court so ruled even though there was no evidence that the State of California was seeking to assert criminal jurisdiction over the Indians at that time. It is interesting that Miller would admit that the tribes' weaknesses were a direct result of activities of the very government which had now received the legal sanction of the Supreme Court to wield even greater—and nonconstitutionally derived—power over Indians.

Miller, besides shunning decades of laws and treaties which had affirmed the sovereign status of tribes, particularly over internal tribal matters, incorrectly asserted that this unlimited federal power had "always been recognized by the Executive and by Congress, and by this court." Perhaps Miller relied upon the statement that the United States in many treaties and in various laws often acknowledged its moral and legal duty to "protect" Indian tribes. Until this decision, however, the concept of "protection" had not been used to legitimate such an unwarranted and extralegal intrusion into intratribal affairs.

Capping off his novel pronunciation of congressional plenary power, laid out meticulously by a Court exercising unlimited interpretive power, Miller concluded his opinion as follows:

> The power of the General Government over these remnants of a race once powerful, now weak and diminished in numbers, is necessary to their protection, as well as to the safety of those among whom they dwell. It must exist in that government, because it never has existed anywhere else, because the theatre of its exercise is within the geographical limits of the United States, because it has never been denied, and because it alone can enforce its laws on all the tribes.[53]

The Mask of Judicial Plenary Power

The Miller Court in the span of a few short pages had cleverly and extraconstitutionally found a way to preclude a nonexistent state threat to exert its jurisdiction over Indians. In so doing, the Court had also given itself and the legislative branch carte blanche to exercise whatever power it believed necessary in the best interests of its "helpless wards." Most contemporary Indian law scholars, political scientists, and historians familiar with this seminal case assert that it is the fountain of congressional plenary and judicial plenary interpretive power, although the word "plenary" never appeared in the decision. These commentators have pointed out the multitude of untenable errors lodged in the Court's statements.

First, how could Congress legitimately apply its laws to tribes which "until that time had not been subject under the Constitution to its legislative jurisdiction?"[54] Second, if the Constitution limits, as *Bailey* had said, the authority of the various branches to enumerated powers, why did the Court cite extraconstitutional reasons for holding a statute to be constitutional?[55] Third, "consent of the governed" is a treasured democratic principle; however, the fact that most Indians were not citizens and were thus unable to vote seemed irrelevant to the Court. As Newton suggests: "Concentrating on justifying federal power the Court reinforced earlier precedents abdicating its role in accommodating the legitimate but competing interest raised by the federal government's interference with tribal rights. Such accommodation was left to the political arena—an arena from which Indians were excluded."[56]

Congress's Major Crimes Act presaged an impressive transformation in the relationship between the tribes and the federal government; however, it was restricted legislation, applying only to seven crimes. Furthermore, some scholars have suggested that theoretically tribal courts still may exercise concomitant jurisdiction along with the United States and that, in fact, the Major Crimes Act merely added federal jurisdiction to preexisting tribal jurisdiction.[57] Finally, while the act was ostensibly comprehensive, the Five Civilized Tribes, as noted earlier, were actually exempted from its provisions. With this major exemption in mind, one is compelled to ask: Who actually determines how a law that involves tribal nations is to be applied? The Congress? The President? The courts? Or local federal bureaucrats?

In *Kagama* the Court went far beyond merely "expounding and executing." Instead, it exercised an interpretive power that very nearly supplanted tribal sovereignty, that completely omitted the doctrine of enumerated powers, and that elevated a simple analogy to wardship into a newly created extraconstitutional power to regulate even internal tribal affairs—the so-called guardianship power.

What accounted for this transformation in the legal consciousness of the Miller Court? All it had been asked to do was simply determine the constitutionality of a single piece of legislation. Yet, it abruptly and inexplicably vested in Congress an unlimited and unauthorized power not connected to any constitutional provisions. In the 1883 Supreme Court opinion *The Civil Rights Cases*, the Court had properly noted that the Commerce Clause gave Congress the exclusive power to deal with tribes. Furthermore, in the case *In re Sah Quah*, decided May 8, 1886, two days before *Kagama*, a federal district court held the following: "From the organization of the government to the present time, the various Indian tribes of the United States have been treated as free and independent within their respective territories, governed by their tribal laws and customs, in all matters pertaining to their inherent affairs, such as contracts and the manner of their enforcement . . . and the punishment for crimes committed against each other."[58]

Broadly put, the answer to this sudden transformation in Supreme Court thought and policy occurred to legitimize the congressional policy of forced assimilation and acculturation of tribal citizens into American society. As Indian Affairs Commissioner John Oberly noted in his 1888 *Annual Report*, it was essential that the Indian "be imbued with the exalting egotism of American civilization, so that he will say 'I' instead of 'we,' and 'this is mine' instead of 'this is ours'."[59] The Miller Court, in its efforts to legitimate the federal government's policy on Americanization and assimilation, developed the extralegal sophistry of "wardship" to further the assimilative process but also to allegedly "protect" Indian people from state interests as well. The Court's extraconstitutional principles sent a message to those seeking to intrude into tribal affairs, excepting the federal government, of course, that unconstrained federal authority over Indian affairs would be used "precisely because [Indians were] outside the protection of the Constitution" and because Congress "needed to be immune from ordinary challenges which might otherwise hamper the wise administration of the affairs of Indians."[60] Unfortunately, the absolute power which the Court arrogated to itself and Congress in *Kagama* set a destructive precedent for tribal nations that continues to affect their daily operations and intergovernmental relations. There is, in the tribes' legal and political reality, no obvious limitation on Congress's presumed plenary power regarding tribal sovereignty "except the moral sensibility of Congress."[61]

Cherokee Nation v. Southern Kansas Railway Company

THE RAILROADING OF TREATY RIGHTS

Congress passed the General Allotment Act[62] in 1887, a year after *Kagama*. Actually a major policy directive, it was hailed, and accurately so, as a "mighty pulverizing engine to break up the tribal mass."[63] By 1934, when the allotment policy was finally stopped, "the government had allotted 118 out of 213 reservations and brought over three-fourths of the Indians under the provisions of the Dawes Act."[64] Again, the Five Civilized Tribes were originally exempt from the act's provisions because they held their territory in fee-simple title as a result of their removal to the Indian Territory under treaties and the Indian Removal Act of 1830.

Preceding and throughout this period of allotment, a multitude of interests, including the powerful railroad companies, were intent on securing right-of-way to tribal lands. By the mid-1880s there were four transcontinental railroad lines: the Union Pacific–Central Pacific; the Atchison, Topeka, and Santa Fe; the Southern Pacific; and the Northern Pacific. Each of these branch lines, along with many tributary lines coursing throughout the country, was already passing through Indian lands. Railroad companies, created by congressional law, occupied a special federal niche and thus were often favorably treated by lawmakers. While admitting that railroads had a critical role insofar as federal relations with tribes were concerned, a commissioner of Indian affairs observed, as early as 1872, that a railroad's right-of-way request would not be considered if it appeared to be a "demand for the disruption of a reservation." The commissioner noted that "the treaty-rights of the Indian are paramount, and must in all honor and conscience be preserved inviolate." [65]

Despite the railroad lobby's power, therefore, securing right-of-way through tribal lands was sometimes problematic. President Grover Cleveland, on July 7, 1886, had vetoed an act that would have granted railroads the right-of-way through a reservation in Montana. The President, while acknowledging the federal government's right of eminent domain when exercised in the public interest, said that neither had the Indians given their consent to the right-of-way, nor had the tribal residents been consulted about the proposed railroad route.[66] Cleveland emphasized that the act under review posed a serious threat to democratic principles. It was, he said, "a new and wide departure from the general tenor of legislation affecting Indian reservations. It ignores the rights of the Indians to be consulted as to the disposition of their lands, opens wide the door to any railroad to what, under the treaty covering the greater portion of the reservation, is reserved to the United States alone . . . [and] it invites a general invasion of the Indian country. . . ."[67]

The powerful railroad companies were not to be denied, and in 1899 Congress enacted an important measure, the Omnibus Railroad Act, which gave them a general right-of-way to construct lines through any Indian reservation, across Indian lands, and even through Indian allotments. All the company needed to do to secure this significant right was to show the secretary of the interior that it had made its "application in good faith and with intent and ability to construct said road" and pay an annual rental of at least 15 dollars for each mile of rail laid "for the benefit of the particular nation or tribe through whose lands the road may be located. . . ."[68] Only tribes within the Indian territory were entitled to receive such payments, presumably because they held their lands in fee-simple title.

HISTORICAL BACKGROUND

The Cherokee Nation was contesting a July 4, 1884, congressional act that had granted, without the consent of the Cherokee Nation, a right-of-way through Cherokee lands to the Southern Kansas Railway Company (SKRC).[69] The act authorized the SKRC to construct the railway as well as a telegraph and telephone line through the heart of the Cherokee Nation's lands. While the constitutionality of the act was itself of deepest importance to the Cherokee, it was section 3 on which some of the principal questions in the case depended. Section 3 stated that "before said railway shall be constructed through any lands held by individual occupants, according to the laws, customs and usages of any of the Indian nations or tribes through which it may be constructed, full compensation should be made to such occupants for all property to be taken or damage done by reason of the construction of such railways."[70]

Other provisions of the act called for the President to appoint "disinterested referees" in the event agreement could not be reached on the amount of compensation to be paid the Indians; for the SKRC to pay the secretary of the interior, "for the benefit of the particular nation or tribes," so much money per mile of track laid; for the company to develop maps showing the exact route of the lines to be constructed; and for the federal courts of Texas, Arkansas, and Kansas to have jurisdiction over any controversies that might arise between the Cherokee and the railroad.

"Controversies" were inevitable and immediate. The Cherokee Nation, through its National Council, enacted a resolution on December 12, 1884, in which they "solemnly protested" the act and filed their protest with the secretary of the interior. Simultaneously, the Cherokee legislature sent instructions to its delegates in Washington to "resist the claim of right or authority on behalf of any railroad corporation to build or maintain any railway through the territory or domain . . . without its consent."[71] The Cherokee Nation argued, more specifically, that "no jurisdiction or authority remained in the United States to grant such right of way . . . nor did the right of eminent domain over such territory remain in the United States, but that by its treaties and patents aforesaid remained solely in your complainant, The Cherokee Nation."[72]

The federal government, through the secretary of the interior, ignored the official pleas of the Cherokee and advised the Cherokee National Council in April 1886 that the secretary had received a map from the SKRC that plotted the construction routes. Again, the Cherokee protested. Rather than accede to their legitimate complaints, the President responded by utilizing a section in the law which authorized him to appoint referees who would provide an analysis of the conflict and render an assessment. Of course, the referees were not Indian, and it was clear in which direction the allegiance of these presidential appointees would tilt.[73] They met in Topeka, Kansas, in August 1886 and made their way to Indian Territory, completed their work within a month, and issued a report to the President on September 25, 1886. They concluded that "said Nation was entitled to receive as adequate compensation for such lands and for damages . . . the sum of $93.00 for each mile, aggregating for the whole distance $3301.50."[74] They also found that in recompense for the lands taken for the branch line, the tribe should receive $4051.44 for 112 miles of line. The commissioners ordered that Southern Kansas Railway, once in receipt of the report from the secretary of the interior, should deposit the amount awarded in the federal treasury.[75]

The Cherokee Nation was notified of the referees' report by the commissioner of Indian affairs on October 29, 1886. Their response, by an act dated December 17, 1886, approved by the Cherokee Senate and concurred in by their House, "dissented from and rejected as unjust, inequitable and without authority of law," the commissioners' award.[76] In particular, the Cherokee lawmakers, led by Principal Chief D. W. Bushyhead, stated that the Nation did not "concede to the United States the rightful power, through its constituted authorities, to authorize any private individual or corporation to enter upon, appropriate, and use any lands belonging to said nation without first obtaining the consent of the constituted authorities of said nation," and was therefore protesting "the action of said Southern Kansas Railway Company in entering upon and appropriating the lands of the Cherokee Nation as an arbitrary and unjust violation of the guaranteed rights of said nation."[77] They also notified the federal government that the referees' award was "insufficient and inadequate . . . the same is reasonably worth the sum of $500.00 per mile." Principal Chief Bushyhead was empowered by the Council to file a lawsuit in the Circuit Court of the Western District of Arkansas against the railway company in an effort to "vindicate the absolute title of the Cherokee Nation to all lands within her borders, and to obtain redress from said company for such damages as may have been sustained by said nation by means of the location and construction of said railroad: Provided, that nothing herein shall be so construed as an acknowledgment by the Cherokee Nation of the right of the United States to appropriate the lands of the Cherokee Nation for the benefit of private corporations without its consent."[78]

These passages evidence the Cherokee officials' clear understanding of their vested aboriginal and treaty-defined property rights, and their keen awareness of the crucial political doctrine—consent. The Cherokee case was filed in District Court on January 26, 1887. Interestingly, the SKRC brought forward another monetary offer. They said that they were willing to double their offer for the purchase of the Cherokee's right-of-way, for a grand total of $14,705.98. The Cherokee declined the offer. The SKRC's attorneys then filed a demurrer to the Cherokee bill, signifying that while the company admitted the matters of fact brought by the Cherokee Nation, they did not believe sufficient grounds existed for the Cherokees to proceed with their case.

Judge Isaac C. Parker, the infamous "hanging judge"[79] who presided over the Fort Smith District Court from 1875 to 1896—a district which included Indian territory—ordered that the demurrer be sustained, denied the injunction sought by the Cherokee Nation, and refused to hold a hearing on the question of damages requested by the Cherokee. Judge Parker perfunctorily dismissed the Cherokee bill and ordered the Cherokee to pay the SKRC five hundred dollars in litigation costs and the costs of an appeal to the Supreme Court, if the appeal was found to be "wrongfully taken."[80] In Judge Parker's opinion: "The controlling question in this case is, did the congress of the United States have the right to grant to defendant a right of way for its railroad across or over the land of the Cherokee Nation, the defendant paying the nation for the same and individual occupants for their improvements?"[81] If Congress had the right, then the Cherokee had no case. And if not, the entire act authorizing the railroad would be void.

Parker, echoing the nationalist/federalist sentiment of the day, and in the *Kagama* tradition, elaborated on the alleged "dependent" status of tribes, saying, "If they are a dependent nation, upon whom are they dependent? Not upon the states, but upon the United States. This dependence is a political one, and its very existence implies political control in some other power than their government."[82] Having placed the Cherokee Nation in an inferior political status, Parker then easily surmised that the federal government had the power of eminent domain and could appropriate Cherokee territory even while title was vested in the Cherokee Nation.

MASKING WITHIN THE DECISION: THE OPINION

The Cherokee Nation was represented by attorneys J. F. McDonald, John C. Fay, and R. J. Bright, who were opposed by the SKRC's lawyers, George R. Beck, A. B. Brown, and A. J. Britton. Justice John Marshall Harlan delivered the Supreme Court's unanimous opinion. It is an opinion built, not surprisingly, on the faulty and startling illogic of *Rogers* and *Kagama*. Harlan began by describing the dual—equitable and legal—nature of the Cherokee's course of action. On the one hand, said Harlan, the Cherokee wanted an injunction against the SKRC to prevent it from constructing the railroad, telegraph, and telephone line. This desire, he stated, was relief of an *equitable* nature. On the other hand, Harlan said, the Cherokees had joined this equitable claim with a *legal* one by asking for "just and adequate compensation" for the lands to be taken and the other "rights, easements, and franchises," if their equitable claim were rebuffed.[83]

Harlan said the lower court had been right in concluding that these two causes could not be united in the same suit; however, he added that the district court had erred in dismissing the Cherokee claims "without making some provision, by appropriate orders, for the protection of its rights as against the Railway Company."[84] Harlan said while the equity suit would not be permissible, he saw no reason why under the terms of the legislation and of "the peculiar relations" which the Cherokee had with the federal government and the American people, "relations which forbid . . . the application of strict rules of interpretation," the Cherokee claims could not be treated as an appeal on the issue of damages.[85]

The so-called strict rules of interpretation Harlan alluded to were also derived from another early Marshall case, *Worcester v. Georgia* (1832). There, Marshall explicitly said, "the language used in treaties with the Indians should never be construed to their prejudice. If words be made use of which are susceptible of a more extended meaning than their plain import, as connected with the tenor of the treaty, they should be considered as used only in the latter sense. . . . How the words of the treaty were understood by this unlettered people, rather than their critical meaning, should form the rule of construction."[86] Similarly, in *The Kansas Indians* (1867) the Supreme Court said "rules of interpretation favorable to the Indian tribes are to be adopted in construing our treaties with them. . . ."[87] And in *Jones v. Meehan* (1899), the High Court reaffirmed Marshall's original language and held that "the treaty must therefore be construed, not according to the technical meaning of its words to learned lawyers, but in the sense in which they would naturally be understood by the Indians."[88]

When this language is compared with that of *The Cherokee Tobacco* and then contrasted to the Court's comments in *Worcester*, *Kansas*, and *Meehan*, the interpretation is not clear as to whom it favors. In this instance all we can surmise is that "it depends," which means that the Court is not wedded to constitutional, treaty, or legal principles so much as it is to ad hoc decision-making based on issues, players, and political circumstances. An analysis of the language used by Harlan in *Cherokee Nation v. Southern Kansas Railway* vividly reveals as much.

Eminent Domain = Imminent Tribal Loss

In his opening lines Harlan had curtly discarded the most important Cherokee contention—the equity claim that the United States did not have the right to construct the railway on Cherokee land without their consent. He then set the Court up as an impartial entity willing, although not required, to consider the Cherokee Nation's petition for monetary damages. With the Cherokee's most vital rights to territorial sovereignty ignored, and having reduced their standing request, without any discussion, to a mere monetary debate for damages, Harlan proceeded to make a most interesting comment:

> We have had some doubt as to whether, in the present attitude of the case, the reasons for this conclusion ought to be now given. But as the questions raised by the demurrer were elaborately examined by the Court below . . . and as the plaintiff ought not to be led to suppose that a new bill in equity, based upon the alleged invalidity of the Act of July 4, 1884, would avail any good purpose, we have concluded to state the grounds upon which we hold that Congress, in the passage of that Act, has not violated any rights belonging to the plaintiff.[89]

One wonders why the Court hesitated to reveal its reasons for a decision which flagrantly violated the fee-simple and treaty-guaranteed land rights of the Cherokee Nation. For instance, what does Harlan mean by saying that "the present attitude of the case" might normally preclude the Court's explaining its decision? The official record does not reveal this. Congress, of course, had overtly violated the Cherokee Nation's property rights. The Cherokee had explicit fee-simple title guaranteed by ratified treaties. The Court, however, in its own unique style, decided to "reveal" the reasons why it ruled the way it did. It appears that Harlan decided to discuss the reasons because he and the Court were embarking on the formation of extralegal reasoning to rationalize the power of the United States to confiscate fee-simple land.

Harlan began by inaccurately stating that "no allegations are made in the bill that would justify a decree perpetually enjoining the railway company from proceeding under the Act of Congress." This statement overlooked the fact that the Cherokee Nation, as far back as 1884, had raised a number of viable points that should have immediately led to the revocation of the 1884 law. The Court simply chose to ignore or transmute the tribe's allegations.

The Cherokee had given five major arguments. First, that the Cherokee Nation was a sovereign state, recognized as such in twenty treaties, and as a sovereign it exercised the powers, jurisdiction, and function of a sovereign in the territory ceded to it under the treaty of February 14, 1833.[90] Second, that in view of their sovereign status, the right of eminent domain remained exclusively vested in the Cherokee nation.[91] Third, that in addition to the cession of the territory by the various treaties, a patent in fee-simple had been granted by the United States to the Cherokee Nation. And since those land rights had been vested, neither Congress nor the states could constitutionally impair those rights without the consent of the Cherokee Nation.[92] The "title, then, being in the Cherokee Nation, the defendant [SKRC] took nothing by its grant of a right of way in the second section of the act. *The United States had no land in the Cherokee Nation to grant.*"[93] Finally, that the United States had no remaining jurisdiction or authority to grant such a right-of-way through Cherokee territory; said jurisdiction and authority remained in the Cherokee Nation by its treaties and patents.[94]

Each of these arguments was historically accurate, legally valid, and, until this case, politically recognized. Nevertheless, Harlan spoke as if the arguments were inconsequential. In keeping with his radically revisionist history, focused myopically on national sovereignty vis-à-vis the states, Harlan stated the following:

> The proposition that the Cherokee Nation is sovereign in the sense that the United States is sovereign, or in the sense that the several States are sovereign, and that that Nation alone can exercise the power of eminent domain within its limits, finds no support in the numerous treaties with the Cherokee Indians, or in the decisions of this court, or in the Acts of Congress defining the relations of that people with the United States.[95]

This statement is without merit and indicates the Court's unwillingness even to acknowledge, much less recognize, the validity of the actual historical record between the Cherokee Nation and the United States. Appropriating selected excerpts and modifying them as he moved from John Marshall's early decisions through the judicial landscape, Harlan said that "from the beginning of the government to the present time, they have been treated as 'wards of the nation,' 'in a state of pupilage,' [and as] 'dependent political communities'. . . ."[96] This statement also errs. There is nothing in the historical or judicial record, prior to the

Kagama decision, that supports Harlan's contention that "from the beginning of the government" Indians were treated as dependent wards.

Harlan then proceeded to contradict himself by correctly citing the *Worcester* precedent that tribes constitute separate and distinct peoples recognized as such by each branch of the federal government; however, he immediately reentered his fictionalized world devoid of tribal sovereignty. Even after quoting *Worcester*, Harlan asserted that the principle established in that case "falls far short of saying that they are a sovereign state, with no superior within the limits of its territory."[97] Harlan then briefly discussed the Cherokee treaties of 1835, 1846, and 1866, wherein the United States confirmed the Cherokee's title to their lands. "But," said Harlan, "neither these nor any previous treaties evinced any intention, upon the part of the government, to discharge them from their condition of pupilage or dependency, and constitute them a separate, independent, sovereign people, with no superior within its limits."[98] What "pupilage" or "dependency" is Harlan referring to? They were not "discharged" from dependency because they were never politically in a dependent status. In support of his questionable contention, Harlan quoted from both *Rogers* and *Kagama*, emphasizing the sections in those cases centering on the assorted "geographical incorporation" of tribes and their alleged "weakness" as somehow correlating with a gross reduction of tribal political rights.

At this point, Harlan felt comfortable enough to enunciate the destructive precedent that even the fee-simple patents—confirmed by treaty—were not strong enough to withstand federal confiscation:

> The fact that the Cherokee Nation holds these lands in fee simple under patents from the United States is of no consequence in the present discussion; for the United States may exercise the right of eminent domain, even within the limits of the several States, for purposes necessary to the execution of the powers granted to the general government by the Constitution. Such authority . . . is essential to the independent existence and perpetuity of the United States, and is not dependent upon the consent of the State.[99]

The Court had effectively blamed the Cherokee's loss of treaty-defined property rights and territorial jurisdiction on their purportedly "dependent" status. This wardship status, conjoined with the nation-building and territorial expansion of the United States, effectively deprived the Cherokee Nation of their land rights. One could ask why

the Cherokee Nation's property rights were considered "of no consequence." It appears that economic development, under the guise of na-
tionalistic expansion, had completely overwhelmed the "rule of law"
as explicitly laid out in ratified treaties. The moral character of the
United States was savaged in the name of corporate and national political
development.

Building upon his nationalist/federalist apparatus, Harlan stressed
that while the states also had a version of eminent domain, this could not
restrict the supremacy of the federal government's power of eminent
domain. "It would be very strange," said Harlan, "if the national government, in the execution of its rightful authority, could exercise the
power of eminent domain in the several States, and could not exercise
the same power in a territory occupied by an Indian nation or tribe, the
members of which were wards of the United States, and directly subject
to its political control." [100] The Cherokee's lands, "like the lands held by
private owners everywhere within the geographical limits of the United
States, are held subject to the authority of the general government to
take them *for such objects as are germane to the execution of the powers granted
to it;* provided only, that they are not taken without just compensation
being made to the owner." [101] Now that he had contrasted the states with
the tribes, it was a simple step for Harlan to say that if the United States
has power over the states, then surely it must have a similar authority
over tribes.

Tribal nations, however, are not states. They are not subject to the
United States Constitution as are the states. Tribal land title, once vested,
cannot be legally confiscated by regular constitutional channels. Harlan
circumvented this matter by relying upon the reified legal mask that Indian tribes were wards, which, of course, meant that the United States
was already the implicit owner of the lands in question. In essence, Harlan was saying that while Indians may have title to their territory, this
title was valid only so long as the federal government had no need of
it. He was arguing that the tribes, even those with fee-simple title, were
only temporary landholders with a secure title only so long as the government had not arrived at a "germane" reason to take it.

Harlan next engaged in a judicial hyperbole of the highest order. In
discussing the merits of the 1884 law, he said that even though the right
of eminent domain was not expressly granted to the United States in the
act, it was not necessary "that an Act of Congress should express, in
words, the purpose for which it was passed." [102] Apparently the question
was not raised as to what the purpose of a congressional law is if not to

identify congressional goals and purposes, or at least to sketch out the legislative terrain and intent. "The court," Harlan stated, "will determine for itself whether the means employed by Congress have any relation to the powers granted by the Constitution."[103] In other words, whenever a congressional intent is not clear, the Court would read an intent into the law.

Finally, Harlan stated that since the railroad was a "public highway," it was permissible for Congress to appropriate "private property" for purposes of a right-of-way, so long as just compensation was paid. Thus, Harlan redefined the legal nature of Cherokee communal territory. In later years, Felix S. Cohen stated that Indian land must be distinguished from both individual Indian property and public property of the United States, although it has "some elements of both titles."[104]

The lower court's judgment was reversed and the case was remanded for further proceedings.

Ward v. Race Horse

RIGHTS OR PRIVILEGES?

As with the American Indian the only way to prevent his extermination is to civilize him, so the only way to preserve the remaining buffalo is to domesticate them.[105]

As the original sovereigns of North America, tribal nations recognized an inherent responsibility to their homelands and the need to care for them properly. However, as colonization ensued, tribes often entered into treaties with the federal government in which they sold or exchanged portions of their territory to the United States or the states. In exchange for these relinquished lands, the tribes reserved all other rights not specifically ceded away, and often received certain other benefits like monetary payments, gifts, etc.

Obviously, Indian lands and the legal protection of their natural resources, both on and off reserved lands, were essential for tribal survival. In *Ward v. Race Horse*, a Wyoming case, the Supreme Court announced a bizarre set of doctrines which severely impacted Indian treaty rights even further. The interested parties were the state, the Shoshone-Bannock Indians of the Fort Hall Reservation, and the federal government as trustee[106] for the tribe's resources. Before proceeding with the Court's decision, we must review some historical data.

HISTORICAL BACKGROUND

The Fort Hall Reservation was fashioned by a provision in the 1868 Treaty, ratified in February 1869, between the Eastern band of Shoshone—the Bannock—and the United States.[107] Article 4 reserved to the Indians their right to hunt on uninhabited federal lands off the reservation as long as peace existed between the whites and the Indians. Earlier, in July 1868, the government had enacted a law establishing a temporary government for the Wyoming Territory. That law contained a provision acknowledging that this act could not interfere with treaty-reserved Indian political and property rights "so long as such rights shall remain unextinguished by treaty between the United States and such Indians."[108]

Wyoming became the forty-fourth state twenty-one years later, in legislation signed on July 10, 1890; this measure, however, lacked a provision recognizing the treaty rights of the resident tribes. With statehood, Wyoming officials and her non-Indian residents, basking in their newly acquired political status, began agitating for jurisdiction over Indian issues and resources. The state's desire was largely supported by the Bureau of Indian Affairs which, on November 1, 1889, had issued a circular to all federal Indian agents urging them to exercise greater control over Indian hunters. The commissioner of Indian affairs, in conformity with the general perception held of Indians by federal officials of the day, said,

> In view of the settlement of the country and the consequent disappearance of the game, the time has long since gone by when the Indian can live by the chase. They should abandon their idle and nomadic ways and endeavor to cultivate habits of industry and adopt civilized pursuits to secure means for self-support.[109]

The circular did, however, acknowledge that Indian treaty stipulations guaranteeing tribes the right to hunt outside their reservation still should be enforced, although this so-called privilege could be exercised only "to supply the needs of the Indians" and should not lead to the "wanton destruction of game."[110] By 1894 the Department of the Interior was being inundated with complaints from whites—including Wyoming's governor, county attorneys, and private citizens—that the Shoshone and Bannock were "wantonly slaughtering elk and deer." The Indian agent, when asked to report on the situation, stated that this was untrue. He did acknowledge that some game had been killed outside the reservation, but he said that the Indians were justified both legally, under article 4, and biologically, because they were starving. "Unless," said the agent, Captain Ray, "they receive sufficient food on the reservation, no power can prevent them from killing game or cattle." [111]

Furthermore, the agent reported that, according to the Indians, whites hunting in the same area were "killing game merely for the pleasure of hunting." [112] These reports were corroborated by other Indian agents, who said that game officials refused to prosecute the whites for violating state game laws because they "did not feel justified in prosecuting white men . . ." as long as "Indians were allowed to hunt." [113]

By July 1895 conditions had deteriorated to the point where a number of Indians were killed by white settlers at what became euphemistically known as the "Jackson Hole disturbance." [114] On July 20, 1895, Wyoming's legislature enacted a comprehensive law to regulate the taking of game throughout the state. As written, the law applied to Indians exercising their off-reservation hunting rights.

Throughout this tense period, the Indian agent at Fort Hall reported continuously on the situation to his superiors in the Interior Department. Invariably, these reports painted a bleak picture for the Indians. In Agent Thomas Teter's words:

> The Indians killed by these settlers were practically massacred. . . .
> One batch, disarmed, were being driven by a body of armed settlers,
> and in passing over a trail . . . made a break for liberty, whereupon the
> guards opened fire at once and killed from four to seven Indians, going
> on the principle that "a good Indian is a dead Indian." [115]

As the truth surfaced about the murdered Indians, public sentiment shifted in favor of the tribes. In contrast to the early reports of an Indian massacre of whites, a more accurate view emerged showing that the Indians were the real victims. [116]

By now even the Indian Affairs office had grudgingly adopted a position supportive of Indian treaty rights. In his 1895 *Annual Report*, the commissioner stated that "the laws of the State of Wyoming which prohibit hunting within that State for certain kinds of game during certain months must be construed in the light of the treaty granting rights to these Indians to hunt on the unoccupied lands within the State, so far as they apply to the Shoshone and Bannock Indians." Therefore, urged Browning, "it is not competent for the State to pass any law which would modify, limit, or in any way abridge the right of the Indians to hunt as guaranteed by the treaty." [117]

Browning further stated that the government was bound under its treaty with the Shoshone-Bannock to prosecute those whites who had violated the Indians' treaty-stipulated hunting rights. He requested that the Department of Justice study the matter and make recommendations on how to proceed with punishing the offenders.[118] On September 20, 1895, the Office of Indian Affairs instructed Province McCormick, inspector for the United States Indian Service, to proceed to Wyoming to meet with the governor and other state officials regarding the hunting dispute. The Indian commissioner's instructions to McCormick indicate the great importance the United States attached to this case:

> I desire you to confer with the governor of Wyoming with reference to the right of these Indians to hunt off their reservation in the territory in question and ascertain his views upon the subject. . . . In case the governor is unwilling to concede the rights of the Indians to hunt as above indicated, you will propose to him that there shall be a *test case* made and a decision arrived at as to the right of the Indians to hunt on public lands under their treaty, either by having an Indian arrested by the State officials for hunting, and an application brought by the United States attorney for Wyoming or a writ of habeas corpus for the release of such prisoner, or in some other way, and that he shall agree that in case it shall be decided that the Indians have a right to hunt, and that the laws of Wyoming are of no effect as against them, then, in that event, he, Governor Richards, shall, by all the means in his power, protect the Indians in such right; and on the other hand, if it shall be decided by the Courts that the Indians have no right to hunt, in violation of the State laws, or, in other words, that the state laws operate to abridge or defeat their said treaty rights, then this Department will recommend to Congress that an agreement be made with them for the relinquishment of the rights guaranteed to them by the treaty of 1868, and which they claim and believe are still in full force.[119] (emphasis mine)

Interestingly, the letter goes on to suggest that McCormick not contact the Indians until after he has concluded his meetings with the governor and his officials. This communication highlights the structural disadvantage of tribes existing in an extraconstitutional standing; the United States was exhibiting a clear willingness to negotiate the treaty rights of the Indians without their knowledge or consent.

McCormick traveled to Wyoming and met with Governor Richards on September 29. The governor, McCormick later said, refused to concede that the Indians had any treaty rights that the State was legally bound to recognize. According to the governor, the Indians' treaty rights had been abrogated by the state's hunting laws. Nevertheless, McCormick reported that Wyoming's chief executive was willing to accept the proposition for a "test case" to let the judiciary decide the matter.[120] After the detailed state-federal agreement had already been worked out, McCormick met with the Shoshone-Bannock to explain the government's strategy. Urging the Indians to "rely implicitly upon the Department," McCormick received near unanimous tribal consent to proceed.[121]

The inspector terminated his report by predicting that the courts would uphold the treaty rights guaranteed to the Indians.[122] Nevertheless, he strongly urged that the government proceed to negotiate with the Indians to have their hunting rights ended because he believed, as the massacre had shown, that "establishing the right of these Indians to hunt on public or unoccupied lands does not protect them in that right."[123]

The legal infrastructure was set. Soon, the "test" Indians, including Race Horse, were arrested. Almost immediately, Gibson Clark, a Justice Department attorney, instituted habeas corpus proceedings seeking the release of the Indians. The case was tried in the Federal District Court of Wyoming on November 21, 1895.[124] Benjamin Fowler, John Ham, and Willis Van Devanter, representing Wyoming, brought the case against Race Horse. Gibson Clark represented Race Horse.

In a sterling opinion affirming Indian treaty rights, District Judge Riner ruled that Wyoming's hunting laws were invalid against the treaty and reserved hunting rights of the Shoshone-Bannock. Judge Riner's decision had three interrelated points: (1) whether an Indian treaty and the rights and privileges claimed under it were void and continued even after Wyoming's statehood; (2) whether a Wyoming statute which was inconsistent with the federally sanctioned Indian treaty was lawful; and (3) whether Wyoming's admission as a state "upon an equal footing with the original States" abrogated the Indian treaty's provision.[125]

Judge Riner began by asserting the supremacy of the federal government's treaty power; "a power which is expressly delegated to the United States and prohibited to the States."[126] Wyoming's hunting laws, therefore, which conflicted with the Indians' treaty rights, were invalid because Congress's intention to violate the treaty was not clear and unequivocal.[127] The district judge also refused to accept Wyoming's "equal footing" argument as nullifying treaty rights. While acknowledging that the act which admitted Wyoming into statehood had not explicitly reserved the tribes' treaty rights, Judge Riner forcefully wrote, "neither does it, in express terms, abrogate the treaty, or any of its provisions."[128] In conclusion, Judge Riner noted that "the act admitting Wyoming into the Union does not, by necessary implication, repeal or abrogate the treaty, and that the treaty provision remains in force."[129]

Despite this impressive judicial ruling, the Shoshone-Bannock soon faced a legislative extinguishment of their hunting rights. Their agent, Thomas Teter, echoing the treaty-rights termination sentiment expressed earlier by Inspector McCormick, strongly urged that the Bureau of Indian Affairs establish a commission to negotiate with the Indians "for a relinquishment of their treaty rights."[130] The rationale given: to "prevent a recurrence . . . of the Jackson Hole troubles of the past July."[131]

H. R. 4444 was introduced by Representative Frank Mondell (R., Wyoming). Mondell sought either a complete "surrender" or at least a major "modification" of the Indians' right to hunt "to such an extent that they shall be amenable to State game laws and regulations."[132] The bill was read, its title was amended, and it was subsequently passed in the House. It was not, however, enacted into law. By the time it was introduced, Willis Van Devanter, Wyoming's lead attorney, had already appealed the district court's ruling to the Supreme Court.

MASKING WITHIN THE DECISION: THE OPINION

The Supreme Court, speaking in majority fashion (seven to one; Justice David Brewer did not participate) through Justice Edward D. White, reversed Judge Riner's decision by declaring that judgment "erroneous" and held that Wyoming's gaming laws had superseded the Shoshone-Bannock's treaty-guaranteed rights to hunt either off-reservation or on unoccupied lands ceded by the two tribes to the United States.

White began the majority decision by denying as "wholly immaterial" the importance of exactly where John Race Horse had killed the elk. This denial language immediately signaled his position on the treaty since that document explicitly recognized the Shoshone-Bannock's right to hunt on "unoccupied lands of the United States so long as game may be found thereon, and so long as peace subsists among the whites and Indians on the borders of the hunting districts."[133] For White, the "sole question" to be considered was whether the treaty "gave" the Shoshone-Bannock the "right to exercise the hunting privilege," which now was in violation of Wyoming's laws.

The Mask of Treaties as "Privileges"

Notwithstanding that the Shoshone-Bannock, like other hunting tribes, had always relied on hunting to sustain themselves, White asserted that this was a right "given" to the tribes. The hunting right assumed an even more paramount nature since the Indian agents had evidence that many Indians were malnourished because of the inconsistent and inadequate federal food supply to the Fort Hall Reservation. These food supplies had been guaranteed to the Indians as part of their 1868 treaty arrangement with the United States. The federal government's rationale for supplying foodstuffs to the Indians on the reservation was to create a sedentary lifestyle which they believed would aid in their assimilation to the American way of life.

White's postulation of hunting as a "privilege," a term he would use throughout the case, says much about the tenuous nature of what actually were vested rights that the tribes reserved for themselves during their treaty negotiations with the federal commissioners. The tribes, in fact, had been very careful to reserve the bulk of those rights that had not explicitly been ceded away in the 1868 treaty. In other words, the Shoshone-Bannock surrendered much of their aboriginal territory to the federal government and, in exchange, secured to themselves all those rights specifically mentioned in the treaty—i.e., hunting—and all other rights not granted away. The issue for White became whether to interpret expressed treaty provisions "as the Indians understood them" or to consider only the Supreme Court's interpretation, even when it conflicted with the Indians' view.

Furthermore, in wording the question in this manner, White held implicit that a state municipal law was superior to a ratified federal treaty. In discrediting the status of treaty-reserved hunting rights, White observed,

> If it [treaty] gave such right, the mere fact that the State had created school districts or election districts . . . could no more efficaciously operate to destroy the right of the Indian to hunt on the lands than could the passage of the game law. If, on the other hand, the terms of the treaty did not refer to lands within a State, . . . then it is equally

clear that, although the lands were not in school and election districts and were not near settlements, the right conferred on the Indians by the treaty would be of no avail to justify a violation of state law.[134]

In this quote, White effectively manipulated the facts to give legitimacy to the state's claim where none existed; specifically, the 1868 treaty could not possibly refer to state lands, because Wyoming did not become a state until 1890. Although it was true that Wyoming achieved territorial status in 1868, shortly after the signing of the Fort Bridger Treaty, the act that established territoriality included an explicit provision stating, "nothing in this act shall be construed to impair the rights of person or property now pertaining to the Indians in said Territory, so long as such rights shall remain unextinguished by treaty between the United States and such Indians."[135]

White's discussion of Wyoming's actual political status insofar as that status overrides Indian treaty rights is an important misconstruction on his part. This is evident in his early statement of the question before the Court, where he equated the establishment of treaty rights (1868) with Wyoming's existence as a state (1890 in fact; 1868 in White's articulation). This is a crucial error, because the tribes' treaty rights predated Wyoming's territorial status by an entire month (July 1868) and statehood by more than two decades (July 1890). The Indians' preexisting treaty rights, according to the U.S. Constitution's treaty clause, entailed the supreme law of the land.

White then returned to an analysis of the language in article 4 of the treaty, especially the word "unoccupied," which earlier he had said was "wholly immaterial" to deciding the case. He had to return to this, however, because the language of that provision was explicit, and in order to circumvent such express language he would have to orchestrate the meaning of words carefully:

> It may at once be conceded that the words "unoccupied lands of the United States," if they stood alone, and were detached from the other provisions of the treaty on the same subject, would convey the meaning of lands owned by the United States, and the title to or occupancy of which had not been disposed of. But in interpreting these words in the treaty, they cannot be considered alone, but must be construed with reference to the context in which they are found. Adopting this elementary method, it becomes at once clear that the unoccupied lands contemplated were not all such lands of the United States wherever sit-

uated, but were only lands of that character embraced within what the treaty denominates as hunting districts.[136]

White had adroitly changed the tribes' heretofore unqualified right to hunt on any of their former "unoccupied" territory ceded to and now under the control of the United States in the treaty. He thus reduced this right to a "privilege" subject to state law via hunting districts which had been nonexistent when the treaty was negotiated. White expanded his exercise in obtuse language:

> This view follows as a necessary result from the provision which says that the right to hunt on the unoccupied lands shall only be availed of as long as peace subsists on the borders of the hunting districts. Unless the districts thus referred to be taken as controlling the words "unoccupied lands," then the reference to the hunting districts would become wholly meaningless, and the cardinal rule of interpretation would be violated, which ordains such construction be adopted as gives effect to all the language of the statute. Nor can this consequence be avoided by saying that the words "hunting districts" simply signified places where game was to be found, for this would read out of the treaty the provision as "to peace on the borders" of such districts, which clearly pointed to the fact that the territory referred to was one beyond the borders of the white settlements.[137]

In short, White was saying that the Indians enjoyed the "privilege" of hunting, but if violence erupted, the privilege could be withdrawn.

The Court then proceeded to give a description of the events surrounding the 1868 treaty's negotiation and the subsequent years up to and through Wyoming's statehood. White, using his own rather than the Indians' interpretation of these treaty proceedings, observed that the Shoshone-Bannock had indeed been granted hunting rights, but only "so long as the necessities of civilization did not require otherwise" and that such rights were "absolutely" dependent "upon the will of Congress."[138]

In constructing his treaty abrogation language, White said that the "privilege" of hunting was available to the Indians "only whilst peace reigned on the borders."[139] With the arguments thus established, White then reached the gist of his justification for abrogating Indian treaty rights:

> To suppose that the words of the treaty intended to give to the Indians the right to enter into already established States and seek out every

portion of unoccupied government land and there exercise the right of hunting, in violation of the municipal law, would be to presume that the treaty was so drawn as to frustrate the very object it had in view. It would also render necessary the assumption that Congress, whilst preparing the way, by the treaty, for new settlement and new States, yet created a provision not only detrimental to their future well being, but also irreconcilably in conflict with the powers of the States already existing.[140]

This quote contains several fallacies and flaws. First, White spoke as if the state existed as a sovereign at the time of the treaty's negotiation. Second, the Court, in a questionable interpretation of the Treaty and Supremacy clauses of the Constitution, and ignoring prior judicial precedent (e.g., *Worcester v. Georgia* [1832]), urged that treaties were of a diminished stature when placed next to "municipal laws." Third, White noted that the treaty's language, if interpreted to allow the Shoshone-Bannock's right to hunt off the reservation, would somehow "frustrate" the purpose behind the treaty's negotiation. And, finally, he created an alleged "irreconcilability" between a state's admission into the Union and treaty rights, when no such conflict existed.

White then made statements about the relationship between the location of Race Horse's killing of the elk and the timing of statehood. He observed,

It is undoubted that the place in the State of Wyoming, where the game in question was killed, was at the time of the treaty in 1868, embraced within the hunting districts therein referred to. But this fact does not justify the implication that the treaty authorized the continued enjoyment of the right of killing game therein, when the territory ceased to be a part of the hunting districts and came within the authority and jurisdiction of a State. The right to hunt given by the treaty clearly contemplated the disappearance of the conditions therein specified.[141]

Following this remarkable demonstration of how it was possible for a treaty to contemplate the disappearance of nonexistent future conditions, the Court arrived at the apex of its abrogation. White stated that the federal government had the sole power of determining who could do what on the lands in question. This sense of unrestrained ownership harkens back to the "doctrine of discovery" principle first unleashed in 1823 by the Supreme Court in *Johnson v. McIntosh*, which held that the United States was vested with absolute title to "discovered" Indian lands, while the tribal inhabitants' land title was diminished to that of occupancy.

According to White's logic, since under the *Johnson* rule the land already belonged to the United States, the Indians' right to hunt logically "cease[d] the moment the United States parted with the title to its land in the hunting district."[142] Again, this is a problematic historical argument. A reserved treaty right, at this time, was just that, a reserved right, and there was nothing in the language of the treaty which indicated that the Indians' right to hunt would cease if or when Wyoming went from territorial status to statehood. White then stated his personal views about Indian treaty rights, citing their "temporary and precarious nature":[143]

> Here the nature of the right created gives rise to such implication of continuance, since, by its terms, it shows that the burden [the Indians' hunting rights] imposed on the Territory was essentially perishable and intended to be of a limited duration. Indeed, the whole argument of the defendant in error rests on the assumption that there was a perpetual right conveyed by the treaty, when in fact the privilege given was temporary and precarious.[144]

In the end, White had provided an interpretation of an 1868 treaty provision which completely clashed with the treaty views held by the Indians, the Bureau of Indian Affairs, and the Department of Justice. The Court had also read a congressional intent into the treaty which was not discernible from the historical record and which conflicted with the arguments of the federal government's lawyers, who had sided with the Shoshone-Bannock.

The Mask of "Equal Footing"

White firmly indicated that Indian treaty rights should not be allowed to be "destructive of the rights of one of the States."[145] To support this, the Tenth Amendment to the Constitution, which expressly states that "the powers not delegated to the United States by the Constitution, nor prohibited to the States, are reserved to the States respectively, or to the people," became another source of state power that White and the majority relied on. This view capsulized the fragile position of Indian/tribal treaty rights when the justices of the Court were ideologically aligned with the doctrine of dual-federalism,[146] which emphasized the states' retention of all sovereign rights not delegated to the federal government via their enabling acts.

Justice White, therefore, maintained that article 4 of the 1868 Treaty (which included the hunting clause) had been repealed because it conflicted with Wyoming's admission act.[147] In an interpretation wholly at odds with District Judge Riner's more constitutionally sound federal supremacy argument and a recognition of the federal government's legal, moral, and political obligation to protect Indian treaty rights, Justice White asserted that the act which admitted Wyoming into the union "declared that that State should have all the powers of the other States of the Union, and made no reservation whatever in favor of the Indians."[148] However, the state's enabling act actually said nothing about Indians. The Constitution's Commerce Clause had conferred the regulation of the nation's Indian affairs on the Congress, not the states.

White quoted liberally from *Escanaba Company v. Chicago* (1883), which discussed the "equal footing theory." In *Escanaba*, the Court held that on admission a state "at once became entitled to and possessed of all the rights of dominion and sovereignty which belonged to the original States. She was admitted, and could be admitted, only on the same footing with them. . . ."[149] This is true. However, none of the original states enjoyed unfettered authority over Indian affairs, Indian lands, or Indian treaty rights. Again, the Constitution's Commerce Clause and the President's well-exercised treaty authority saw to that.

Justice White stated that the treaty right had been repealed because of "the conflict between the treaty and the act admitting that State into the Union." "The two facts," said White, "the privilege conferred and the act of admission, are irreconcilable in the sense that the two under no reasonable hypothesis can be construed as co-existing."[150] This interpretation, however, directly conflicts with an earlier federal district court opinion, *United States v. Berry*,[151] which involved the attempt of a state (Colorado) to construe its enabling act in a way to repeal the treaty rights of the Ute Indians.

In *Berry*, it was held that "according to a well settled rule of construction, since there is no express repeal of any part of the treaty, that instrument and the statute should be construed together, and as far as possible, the provisions of each should be allowed to stand."[152] More importantly, *Berry* said that an enabling act could not be so construed because it would deprive the United States "of the power of fulfilling the solemn obligations imposed upon them by said treaty." [153] "The treaty by its terms was to be permanent, and the rights conferred thereby were not to be taken away without the consent of the Indians." [154] And while conceding that the United States could abrogate or repeal treaty provisions, "it is clear to my mind that such repeal can only be enacted in express terms, or by such language as imports a clear purpose on the part of congress to effect that end." [155]

While paying lip service to the constitutional delegation of federal authority in relation to Indian tribes, White said that "nothing in this case shows that this power has been exerted by Congress." [156] The Shoshone-Bannock, however, were under the distinct impression, reinforced by the legal support rendered by the government, that their treaty hunting right was not subject to control by any other party, absent tribal consent or a bilateral modification of the preexisting treaty arrangement.

Nevertheless, wedding public faith, state sovereignty, and congressional will together, White concluded by saying that the lower court's decision was "erroneous," and the case was reversed and remanded.

JUSTICE BROWN'S DISSENT

Justice Henry Brown was aware of the destructive precedent being established by the Court's opinion. He said that the majority's ruling was a "distinct repudiation by Congress of a treaty with the Bannock Indians." [157] The continuing validity of the treaty, and the fact that Wyoming's admission to statehood abrogated the treaty *pro tanto* and left tribes "at the mercy of the state government" [158] was enough to rankle Brown's sense of justice. While claiming that Congress retained the power to abrogate treaties, Brown stated that such an extinguishment should not occur except and unless the intent was clear and unambiguous. [159] After describing the history of the treaty—coming as it had at the close of a series of deadly skirmishes—Brown noted that the tribes agreed to the terms of the treaty and ceded certain sections of their land, reserving all other rights to their remaining territory and specific rights in the ceded land. The United States, Brown said, solemnly pledged to protect the tribes and their retained rights, including the essential hunting right. Brown's interpretation of article 4 was radically different from the majority's and closely conformed to what the federal government was arguing on behalf of the Indians. He said that the Shoshone-Bannock retained the right to hunt, as long as there was game and peace. More importantly, Brown noted:

The right to hunt was not one secured to them for sporting purposes, but as a means of subsistence. It is a fact so well known that we may take judicial notice of it, that the Indians have never been an industrial people; . . . and that their chief reliance for food has been upon the chase. The right to hunt on the unoccupied lands of the United States was a matter of supreme importance to them, and as a result of being deprived of it they can hardly escape becoming a burden upon the public. It is now proposed to take it away from them, not because they have violated a treaty, but because the State of Wyoming desires to preserve its game. Not doubting for a moment that the preservation of game is a matter of great importance, I regard the preservation of the public faith, even to the helpless Indian, as a matter of much greater importance.[160]

Brown also refused to accept the "equal footing argument." He argued, in line with the Court's precedent in *The Kansas Indians*,[161] that Indian treaty rights could not be adversely affected except "by purchase or by a new arrangement [treaty] with the United States."[162] Since neither of these stipulations had been met, there was no lawful basis for the Court to accede to Wyoming's abrogation of the Indians' treaty rights. In closing, Brown gave a more historically justified appraisal of the words "unoccupied lands of the United States." He said that although the language referred "not only to lands which have not been patented, but also to those which have not been settled upon, fenced or otherwise appropriated to private ownership," he did not believe that "the admission of a Territory into the Union changes their character of unoccupied to that of occupied lands."[163]

CONCLUSION

Although *Ward* was thought to have been implicitly overruled in *United States v. Winans* (1905) and has been a much criticized opinion,[164] this decision nevertheless continues to pose a viable and recently reinvigorated threat to tribal sovereignty and the exercise of off-reservation treaty rights.[165] *Ward* dealt a paralyzing blow to the sanctity of Indian treaties by ignoring earlier case precedent[166] and elevated state power not only over tribes' vested rights, but also over the federal government itself as trustee for the Indians. This last element was in direct contrast to what the Court had maintained in the two most recent cases examined, *Southern Kansas Railway* and *U.S. v. Kagama*.

Lone Wolf v. Hitchcock

JUDICIAL MYOPIA — WHAT INDIAN RIGHTS?

In the March 29, 1902, edition of *The Outlook* magazine, an article appeared entitled "Have Reservation Indians Any Vested Rights?" Its author was George Kennan, *The Outlook*'s Washington correspondent. Kennan examined the federal government's policy of leasing tribal lands on the Standing Rock Sioux Reservation and concluded that Indian lands were not being protected, and were, in fact, being confiscated without tribal consent.[167]

As evidence that this actually had happened, Kennan quoted from a decision rendered March 4, 1902, by the Court of Appeals of the District of Columbia in *Lone Wolf v. Hitchcock*.[168] In this case, the court had held that the pertinent provisions of the 1868 treaty between the Kiowa, Comanche, and the United States did not give the tribes legally enforceable title to their lands. In the appeal judge's own amazing and prophetic words:

> The treaty of 1868 certainly did not vest in the Indians, either in their individual or tribal capacity, anything more than the right to occupy the lands as against the United States until it was found necessary to make other provisions for them. There was no grant of estates either of freehold or a leasehold; only a mere right to occupy and use the lands, according to the habits and customs of the Indians; but those rights of the Indians were sacred to them as against every one, until Congress made provision for assuming control over the lands, and making other disposition thereof, upon such terms and conditions as Congress should prescribe.[169]

The issue of Congress's power to abrogate foreign and Indian treaties had been dealt with by the federal courts in several earlier cases.[170] Those decisions, at least the ones involving Indian treaties, however, are clearly differentiated from *Lone Wolf* because they did not specifically involve a deprivation of tribal property rights previously acknowledged under a ratified treaty.[171]

HISTORICAL BACKGROUND

On October 21, 1867, representatives of the Kiowa and Comanche tribes (the Apache Tribe joined by separate treaty later) entered into a treaty with the seven-member delegation of the congressionally created Indian Peace Commission at Medicine Lodge Creek in Kansas.[172] This multi-purpose treaty entailed land cessions, the establishment of peace, and the creation of reservation boundaries. Moreover, it contained several "civilization" provisions, including the following: Indian parents agreed to send their children to schools; heads of households could select up to 320 acres for farming; and the Indians agreed to remain within boundaries of their newly established homelands.

The most relevant provisions, however, are found in articles 2 and 12 which deal with the establishment and protection of the three-million-acre reservation. Article 2 reads in pertinent part that the reservation was to be "set apart for the absolute and undisturbed use and occupation of the tribes herein named. . . ."[173] The germane section of article 12 reads as follows:

No treaty for the cession of any portion or part of the reservation herein described, which may be held in common, shall be of any validity or force as against the said Indians, unless executed and signed by at least three-fourths of all the adult male Indians occupying the scene. . . .[174]

Notwithstanding these legal and moral assurances, the fervor to individualize tribal land holdings following the passage of the 1887 General Allotment Act soon reached the confederated Kiowa, Comanche, and Apache (KCA) reservation.

In 1892, the three-member federal Cherokee Commission (also known as the Jerome Commission), established by Congress in 1889 to engage certain Oklahoma tribes in land cession agreements,[175] concluded a pact with representatives from the KCA tribes for the allotment of their lands. The remaining "surplus" lands were to be opened for non-Indian settlement. Although a number of Indian signatures were obtained, the three-fourths requirement was not met. Nevertheless, the agreement was sent to Washington, D.C., for congressional ratification.

On October 20, 1893, 323 KCA tribal members memorialized the Senate, strenuously arguing that the October 6, 1892, agreement should not be ratified for several reasons. First, they stated that negotiating sessions had not, as required by law, been conducted "in open council nor in the presence or with the knowledge of their people [tribal leaders] and constituents. Second, they stressed that the commission, after having fraudulently obtained an inadequate number of signatures, then "caused numerous pretended councils of said Indians to be held under the guns of said fort" (Fort Sill), where additional—though still too few—signatures were gathered "by misrepresentation, threats, and fraud. . . ." Finally, that the government's commission then relocated to the Indian agency headquarters of Anadarko where, for "more than a month . . . it continued its campaign of mendacity, fraud, and coercion until the alleged signatures of 456 Indians were claimed to have been obtained."[176] The tribal memorialists then asserted that once the 456 signatures had been collected, the "said agreement was, without the loss of an hour, but upon the same day, transmitted to Washington. . . ."[177]

Despite the haste with which the agreement was shuttled to the Capitol, the ratification process would not be so quick. In 1898, five years from the date of the agreement's arrival in Washington, and after several previous attempts, a bill was finally reported out of committee on the House side favoring enactment of the 1892 agreement. This bill, however, substantially altered the original agreement by inserting a provision to hasten the settlement of Choctaw and Chickasaw claims to the Leased District. The KCA tribes had fought every legislative attempt to approve the agreement; nevertheless, the House bill was passed on May 16, 1898.[178]

The Senate, however, bowing to pressure from the KCA tribes and a prestigious and influential interest group, The Indian Rights Association, adopted a resolution in January 1899 which directed the secretary of the interior to inquire whether the requisite number of signatures had been obtained.[179] When Secretary Hitchcock responded on January 13, 1900, his startling findings confirmed the major contentions of the KCA tribes and their supporters. Hitchcock acknowledged that not only had "less than three-fourths of the adult males . . . signed" the agreement, but that the agricultural acreage provided for in the 1892 agreement was inadequate to meet the needs of the Indians.[180]

W. A. Jones, the commissioner of Indian affairs, submitted equally revealing findings. The commissioner gave three reasons why he felt the agreement should not be ratified: (1) he questioned "when, if ever, the Indians [would] receive any compensation for their lands"; (2) he stated that "if the lands are paid for there is no certainty that the Comanche, etc., Indians will ever receive one cent"; and (3) he complained that the agreement, as amended, "made no provision for the payment of the interest to the tribes."[181] The commissioner ended his remarks by suggesting that "the agreement should be rejected by Congress, or that it be ratified with the proposed amendments and submitted to the Indians for their acceptance or rejection."[182] After all, noted Commissioner Jones, "it is certainly a novel proposition in law that one party to an agreement may, without the consent of the other, alter or modify an essential part of such contract." He concluded with, as it turned out, unwarranted faith in the legal system, that "no court of law would uphold or enforce any contract so altered or amended." [183]

However sound these and the KCA tribes' arguments were, it was obvious that certain members of Congress intended to ratify the agreement over the considered opposition of the tribes and the Indian Affairs commissioner. This is apparent in the manner in which the agreement was ultimately approved. It was simply attached as an amendment (section 6) to Senate Bill S. 255, which was a pending agreement between the United States and the Indians of the Fort Hall Reservation in Idaho. The House report accompanying the Senate bill described the 1892 KCA agreement this way:

> This agreement . . . embraces 2,969,893 acres of land; and after allotting or giving to each Indian 160 acres, it cedes to the United States 2,517,853 acres, which will be opened to settlement. There are only 2,679 of these Indians. . . . This reservation contains very valuable farm and grazing lands. For years the most of it has been used by cattlemen for the grazing of large herds of cattle. Your committee are advised that these Indians have made great advancement during the last few years under the management of acting agent Captain Baldwin and those who have succeeded him.[184]

In closing the report, the committee quoted Oklahoma's territorial governor, who said: "I can not refrain from urging, as I have heretofore, that these reservations be at once opened to settlement. They embrace some of the finest lands in Oklahoma Territory, and would be capable of supporting a large population."

Entered into the *Record* on April 2, 1900, a month before Congress acted on the measure, the comments of Representative Charles Curtis (the sponsor of the devastating Curtis Act of 1898 which legally dismembered the Five Civilized Tribes) reveal the political strategy used by the House to get both the KCA and Fort Hall bills enacted. Curtis stated: "The bill to ratify the Kiowa [KCA] treaty has passed this body upon two different occasions. It has never passed the Senate. The Fort Hall bill has passed the Senate twice, but has never passed the House. The Committee on Indian Affairs reported this bill unanimously. This, I believe, is all there is to say about this bill." [185]

The House proponents, in desperation, had attached their two-year-old bill as a rider to the Senate Indian bill on Fort Hall. The House passed the merged measure, and it went to the Senate. On June 6, 1900, nearly eight years after the original agreement was signed, the Senate passed the amended agreement without debate at the end of the session. Nothing in the title of the act indicated that section 6 was a ratification of the contested Jerome Agreement of 1892.[186] Three supplementary acts enacted in 1901 expanded the manner in which ceded tribal lands were to be handled.

THE JUDICIAL PROCESS BEGINS

Lone Wolf, a well-known Kiowa headman, supported by the Indian Rights Association, filed suit in the Supreme Court of the District of Columbia on June 6, 1901, to obtain an injunction to prevent implementation of the acts confirming the 1892 agreement. Lone Wolf and his associates lost in the District Court. They then appealed to the district court of appeals. Even as this appeal was pending, President McKinley issued a proclamation on July 4, 1901, which said that the KCA-ceded surplus lands were to be opened for settlement from August 6, 1901.[187]

The court of appeals also ruled for the United States. The court stated that reservation Indians with "assigned lands" had no vested rights but only a right to occupy "at the will of the government." The judges, however, after having savaged tribal treaty and property rights, ironically ended their opinion by piously intoning, "We shall be greatly gratified if that high tribunal [U.S. Supreme Court] may be able to find a way for affording a remedy for what is alleged to be a grievous wrong to the Indians."[188]

Lone Wolf, also known as A. Kei-quodle, was joined by Eshitie, principal chief of the Comanche; White Buffalo, Ko-Koy-Taudle, Marmo-sook-car-we, Narwats, Too-wi-car-ne, William Tivis, and Delos K. Lone Wolf (Lone Wolf's interpreter). They were represented by William Springer and Hampton L. Carson. Ethan A. Hitchcock was joined by William A. Jones, commissioner of Indian affairs, and Binger Herman, commissioner of the general land office, as appellants.

Springer and Carson, on behalf of the KCA tribes, raised a number of compelling treaty and constitutional arguments in their brief before the Supreme Court that stress the importance of this case. First, they argued that the Court of Appeals had made a "fundamental error" in stating that Indians "had always been treated as wards with assigned lands and no defensible title." They noted that this was a "historical error and ignore[d] the feature of Indian consent."[189]

Second, they cited the precedent established in *Mitchel v. United States* (1835) and reaffirmed in *Holden v. Joy* (1872) that Indian title was as "sacred as the fee-simple title of whites." And they brought forth another principle established in *Holden*—that Congress has no power to interfere with treaty rights, "except in cases purely political."[190]

Third, they argued that the 1867 Medicine Lodge treaty was a binding contract. They said that agreements executed and confirmed by which the tribes "in consideration of the relinquishment of the right to use and occupy other lands," were binding upon both parties and could not "be annulled or abrogated without the consent of both parties."[191]

Fourth, the tribes' attorneys maintained that the central issues in the case were not "political questions" and reminded the justices that the court of appeals itself had concluded its decision by stating that it hoped the Supreme Court would find a remedy for the Indians.[192]

Fifth, the attorneys stated that tribal objections to the original amendment and Congress's unilateral amendments to the treaty, which were not submitted to the Indians for approval, portrayed a situation which "shocks the conscience of every person who believes in justice and fair dealing."[193]

Sixth, Springer and Carson argued that the Indians had a vested right to their property and that under existing law legislative acts impairing such rights were void.[194] They then cited *Marbury v. Madison*, and argued that since the essence of civil liberty was the right of every individual to have the protection of the law when an injury was sustained, the Supreme Court had the authority to provide a forum for the determination of what constitutes vested rights.[195]

Seventh, they asserted that the Indians had a perpetual right of occupancy, that they were entitled to due process of law, that Indians were "persons" under the Constitution, and that the tribes' property had not been taken for "public use."[196] This action by the government, argued the attorneys, was without precedent. Prior to the act of June 6, 1900, Congress had "never passed an Act which deprived Indians of the right to the use and occupancy of lands secured to them by treaty, without their consent, except by due process of law."[197]

Eighth, Springer and Carson rejected the government's contention that as "wards," Indians had few rights. Moreover, they astutely noted that even if the Court insisted on treating the Indians as wards, even wards could not be divested of their title to lands without some kind of hearing.[198]

Finally, Springer and Carson gave Congress the benefit of the doubt and said "there is some doubt even as to whether Congress really intended to ratify the so-called Jerome Agreement...."[199] They noted that the KCA Agreement, which had never been ratified by the Indians, had been dovetailed with the tribally approved Fort Hall Agreement. And they expressed doubt that a majority of Congress knew what was transpiring: "The fact that it was being amended and ratified without submission to the Indians for ratification or rejection does not appear to have been called to the attention of either House of Congress. It is highly probable, therefore, that but few Senators or members understood the full import of the measure."[200]

The United States attorneys, Assistant Attorney General Willis Van Devanter (Wyoming's lead attorney in *Ward*, and a future Supreme Court justice) supported by William C. Pollock and Anthony C. Campbell, reached for and relied on the entrenched rhetoric of Indian "wardship" and argued that as "wards" tribes were fully controlled and cared for by Congress. Van Devanter said:

> It was demonstrated that the Indian [by this period] was absolutely incapable of protecting himself in his new surroundings or of determining what was for his advantage. . . . [T]o afford the Indian that protection which the laws of humanity demanded should be given him, and to prevent as far as possible the evil consequences to both parties which would necessarily flow from the clash between civilization and savageism, it was necessary that the Government should intervene and assume complete control over the Indians.[201]

Another telling quote from Van Devanter's brief indicates how deeply the guardianship-wardship theory had seeped into the consciousness of government lawyers and policymakers. "While sentimentality may characterize the exercise of absolute authority over the affairs of the Indians as an arrogation of power because of might, yet the exigencies of the situation demanded its assumption and results have justified it."[202]

Finally, Van Devanter reiterated a classic Darwinian cultural argument—that the federal government had legitimate authority to force the Indians to emerge from their alleged "savage" state. The essential step in this "cultural evolution" was individual ownership of land. As Van Devanter argued:

> There was nothing in his [Indian] connection with the land that tended to his civilization or improvement, financially, or otherwise. . . . The Indians had not become self-supporting and had made no advance in

that direction which would justify a hope that they ever would become so under the old system. It was not only the right, but the imperative duty of the United States to change this condition of affairs and to make such provision for these people as would start them upon the road to self support and civilization. To successfully accomplish this it is necessary that each individual should be invested with the ownership of a tract which he should look upon as his own. . . . The indefinite, intangible, undivided, and indivisible interest of the individual in the tribal right of occupancy must be replaced by a defined, separate, and distinct personal right in and to a specific tract of land.[203]

In the Records and Briefs file of the case are two heart-rending letters written by Lone Wolf to his attorney, William Springer. The first, written December 27, 1901, reveals a man who was defiantly opposed to the selling of tribal lands, and who remained optimistic that the federal political and legal systems would protect his people's property and treaty rights. Lone Wolf informed Springer that the Kiowa Nation had instructed him to inform the government that they would not accept any monetary settlement offered by the United States for tribal lands being squatted on by whites. "We believe," said Lone Wolf, "that while everything seems to be against us, we will succeed. There is [a] just God who rules the affairs of this government."[204] By July 1902, Lone Wolf's tone was noticeably more depressed. In a letter to Springer signed by Lone Wolf and sixteen other Indians, one senses the severe level of frustration now experienced by the tribesmen regarding their inability to protect their lands from white encroachment, notwithstanding their seemingly invincible legal and moral arguments. "Good friend," wrote Lone Wolf, "we, the undersigned members of the Kiowa and Comanche tribes, wish to write to you concerning our affairs. We think we ought to have by rights the say so in some things, but the way things are running we have no rights whatever." Lone Wolf's fears were soon to be realized.

MASKING WITHIN THE DECISION: THE OPINION

The fate of the KCA tribes now lay at the Supreme Court's doorstep. In the ensuing decision, however, their hopes and, by implication, those of all tribes with treaty-based rights and desirable lands, were crushed. The Court's unanimous opinion represented a perfect and deadly synthesis of the plenary power concept and the political question doctrine. The Court refused, citing the political question doctrine, to even consider the tribes' core argument of "fraudulent misrepresentation" by government officials. The justices also refused to consider the issue of the Senate's unilateral alteration of the 1892 agreements provisions. Additionally, the Court ignored the fact that the KCA were not in a relation of dependency when they negotiated their treaty with the U.S. in 1867.

The only question the Court considered was whether the Act of June 6, 1900, was constitutional. Despite Lone Wolf's treaty and constitutional arguments, Justice White accepted the "wardship" arguments of Van Devanter and said that the Indians' treaty-defined property rights had vested not in themselves but in the federal government. This "contention" of the Indians, said White, "in effect ignores the status of the contracting Indians and the relation of dependency they bore and continue to bear toward the government of the United States." White was retroactively bestowing wardship status on the tribes to make the abrogation of their treaty rights appear legal. He went on: "To uphold the claim would be to adjudge that the indirect operation of the treaty was to materially limit and qualify the controlling authority of Congress in respect to the care and protection of the Indians, and to deprive Congress, in a possible emergency, when the necessity might be urgent for a partition and disposal of the tribal lands, of all power to act, if the assent of the Indians could not be obtained."[205]

The Masks of Dependency, Security, and Christian Morality

On the status of tribal lands, White first cited prior language in which the Court had equated Indian title with fee-simple title, and then proceeded to set up a situation in which he was able to circumvent these decisions. He said, "In none of these cases was there involved a controversy between Indians and the government respecting the power of Congress to administer the property of the Indians."[206] This is correct, as written. Prior to this date, Congress had historically acknowledged that it had no right to challenge treaty-recognized property rights which, despite what White said, did indeed vest in the retaining party. One of the cases cited by White, however, *Beecher v. Wetherby* (1877), had stated that the United States had a superior authority over Indians based on guardianship and that such authority "might be implied, even though opposed to the strict letter of a treaty with the Indians."[207] This "abrogation by implication" argument was then meshed with another *Beecher* precedent: that the United States' actions regarding tribes would be governed "by such considerations of justice as would control a Christian people in their treatment of an ignorant and dependent race."[208] Here we see Christian theology being used to rationalize violations of constitutionally recognized treaty rights.

Displaying a lucid and self-contradictory ability to rewrite history in a way that legitimized congressional power over tribes, Justice White asserted that "[p]lenary authority over the tribal relations of the Indians has been exercised by Congress from the beginning, and the power has always been deemed a political one, not subject to the control of the judicial department of the government."[209] Both of these statements are judicial myths, without historical justification. Congress has not had plenary power over the tribes from the beginning; nor has the power always been determined to be political.

White apparently said Congress *always* had plenary authority not subject to judicial review because the Court was intent on legitimating the congressionally inspired and presidentially executed breakdown of communally held tribal lands which, the Court had determined, was essential before Euro-American civilization could be approximated by detribalized Indian individuals.

For White, as for the *Kagama* Court, the 1871 treaty-ending law was pivotal. Until that year, "the policy was pursued of dealing with the Indian tribes by means of treaties, and, of course, a moral obligation rested upon Congress to act in good faith in performing the stipulations entered into on its behalf." White then cited *Ward* and *The Cherokee Tobacco* as support. He was asserting that after 1871 Congress could selectively decide whether it wanted to act in a morally responsible way by fulfilling the provisions of extant treaties. White then stated the most powerful lines of the decision:

> The power exists to abrogate the provisions of an Indian treaty, though presumably such power will be exercised only when circumstances arise which will not only justify the government in disregarding the stipulations of the treaty, but may demand, in the interest of the country and the Indians themselves, that it should do so. When, therefore, treaties were entered into between the United States and a tribe of Indians it was never doubted that the *power* to abrogate existed in Congress, and in a contingency such power might be availed of from considerations of governmental policy, particularly if consistent with perfect good faith towards the Indians.[210] (emphasis original)

White does not define the "contingency" spoken of or what the considerations of "governmental policy might be," or how overt treaty abrogation can be consistent with "perfect good faith" toward Indians when the Indians consider it a direct exercise of bad faith and a contravention of their treaty rights. This is a prime example of the Court's use of legal masks to deny the humanity of the Indians and mask their own violations of the law. The judiciary, acting purely and deferentially as a legitimator of congressional policy, simply "presumed" that Congress had acted in good faith in dealing with the tribes because subsequent to the treaties' ratification it could find no historical or legal assurance that Congress had "in reality" acted in good faith.

Congress, said the Court, had not only unlimited but unreviewable authority over Indian tribes, their treaties, and their properties. White and the Court were acknowledging that even if Congress had violated the treaty, had violated the Constitution's Treaty Clause, and had violated the principles of consent, fairness, and justice, the judiciary would not look behind the actions of the legislative bodies.

White concluded by reiterating his presumption of good faith in Congress's right to exercise plenary authority to transform tribal communal lands to individual parcels—a transformation Indians could not resist by challenging the government's actions in Court. As in *The Cherokee Tobacco*, the Indians learned that to gain any measure of justice they would have to petition Congress, the very branch intent on destroying the basis of tribalism—tribal lands. In White's words:

> The controversy which this case presents is concluded by the decision in *Cherokee Nation v. Hitchcock* . . . decided at this term, where it was held that full administrative power was possessed by Congress over Indian tribal property. In effect, the action of Congress now complained of was but an exercise of such power, *a mere change in the form of investment of Indian tribal property*, the property of those who, as we have held, were in substantial effect the wards of the government. We must presume that Congress acted in perfect good faith in the dealings with the Indians of which complaint is made, and that the legislative branch of the government exercised its best judgment in the premises. In any event, as Congress possessed full power in the matter, the judiciary cannot question or inquire into the motives which prompted the enactment of this legislation. If injury was occasioned, which we do not wish to be understood as implying, by the use made by Congress of its power, relief must be sought by an appeal to that body for redress and not to the courts. The legislation in question was constitutional, and the demurrer to the bill was therefore rightly sustained.[211] (emphasis mine)

In sum, *Lone Wolf* mangled tribal sovereignty. Congressional plenary power, unconstrained by the Constitution, was interwoven with the political question doctrine and judicial deference to the legislature to form an almost impregnable shield which ignored the fact that tribal interests and federal interests could be in fundamental conflict. Although the Supreme Court had asserted that Congress's action was for a public purpose, one could powerfully argue that this was not the case since the lands taken were sold to white homesteaders. The 1900 agreement, therefore, "probably would not have been constitutional had the property been held by non-Indian owners."[212]

A month after the decision, Senator Orville Platt (R., Connecticut) requested that extra copies of the decision be printed as a Senate document because "there is a great demand for it."[213] When the Senate could not agree on the number of copies to be printed—500 or 1,000—Senator Matthew Quey (R., Pennsylvania) stepped forward and insisted that 1,000 copies were needed. His justification: "I think we better make the number of additional copies 1,000. It is a very remarkable decision. It is the *Dred Scott* decision No. 2, except that in this case the victim is red instead of black. It practically inculcates the doctrine that the red man has no rights which the white man is bound to respect, and, that no treaty or contract made with him is binding. Is that not about it?"[214]

CONCLUSION

As federal political, economic, and military power waxed in the late nineteenth century, with the corresponding waning of tribal power in these areas, there was a change, sometimes gradual, sometimes abrupt, in the way tribal sovereignty was conceptualized by the Supreme Court. In Barsh and Henderson's words, by the time of *Lone Wolf*, "[t]ribal domestic sovereignty had been surreptitiously transmogrified, from exclusive to residual, from presumptively inherent to presumptively delegated."[215] The concept "guardianship/wardship" was a principal element in this legal transformation.

In Marshall's *Cherokee Nation* (1831) decision, there was an illusion of tribal wardship; beginning with *Kagama* (1886) and continuing, albeit inconsistently, throughout the next several decades, wardship had become a delusion. Marshall used the analogy of "Indians as wards" in 1831 to justify or rationalize the federal government's self-imposed right or power to "protect" Indian tribes, both from states and foreign nations. He said that the relationship between tribes and the states "resemble[d] that of a ward to his guardian," and that tribes, "as domestic-dependent nations," were in a "state of pupilage." In the Court's legal consciousness, by the last two decades of the nineteenth century and into the first several decades of the twentieth century, tribes were, and according to *Lone Wolf*, "had always been," wards subject to the plenary authority of the federal government, despite ample invalidating evidence. Reified in the Court's consciousness, the justices employed masks like "wardship," "dependency," "savagery," "primitivism," "plenary power," "political question" in various ways to achieve whatever ends they deemed viable. And it was the Court, not the tribe, the individual, the states, or even Congress, which retained plenary discretion to decide the scope of Congress's powers, and the degree, if any, to which treaty tribal rights were to be protected.

CHAPTER 4

The Era of "Myths": Citizenship, Nomadism, and Moral Progress

Derived from the work of Felix S. Cohen,[1] the subtitling phrase for this chapter serves as a unifying factor for the cases discussed herein—from the muffled rights of individual Indians as federal citizens (*United States v. Nice*), to the denied treaty-based land claims of recognized tribes (*Northwestern Bands of Shoshone Indians v. United States*), to the violation of aboriginal land rights of some of Alaska's indigenous peoples (*Tee-Hit-Ton Indians v. United States*). These cases are also different from the ones we have examined in that they are sandwiched around an era of congressional reform, commonly referred to as the Indian Reorganization period, 1934–1945, which represented a legitimate but inadequate effort on the part of Congress to protect, preserve, and strengthen tribal art, culture, and political and social organization. The Indian Reorganization Act (IRA)[2] of 1934 officially initiated this era. The new federal philosophy, argued eloquently and forcefully by Commissioner of Indian Affairs John Collier, "offered an alternative answer to Indian dependency: reconstitution and strengthening of Indian tribes in some sort of autonomy, self-sufficiency, semi-sovereignty, or self-determination."[3]

Although this short-lived era of Indian policy reform was effective in undercutting the previous era's three federal goals of Indian acculturation, assimilation, and Americanization, it was not without its own set of inherent flaws and conflicts.[4] But, as a number of scholars have observed, John Collier and the Indian Reorganization Act years succeeded in terminating the notorious allotment policy, gave rise to widespread empathy for Indian culture, allowed a measured degree of Indian self-government, and garnered congressional support for Indian education, Indian preference, and other necessary economic development projects.[5]

Notwithstanding this renaissance among Indian nations, the Supreme Court would continue along its singular path as a political-legal entity and would render the rulings that left both individual Indians and tribal collectives, as late as the 1950s, wondering why, despite years of progressivism, social reform, and the United States' emergence as a dominant world power after World War II, they still had so little in the way of treaty and property rights.

United States v. Nice

SUBJECT CITIZENS

The 1887 General Allotment Act's major provisions included (1) that formerly communal Indian lands be converted to individual ownership, after which a twenty-five-year trust period would follow in which the United States was to protect the allottee's parcel against private or state encroachment; and (2) that citizenship be granted the patented allottee. It is this last issue—citizenship—which is the essential question in the 1916 case, *United States v. Nice*, that focused explicitly on the individual Indian's status as a propertied American citizen.

The Allotment policy's provision granting immediate citizenship to Indian allottees was explicit. Section 6 stated:

> That upon the completion of said allotments and the patenting of the lands to said allottees, each and every member of the respective bands or tribes of Indians to whom allotments have been made shall have the benefit of and be subject to the laws, both civil and criminal, of the State or Territory in which they may reside; and no Territory shall pass or enforce any law denying any such Indian within its jurisdiction the equal protection of the law. And every Indian born within the territorial limits of the United States to whom allotments shall have been made under the provisions of this act, or under any law or treaty . . . is hereby declared to be a citizen of the United States, and is entitled to all the rights, privileges, and immunities of such citizens, whether said Indian has been or not, by birth or otherwise, a member of any tribe of Indians, within the territorial limits of the United States without in any manner impairing or otherwise affecting the right of any such Indian to tribal or other property.[6]

This provision reflects general congressional sentiment that United States citizenship was conceived "as both a means to civilization, and an end to the civilization process."[7] The legislation was, in part, a direct congressional response to an earlier Supreme Court decision, *Elk v. Wil-*

kins (1884), in which John Elk had "voluntarily" left his tribe and moved to Omaha, Nebraska. Elk had registered to vote, but his application was rejected by Wilkins, the city registrar, because he was an Indian. The Supreme Court agreed with Wilkins's decision and denied Elk's citizenship request. It was held that Indians, like "the children of subjects of any foreign government" were not subject to the Fourteenth Amendment's provision since they belonged to "alien nations, distinct political communities, with whom the United States might and habitually did deal as they thought fit, either through treaties . . . [or] legislation."[8] In effect, the court said that even if individual Indians met the same basic citizenship requirements expected of other noncitizens they still could not be enfranchised unless Congress made an affirmative declaration authorizing such a change in their standing.

When Congress responded with the General Allotment Act, it was thought that the issue of Indian citizenship had been settled. Such was not to be the case, however, as uncertainty prevailed among federal lawmakers regarding whether or not Indian citizens were still "wards." The following passage, extracted from the *Congressional Record* of 1897, indicates the high degree of confusion on the precise political status of Indian allottees, especially as regarded the prohibition of liquor sales to reservation Indians.

> *Mr. Gamble:* It occurs to me, as suggested by my friend from Nebraska (Mr. Meiklejohn), that the Indians are still wards of the Government [even after having received an allotment]. They simply hold a title under the jurisdiction of the Government, which may be extended even during twenty-five years.
> *Mr. Bailey:* Will the gentleman permit an inquiry?
> *Mr. Gamble:* Certainly.
> *Mr. Bailey:* Does not the act provide that when they [Indian allottees] take this land in allotment, they become citizens?
> *Mr. Gamble:* They become citizens.
> *Mr. Bailey: Then it is utterly impossible for them to be citizens and pupils of the United States at the same time.* It is very clear that the Government has the right to continue them in the state of tutelage and dependence, but when it terminates that condition and makes them citizens of the United States, then it has no more power to legislate specifically for them than for any other citizens.
> *Mr. Gamble:* This is entirely a question of jurisdiction. It is a matter that ought to be passed upon and determined by the courts.[9]

THE MASK OF INDIAN WARDSHIP: IN PERPETUITY?

Representative Robert Gamble's (R., South Dakota) desire to have a judicial determination of this crucial question was first realized in a 1901 United States Federal Circuit Court of Appeals case, *Farrell v. United States*. In *Farrell*, the court adopted the position that the extension of federal citizenship to an individual Indian did not prevent the government from continuing to treat the Indian as a "ward" in need of "protection" from the evils of alcohol. Circuit Judge Walter H. Sanborn, who wrote the opinion, conceded that the Indian plaintiff (from the Sisseton and Wahpeton Band of Sioux) "was a citizen of the United States and the state of South Dakota in 1897, and that the argument . . . that he thereby became exempt from the jurisdiction of congress to regulate commerce with him is very persuasive and entitled to grave consideration." [10] However, Sanborn questioned whether the argument was "sound." "May not," he inquired, "the government confer all the privileges and immunities of citizenship upon its wards, and yet retain its power to regulate commerce with them; to protect them against their appetites, passions, and incapacity?" [11] This opinion establishes the rationale—once a ward, always a ward—used by Sanborn, which is remarkably similar to that used much later by Justice Willis Van Devanter in *Nice*. Sanborn stated that Congress clearly retained the power to regulate liquor traffic among Indians. This was a power which had been originally sanctioned by tribal leaders in their efforts to keep liquor traders away from their people, but which the United States agents and Christian missionaries had unilaterally expanded to the point of declaring it illegal for individual Indians to drink, whether on or off Indian lands. Sanborn said:

> These Indians are citizens, but they were originally wards. The nation had the right to prohibit the sale of liquor to them and to control and to superintend their acts and proceedings. They were reasonable, friendly, peaceable, when sober; wild, passionate, and dangerous when drunk. It adopted the settled policy of prohibiting the sale of intoxicating liquors to them to protect Indians and white men alike. Had it not the right to grant them all the privileges and immunities of citizens, and still retain its power to protect them and their neighbors from the baleful effects of intoxication? The question is susceptible of but one true answer. It had the same right and authority to retain this power of control over the commerce with these Indians that it had to retain the title to their lands in trust for them for 25 years or longer . . . The

truth is that the deprivation of these Indians of the right to buy intoxicating liquors is not the taking away from them of any privilege or immunity of citizenship, but it is an attempt to confer upon them an additional immunity which some citizens do not possess, an immunity from drunkenness and its pernicious consequences.[12]

This extended quotation reveals how entrenched and seemingly perpetual Indian "wardship" status was in the Court's opinion. Citizenship, theoretically, involves three separate components—civil, political, and social rights. But, as Judith Shklar recently noted, "there is no notion more central in politics than citizenship, and none more variable in history, or contested in theory. In America it has in principle always been democratic, but only in principle, . . . The equality of political rights, which is the first mark of American citizenship, was proclaimed in the accepted presence of its absolute denial."[13]

No African slave, until after the Civil War, would become a citizen. And individual Indians, as citizens of separate nations, were certainly not American citizens, even though the Indian situation was much more complex than that of African Americans. An overwhelming majority of African Americans have, over most of their history in the United States, pursued or even demanded inclusion in the American polity. Conversely, a majority of Indians have sought to maintain their exclusion from the American political system. And often when federal and state citizenship rights have been extended to them, Indians have learned, as did the Sisseton and Wahpeton Sioux in *Farrell*, that their social rights lagged far behind the civil and political rights they allegedly secured upon their enfranchisement.

Sanborn brought forth cultural and moralistic reasons to deny Indians their legal, social, and political rights; but four years later Sanborn's citizen-subject depiction of Indians was shattered by the Supreme Court in the decision *Matter of Heff* (1905). The Supreme Court held in *Heff* that upon receiving an allotment, an Indian immediately became an American citizen, and therefore federal laws prohibiting liquor sales to Indians were declared unconstitutional. Contrary to the *Farrell* case, Justice David J. Brewer said that Congress's commercial and guardianship power over tribes was not meant to last indefinitely. "Can it be," said Brewer, "because one has Indian blood, and only Indian blood in his veins, he is to be forever one of a special class over whom the General Government may in its discretion assume the rights of guardianship which it had once abandoned, and this whether the State or the individual himself consents? We think the reach to which this argument goes demonstrates that it is unsound."[14] The Court carefully distinguished Indian property rights from the civil or political status of allottees, and held that even if preconditions were attached to the allottees' lands this did not affect the allottees' political status. In closing, the Court said: ". . . [W]hen the United States grants the privileges of citizenship to an Indian, gives to him the benefit and requires him to be subject to the laws, both civil and criminal, of the State, it places him outside the reach of police regulations on the part of Congress. . . ."[15]

The outcry from many federal policymakers over this straightforward ruling was immediate and vehement. In the words of Commissioner of Indian Affairs Francis Leupp, the decision "startled the country." Although Leupp admitted the ruling was "eminently logical" he maintained that the decision "simply places the ignorant, incapable, and helpless Indian citizens at the mercy of one class of evil doers."[16] Congress also reacted swiftly and the following year passed the Burke Act.[17] This act effectively circumvented but did not overthrow the *Heff* principle. It withheld citizenship from allotted Indians until the twenty-five-year trust period had expired and the allottees had secured a fee patent to their acreage. The secretary of the interior, however, enjoyed the discretion to bestow citizenship and fee-simple title at any time if he determined that an allottee was "competent" to manage his own affairs.[18] Additionally, subsequent Supreme Court cases began to narrow the broad *Heff* precedent.[19] Hence, by 1916, *Heff's* principle had been considerably diluted. *United States v. Nice* represented the death sentence for *Heff* and would enigmatically thrust together the two incongruous perspectives noted by Representative Bailey in the 1897 congressional exchange reproduced above and echoed by Judge Sanborn in *Farrell:* Indians as citizens and Indians as dependent peoples.

HISTORICAL BACKGROUND

In this case, Fred Nice, a white from the town of Carter in Tripp County, South Dakota, had been indicted for selling liquor to George Cartier, a Rosebud Sioux. This sale was alleged to be a violation of an 1897 law which prohibited the sale of liquor to Indian allottees whose land was still held in trust by the United States, or to Indians adjudged to be "wards" under Indian agents, or any other Indians of full or mixed blood "over whom the Government, through its departments, exercises guardianship."[20] The Rosebud Reservation had been allotted under an 1889 law,[21] and Cartier had received his allotted acreage on April 29, 1902. Nice filed a demurrer on the grounds that the charges were "not sufficient in law, and that the said Fred Nice is not bound, by law, to answer the same; and that said indictment does not state facts constituting a public offense against the laws of the United States." [22]

Judge James D. Elliott of the Federal District Court of South Dakota issued a ruling on September 8, 1915, sustaining Nice's demurrer to the indictment on the grounds that the 1897 statute "insofar as it purports to embrace such a case, is invalid, because [it was] in excess of the power of Congress." [23] In other words, based on the *Heff* precedent, the General Allotment Act of 1887, and the Burke Act of 1906, the 1897 law was unconstitutional and Congress did not have jurisdiction over Nice or the offense he was charged with. Cartier, in short, was within his rights as an American Indian citizen of the United States to buy liquor, and Nice by extension, had the right to sell liquor to an allotted Indian.

The United States through its attorney, Richard P. Stewart, took exception to this decision and immediately filed a writ of error to the Supreme Court. This was not surprising, considering that since the *Heff* case, the federal government, beginning with Theodore Roosevelt's administration in 1905, had decried the idea that Indian allottees were equal citizens no longer subject to federal control. Roosevelt asserted that the *Heff* ruling had "struck away the main prop on which has hitherto rested the Government's benevolent effort to protect [the Indian] against the evils of intemperance." [24]

Moreover, the acting attorney general was asked in May 1905, a month after *Heff*, to issue an opinion on the impact of the *Heff* case on the sale of liquor to both reservation and nonreservation Indians, since *Heff* had involved an allotted Indian purchasing liquor in a town off the reservation. The attorney general opined:

> The [*Heff*] decision is undoubtedly conclusive as to the want of power in Congress to exercise police jurisdiction over Indian allottees off the reservations in the States. But its jurisdiction over the reservations is a very different thing . . . . The most that can be claimed for the *Heff* decision is that it holds that, by making Indian allottees citizens and subject to the laws of the State, Congress has divested itself of this purely personal jurisdiction over them. But the jurisdiction which Congress exercises over them upon the reservations is authorized by the fact that they are inmates, so to speak, of Federal institutions; and, while subject generally to State jurisdiction, that jurisdiction can not

be exercised so as to interfere with the conduct of these institutions or to defeat the treaty stipulations which the United States may have made with the Indians.[25]

Although all Indian allottees, regardless of their location, after *Heff* may have initially felt that they finally had some civil and political rights equal to those of whites, it was clear from the interpretation of that decision and the responses of the President, the Department of the Interior, the Commission of Indian Affairs, and the Justice Department, that Indians on reservations and in territories were still largely devoid of those same rights despite what the Supreme Court had explicitly held in *Heff*. Hence, the United States, through its principal administrators of the federal government's affairs with tribes, had already cut deep swaths in the *Heff* ruling, as had subsequent Supreme Court rulings.

Assistant Attorney General Charles Warren, in his brief before the *Nice* Court, could therefore vigorously contend that the *Heff* case had been substantially overruled by a 1914 decision, *United States v. Pelican*. That decision held that the allotted land where an Indian had been murdered by a white man was still considered Indian Country and that federal rather than state law applied. Warren's argument was that "if an allottee Indian is still capable of protection by Federal law against murder, as a ward, he is capable of protection, as a ward, by Federal law against sale of liquor."[26]

Attorney General Warren's sixty-page brief (compared to the one paragraph brief of Nice's attorneys) opened with an argument that Congress's power over tribes was derived from three sources. First, Warren said that congressional power came from the constitutional clause giving Congress the right to make all "needful rules and regulations respecting the territory or other property belonging to the United States." The second source was the oft-mentioned Commerce Clause. But it is the third source that is most interesting since it lacks a substantial political or legal foundation. This form of congressional power over Indians "is of an anomalous character and has arisen out of the *necessities of the situation rather than from any express constitutional sanction* [emphasis mine]. It involves the conception of the Indians as dependent peoples in a state of pupilage under the guardianship of the Federal Government. When the Indians are spoken of as 'wards of the government,' it is with this peculiar conception in view."[27]

Attorney General Warren credited the *Kagama* decision for establishing this extraconstitutional plenary power which, as he said, is "not referable to the powers of Congress under the Commerce Clause. . . ."[28] This "theory" of Indian wardship which arose from the idea of the "necessities of the situation," generated solely by the United States between tribes and the United States, would figure prominently in Van Devanter's final opinion. In the face of such tenuous legal arguments, Attorney General Warren resorted to more moralistic and paternalistic reasons in an effort to win the suit. "No sooner was the *Heff* decision made," said Warren, "than its injurious effects were at once shown. The State, having no power to tax these Indian allotments, had no particular interest in the Indian's welfare; the State, county, and municipal authorities were somewhat apathetic; they were loath to give the Indian the benefit of their schools and other public institutions or to incur the expense of prosecuting offenses in his behalf."[29] What followed, according to Warren, was the "usual cycle of dissipation, drunkenness, disease, disaster, and death."[30] These so-called Five-D's were explicitly associated with Indians and alcohol, according to the government. After reciting a litany of other arguments, Warren arrived at his most definitive position:

> The grant of citizenship does not ipso facto terminate tribal status. . . . It will thus be seen that citizenship and tribal status are entirely distinct subjects, and not necessarily mutually exclusive. Both may coexist. The question whether Indians have become fully emancipated and merged into the uncontrolled citizenry of the country depends not on any grant of citizenship by Congress or on the status as recipients of allotments or of fee simple patents, but necessarily depends upon the question whether they are still recognized as a dependent people with continued tribal relations by the executive or legislative branches of the Government.[31]

Warren had made, and the Supreme Court would follow, a crucial blunder of fact and perception. He and the United States were equating the rights of individual Indians as citizens with the sovereign, collective status of tribes as political entities. A similar situation had arisen in *The Cherokee Tobacco* where, although the case had been taken to the Court by two individual Cherokees and tribes as sovereigns were not parties to the litigation, the collective treaty rights of the tribes were diminished.

This equating of individual rights with tribal sovereign rights actually dates back to *Cherokee Nation v. Georgia* in 1831. In *Cherokee Nation*, the question that should have been the focus throughout was did "the Cherokee Nation constitute a foreign nation as defined by the constitution?" Instead, Marshall and the majority waffled—sometimes treating the Cherokee tribe as a political entity in a corporate sense and sometimes treating the tribe merely as a conglomeration of individuals.

When Indian allottees secured their individualized share of tribal property, they were individually recognized as federal and state citizens. Attorney General Warren, however, inaccurately maintained that the question of enfranchisement depended on whether "they are still recognized as a dependent people with continued tribal relations." It was not tribes that received the franchise and allotments, but individual Indians. The two are not synonymous, yet Warren and the Court would treat them synonymously.

The government's argument also reflected a significant change in the federal attitude about the continuation of tribal polities. Historically, some early treaties between the United States and tribes contained provisions granting federal citizenship to individual Indians provided they met certain conditions—that is, they accepted an allotment, physical removal from communally held tribal lands, or the adoption of Euro-American values and lifestyle. This early arrangement implied that "citizenship was incompatible with continued participation in tribal government or tribal property."[32] By the 1880s, however, the government had arrived at conflicting variations on when and how tribal status ended and federal/state status began; *Elk* was followed by the General Allotment Act, *Farrell*, and *Heff*. But after *Heff* (1905), a majority of the important players involved in Indian affairs had arrived at the unique position that federal citizenship was no longer incompatible with tribal status. That Indians could, in fact, be treated simultaneously as wards and as citizens.

Nice's attorneys, in contrast to the extended brief presented by the federal government, succinctly asserted that the *Heff* decision was controlling and that Nice was therefore innocent of any crime against the United States.

VAN DEVANTER AND INDIAN LAW

Willis Van Devanter, the former chief justice of the Wyoming Supreme Court and later an assistant attorney general in the Department of the Interior specializing in matters involving public lands and Indian affairs, was a rigid conservative in his views respecting constitutional interpretation and Indian rights.[33] Recall that Van Devanter, a Republican, was the prosecuting attorney who argued against the hunting rights of the Shoshone-Bannock Indians in *Ward v. Race Horse*. Before his appointment to the Supreme Court, Van Devanter had developed a long-standing association with powerful western business interests. In his twenty-six years on the bench (1911–1937), Van Devanter actually wrote "fewer opinions not only than any other justice that served with him, but also than any justice appointed between 1853 and 1943."[34]

Van Devanter's judicial disengagement from other subjects and matters of law did not, however, spill over into the area of Indian law. In fact, Van Devanter seemed to save his most virulent views and opinions for Indian cases. His arguments as a prosecutor in *Ward* reflected his conservative, business-oriented approach, as did his tactics as an assistant attorney general opposed to Indian treaty rights in *Cherokee v. Hitchcock* (1902) and *Lone Wolf v. Hitchcock* (1903). On the other hand, in another 1903 case, *United States v. Rickert*, Van Devanter argued for the government that neither individual allottees' lands, their personal property, nor their permanent improvements were subject to state or local taxation during the twenty-five-year trust period. While seeming to signal a victory for individual Indian rights, the language used by the justices actually masked a victory for the U.S. policy of assimilation since, according to Justice John M. Harlan, "these lands are held by the United States in execution of its plans relating to the Indians—without any rights of the Indians to make contracts in reference to them or to do more than to occupy and cultivate them—until a regular patent . . . was issued."[35] Harlan further stated that taxing these lands would be tantamount to taxing "an instrumentality employed by the United States for the benefit and control of this dependent race. . . ."[36] The Van Devanter Court's basic contention was that Indian allottees as "federal instrumentalities" could not be taxed. The Court, in other words, was defending a vested federal right, not an Indian right per se. As a Supreme Court justice, Van Devanter wrote similar opinions usually deferring to the "superior" Congressional power to oversee the inevitable transformation of tribes from their "inferior" political and cultural status to that of a civilized people.[37]

A notable exception in Van Devanter's Indian track record was his opinion for a unanimous Court in *United States v. Quiver* (1916), issued the same day as *Nice*. *Quiver* involved the offense of adultery committed between two Indians on an Indian reservation. The Department of Justice argued that federal courts should have jurisdiction over such crimes. Van Devanter, however, emphatically held "that the relations of the Indians, among themselves—the conduct of one toward another—is to be controlled by the customs and laws of the tribe, save when Congress expressly or clearly directs otherwise."[38] Having perused all the relevant statutes, including the Major Crimes Act of 1885, Van Devanter concluded that none dealt with bigamy, polygamy, incest, or adultery, "these matters always having been left to the tribal customs and laws. . . ."[39] Without so stating, Van Devanter's opinion expressly reaffirmed the theory of exclusion, a long-standing principle of law: a general act of Congress is inapplicable to tribes unless it expressly includes them.[40]

How is it possible to account for these seemingly disparate opinions delivered the same day, by the same verdict, by the same justice? The most plausible explanation is that *Nice* involved, from Van Devanter's perspective, the power relationship between Congress and the tribes (Congress must always be dominant); whereas *Quiver* dealt with what Van Devanter considered a strictly internal tribal issue posing no threat to federal authority or any federal interest. Also, by this period, the Christian reformers who had played a major role in the development of federal Indian policy since the late 1800s had lost their "privileged place."[41] Although federal Indian policy for a number of years continued to focus on the individualization of American Indian rights, its "strongly religious orientation . . . had faded away."[42] Thus, there was less overt moral pressure to dismantle Indian customs or traditions which were said to violate the Judeo-Christian ethic.

MASKING WITHIN THE DECISION: THE OPINION

Van Devanter indicated his position early on by stating that Nice's liquor sale was to Cartier, "a member of the Sioux tribe, a ward of the United States, and under the charge of an Indian agent."[43] However, under the *Heff* rule, Cartier was not a ward despite his continued tribal membership and relationship with an Indian agent. The fact that Van Devanter asserted as much at the beginning of the decision colored the rest of this opinion since his premise was that of Indian wardship and not citizenship.

Van Devanter then moved to an analysis of exactly what allotment of the Rosebud Reservation meant and whether individual Indian allottees were immediately enfranchised. Despite the explicit language of section 6 of the General Allotment Act of 1887 and the *Heff* precedent, Van Devanter manipulated the language of section 11 of the Rosebud Allotment Act of 1889 "which provided that each allotment should be evidenced by a patent, *inaptly so-called* [emphasis mine], declaring that for a period of twenty-five years—and for a further period if the President should so direct—the United States would hold the allotted land in trust for the sole use and benefit of the allottee. . . ."[44] Why did Van Devanter say that the patent was "inaptly" termed? It may be because he was trying to divert attention from the fact that a patent provides an exclusive ownership right in the patentee, which according to the terms of the allotment policy was to form the basis of the right to citizenship. He was, in other words, attempting to minimize the significance of the term by unilaterally and retroactively saying that the government did not really intend to give a patent. If he could successfully make the argument that the United States still retained title over the allotment, this would entitle the government to continue to govern the allottees and treat them as wards with diminished citizenship rights. Van Devanter, before reaching the questions involved in the case, asserted that neither the 1889 Rosebud Allotment legislation nor the 1887 General Allotment Act intended to immediately dissolve the "tribal relation" which "while ultimately to be broken up, was not to be dissolved by the making or taking of allotments . . . ."[45]

The express congressional goal, especially in the late 1880s, for Indians was "to promote the speedy transition of Indians into industrious self-supporting citizens, free from government supervision."[46] By the early part of the twentieth century, however, and as the general assimilation campaign continued, it became evident to many federal policymakers and administrators that Indians could not and would not be so easily transformed and that the "complete" assimilation goal of the late nineteenth century would not be realized as quickly as they had envisioned. "The problem," as Hoxie noted, ". . . was to devise a means of providing greater federal protection without appearing to retreat from the government's commitment to Indian citizenship."[47] The solution was Van Devanter's remarkable *Nice* precedent—Indian *citizenship* is perfectly compatible with Indian *wardship*.

Tribal v. Individual Indian Status

Van Devanter raised the first two of three questions for the Court's consideration: "What was the status of this Indian at the time the whiskey and other liquors are alleged to have been sold to him? And is it within the power of Congress to regulate or prohibit the sale of intoxicating liquors to Indians in his situation?"[48] Van Devanter wasted little time in declaring that Congress's power to regulate or prohibit the traffic in liquor to "tribal Indians" whether on or off a reservation was self-evident. This political power, said Van Devanter, had both a constitutional (Commerce Clause) and an extraconstitutional (so-called dependent relationship) base. In describing Congress's power base, Van Devanter expressly said that this power was over "Indian tribes." This was problematic, since the Commerce Clause only authorizes Congress to regulate commerce "with" tribes, and tribes never consented to a loss of their rights based on the federal government's unilateral declaration that tribes were in a "dependent relationship." But what was more troublesome was that "tribes" were not even involved in this case. That it focused on the rights of an individually allotted Indian to purchase and drink liquor rather than the rights of tribal nations points out a major fallacy in Van Devanter's reasoning.

Having established a questionable basis for congressional power—and over *tribes*, not *individual Indians*—Van Devanter then laid out the essence of his conception of Indian status:

> Of course, when the Indians are prepared to exercise privileges and bear the burdens of one *sui juris*, the tribal relation may be dissolved and the national guardianship brought to an end, but it rests with Congress to determine when and how this shall be done, and whether the emancipation shall at first be complete or only partial. *Citizenship is not incompatible with tribal existence or continued guardianship*, and so may be conferred without completely emancipating the Indians or placing them beyond the reach of congressional regulations adapted for their protection.[49] (emphasis mine)

Van Devanter spoke as if Congress had not already acted on this issue, when in fact it had. Congress in 1887 had determined that the "tribal relation" would be dissolved once reservations were allotted. As described earlier, however, by the early 1900s Congress's views on Indian citizenship had substantially changed, as evidenced in the Burke Act of 1906, which withheld citizenship until the end of the twenty-five-year trust period or until individuals were declared "competent." But more important was the definition of "citizenship" being employed by Van Devanter.

Citizenship supposedly entitles citizens to protection *by* as well as *from* the government; it vests in citizens the right to acquire and possess property of all kinds. It entitles the holder to pursue and obtain happiness and safety. It gives the holder the right to travel from state to state, to petition Congress, and to act and to vote for national office.[50] It also exacts commitments from the citizen; for example, the payment of taxes and military service if called upon. So it is unclear from the passage what rights allotted Indians could look forward to exercising. What is clear is that Van Devanter was speaking of a radically different standard of citizenship for Indians: a diminished citizenship modified by whatever conditions Congress decided to impose. Congress, in bestowing citizenship upon allotted individuals, often against their will, empowered itself with the right to set and, if necessary, to reset the conditions upon which that citizenship was received and which rights or privileges could thereafter be exercised.

After warning Indians that, should they become enfranchised, the constitutional protection they expected and were entitled to receive would not be forthcoming because of Congress's self-declared right to enact laws "for their protection," Van Devanter anticlimactically raised what he termed the "ultimate question" for consideration by the Court: whether section 6 of the General Allotment Act—the citizenship provision—had previously disbanded the tribal relation and extinguished federal guardianship? After having examined the entire act, albeit ignoring the plain import of section 6, Van Devanter would only say that while it was obvious that the breakup of tribes in the General Allotment Act was "in contemplation" by the government, such dissolution was not supposed to occur upon the actual issuance of patented allotments. Van Devanter, in fact, also expressly analyzed section 5 of the Allotment Act which provided for Congress's use of money received by a tribe in the sale of its surplus land to make appropriations "for the education and civilization of such tribe . . . or the members thereof."[51] This provision, along with the twenty-five-year inalienability provision, "show that the Government was retaining control of the property of these Indians, and the one relating to the use by Congress of their moneys in their 'education and civilization' *implies the retention of a control reaching far beyond their property* [emphasis mine]."[52]

The direct implication here was that Congress, according to the Court, had virtually unlimited authority over both the property *and* person of the Indian allottee. The actual language of the allotment law, however, actually said something quite different. The United States was supposed to protect the allottees' lands and was to occasionally appropriate money for their education and civilization. This is not the language of perpetual bondage, yet Van Devanter's reading of it would lead one to think that Congress had direct and implied power over Indian property and everything "beyond their property." This was the Supreme Court's way of providing carte blanche legitimization of whatever Congress intended for even individualized and theoretically constitutionalized Indians.

Finally, and in keeping with his vision of federal supremacy over states' rights in the field of Indian affairs, Van Devanter had to deal with the clear wording of section 6 which stated that once allottees had received their trust patents, they immediately received the benefit of and became subject to the civil and criminal laws of the state they resided in. This explicit language was undeniable proof that Indian allottees received state citizenship in addition to federal citizenship. Van Devanter, however, minimized and redirected this section's clear meaning. "But what laws," said Justice Van Devanter, "was this provision intended to embrace? Was it all the laws of the State, or only such as could be applied to tribal Indians consistently with the Constitution and the legislation of Congress? The words, although general, must be read in the light of the act as a whole and with due regard to the situation in which they were to be applied."[53]

This is another example of the Court's retroactively reading its own intent into the allotment law. Van Devanter's next statement is evidence of this: "That they [the words] were to be taken with some implied limitations, and not literally, is obvious."[54] Obvious to whom? The Congress, especially in Indian affairs, is presumed, as *Lone Wolf* held, to be not only the sole constitutional authority, but also the most knowledgeable source when it comes to the development and implementation of Indian policy. And it was apparent to nearly everyone in the articulation of federal Indian policy in the General Allotment Act in 1887 that Congress's express desire was to dissolve tribes and assimilate the individualized Indians as rapidly as possible.

The fact that Congress had modified its policy views by the early 1900s, perceiving that the absorption of Indians would take much longer than originally forecast, is something the Court was most likely aware of. Several earlier decisions had distinguished and narrowed the original *Heff* ruling so that there was little reason to maintain the pretense that Congress had not intended to eliminate tribes in 1887, when that was the stated goal. The Court in this case was acting in a deferential manner to the political branch and did not want it to appear that Congress had made a mistake in wrongly estimating how and when tribes should be terminated, nor did it want to provide the states with any evidence that they could use to enhance their own political position with tribes.

Evidence for the latter statement is found in this Van Devanter pronouncement:

> The act also disclosed in an unmistakable way that the education and civilization of the allottees and their children were to be under the direction of Congress, and plainly the laws of the State were not to have any bearing upon the execution of any direction Congress might give in this matter. The Constitution invested Congress with power to regulate traffic in intoxicating liquors with the Indian tribes, *meaning with the individuals composing them.* That was a continuing power of which Congress could not divest itself. It could be exerted at anytime . . . .[55] (emphasis mine)

This passage contains several startling revelations. First, Van Devanter had again equated the collective concept of the *tribe* with the *individuals* belonging to the tribe. A tribe, on the one hand, is certainly a conglomeration of all its individual citizens. But the constitutional recognition of tribes has a political basis, a corporate and collective connotation. If an individual Indian becomes a U.S. national via citizenship, then that single person, and not the tribe itself, has a new legal relationship which implies both a duty of allegiance on the part of the person and an obligation for protection on the part of the state. And while the concepts of nationality/citizenship are not restricted to people, since corporations or ships assume the nationality of the states that charter or register them, there has never been a law declaring tribes qua tribes to be citizens. By extension, the federal government's treaty negotiations with tribes were conducted on a nation-to-nation basis, not a nation-to-individual basis.[56] Van Devanter's effort, therefore, to equate the two terms—tribe and individual—in the manner described is invalid.

Second, when Van Devanter stated that Congress's "continuing power" over tribes could not be divested, he was contradicting himself. Earlier in the opinion, he had observed that the tribal relation could be terminated, but that such termination "rests with Congress to determine when and how this shall be done. . . ."[57] In *Nice,* however, the Court maintained that the United States government, even after the granting of citizenship for individual Indians, retained boundless plenary authority over both tribes and their dual citizen members because of their allegedly "dependent" standing. The Court's ruling is not supported by constitutional principles, theories of citizenship, or congressional laws. It is supported solely by puzzling judicial language bent on retaining federal guardianship over Indian citizen-wards regardless of the political or legal costs to the individual Indians.

When individual citizens of foreign nations or tribes are nationalized via U.S. citizenship, then, explicitly and implicitly, the relationship is dramatically transformed. The individual is now theoretically endowed with a set of constitutional rights which protect that person's basic civil rights. Constitutionalism, in short, is the notion of a limited government whose ultimate authority is the consent of the governed.

In conclusion, Van Devanter restated that neither the General Allotment Act nor the Rosebud Allotment Act of 1889 was meant to dismantle the "tribal relation" or the "wardship of the Indians." Therefore, "allottees remain tribal Indians and under national guardianship," and Congress's power to regulate the sale of liquor is "not debatable."[58] In candidly canceling out the *Heff* decision, the Court said, "after reexamining the question in the light of other provisions in the act [General Allotment] and of many later enactments clearly reflecting what was intended by Congress, we are constrained to hold that the decision in that case [*Matter of Heff*] is not well grounded, and it is accordingly overruled."[59] *Nice* was immediately hailed by Commissioner of Indian Affairs Cato Sells as a "very important" decision which would enable his office "more successfully to cope with the liquor situation among the Indians."[60] This case energized the BIA and reform organizations to renew their efforts to stop the consumption of liquor by Indians. (A contemporaneous national movement to address the alcohol issue culminated in the nationwide prohibition of alcohol which became effective in 1919 with the passage of the Eighteenth Amendment to the Constitution.)

Nice was decided three years before American Indian World War I veterans were given the opportunity of becoming citizens,[61] and eight years before Congress enacted the general Indian citizenship law which mandatorily extended federal citizenship to all Indians who were not yet enfranchised.[62] The veterans' citizenship law declared that every Indian who had served in the armed forces and who had received an honorable discharge should, "on proof of such discharge and after proper identification . . . and without other examination . . . be granted *full citizenship with all the privileges pertaining thereto*, without in any manner impairing or otherwise affecting the property rights, individual or tribal, of any such Indian or his interest in tribal or other Indian property."[63] More dramatically, the 1924 General Citizenship Act unilaterally declared all other noncitizen Indians as federal citizens, though the act retained the section which confirmed that such citizenship would not diminish the Indians' right to tribal or other property.[64]

Clearly, Indians were not *full citizens* as Congress had declared. The citizenship they had secured, whether under prior treaty or later congressional legislation, was an attenuated, partial citizenship. While Congress inserted provisions in both the 1919 and 1924 laws protecting treaty-drawn property rights of Indians as citizens of their nations, these clauses have proven insufficient to protect the cultural, political, civil, or sovereign rights of individual tribal citizens. Paternalistic in tone and substance, *Nice* had legally mandated perpetual federal guardianship over citizen Indians who were still considered incapable of "handling liquor." More dangerously, as Hoxie points out, since "individual liberties could be circumscribed in an area in which the Indian Office felt that Native Americans did not measure up to their fellow citizens, they could surely be limited in others."[65]

Nice remains a legal travesty. This case sealed the Indians' status as individuals in perpetual legal and political limbo as federal/state *citizens* with rights circumscribed by their alleged perpetual *wardship* status. In order for tribal members to receive any nontribal rights or privileges, they often have had to exhibit a desire to have their tribal identity liquidated, at which point they might be, but not necessarily, considered worthy or "competent" to receive their set of American political rights and privileges. *Nice*, moreover, dramatically informed these individuals that even direct receipt of federal citizenship would not afford them basic constitutional protections because they remained "Indians" over whom the government retained "a control reaching far beyond their property."[66]

Northwestern Bands of Shoshone Indians v. United States

ABORIGINAL INDIAN TITLE THROUGH THE EYES OF THE JUDICIARY

Like any sovereign nation, the United States is exempt from lawsuit unless it has expressly granted its consent to be sued. This is the sovereign immunity doctrine. In 1855 Congress established the Court of Claims, which provided a legal forum wherein aggrieved parties, including tribes, could bring suit against the Federal Government.[67] Tribes began to frequent the Court, seeking legal redress for wrongs they had sustained in violation of treaty rights. When the Civil War arose, however, and because some tribes had allied themselves with the Confederate States, Congress unilaterally and retributively decided in 1863 to amend the Court of Claims Law. The amendment stated: "That the jurisdiction of the said Court shall not extend to or include any claims against the Government not pending in said Court on the first day of December, A.D. 1862, growing out of or dependent on any treaty stipulation entered into with foreign nations, *or with the Indian tribes* [emphasis mine]."[68] Tribes were effectively denied legal recourse, and since they were extraconstitutional entities, they had very little hope for political redress.

As Cohen remarked, "whatever justification there may have been for discriminating against the contracts [treaties] we had made with the original owners of the country in giving the Court of Claims general jurisdiction over contract claims against the government, the effect of this discrimination has been to inject gross delays into our judicial settlements of treaty claims."[69] It was not until 1920 that a number of bills were introduced which allowed particular tribes (tribes of the Fort Berthold Reservation: Iowa, Klamath, and Modoc; and the Sioux Nation, Cheyenne, and Arapaho) to sue the government through the Court of Claims. While this was at least an avenue for some political redress, it was ad hoc and self contradictory, since access to the Court of Claims was dependent on a significant amount of Indian lobbying sufficient to move Congress to act. Of course, tribes were virtually without political power during the years they had lost their lands, and had become even less powerful during the zenith of Bureau of Indian Affairs authority over Indian lives and property from the 1880s to the 1920s.[70] Altogether, an estimated 133 such acts were established. Of the resultant legal actions, tribes actually had monetary recoveries in fewer than one third of the suits.[71] In part, the recovery rate was so low because the grounds for the suit were often narrowly construed. Moreover, it would sometimes take several decades for the Court of Claims to reach a decision.[72]

SHOSHONE–U.S. RELATIONS

The Shoshone Nation, now some ten thousand strong, which historically maintained jurisdiction over some eighty million acres of land, is actually composed of four distinct groups—the Eastern (or Wind River) Shoshone, who inhabited the Wind River Mountains and the high plains; the Western Shoshone, inhabiting lands in present-day Nevada, Idaho, California, and Oregon; the Northern Shoshone, who occupied lands in

Utah, Nevada, Wyoming, and Idaho; and the Comanche-Shoshone. The vast Shoshone homeland was not really penetrated by Euro-American travelers and settlers until the 1840s. A small number of Mormons had settled around the Great Salt Lake, and forays by explorers or hunters had occurred from time to time; in fact, the Shoshone Nation, through Sacajawea, had provided guidance to members of the Lewis and Clark expedition (1804–1806) on their western travels. Shoshone physical isolation from whites, however, changed forever when gold was discovered in the mountains of California near Sacramento. This "discovery," like that of Columbus in 1492, had devastating consequences for the indigenous inhabitants in both California and Shoshone territory. The flood of whites pouring into Shoshone lands led to a dramatic depopulation of the animal herds that the tribe had depended upon for subsistence and also denuded the grasslands, "causing great dissatisfaction among the Indians, aggravated frequently by the conduct of the wilder and more reckless element among the travelers."[73]

In 1849, federal Indian agents and superintendents recommended that the United States negotiate treaties with the various tribes, including the Shoshone, Sioux, Cheyenne, Arapaho, Crow, Assiniboine, and others who were defending their territories. In the first six months of 1850 alone, more than forty thousand persons passed through Fort Laramie, Wyoming.[74] The federal government decided it was necessary to construct roads and military posts through Indian territories which would allow for the safe passage of the whites.

This led to one of the greatest gatherings of indigenous nations ever assembled. The convening took place at Fort Laramie (in eastern Wyoming) in September 1851. This impressive assemblage of indigenous peoples and federal officials included a delegation of sixty Shoshone chiefs and headmen, led by their esteemed leader, Washakie. The invitation of the Shoshone was an explicit recognition that the Shoshone were an important presence and that any treaty would have to consider their sovereign rights to the immense lands they controlled. The Shoshone, however, left the treaty proceedings prematurely and were not signatories to the 1851 treaty. There are conflicting accounts as to why the Shoshone left. Deloria asserts that when Washakie and his delegation arrived, the Sioux objected to their presence because of a battle in which a group of Shoshone had killed a number of Sioux. A Sioux warrior, Deloria says, even attempted to assassinate Washakie. The federal government, according to this account, "realizing there was no practical way to make the Sioux and the Shoshones agree to peace terms . . . decided to make a separate treaty with the Shoshones at a later time."[75]

Another account, however, suggests that the government's treaty commissioner, Colonel D. D. Mitchell, doubted whether his instructions from Washington authorized the inclusion of the Shoshone Nation. Commissioner of Indian Affairs Luke Lea reported the following in his *Annual Report* of 1851:

> A delegation of the Shoshones or Snake Indians, a disaffected and mischievous tribe, infesting one of the principle routes of travel to Oregon and California, was conducted by the agent to the grand council recently held at Fort Laramie with the wild tribes of the prairies. These Indians were not considered by the Superintendent as embraced in his instructions, and were, consequently, not parties to the treaty negotiated with the other tribes. The delegation, however, were kindly received, suitable presents were bestowed upon them, and they returned to their people with more friendly feelings toward the government and the whites.[76]

Whichever account is honored, the fact remains that the Shoshone Nation had the requisite political and military standing to be treated as a sovereign entity by the United States. The fact that their treaties with the United States were delayed until 1863 in no way diminishes their legal affect.

THE SHOSHONE TREATIES

As whites continued to stream westward, their depredations against the tribe and the game of the area continued unabated. Such actions understandably outraged the Shoshone. Furthermore, stagecoach lines had been established and telegraph and overland mail lines had been constructed without the consent of the Shoshone. By 1861, Commissioner of Indian Affairs William P. Dole reported that "the Shoshones, or Snakes, and the Flathead, are wealthy and powerful, and can cause their hostility to the remoter settlements and the overland emigration to be severely felt. Hence, the pressing necessity of some speedy arrangement with them, which with the Snakes [Shoshone] it is suggested should be (as a temporary measure) a treaty granting annuities in consideration of a right-of-way across their country."[77]

The subsequent discovery of additional gold veins in the early 1860s in the Beaver Head, Salmon River, and Boise areas in Idaho, along with the expansion of the Civil War, exacerbated an already delicate inter-racial situation. The Civil War compelled the United States to confront the reality of tribal military powers west of the Rocky Mountains. And since gold provided the economic stability that the North needed to continue the war, the struggle for the control of roads on which to transport this precious material was critical.[78]

On July 5, 1862, Congress appropriated twenty thousand dollars for the purpose of negotiating a treaty with the Shoshone Nation.[79] U.S. military expeditions, sent to provide safety for their westward-bound citizens, felt the need to maintain the roads for the transport of gold and other supplies, and to ensure the passage of mail and other freight items. Although the superintendent of Indian affairs for Utah had earlier recommended that the treaty have as its main objective the extinguishment of the Shoshone's right of occupancy, Congress, in authorizing the appointment of the treaty commission, emphatically chose not to terminate Shoshone land title. Acting under the statute, the commissioner of Indian affairs instructed the treaty commissioners as follows:

It is not expected that the treaty will be negotiated with a view to the extinguishment of the Indian title to the land, but it is believed that with the assurances that you are authorized to make of the amicable relations which the United States desires to establish and perpetuate with them, and by the payment of Twenty thousand dollars of annuities . . . you will be enabled to procure from them such articles of agreement as will render the routes indicated secure for travel and free from molestation; also a definite acknowledgment as well of the boundaries of the entire country they claim, as of the limits within which they will confine themselves, which limits it is hardly necessary to state should be as remote from said routes as practicable."[80]

The only specifics sought by the United States in the appropriating legislation were peaceful relations with the Shoshone and safe passage for American citizens and U.S. mail. The federal government also hoped to learn what the outer boundaries of Shoshone territory were. Shoshone lands, importantly, were given specific acknowledgment. These lands were, from the government's viewpoint, considered "largely unfit for cultivation" and were not considered even remotely attractive enough to warrant white settlement "for many years."[81]

In January 1863, several months before the treaty negotiations began, several hundred Northwestern Shoshone who had gathered at one of their customary winter encampments at Bear Lake in Southeastern Idaho were brutally attacked by Brigadier General P. Edward Connor of the U.S. Volunteers, District of Utah, and his 250 men, fresh from a campaign to crush California Indian resistance to white intrusion. When the Bear Lake massacre had ended, some 224 Shoshone lay dead. The United States lost 14 men. The senseless killing of so many Indians left an indelible mark on the Shoshone people. It was the last time the Northwestern Band ever took up arms against the United States.[82]

Between July 2 and October 14, 1863, the United States negotiated five treaties with the geographically dispersed bands of the Shoshone Nation. These were: Eastern Shoshone Treaty, held at Fort Bridger, Wyoming, on July 2, 1863;[83] Northwestern Shoshone Treaty, held at Box Elder, Utah, on July 30, 1863;[84] Western Shoshone Treaty, held at Ruby Valley, Nevada, October 1, 1863;[85] Shoshone-Goship Treaty, held at Tuilla Valley, Utah, October 12, 1863;[86] and the Mixed Band of Bannocks and Shoshones Treaty, held at Soda Springs, Idaho, on October 14, 1863. All five treaties were subsequently ratified by the Senate, though an important amendment was tacked onto each of the treaties except for the Western Shoshone agreement. This amendment affirmed that the Indians' unspecified title to their lands was comparable to the title or interest they had held when Mexico ceded control of the area to the United States in 1848. This amendment, article 5 of the Northwestern Shoshone Treaty, was an explicit, if ill-defined acknowledgment that the Shoshone groups had a title to their territory which had been recognized by both Mexico and the United States.

The Fort Bridger agreement negotiated with the Eastern Shoshone (the largest of the bands) was a prototype for the rest, but it was unique in that Washakie, the principal chief of the Eastern Shoshone Nation and a pivotal player in long-term Shoshone/U.S. relations, presided over this agreement for his people. As was the case with all five treaties, the major emphasis lay in securing from the tribe their permission to allow white travelers safe passage and to allow the construction of stagecoach stations, telegraph lines, and projected railroads.

The Northwestern Shoshone Treaty (held at Box Elder, Utah) is the one most salient for our purposes because it is the treaty the petitioners to this suit based their case on. It was negotiated, on the part of the federal government, by James Duane Doty, the governor and acting superintendent of Indian affairs for the Utah Territory, and General Connor. The Northwestern Shoshone were led by their principal chief, Pokatello. The treaty is brief enough and substantive enough to warrant full recitation:

Articles of agreement made at the Box Elder, in Utah Territory, this thirtieth day of July, a.d., Eighteen hundred sixty-three, by and between the United States of America, represented by Brigadier-General P. Edward Connor, commanding the military district of Utah, and James Duane Doty, commissioner, and the northwestern bands of the Shoshonee Indians, represented by their chiefs and warriors:

Article I. It is agreed that friendly and amicable relations shall be re-established between the bands of Shoshonee Nation, parties hereto, and the United States, and it is declared that a firm and perpetual peace shall be henceforth maintained between the said bands, and the United States.

Article II. The treaty concluded at Fort Bridger on the 2nd day of July, 1863, between the United States and the Shoshonee Nation, being read and fully interpreted and explained to the said chiefs and warriors, they do hereby give their full and free assent to all of the provisions of said treaty, and the same are hereby adopted as a part of this agreement, and the same shall be binding upon the parties hereto.

Article III. In consideration of the stipulation in the preceding articles, the United States agree to increase the annuity to the Shoshonee Nation, to five thousand dollars, to be paid in the manner provided in said treaty. And the said northwestern bands hereby acknowledge to have received of the United States, at the signing of these articles, provisions and goods to the amount of two thousand dollars, to relieve their immediate necessities, the said bands having been reduced by the war to a state of utter destitution.

Article IV. The country claimed by Pokatello, for himself and his people, is bounded on the west by Raft River and on the east by the Porteneuf Mountains.

Article V. Nothing herein contained shall be construed or taken to admit any other or greater title or interest in the lands embraced within the territories described in said treaty in said tribes or bands of Indians than existed in them upon the acquisition of said territories from Mexico by the laws thereof.[87]

At the conclusion of this bilateral agreement in the autumn of 1863, Commissioner Doty, chairman of the treaty commission, was able to draw a crude map of Shoshone country which he then sent to the commissioner of Indian affairs. This map sketched out "the exterior boundaries of the territories claimed by the Shoshonees in their recent treaties, as also the lines of the country occupied by different positions of the tribe indicated upon it as correctly as the map will allow." [88] The commissioner in his 1863 *Annual Report* recommended "that measures be taken for the negotiation of further treaties with the [Shoshone] Indians, having for their object the extinguishment of their title to the soil. . . ." [89] And while Congress subsequently passed two laws [90] for the squelching of Indian title in Utah, and for dealing with so-called hostile Indians, the only Shoshone that entered political arrangements for cessions to their territory were the Eastern Band. On July 3, 1868, the Eastern Shoshone ceded all claim to the territory "except a reservation in Wyoming of 3,047,730 acres." [91]

Nevertheless, between 1863 and the 1920s, practically all the land claimed by the Northwestern Shoshone, some 15,643,000 acres that would be valued at fifteen million dollars in the 1930s, was openly encroached upon by the United States and its citizens.

CONGRESS AND THE COURT OF CLAIMS

From the January 1863 massacre of more than 200 Northwestern Shoshone to the negotiation of their treaty at Box Elder later that year, the tribe had been placed in a dependent position relative to the United States, forced to stand by as the federal government, without the consent of the Shoshone Nation, began to grant their territory for the construction of public schools, to establish a national forest within Shoshone territory, and to allow public settlement of tribal lands under federal homestead laws. [92] Although in 1926 the tribe hired two claims attorneys, Charles H. Merrillat and Charles Kappler, the government made no formal efforts to allow the Shoshone any redress for the multitude of intrusions into their territory until December 9, 1927, when Senator King of Utah introduced a bill which conferred jurisdiction on the Court of Claims to "hear, adjudicate, and render judgment in any and all claims which the Northwestern bands of Shoshone Indians may have against the United States arising under or growing out of the treaty of July 2, 1863, treaty of July 30, 1863, Act of Congress approved December 15, 1874, and any subsequent treaty, Act of Congress, or Executive Order. . . ." [93]

The bill was sent to the secretary of the interior for his analysis and recommendation. The secretary acknowledged that the Shoshone band in question had indeed been party to the treaty of July 30, 1863, and that they were asserting claims for lands in Utah, Nevada, Oregon, and Idaho which they believed had been disposed of by the government without tribal consent.[94] Senator King's bill, without amendment, was enacted into law and became the jurisdictional act under which this lawsuit was initiated.[95] The Shoshone filed their petition in the Court of Claims on March 28, 1931. Prohibited from actually recovering any land, the tribe sought to recover 15 million dollars for what they claimed had been the unlawful taking of their 15 million acres in violation of the 1863 treaty. They also sought to recover $70,000 of the treaty annuities which had been promised to them for twenty years under the treaty. The government contended that the 1863 treaty was simply one of peace and amity and that the agreement failed to recognize in the Shoshone an exclusive use and occupancy right to the lands. Instead, the government claimed that it had exercised dominion and complete ownership of the territory in question.[96]

The Court of Claims ruled in 1942 that the Shoshone were not entitled to any recovery under the treaty of July 3, 1863, or any other treaty for a taking of any portion of their lands described in the agreements. The Shoshone were initially informed that they were entitled to recover $10,800 [17] for unfulfilled treaty annuities. But, upon a further hearing, even this amount was dismissed on the grounds that the United States' gratuitous expenditures offset this amount. The Court of Claims, in a strange twist of logic, said:

> Although the plaintiff bands . . . may have exclusively occupied and used all or a portion of the territory involved in their present claim as their aboriginal home (and the record is sufficient to show that they did), they are not entitled to recover for the reason that the jurisdictional act only authorizes this court to consider, adjudicate, and render judgment on a claim "arising under or growing out of the treaty" with them. Such a claim must be one that is within the terms of and supported by the provisions of the treaty. Aboriginal occupancy and use is not such a claim.[97]

This statement, denying any legitimacy to aboriginal land rights and effectively diminishing the status of the 1863 treaty to the equivalent of a handshake, is one of astonishing dimensions. "It means," one commenter has noted, "that the litigation of Indian rights begins with the proposition that Indians really have nothing. It also means that the task of courts and claims commissions is to find a way to justify present conditions by using words with apparent legal importance to cover up the very peculiar historical circumstances that determined in a large part the present status, lands and rights of the respective Indian tribes."[98] This was evident when the court acknowledged that, yes, the Shoshone had inhabited the lands in question since time immemorial, but no, this did not imbue them with any recognized rights to those lands, even when a treaty identifying their lands had been negotiated and ratified.

The tribes' attorneys, Ernest L. Wilkinson and Joseph Chez, shortly thereafter appealed to the Supreme Court. They maintained that the Court of Claims had erred in a number of ways: first, by failing to hold that the word "claim" as used in Indian treaties actually constituted an acknowledgment or recognition by the United States of Indian title; second, by holding that a "peace" treaty with a tribe did not constitute a recognition by the federal government of Indian title; and third, by holding that the Box Elder treaty with the Northeastern Shoshone was not an acknowledgment of their title to land. They noted several other mistakes in the Court's decision but ended with what, to them, was the most flagrant error—that the Shoshone, under the treaty of 1863 and related treaties, were not entitled to recover damages for the taking of their lands.[99]

"Despite the treaty," said the attorneys, the court "disposed of the case as though petitioners were not under the treaty with the United States." In doing so, it overlooked the normal principle of international law that a treaty necessarily implies some lawful national domain on the part of the respective parties.[100] Charles Fahy (the solicitor general), Norman M. Littell, and Norman MacDonald for the federal government challenged the tribe's petition for a writ of certiorari on the grounds that "a mere Indian title is subordinate to the United States title unless recognized as something more." Furthermore, the opposition brief argued that "petitioners confuse aboriginal title with title valid as against the United States. The former was indeed extinguished; the question is whether the latter ever was created. The Court below correctly held that it was not."[101]

The prevailing sentiments of the Supreme Court at the time of the *Shoshone* case are well illustrated by the Court's 1944 decision, *Korematsu v. United States*.[102] In what was arguably the most unsettling use of executive military authority in U.S. history, President Roosevelt had ordered, and the military in California carried out, the compulsory evacuation of virtually all persons of Japanese ancestry. A sharply divided Supreme Court held in a 6–3 decision that this racially discriminatory mass evacuation of Japanese-Americans, many of whom were citizens, was a valid exercise of authority by the military branches of government. Justices Owen Roberts, Frank Murphy, and Robert Jackson wrote stinging dissents. Justice Murphy had this comment: "This exclusion of 'all persons of Japanese ancestry, both alien and non-alien,' from the Pacific Coast area on a plea of military necessity in the absence of martial law ought not to be approved. Such exclusion goes over 'the very brink of constitutional power' and falls into the ugly abyss of racism." [103] Murphy robustly dissented from what he termed "this legislation of racism." [104]

This Court's decision of the *Shoshone* case was also deeply fragmented, but in an even stranger way. While technically a 5–4 decision, with Justices Stanley Reed, Wiley Rutledge, Robert Jackson, Hugo Black, and Harlan F. Stone concurring in the result and Justices Owen Roberts, William Douglas, Felix Frankfurter, and Frank Murphy in opposition, it was actually even more fractured than the raw number shows. For example, and most notably, the concurring opinion of Justices Jackson and Black actually read more like a dissenting opinion, until they concluded by saying that despite the injustice sustained by the Shoshone, they were not entitled to recover any damages. There were two dissenting opinions. The first, written by Justice Douglas, was joined by Justices Frankfurter and Murphy. Murphy, however, opted to write his own dissenting opinion which was then also joined by Frankfurter and Douglas.

MASKING WITHIN THE DECISION: THE OPINION

After briefly restating the background of the case, Reed noted, "Certiorari was granted in view of the importance of the question in Indian affairs." [105] This is an understatement. A solid case can be made that nothing less than the nation's integrity was involved. Either the United States was bound and would support its constitutionally sanctioned Indian treaty commitments to a now impoverished and dependent nation, or it would not. Either tribes had preexisting rights based on their aboriginal standing and de facto existence, or they did not. These are not trivial concerns, nor are they simply questions of "Indian affairs."

Reed went on to observe that certiorari had been granted "to determine whether there was 'recognition' or 'acknowledgment' of the Indian title by this treaty through the language employed or by the act of entering into a treaty with the Indians as to the use by the United States of lands which were claimed by the petitioners." [106] In other words, did either the fact of the 1863 treaty's negotiation and subsequent ratification, or specific language employed, affirm land rights of the Northwestern Shoshone?

Other questions might have been considered by the Court, such as the very fact that the treaty process involves two separate nations, an acknowledgment of the distinctive political and geographical status of *each* nation. Moreover, if the treaty does not explicitly take away rights, then under the reserved rights doctrine established in *U.S. v. Winans*,[107] and the tribes' general understanding of treaty processes, they are retained by the tribe. The Court, therefore, could very easily have looked at what the United States sought in entering into treaty negotiations with the Shoshone, and what it specifically and broadly acquired as a result of that treaty.

The Masks of Recognized versus Aboriginal Title

Reed's next step set an ominous tone that held throughout his opinion. He began by citing a 1937 ruling, *Shoshone Tribe of Indians v. United States*,[108] which also involved the Shoshone people, specifically the band inhabiting the Wind River Reservation in Wyoming. In this case, an important victory for the Shoshone, a unanimous Court held that the United States had been wrong to settle a group of Arapaho on the Wind River Reservation without the consent of the Shoshone people and without just compensation to the latter. The federal government was compelled to pay the Shoshone over 4 million dollars plus interest. The Arapaho, however, were not relocated.

One of the differences between the Wind River decision and the present case is that the Wind River Shoshone, by an 1868 treaty with the United States,[109] had ceded over 44 million acres of their land in the high plains and the Rocky Mountains in exchange for a reservation of over 3 million acres in Wyoming. The Northwestern Shoshone, on the other hand, never had a reservation expressly created for them. Their territory was held under aboriginal (original or Indian) title, which exists where "it is established as a fact that the lands in question were included in the ancestral home of a tribe of Indians, in the sense that they constituted definable territory occupied exclusively by that tribe as distinguished from being wandered over by many tribes."[110]

Citing this decision, Reed stated that "[e]ven where a reservation is created for the maintenance of Indians, their right amounts to nothing more than a treaty right of occupancy."[111] Under Reed's logic, if an established Indian reservation's title is "nothing more" than a treaty right of occupancy, then surely a situation like that of the Northwestern band, whose 1863 treaty was neither a land cession or treaty establishing one, cannot be one which creates strong land rights. This, of course, is one of the perpetual debates in Indian law, as to precisely what the Indian right of occupancy entails. Is it a defensible and permanent title, or is it merely a temporary use permit? Reed obviously believed it was nothing more than a temporary right.

Evidence of this assumption is found in Reed's next statement:

> Prior to the creation of any such area, formally acknowledged by the United States as subject to such right of Indian occupancy, a certain nation, tribe or band of Indians may have claimed the right because of immemorial occupancy to roam certain territory to the exclusion of any other Indians and in contradistinction to the custom of the early nomads to wander at will in the search for food. . . . This claim has come to be known as Indian title and is likewise often spoken of as the right of occupancy. To distinguish from a recognized right of occupancy, we shall refer to the aboriginal usage without definite recognition of the right by the United States as Indian title.[112]

Here Reed accomplished two things. First, he quietly dichotomized Indian land title: recognized versus aboriginal title. Second, he raised an even more stunning premise: that because Indians were "nomads" and in his opinion "roamed" over vast acreage, they had diminished rights to the land. According to Felix Cohen, this "Myth of the Nomadic Homeless Indian" has frequently been "accepted as a fact even by judges who are trained in the difficult art of reserving judgment in the absence of evidence, outside the field of anthropology."[113] Both factors damaged Shoshone land claims, but the ambiguous classification of land title as "recognized" versus "aboriginal" has continued to haunt tribal nations. The search for what constitutes "recognition" necessitates finding out from the federal government who is empowered to act and in what way they do act when "recognition" is extended or denied. Pinning down who does the acting—the president, the Congress, the Supreme Court, the secretary of the interior, the commissioner of Indian affairs, or other governmental bureaucrats—is more difficult. Furthermore, if the national government has treated with a tribe, as in the case under discussion, how can such action be determined *not to be* recognition, particularly when such political treating is coupled with the reserved rights doctrine.

Reed found support for his "Indian occupancy" theory in the *Johnson v. McIntosh* decision discussed in Chapter 1. Reed, however, gave *Johnson* a unique and questionable interpretation. He said that as a result of Marshall's decision "the extinguishment of Indian title . . . has proceeded, *as a political matter*, without any admitted legal responsibility in the sovereign to compensate the Indian for his loss." The post-*Johnson* historical record is replete with negotiations in which the United States paid out millions of dollars for the lands tribes had ceded. Cohen noted the vast extent of such purchases: "the purchase of the land of the United States from the Indians was, I suppose, the largest real estate deal recorded in the history of the world." [114] These dealings stretched over two centuries and involved expenditures of "several hundred million dollars." [115] Both the treaty process and history attest to the fact that although the federal government has often arbitrarily and nonconsensually appropriated Indian territory, it has not thereby acquired the lawful right to do so.

But Reed turned aside from this body of historical fact and again quoted Marshall from *Johnson:* "Exclusive title," said Reed, "passed to the white discoverers, subject to the Indian title with power in the white sovereign alone to extinguish that right by 'purchase or conquest.' . . . The whites enforced their claims by the sword and occupied the lands as the Indians abandoned them." [116] Reed acknowledged, moreover, that there had been no purchase of Northwestern Shoshone lands, nor had the Shoshone been "conquered" or "abandoned" their country. In fact, none of Reed's contentions regarding the historical or legal record between the Shoshone tribe and the United States are supported by the facts.

Reed then approached one of the more crucial issues. He stated that success for the Northwestern Shoshone was not contingent on the proof of their Indian title which, he said, "may be admitted," but depended instead on whether that title had received recognition in the 1863 treaty. [117] This new twist to make Indian title contingent upon express federal recognition of said title in a bilateral treaty, especially when the United States concedes preexisting proof of Indian title is interesting. To believe that the Shoshone did not have title questions the nature of the right-of-way for which the United States had treated with the Northwestern Shoshone originally. The federal government gained tangible rights through the treaty process which it immediately and subsequently exercised. So to argue that the Shoshone lacked recognized title despite the treaty would also mean that the government gained no substantive rights or should be required to return those it has exercised until and unless it properly acknowledges Shoshone land title. The very foundation of a treaty is that it typically involves the political give-and-take between two or more not necessarily equal nations. More often than not, as the Court said, it also involves a grant of rights from one or both parties and a reservation of rights not granted away, an affirmation of those rights expressly named. A nation does not make treaties with itself or non-nations.

Reed followed with a perplexing statement which bears repeating:

> It is quite understandable from the point of view of both petitioners [Shoshone] and Congress that the Government should limit its submission to suits to claims under the boundaries if acknowledged by the treaty rather than to consent to judicial examination of claims for taking the unknown area of their possible Indian title. The Shoshone Indian title was in Indian country . . . and as a consequence [was] subject to all the uncertainties of definition of boundaries and difficulties of proof to establish aboriginal title for tribes with a shifting habitat.[118]

Justice Stanley Reed appeared to be blaming the Indians for not having land boundaries delineated in a manner with which he was familiar. Furthermore, he was making prejudicial assertions to deny land rights to tribes who maintained what he termed a "shifting habitat." Reed had now effectively collapsed both a purportedly legal standard—nonrecognition—with a sociological or demographic standard—shiftless nomads—to subjugate the land rights of the Northwestern Shoshone.

Thus, by the time Reed finally raised what he termed "the decisive question"—whether the Box Elder Treaty of July 30, 1863, recognized "by implication" a Shoshone title to their admitted ancestral lands[119]— his answer was manifest. The Box Elder treaty provided no such recognition, according to Reed. Therefore, the Shoshone were not entitled to the 15 million dollars in compensation they had sought under the 1929 jurisdictional act. So clear was it that the majority were refusing Shoshone rights to compensation (the possibility of an actual recovery of land was never even broached) that Reed could use the phrase "by implication" without reservation. That the 1863 Box Elder Treaty had not been about land per se, since according to the United States' own officers, they had no interest in securing any of the territory at the time of the treaty, seemed to be of no interest to the majority.

Over the course of tribal-federal relations, tribes and the government have entered into a wide array of treaties and agreements—peace and friendship, military alliance, physical removal, boundaries, trade, land cession, reservation establishment, and continuation and protection of certain rights by either or both parties.[120] Many treaties were negotiated for more than one reason. Essentially a treaty of peace and friendship, the Box Elder Treaty also contained reassurances, sought by the United States from the Shoshone, for the protection of ever-intrusive white settlers. The Box Elder Treaty was not about expanding, acknowledging, or curtailing Shoshone land title.

Over the next several paragraphs, Reed injected his ethnocentric views of indigenous people into the law. He called the Shoshone "a nomadic Indian nation," numbering fewer than 10,000, who "roamed over" 80 million acres of land in several western states. In his recounting of the intrusion of a multitude of gold-seeking whites upon Shoshone territory on their way to California, Reed stated that a result of this mingling was that the "Indians' game disappeared from their hunting grounds."[121] "Racial relations," said Reed, "degenerated to the point that Indian depredations interfered with travel and settlement, the overland mails and the new telegraph lines."[122]

Despite Reed's acknowledgment of white blameworthiness in the struggle, a portrait emerged of the Shoshone as a sinister force, the whites as victims entitled to safe passage through Indian lands. In describing events leading to the 1863 Shoshone treaties, Reed noted that Congress was aware that the Shoshone lands were not deemed suitable for Anglo-American settlement. Thus, the treaty, as Reed acknowledged, was not about the extinguishment of Indian title but was actually designed to secure for whites freedom from Shoshone raids and an "acknowledgment . . . of the boundaries of the entire country they claimed. . . ." Despite this admission by Reed, he insisted upon describing the treaty as a document which, since it did not involve an express articulation of Shoshone land rights, could not be used as the basis upon which to recover compensation. In actuality, if the 1863 treaty did not extinguish the Shoshone title, then obviously that title still rested with the tribe. That Reed was able to draw any other conclusion defies logic.

Judicial Accretion and Lost Tribal Ground

After laying out the details of the Box Elder Treaty, the Court made its most astounding assertion on how the land in dispute came to "belong" to the United States. "Without seeking any cession or relinquishment of claim from the Shoshone [except of the Eastern band in 1868], . . ." said Reed, "the United States has treated the rest of the Shoshone territory as a part of the public domain." [123] Using the rationale put forth by Milner Ball, "if an Indian nation is a nation, then its governmental powers cannot simply evanesce and reappear in the hands of another nation's government." [124] Such a statement is even more true for a tribal nation's property. If the tribe has not lost their lands by treaty provision (and Reed admitted that the 1863 treaty was not a land cession agreement); and if they had not lost their lands through conquest (which Reed never suggested); and if the tribe had not lost their lands by statute (Reed said this had not happened); then on what basis did he claim that the federal government had acted as if the land belonged to them? As proof of federal dominion, Reed said that school lands had been granted, that a national forest or two was established, and that the lands were opened for settlement under federal homestead laws. "Thus," said Reed, "we have administration of this territory by the United States proceeding as though no Indian land titles were involved." [125]

Here the Court simply asserted, on behalf of the United States, that all of Shoshone territory simply dissipated like vapor and reappeared under federal dominion. The Court's anomalous action in this instance seems to call for the coining of a phrase: I submit *judicial accretion*. In water law, the term *accretion* means a gradual, incremental increase of land along the shores of a body of water. In biology, it refers to any growing together of plant or animal tissues that are normally separate.

In this manifestation of judicial accretion, the Supreme Court unilaterally provided a nonlegal and ahistorical rationalization for the gradual extension of federal sovereignty over tribal lands without the essential support of a constitutional foundation. Changes in the political relationship between tribes and the U.S. might legitimately occur through a legal transmittal (via treaty or statute), a conquest, a voluntary cession, or the extinction of one of the parties. None of these situations had transpired between the Shoshone and the federal government.

The model of judicial accretion, in which the Court vests the United States government with virtually unlimited authority, is an imposing display of judicial deference to the political branches, for by it, the Court simply and semantically can grant to the federal government whatever is in dispute—whether it is lands, powers of government, or rights and responsibilities. The second party, the Northwestern Shoshone Nation in this case, is treated as a nonentity. In effect, the Shoshone were denied any credibility as a viable actor. This model of a gradual, incremental usurpation of tribal lands, power, or rights without corresponding legal or political authorization unfortunately has wide applicability to a number of subsequent Supreme Court opinions.

The Court, having artfully legitimated the federal accretion of assumed sovereignty over Shoshone lands, could have rested. Reed, however, felt the need to expand his already peculiar opinion in directions that added more layers of myth over tribal standing. He proceeded to further blame the tribal victims by fixing the burden of proof on the Shoshone Nation to show that the land actually belonged to them. Reed set this up by noting that "[w]hether the issue as to acknowledgment by a treaty of Indian title to land is treated as a question of fact, like Indian right to occupancy itself, . . . or as a matter of inference to be drawn by the trier of fact from the treaty and surrounding circumstances or as a conclusion of law to be reviewed by this Court upon the record, this finding places the burden on petitioners [the tribe] to overthrow the judgment of the Court of Claims."[126]

Next, Reed considered the specific phraseology of the 1863 treaties of the Shoshone Indians. Although admitting that the Government's treaty commissioners had clear instructions to negotiate not for the termination of Shoshone land rights, but only for route security, Reed still pursued his own arguments that the Northwestern Shoshone band's treaty, by not providing a "specific acknowledgment of Indian title," which was never its purpose, was therefore deficient and could not serve as a basis for compensation to the Indians. For Reed, Shoshone boundary uncertainty, as defined by federal officials, meant the complete loss of tribal lands.[127]

Once again, the "myth of the nomadic homeless Indian," worked to the stark detriment of Indian rights. As Cohen has observed, "on the whole each Indian group knew its own territory and the life of each of its members depended upon an exact knowledge of the boundaries and resources of a particular area."[128] The semiarid conditions that predominated in many of the western states were simply unsuited for permanently established communities, and seasonable moves were often necessary. Such periodic moves did not mean that indigenous peoples lacked recognized homes for the different seasons. Many traditional Navajo, for example, still connected to a pastoral lifestyle in a semiarid environment, have separate summer and winter homes. The practice of owning more than one home did not cause indigenous peoples to lack a clearly defined sense of property rights. It was simply a different property, in kind, from that of their industrialized neighbors.

The Shoshone argued that the federal government, in seeking permission to travel through Shoshone country and for the construction of telegraph and transportation facilities, had implicitly recognized their land title. The very act of seeking permission for land use is an acknowledgment by the seeker of the inherent right of the one who owns or controls the land in question. The Shoshone attorneys quoted a passage from John Marshall's important *Worcester v. Georgia* decision of 1832 in which the Cherokee had been asked to grant safe passage for whites. Marshall said that "the acceptance of these cessions [was] an acknowledgment of the right of the Cherokees to make or withhold them."

Reed asserted that the *Worcester* case was somehow "inapposite" to the Shoshone situation because the Cherokee treaties had other provisions which "specifically set apart and solemnly guaranteed" them their lands and that "no such specific recognition" was found in the Shoshone treaty. This difference, he argued, occurred because the Cherokee had signed removal treaties, whereas the Northwestern Shoshone had merely signed a peace and amity treaty, therefore creating a very different sort of legal document.

In an effort to strengthen his frail legal position on the 1863 Box Elder Treaty, Reed ventured into the realm of philosophy with the speculation that "[t]he United States undoubtedly might have asserted, at the time of the treaty, its purpose to extinguish Indian title or it might have recognized Indian title or it might, as the Court of Claims held, have sought only freedom from hostile acts . . . . The treaties were made in the midst of Civil War and before the outcome of that conflict was clear."[129] What the United States theoretically might have done, however, was irrelevant. The Court might have focused on what was done, on what the treaty actually said, on what the United States actually gained. Had it done so it would probably have had to admit that the federal government only secured certain rights-of-way through Shoshone territory. Reed's gratuitous comment about the uncertainty of the Civil War's outcome and his use of the expression "undoubtedly might have" speak volumes about the precision of his legal arguments.

In several succeeding paragraphs Reed challenged Shoshone arguments that their presence and early departure at the 1851 Fort Laramie Treaty provided implicit recognition of their title. If a treaty is a "grant of rights from the Indians, a reservation of those not granted away,"[130] then clearly the Shoshone lost no rights by either the Fort Laramie or the Box Elder treaties.

More disturbing evidence in Reed's discussion on these points is found in footnote number 8, where he casually remarked: "We note but consider unimportant, because this issue was not involved, casual references by this and other courts that the Shoshone treaties recognized Indian title in the Shoshones."[131] He cited as evidence *Shoshone Tribe of Indians v. United States,*[132] *United States v. Shoshone Tribe,*[133] *Shoshone Indians v. United States,*[134] and *United States v. Board of Commissioners.*[135] It is perplexing that such prior references acknowledging Shoshone title by the Supreme Court and other federal courts could be called "unimportant." This was, after all, the very crux of the decision. Reed continued his footnote by denying other crucial evidence provided by federal officials which recognized Shoshone land title: "We do not consider the references of the administrators in routine communications called for in the preparation of this case before the Court of Claims to the 'Shoshoni Indian Reservation' [Northwestern Band] to the fact that the territory of the Shoshone 'was recognized by the United States' or 'set apart for the Shoshone Indians' [to be] of any more weight."[136] "Nothing in these statements," said Reed, "shows that the attention of the administrators was focused on the problem of recognition or that they reflected a contemporaneous interpretation."[137] Thus Reed brushed aside the federal government's own primary Indian policy officials who, on numerous reported occasions, talked about the Shoshone as a tribe with recognized status.

At the end of the footnote, Reed derided the idea that the Court of Claims in refusing to consider administrative evidence in the form of maps of the territory in question had "abused its discretion."[138] In short, this single footnote contained substantial discarded, but highly credible, evidence recognizing Shoshone land rights. Reed and the majority were unwilling to let an array of solid documentary evidence stand in the way of their determination that the Shoshone had no land rights and were entitled to no compensation.

Justice Reed then challenged the Shoshone interpretation of the Senate amendment to the 1863 treaty. The Shoshone argued that the amendment showed that there would have been no need for the Senate to prescribe such a limitation had the treaty not recognized their preexisting land rights. Reed and the majority took the converse position. He said that "[w]hile such a limitation would not have been needed if the Senate *of that day* were positive, on weighing the issue as *we now do*, that the treaty was ineffective to give any additional color to Indian titles within or without the Mexican cession, it is unlikely that the ratifying body could or did appraise the several possibilities *which are now pre-*

sented"[139] (emphasis mine). In this passage Reed, using a mid-twentieth-century interpretation of the Senate provision, seemed to be lecturing the 1860 Senate for their inability to do this, in effect disparaging the Senate of the 1860s for not being able to foresee the future.

Finally, Reed challenged one of the better-known legal rules of treaty interpretation, the canons of construction, which holds that treaty phraseology should never be construed in a way that is damaging to Indians because of their relatively disadvantaged linguistic and military position during the forging of the treaty. Nearly a half-dozen cases had followed this rule,[140] although other cases ignored the principle.[141]

Reed's interpretation of the principle went something like this: The Court should attempt to ascertain what the language used in the treaty means according to the tenor of the agreement. The judiciary should simply seek to gauge what both parties meant by their participation. The Court should not change the terms of the treaties to correct an alleged injustice. If this kind of "generosity" is to be wielded, it is for the Congress to act.[142] Reed's construction of the treaty rule, therefore, is at odds with that of a number of prior Courts, for he assumes an equitable negotiating position between tribes and the federal government. More worthy of consideration is the fact that there was very little ambiguity in the language of the Box Elder Treaty. The tone was straightforward and the tribe's attorneys should not even have had to raise the rule of treaty interpretation. It was basically a document establishing peace and allowing sheltered passage for whites, their supplies, and their transportation and communication equipment.

Through Reed, the claims door had been slammed in the face of the Shoshone on the grounds that their rights to property, which were not specifically determined, did not spring from the 1863 Box Elder Treaty. Hence, the Shoshone could hope for no recovery under Congress's 1929 jurisdictional act, which was the original measure used by the Shoshone to bring their suit against the U.S. before the Court of Claims.[143]

The Concurring Opinion of Justices Jackson and Black

Jackson and Black's concurring opinion was a remarkable one indeed. Unlike Justice Reed, who appeared to have virtually no regard, empathy, or even sympathy for the depth of the loss the Court was legitimating, these two justices, on first blush, had a clear sense of the injustice being leveled against the Shoshone and denounced it in vivid terms. Jackson and Black appeared to support Shoshone claims; however, in the end, they concurred with Reed's opinion. Their arguments have been re-cycled in liberal quotations through the years and demand intense scru-tiny, because they continue to resurface periodically as legal strategies which have sometimes benefited tribes but more often have worked to their disadvantage.

Jackson and Black set a somber and reminiscent tone for their concur-rence by asserting at the start that the Shoshone grievance was not suited to a legal proceeding but rather to a congressional action. This harkens back to the Court's telling Indian claimants with regularity that Indian claims were political questions which only Congress could address. The fact that Congress had already acted by passing the 1929 judicial act which allowed the Shoshone to sue in the Court of Claims seems to have slipped the attention of the two justices: "It is hard to see how any judi-cial decision under such a jurisdictional act can much advance solution of the problem of the Shoshone."[144] They feared that any judgment in the Shoshone's favor would actually provide "neither lands nor money."[145] This statement is only partially correct. It is true that the Shoshone had no chance of reclaiming lost land, but the question of money is more complicated. If the tribe were to win the case, the 15 million dollars sought would be deposited in the Federal Treasury "for their benefit." And, while they would not have had direct access to those funds, the money would have belonged to the tribe. Jackson and Black, however, attacked the jurisdictional act's provisions that any funds tribes secured be placed in the United States Treasury for the benefit of the Indians, but subject to congressional appropriations. That it was Congress which denied the Indians the right to receive their monies was a direct result of the paternalism rampant throughout federal Indian policy channels which viewed Indians as incompetent to handle their own affairs. This seems not to have phased the concurring justices.

Jackson and Black also pointed out, in apparent irritation, that attor-neys were the only parties who received cash payments in the event the Shoshone were successful. Again, this was a federally created problem, out of the tribe's control. The issue of attorneys' fees was also problem-atic for the Indian Claims Commission which was just gearing up.

Further evidence of the justices' anger at both the lawyers and Con-gress is found in this passage: "After counsel are thus paid, not a cent is put into the reach of the Indians; all that is done for them by a judgment is to earmark some funds in the Treasury from which Congress may as it sees fit from time to time makes appropriations. . . ."[146] But this has little to do with the actual Shoshone claim. It is not the normal business of the Court to determine how the United States administers its policies, at least that is what the Court had said in *Lone Wolf*; yet the concurring justices were questioning the congressional administration of Indian monies which, in this case, were not even forthcoming.

The justices proceeded to coin and rely upon what Felix Cohen called the "Myth of Moral Progress." [147] This myth allows Euro-America to attribute contemporary exploitations to their ancestors while continuing to "draw a profit therefrom." It further maintained that all injustices committed against Indians were "ancient wrongs committed by our forefathers in the distant past against remote ancestors of the present claimants." [148] The Shoshone argued that although the wrongs did indeed have a historical basis, history had done nothing to reverse the ongoing process of exploitation.

The moral progress myth was related to another crucial issue—the moral obligation of the United States to the tribes and the relationship, if any, of morality to legality. Jackson put it this way:

> We would not be second to any other in recognizing that—judgment or no judgment—a moral obligation of a high order rests upon this country to provide for decent shelter, clothing, education, and industrial advancement of the Indian. Nothing is gained by dwelling upon the unhappy conflicts that have prevailed between the Shoshones and the whites—conflicts which sometimes leave one in doubt which side could make the better claim to be civilized. The generation of Indians who suffered the privations, indignities, and brutalities of the westward march of the whites have gone to the Happy Hunting Ground, and nothing that we can do can square the account with them. Whatever survives is moral obligation resting on the descendants of the whites to do for the descendants of the Indians what in the conditions of this twentieth century is the decent thing.[149]

The question of the federal government's *moral obligation* to tribes is a recurring one. When the United States signed the various treaties with tribes, it drew upon its character as a political culture steeped in a moral tradition, with the assumption that morality and the democratic ideals acknowledged in the Constitution formed the basis of the political and legal obligations the United States has to tribes. Thus, the assertion that the national government has a moral obligation to provide housing, clothing, and education but is somehow not morally bound to uphold its legal and political obligations, as stated in treaties, gives evidence of a curious double standard at work in the minds of the justices.

The justices continued their journey through the unusual world of morality divorced from reality: "It is most unfortunate to try to measure this moral duty in terms of legal obligations and ask the Court to spell out Indian legal rights from written instruments made and probably broken long ago and to put our moral duty in figures as legal damages. The Indian problem is essentially a sociological problem, not a legal one. We can only make a pretense of adjudication of such claims, and that only by indulging in the most unrealistic and fictional assumptions." [150]

From the unusual bifurcation of the federal government's relationship to tribes into (1) moral obligations and (2) legal obligations; to the justices' harmful assertions that Indian issues were sociological and not legal in nature; to their conclusion that any judicial effort to ameliorate these issues could only take place by indulging in "unrealistic and fictional assumptions," this passage shows that even those justices harboring some degree of sympathy for American Indian rights were overwhelmed by the masks applied to the Indians by the justice system and thus had failed to understand the basic political relationship between indigenous groups and the United States. For example, Jackson's statement that the Court could not deal with Indian claims without delving into "unrealistic and fictional assumptions" is problematic. We are not told what these "assumptions" are, though Jackson did hint that they had something to do with time and Indian treaties. Jackson wrote as if the 1863 treaty were actually a document of remote antiquity in a language he was unfamiliar with. What else explains this statement: "Here we are asked to go back over three-quarters of a century to spell out the meaning of a most ambiguous writing made in 1863." [151] As seen above, there was nothing ambiguous about the treaty, and the Court is frequently called upon to revisit events of the eighteenth and nineteenth centuries to interpret provisions of the federal and state constitutions and other documents and prior precedent, which happen to have been written in the same "ambiguous" language as the treaty—English.

"Even if the handicap of time could be overcome," said Jackson, "we could not satisfactorily apply legal techniques to interpretation of this treaty." [152] In Jackson's words, legal interpretation would not be possible because the Shoshone were racially and socioculturally inferior. "The Indian parties to the treaty were a band of simple, relatively peaceful, and extremely primitive men." [153] The allegedly inferior status of the Shoshone was worsened by their numerical inferiority—1,500 Indians occupying 15 million acres of land. This dual "inferiority" made it easy, according to Jackson, for the "more aggressive and efficient whites" (he distributed the stereotypes evenly enough) who happened to be "better killers" to come to dominate the Shoshone.[154]

Jackson then examined the doctrine that Indian treaties were to be construed as comparable to contracts between whites. He agreed that in some simple cases this was practicable but called it "far fetched" for the case at hand. It was far-fetched, in Jackson's opinion, because the Shoshone lacked equal bargaining power. Very few historians would argue that in 1863 the Shoshone had the military muscle of the federal government. But, as John Marshall said in *Worcester v. Georgia* in 1832, "the law of nations is that a weaker power does not surrender its independence— its right to self-government, by associating with a stronger and taking its protection."[155] It is the end result—the treaty which emerges—that matters and is legally enforceable.

Jackson went on to describe how "dominant, powerful, shrewd, and educated" were the whites, in contrast to the "destitute, illiterate Indians."[156] Indeed, if the tribe were so disadvantaged, should its weakness not give all the more reason for the Supreme Court to adhere to the law as negotiated between the tribe and the federal government? Jackson seemed to be arguing that disparate and unequal relations allowed illegalities to be condoned. Jackson, like Reed, said that because the Indians were ignorant of certain western concepts like property ownership and land title, they were not entitled to legal protection:

> Acquisitiveness, which develops a law of real property, is an accomplishment only of the "civilized." Of course, the Indians may have had some vague idea that thereafter they were to stay off certain lands and the white man in return were to stay off certain other land. But we do not think it possible now to reduce such a nebulous accord to terms of common-law contract and conveyancing. The treaty was a political document. It was intended to pacify the Indians and to let the whites travel in peace a route they were somehow going to travel anyway.[157]

Jackson struggled in conclusion to find some way to acknowledge the loss to the Shoshone without according them any legal right to compensation. His compromised conclusion was as follows:

> We agree with Mr. Justice Reed that no legal rights are today to be recognized in the Shoshones by reason of this treaty. We agree with

Mr. Justice Douglas and Mr. Justice Murphy as to their moral deserts. We do not mean to leave the impression that the two have any relation to each other. The finding that the treaty creates no legal obligations does not restrict Congress from such appropriations as its judgment dictates "for the health, education, and industrial advancement of said Indians," which is the position in which Congress would find itself if we found that it did create legal obligations and tried to put a value on them.[158]

JUSTICE DOUGLAS'S DISSENT

Justice Douglas issued a powerful dissent, which was joined by Frankfurter and Murphy. Murphy, however, opted to write his own opinion, which was then joined by Frankfurter and Douglas. Douglas essentially argued that when federal negotiators approached the Shoshone requesting, not demanding, safe passage for its settlers, seeking the right to establish military posts and the right to construct a railroad, as well as establish and maintain telegraph and stage coach lines, it was admitting to and recognizing Shoshone ownership of the lands they inhabited. And while the United States could have attempted to extinguish Shoshone title by military conquest or by purchase, they chose not to exercise those options. What the government did, as the historical record clearly showed, was to negotiate a treaty. Whether the treaty was negotiated by relative equals was unimportant. It was the act of negotiation, the subsequent ratification, and the proclamation of the document that vested or diminished rights in the respective parties.

In contrast to Reed, who had argued that the Shoshone's right of occupancy to their lands was an inferior title to that of the United States, Douglas cited *Mitchel v. United States* (1835), wherein the Supreme Court unanimously held that Indian title was "as sacred as the fee simple of the whites."[159] Douglas also gave much greater weight to the Senate amendment, and to the little-discussed provision of the 1863 treaty which described "country claimed by Pokatello, for himself and his people...."[160] He stated that although the majority "brushed aside" the Pokatello provision, the fact was that "[i]f the standards of the frontier are to govern, his [Pokatello's] assertion of ownership and its recognition by the United States could hardly have been plainer."[161]

The Douglas dissent also reminded the majority about the canons of Indian treaty construction. "When the standard is not observed," said Douglas, "what these Indians did not lose to the railroads and the land companies they lose in the fine web of legal niceties." [162] Douglas concluded by noting that for a pittance the Shoshone had granted not the land itself, but certain valuable rights in their lands, to the federal government. Quoting from the amicus curiae briefs of the attorneys general of Idaho and Utah, which had been filed on behalf of the Shoshone, Douglas opined that this denial of the Shoshone claim was "unworthy of our country." [163] "The faith of this nation," said the amici, "having been pledged in the treaties, the honor of the nation demands, and the jurisdictional act requires, that these long-unsettled grievances be settled by this Court in simple justice to a downtrodden people." [164]

JUSTICE MURPHY'S DISSENT

Murphy's dissent focused on the meaning of the 1863 Box Elder Treaty. The question, he said, was whether the treaty recognized the Shoshone claim to land which, if recognized, would make them eligible for compensation under the 1929 jurisdictional act. Murphy said there was no doubt that the treaty provided such recognition, based both on the clear language of the treaty and on the circumstances preceding and succeeding the treaty's negotiation and ratification.

Justice Murphy gave a political and historical analysis examining the significant evidence in which various government officials had openly said that the lands involved were "owned by the Indians." [165] He quoted liberally from reports and communications of the secretary of the interior, the commissioner of Indian affairs, the House Committee on Indian Affairs, the treaty commissioners, and Congress itself. "The fact," said Murphy, "that the United States thought it necessary to make a treaty concerning rights of way and the fact that the United States expressly did not desire to negotiate 'with a view to the extinguishment of the Indian title to the land' strongly indicate that the United States considered the Indians as owners of this ill defined area of land." [166] More to the point, the securing of rights-of-way "would have been a needless formality had title to the underlying land been thought to be in the name of the United States." [167]

Murphy briskly continued his assault on the majority's ruling by stating the obvious: "The Box Elder and the four other treaties would have been meaningless had the United States not recognized the Indian title to the land claimed." It also did not matter, according to Murphy, whether the land in question was based on aboriginal possession or whether it had been expressly set aside. And Murphy deemed it "immaterial that the main purpose of the treaties was to secure rights in the land rather than to acknowledge or secure title. The securing of those rights necessarily presupposes Indian title and necessarily recognizes such title."[168]

For Murphy, the established rule of canons of construction, that ambiguities in Indian treaties were to be resolved in favor of the Indians, demonstrated that the United States had recognized Shoshone title. In closing, Murphy chastised Jackson who, in his dissent, had expressed qualms that the money, if it had been secured, would not have been directly sent to the Shoshone but would have been deposited in the United States treasury. While concurring in this prediction, Murphy declared that such an eventuality "does not justify ignoring the rights of the Shoshone Indians recognized under solemn treaties entered into with the United States."[169] Moreover, noted Murphy, "[i]t does not command us to overthrow the moral obligation of the United States to fulfill its treaty obligations. And it does not warrant the application of narrow principles of construction to the injury of the Indians' interest. If Congress desires to place in the Treasury any money that might be recovered by the Indians in this suit that is the business of Congress, not ours."[170]

THE AFTERMATH

There was an immediate outcry on behalf of the Northwestern Shoshone by a variety of individuals, organizations, and political groups. Requests for a rehearing of the case were filed by the tribe's attorneys, the House and Senate Committees on Indian Affairs, Judge Manley O. Hudson of the Permanent Court of International Justice, the Department of the Interior, the American Civil Liberties Union, the fledgling National Congress of American Indians, and the attorneys general of Utah and Idaho—a diverse assortment, to be sure. Such requests for rehearing are not unusual. Only rarely, however, are such rehearings granted.[171] Some of the arguments invoked by the Shoshone and their advocates warrant attention.

Congressman Karl E. Mundt (R., South Dakota) was one of the first persons to register his displeasure with the Court's opinion. In remarks logged in the *Congressional Record* on March 15, 1945, Mundt said that this decision was "one of the most complete reversals of form ever witnessed . . . reversing the policy of 150 years in liberally construing Indian treaties."[172] Mundt also inserted in the record an anonymous editorial entitled "Lo! The Poor Indian." The editorial attacked the Court's holding and ended by interjecting an international dimension: "Incidentally, these opinions, revealing as they do the shameful conduct of the master race in America toward conquered people, will make good reading for those critics who think that full justice in all parts of the world must be a condition precedent to our joining an international organization [the United Nations] to keep the peace."[173]

Judge Manley O. Hudson of the Permanent Court of International Justice accused the majority of misconstruing and misapplying the Box Elder Treaty and pointed to the global implications of the issue in this case. "What is at stake here," said Judge Hudson, "is the declared and historic policy of the United States in the treatment of a racial and linguistic minority. And this at a time when the whole world is aflame on the subject of the treatment of minorities."[174] Hudson also called for international recognition of indigenous rights by noting that the Shoshone had gone before the Supreme Court because they deemed it the only forum where their rights would be recognized. "It is," he astutely remarked, "a tribunal of the other party to the treaty, but the petitioners have no other choice. No international tribunal exists to which they may have access."[175]

Ironically, because tribes and states are often posed at opposite ends of frequently adversarial proceedings, one of the strongest and most moving arguments requesting a rehearing came from the attorneys general of Utah and Idaho. Grover A. Giles, the attorney general of Utah, and Frank Longley, Idaho's attorney general, rendered a stirring, almost apologetic argument in support of the Shoshone claim:

> The *amici* despair of being able to explain to petitioner Indians that they are without redress for the taking of their country because nothing in the records of the United States shows that the United States intended to recognize their title. . . . Specifically, how are these bands of Indians—as of the time of the Treaty of July 30, 1863 or at the present time—to understand that when they grant the United States a limited permission to use their country, the United States (in its own Courts) is not merely guiltless but guileless when it takes not only what it bargained for but the entire use and benefit of their country? How are the bands to understand that when they had their claim to their ancestral country set to paper by the representative of the United States and delineated with natural landmarks, nevertheless because they did not insist, in accordance with what this Court holds to be the white man's law, that the United States agree never to take their land from under them, they have no substantive rights on their part as against the

United States? . . . How can the bands—who in common with other Indian peoples of our country have relied on this Court of all Courts for an assessment of their rights in accordance with what they understood their treaty to provide—be expected to be convinced of the white man's justice when their understanding, heretofore furnishing the rule, is now held to mean only what the "tenor of the treaty" as written and interpreted by the white man may indicate? [176]

They also challenged Jackson's assertion that Congress could still be expected to provide for the health, education, and welfare needs of the Shoshone. "The fact is," said Giles and Longley, "that Congress has done precious little for these wards. They are the object of charity; they have (except for those at the Fort Hall Reservation in Idaho) no Indian agent to communicate their needs; they have no program of government assistance in education or industry; they are scattered throughout the states we represent, truly men without a country of their own." [177]

Lastly, the National Congress of American Indians (NCAI), which had been organized in 1944, then consisting of approximately fifty tribes (including the Northwestern Shoshone) in twenty-one states, was especially and understandably disturbed by this decision. The NCAI realized that "the language of the majority opinion here expressed may by analogy throw grave clouds upon the titles of these respective tribes and set up new tests that may have the effect of excluding recovery. . . ." [178]

Despite the force of these legal and moral arguments, and despite the breadth of dissent, the request for rehearing was denied without opinion. The massive and ongoing Shoshone land loss was let stand. Most disturbingly, by the 1940s there were actually fewer whites making their living in the disputed area than there had earlier been Shoshone, so in the long run the dispossession of the Shoshone served not even the goals of scientific exploration and national expansion that had dictated the decision. And finally, it must be remembered that although the Court of Claims and the Supreme Court assumed that the entire area of over 15 million acres had been taken as of the 1863 treaty, there was never a precise finding by the Claims Court of the actual amount of land taken or when it had been taken. In other words, the actual "taking" of Shoshone lands was an ongoing physical accretion process which was now sanctioned by the judiciary. As the tribe's attorneys argued in their request for rehearing, "there is, therefore, no basis for the assumption that this is an ancient wrong. A considerable amount of land has been taken from the present generation." [179]

Tee-Hit-Ton v. United States

THE MASKED "DISCOVERY" AND
"LEGAL CONQUEST" OF ALASKAN NATIVES

By 1955 the federal government was well into what could rightly be termed the United States' last systematic and well-defined Indian policy—the termination of the federal government's lawful treaty and moral trust relationship with a host of tribal nations. Termination was forcefully begun in 1950 under Commissioner of Indian Affairs Dillon S. Meyer. He argued that Indians would have to be "moved to accept their status along side their non-Indian neighbors."[180] The government set about the task of divesting itself of its legal obligations and moral responsibilities to certain tribes in the nation when it was determined that they, in the words of Meyer, met the "qualifications to manage their own affairs without supervision by the Federal Government."[181]

The most tangible evidence of this fundamental shift in policy occurred in 1953 with the enactment of two measures—a House Concurrent Resolution and a federal law. HCR 108, passed on August 1, declared it to be the new policy of the federal government to abolish federal supervision over the tribes as soon as practical, and to then subject the terminated Indians "to the same privileges and responsibilities as are applicable to other citizens of the United States, to end their status as wards of the United States, and to grant them all the rights and prerogatives pertaining to American citizenship."[182] Assimilation was one of the driving forces, although certainly not the lone force, behind this policy. There was a renewed sense that Indians should be allowed to "assume their full responsibilities as American citizens," a status that many in Washington, D.C., and elsewhere felt that Indians had been deprived of because of the Bureau of Indian Affairs' heavy-handed paternalism and the Indians' own unwillingness to "let go" of their tribal rights.[183]

Public Law 280,[184] the second measure, was enacted two weeks later. This act brought Indian lands and their tribal residents in California, Minnesota (except the Red Lake Reservation), Nebraska, Oregon (except the Warm Springs Reservation), and Wisconsin (except the Menominee Reservation) under the criminal and, to a lesser extent, the civil jurisdiction of state governments, and authorized any other state to pursue such a jurisdictional coup. This omnibus act was "in principle" a unilateral repudiation of treaties between tribes and the United States and severely reduced the tribal governments' inherent powers over civil and criminal issues.[185]

Public Law 280 was enacted in part to relieve the Bureau of Indian Affairs of costly law enforcement duties and to continue narrowing the scope of federal responsibilities to tribes. President Eisenhower signed the bill into law, although he had "grave doubts" about some provisions of the measure and declared it "unfortunate" that the bill contained two sections which "permit other states to impose on Indian tribes within their borders," the same level of jurisdiction "while removing Indians from Federal jurisdiction, and, in some instances, effective self-government." [186]

The devastation of tribal treaty rights and property rights and the abrogation of the constitutional rights of tribal members unleashed with the enactment of these two pieces of legislation were combined with the already established threat to individual Indians under the government's policy of physical relocation of Indians into urban areas where their absorption into American society would be quickened. These enterprises were to be financially supported, in part, by the Indian Claims Commission (ICC) settlements; that is, the government would appropriate money won in court by the Indians to finance its ultimate goal of gradually severing all remaining federal trust and treaty obligations to tribes. Tribes, in effect, were to pay for their own termination. The legal liquidation of tribes, the enforcement of state jurisdiction over reservations, and the relocation of Indians to urban areas "were thought by the Federal Government and by many of the public concerned with these issues to be programs that could be managed with minimal new state and federal resources, all because of the potential of the Indian Claims Commission's anticipated allocations." [187] (The presumption that tribes would be "successful" in pursuit of claims settlements, as we have seen, was not always realized.)

The 1946 Indian Claims Commission Act (ICC) was supposed to settle tribal grievances against the United States with finality. The act initially stated that Indian tribes had five years to file their claims. The ICC was to conclude its work within ten years from the time of its first meeting. Because of the enormous number of cases filed, however, over 850, the act was extended in 1956 for another five years, until April 10, 1962.[188] Several additional time extensions became necessary. Finally, Congress, weary of the process, terminated the Commission's life in 1978 and sent the more than 100 pending cases to the Court of Claims. Many of these claims remain unsettled. "Indian people," said Charles Wilkinson, "complain that the long delays in settling their claims are another injustice. There is no other area in the judicial system, even antitrust, where you have delays of that magnitude."[189]

The role of the ICC has a strong connection with the *Tee-Hit-Ton* case. Although the Tee-Hit-Ton had filed their case in the Court of Claims and not in the ICC forum, it was clear that whatever the Supreme Court decided would have broad implications for all Indian claims against federal takings of aboriginal lands. This was an interesting case for several reasons. First, it arose in Alaska, that territorial giant with largely untapped economic potential. Second, it involved Alaskan natives, Inuit and Aleut, who held virtually all their land under aboriginal title since no treaties were ever negotiated directly with any Alaskan indigenous group. And finally, there was the likelihood that the decision would establish a precedent reaching throughout the territory of Alaska (statehood was not gained until 1959) and the lower forty-eight states.

HISTORICAL BACKGROUND

The Tee-Hit-Ton were, at the time of the decision, a small clan numbering about seventy, living in southeastern Alaska near present-day Wrangell. They identified themselves as the Sti-Kine-Quon (or Stikine) people. They spoke the Tlingit language and had customs, laws, and traditions similar to other Tlingit peoples.[190] The area claimed by the Tee-Hit-Ton entailed approximately 357,802 acres of land and 150 square miles of water. They had inhabited the region for thousands of years, and the area in question was recognized as theirs by neighboring tribes. The Tee-Hit-Ton maintained that although they had never signed a treaty with either Russia (which had occupied portions of Alaska from 1741 to 1867) or the United States, their aboriginal rights to the land had been confirmed and recognized in section 8 of the 1884 organic law which created the Alaskan territory,[191] in section 14 of the Act of 1891,[192] and in section 27 of the Act of June 6, 1900,[193] establishing a civil government for Alaska. Furthermore, as an identifiable tribe, band, or clan, they also stressed that even if the federal government refused to recognize their full proprietary ownership of the area, the government under the trust principle, "still held title to the land, water, and natural resources of the Tee-Hit-Ton in trust for the Tee-Hit-Ton Indians."[194]

In the early 1900s several reservations were established for Alaskan native groups by presidential executive orders. With a general act, Congress stopped the executive order reservation process in 1919; however, when the Indian Reorganization Act of 1934 was extended to Alaskan peoples in 1936, the Department of the Interior was specifically authorized again to establish executive order reservations for Alaskan natives.[195] Six small reservations were set aside in the 1940s, while others were under consideration. An intensive campaign, however, "was launched by local interest to frighten the natives into rejecting them."[196] The Alaskan native groups were misled into thinking that they would be "confined" and would lose the valued American citizenship they had acquired under the 1924 law.

The campaign to prevent the establishment of Indian reservations was led by the burgeoning fishing, timber, mineral, and oil interests which had been streaming into Alaska since the end of World War II. Their rationale, supported by some in Congress and by the Department of the Interior, in preventing the establishment of more Indian reservations was self-evident. Reservations have a recognized status in law and are subject to federal trust protection. Nonreservation Indian communities lack any such safeguards and have little in the way of effective weaponry to fend off corporate or governmental interests intent on exploiting the resource base of tribes. Alaskan native communities, including the Tee-Hit-Ton band, as a result of this disinformation campaign, voted against continued reservation establishment.[197] By the early 1950s, some 90 Alaskan villages reconsidered their position and decided to petition to have their lands reserved. The Interior Department, however, was already well into its termination phase and refused their request.

The first dramatic signal that the Tee-Hit-Ton were in a precarious position regarding their land title came when the House issued a report on July 10, 1947, "authorizing the Secretary of Agriculture to sell timber within the Tongass National Forest." The Tongass National Forest encompassed an important segment of the Tee-Hit-Ton's land claim. The Committee on Agriculture, which submitted the report, recommended that the Tongass resolution pass with only minor amendments. The legislation was supported by Secretary of the Interior J. A. Krug for reasons of national interest, though he was well aware of the unresolved nature of the Indian claims. Krug said that "the question of native land titles in the Territory of Alaska has remained, in the large, unresolved throughout the history of that territory." He noted, "It is not yet authoritatively settled whether the Alaskan Cession Treaty of 1867 (15 Stat. 539) preserved or extinguished the native or aboriginal title to lands. If not extinguished, and if not subsequently abandoned, these rights exist in some form as a valid type of land ownership."[198]

Krug, however, despite this legal uncertainty, showed where his political loyalties lay when he stated, "For almost 25 years it has been the very strong desire of all persons concerned with the development of Alaska to put the rich timber resources of southeastern Alaska to use, upon a sustained yield basis, for the production of newsprint and other paper products. This potential development is now of a great general interest because of the acute shortage of paper pulp."[199] There remained, however, one small stumbling block. "Only the cloud," said Krug, "on the Forest Service title which is cast by the native claims remains as a formidable obstacle.[200]

Krug's arguments, and his concern that litigation to determine title "would take a considerable number of years to settle," were enough to persuade the committee to support the measure. Sacrificing the property rights of the Tee-Hit-Ton band would meet the needs of the "hard pressed consumers of wood pulp," the Alaska territory, and would add to the "national security of Alaska." The national security argument is interesting, for this case arose during the height of America's unbridled crusade against communism. As the committee concluded in its report, the development of this timber stand would be good for business enterprises, would raise employment, and would create "sorely needed products." Even more important, it would be pivotal "from the standpoint of promoting the national defense through increasing the population and industrial capacity of Alaska as our northern rampart."[201]

With such a wide-ranging set of economic, cultural, and ideological arguments, the Tee-Hit-Ton stood little chance of protecting their property rights. Less than three weeks later, Congress, by joint resolution, enacted a law authorizing the secretary of agriculture to sell the timber of the Tongass National Forest. The secretary, in section 2, was authorized to sell any timber "notwithstanding any claim of possessory rights" claimed by Alaskan natives.[202] In short, the property rights of the Tee-Hit-Ton and other native groups or individuals, whether based on aboriginal possession or title, were disregarded. Felix S. Cohen, former solicitor general and author of the classic treatise on federal Indian law, once again came to the defense of indigenous peoples. In an article appropriately titled "Alaska's Nuremberg laws: Congress Sanctions Racial

Discrimination,"[203] Cohen argued that "for the first time in our history, it has been decreed by Congress that a government bureau may seize the possessions of Americans solely because they belong to a minority race. That is the meaning of the Tongass Act, which deprives Alaskans of their land and timber if two or more of their grandparents were Indian, and which quietly became law on August 8, 1947."[204]

The only consolation insofar as the Tee-Hit-Ton were concerned was section 3a of the resolution. While the Tee-Hit-Ton could not prevent the sale of land or timber, section 3a declared that all receipts from the timber or land sold were to be kept in a special account in the Treasury Department "until the rights to the land and the timber are finally determined."[205] Even this concession, however, would be negated by the Supreme Court's decision.

A year after the Tongass Resolution, President Truman, in a special message to Congress on May 21, 1948, warned that "a special legal problem is at present hampering the development of Alaska. This is the question of whether or not Alaska natives have claims to the ownership of certain lands."[206] Three years later, on August 20, 1951, the U.S. Forest Service, acting under authority prescribed by the joint resolution, sold to Ketchikan Pulp and Paper Company, a Washington state–based corporation, the right to all harvestable timber in the Tongass National Forest, estimated at 1,500,000 cubic feet. The agreement gave the corporation exclusive rights to the timber until June 30, 2004.[207]

Within two months, the Tee-Hit-Ton had retained James C. Peacock and the law firm of William, Myers, and Quiggle, who promptly filed suit in the Court of Claims. They argued that the Tee-Hit-Ton were the sole owners of the land and water in dispute; that they had never sold or conveyed the land to any other party; and they asked for a judgment for the losses and damages from the Tongass taking, plus interest. The United States responded that the Tee-Hit-Ton were not even a recognized tribe, band, or group, and were, therefore, not even authorized to sue the United States. Furthermore, the government maintained that even conceding that the Tee-Hit-Ton were a tribe, they lacked collective rights to the lands or water in dispute and were therefore not entitled to any compensable interest in the land or resources involved. In other words, the United States denied that the Tee-Hit-Ton "owned anything."[208]

The Court of Claims ruled on April 6, 1954, that the Tee-Hit-Ton were indeed an "identifiable group of American Indians" and were in

172 ║ AMERICAN INDIAN SOVEREIGNTY AND THE SUPREME COURT

fact asserting "ownership" of the land in question. However, the Court refused to say that the tribe did own the land in question and hinted that they had serious "doubt" whether they had any claim that survived the United States' assumption of jurisdiction in Alaska in 1867. The Court would only say that if the Tee-Hit-Ton's rights in the lands survived the federal government's 1867 treaty with Russia, their only legal share would be rights of occupancy "with its weaknesses and imperfections."[209] Finally, the Court denied that the pieces of legislation relied upon by the tribe to assert recognized title—the acts of 1884, 1891, 1900, and 1947—provided any unqualified rights to the territory involved.

The tribe then appealed to the Supreme Court. This case had broad-ranging implications for (1) the tribe's potentially extensive claims to the Tongass lands; (2) the hundreds of pending ICC claims in Alaska and the "lower forty-eight" states based on aboriginal title; (3) the Alaska territory—especially the potential cost of developing the vast resources of that massive land mass; and (4) the field of federal Indian law.

The tribe's lead attorney, James C. Peacock, recognized as much when he stated that "the instant case has been shaped from the very outset to serve as a test case. . . ."[210] Peacock noted how in several other pending cases the United States had sought and been granted an extension of time until after the *Tee-Hit-Ton* case was to be decided. Furthermore, the Yakutat clan, which Peacock also represented, had recently received 30,000 dollars in commitments from two oil companies in exchange for the groups' pledge "not to sue those companies operating under leases granted by the United States."[211] The Yakutat had made a substantial cash contribution in support of the Tee-Hit-Ton band's expenses in bringing this suit to the Supreme Court.

Congress was likewise concerned, evidenced by the introduction of HR 192 which would have established a sort of declaratory judgment for the settlement of possessory land claims in the territory. This move unnerved the Ketchikan Pulp Company. In a letter to the Forest Service, the company's chief executives expressed deep trepidation that under the bill as drawn, the tribe would succeed to the rights of the government and the company would have to deal directly with the tribe and not the Forest Service, if, that is, aboriginal rights to the Tongass lands were affirmed. "This," said the company, "would create an intolerable situation . . . it would, in our opinion, amount to a breech of good faith on the part of the United States if the title to the lands covered by the company's contract would in the course of time vest in third parties. . . ."[212]

The United States, in its brief arguing the correctness of the Court of Claims' decision, asserted that the potential impact of the case was such that it warranted a Supreme Court ruling. "There are," said Solicitor General Simon E. Sobeloff, "now pending before the Indian Claims Commission approximately 400 cases, involving some 800 separate claims or causes of actions by Indians in the continental United States. Of these 800 claims, about half involve in some form or other the question of the compensability of 'original Indian title.' With specific reference to Alaskan Indians, there is one case pending in the Court of Claims and twelve others in the Indian Claims Commission. Moreover, so long as it is contended that the questions remain unsettled, there may be a cloud upon the title to much of the land in Alaska and its further development may be thereby impeded."[213] The federal government hoped for a final resolution denying any aboriginal title to clear the way for unimpeded economic development.

Amicus curiae briefs were filed by the attorneys general of Idaho, New Mexico, and Utah. All three feared that a decision adverse to the Tee-Hit-Ton would have devastating consequences for their state's resident tribes, each of whom had filed claims with the ICC. It may be that the attorneys general were less concerned with the justness of the tribes' legal and moral claims against the United States than they were worried that the tribes, having lost their chance for compensatory settlement with the United States and facing federal liquidation, would then become a major financial burden upon the state.

There is some evidence of this in the amicus brief of Idaho's chief lawyer, Robert Smylie, who described the pending Indian Claims Commission cases of that state's four tribes—Shoshone-Bannock, Coeur d'Alene, Kootenai, and Nez Perce. Smylie observed that the federal government's termination policy would eventually "leave this State the serious problems of providing community and social services and supervising the adjustment of its Indian citizens to the proposed new status of unregulated responsibility."[214] Smylie concluded by stating that the ICC Act should not be "frustrated by an improvident interpretation which would deny the Indians the opportunity to settle their ancient grievances against the Federal Government before its responsibilities to the Indians of Idaho are terminated."[215]

More directly, New Mexico Attorney General Richard Robinson said this case was "merely a weapon." "The real target," he urged, "was the claims filed before the Indian Claims Commission. . . ."[216] This was, indeed, a real concern, and one that many Indians were extremely anxious about since significant amounts of Indian land were still held under aboriginal title throughout the United States.

MASKING WITHIN THE DECISION: THE OPINION

In Justice Stanley F. Reed's opinion, the Tee-Hit-Ton began with two strikes against them. First, unlike the Northwestern Shoshone, they had no treaty relationship with the United States. And second, the Court was under no statutory direction to consider the tribe's claims, as it had been in the *Shoshone* case. However, even if they had met one or both of these requisites, as the Shoshone had done, there was still no guarantee they would emerge victorious in court. On the positive side, the Court of Claims had acknowledged the Tee-Hit-Ton clan as an "identifiable group of American Indians." Reed had already shown, however, in *Shoshone*, that in his view Indians had no enforceable natural rights to their inhabited property, regardless of the length of their tenure or their status as a treaty-recognized nation. He had also stated his opinion that the fact that individual Indians were citizens of the United States was not a bar to federal actions aimed at the taking of tribal rights.

Speaking for a majority, six to three, with Justices William Douglas and Felix Frankfurter joining Chief Justice Earl Warren in dissent, Reed began his opinion by restating the Tee-Hit-Ton's claim. Since this case, like the preceding *Shoshone* decision and all the pending ICC cases, centered on compensation and not land recovery, Reed said, "Payment, if it can be compelled, must be based upon a constitutional right of the Indians to recover." Reed then immediately established a questionable legal distinction between the status of Alaskan natives and tribes in the lower forty-eight states:

> This is not a case that is connected with any phase of the policy of the Congress, continued throughout our history, to extinguish Indian title through negotiation rather than by force, and to grant payments from the public purse to needy descendants of exploited Indians. The legislation in support of that policy has received consistent interpretation from this Court in sympathy with its compassionate purpose.[217]

Reed was denying the Tee-Hit-Ton the legal status they had enjoyed under federal law since at least the 1930s. As Cohen stated, "the legal position of the individual Alaskan natives has been generally assimilated to that of the Indians in the United States."[218] "In fact," said Cohen, "it is now substantially established that they occupy the same relation to the Federal Government as do the Indians residing in the United States; that they, their property, and their affairs are under the protection of the Federal Government; that Congress may enact such legislation as it deems fit for their benefit and protection; and that the laws of the United States with respect to the Indians . . . of the United States proper are generally applicable to the Alaskan natives."[219]

Although the federal government never signed treaties with the Alaskan natives, a fact also pertinent to a number of well-known tribes in the lower forty-eight states—Hopi, Tohono O'odham, Yaqui, and others— it was a weak excuse to deny that the Alaskan native groups had comparable political dealings with the federal government. The additional fact that the benefits of the Indian Reorganization Act, a major federal Indian policy, were in 1936 made available to those Alaskan native communities which chose to adopt the act, was ignored by Reed.[220] Although the Tee-Hit-Ton chose not to avail themselves of the 1936 act's provisions— a decision other tribes in the lower forty-eight states also made—their "identifiable" status as an indigenous community had already been conceded by Reed.

Reed restated the Court of Claims' findings as to the Tee-Hit-Ton's status as an identifiable group with occupancy rights to their lands. He said, "Because of general agreement as to the importance of the question of compensation for congressionally approved taking of lands occupied in Alaska under aboriginal Indian use and claim of ownership, and the conflict concerning the effect of federal legislation protecting Indian occupation between this decision of the Court of Claims . . . and the decision of the Court of Appeals . . . in *Miller v. United States* . . . we granted certiorari."[221]

Reed had selectively chosen to look at the alleged conflict between two lower court cases without considering the possibility that the 1947 Tongass Act itself deserved constitutional scrutiny as a possibly unconstitutional taking of Indian title. Reed, ignoring the Court of Claims' finding that the Tee-Hit-Ton had rights of occupancy in their lands, said that "the problem presented is the nature of the petitioner's interest in the land, if any."[222] The Tee-Hit-Ton argued that they had "full proprietary ownership" in their lands or they had at least a recognized right to unrestricted possession, occupation, and use. In either case, the right would be compensable if taken. The United States, by contrast, denied the Tee-Hit-Ton any compensable interest. The solicitor maintained that if the Tee-Hit-Ton had any property interest at all, it was only "that of the right to the use of the land at the Government's will. . . ."[223] Congress, in other words, in having never "recognized" in the Tee-Hit-Ton any legal interest in the lands they occupied, could take those lands and was not responsible for providing any compensation. It was as if the Tee-Hit-Ton had never existed. Otherwise, how could their very presence not establish their rights to territory?

The Mask of "Permissive Occupancy"

Not surprisingly, Reed endorsed the United States' position. He focused his rationale on two aspects: (1) What constitutes "recognition"? and (2) What is "Indian title"? As for the question of recognition, Reed noted that this could be "disposed of shortly."[224] He indicated that when Congress "by treaty or other agreement" had stated that Indians may hold their lands "permanently," then the United States was required to pay compensation if there was a later taking. Reed cited as support several earlier Supreme Court cases including the 1937 *Shoshone Tribe of Indians v. United States* involving the Wind River Reservation. He threw out the ample evidence provided by the Tee-Hit-Ton's attorneys—evidence that had been accepted as convincing proof of recognition by the *Miller* Court in 1947—which had held that Indian title was compensable under the Fifth Amendment.

In discounting this explicit statutory evidence, Reed said that he could find "nothing to indicate any intention by Congress to grant to the Indians any permanent rights in the lands of Alaska occupied by them by *permission of Congress* [emphasis mine]."[225] This is a classic Reed statement. He had taken a congressionally recognized and vested tribal right—recognized also in *Worcester*, *Mitchel*, and elsewhere—and reduced it to a conditional occupation subject to the whims of the federal government. Since the Tee-Hit-Ton were living in Alaska before the federal government's presence, then they occupied the land under their own authority. By Reed's logic, however, the Tee-Hit-Ton could not have had a viable presence before the United States' arrival. Even if one accepts Reed's inaccurate assertion that the Alaskan natives occupied their land with Congress's "permission"—and the historical evidence would make such an acceptance impossible—this permission would itself be an acknowledgment of ownership.

Reed insisted that the Tee-Hit-Ton's evidence of recognized occupation showed nothing more than a "permissive occupation" and was not "the definite intention by congressional action or authority to accord legal rights. . . ."[226] As in *Shoshone*, with his misreading of the 1863 treaty,

Reed construed an intent and purpose in the organic and civil government act which they never had. These acts had nothing to do with the establishment of Indian reservations. The rights of the Alaskan natives were already understood as preexisting. Moreover, nothing had legally occurred that would represent a loss or reduction of their land rights. In other words, if a land cession treaty was a reduction of Indian land rights, then the Tee-Hit-Ton retained all their natural, political, and territorial rights since by not having entered into a treaty with Russia or the United States, they had not bargained any of those rights away.

For Reed, the Tee-Hit-Ton's nontreaty status guaranteeing their lands, combined with the 1946 Tongass Joint Resolution, was enough to disavow any enforceable property rights for the Tee-Hit-Ton. In Reed's opinion, the Tongass Act and Congress's general termination policy affirmed that Alaskan native groups had no territorial or natural resource rights that could withstand federal taking. The Court then moved to a surprising discussion of "Indian title." This section is so rife with historical inaccuracies, misstatements of fact, and misinterpretations of Supreme Court precedent, that an extended quotation is warranted:

> The nature of aboriginal Indian interest in land and the various rights as between the Indians and the United States dependent on such interest are far from novel as concerns our Indian inhabitants. It is well settled that in all the States of the Union the tribes who inhabited the lands of the States held claim to such lands after the coming of the white man, under what is sometimes termed original Indian title or permission from the whites to occupy. That description means mere possession not specifically recognized as ownership by Congress. After conquest they were permitted to occupy portions of territory over which they had previously exercised "sovereignty," as we use that term. This is not a property right but amounts to a right of occupancy which the sovereign grants and protects against intrusion by third parties but which right of occupancy may be terminated and such lands fully disposed of by the sovereign itself without any legally enforceable obligation to compensate the Indians. This position of the Indian has long been rationalized by the legal theory that discovery and conquest gave the conquerors sovereignty over and ownership of the lands thus obtained.[227]

This passage contains a multitude of errors that Reed argued without hesitation. First, Reed treated recognized original Indian title as synonymous with white "permission" to occupy, whereas most prior courts had held it to be equal to or the equivalent of fee-simple title. By contrast, the United States' "permission" is merely a gratuity bestowed or delegated by the federal government on tribes. Second, Reed presumed that all Indian groups had been *conquered*, thus erasing any prior rights they may have had to the land. This statement is also incorrect; as Marshall had previously noted in both *Johnson v. McIntosh* and *Worcester v. Georgia*, the notion of "conquest" was largely inapplicable to the tribal-federal relationship. If tribes had actually been conquered, the United States probably would not have felt compelled to negotiate the hundreds of treaties and agreements it entered into with tribes. Nor would the United States, based on those same documents, have paid out millions of dollars for Indian lands. President Truman stated in 1946 upon signing the ICC Act, "This bill makes perfectly clear what many men and women, here and abroad, have failed to recognize, that in our transactions with the Indian tribes we have at least since the Northwest Ordinance of 1787 set for ourselves the standard of fair and honorable dealings, pledging respect for all Indian property rights. Instead of confiscating Indian lands, we have purchased from the tribes that once owned this continent more than 90 percent of our public domain, paying them approximately 800 million dollars in the process."[228]

Tribes, in selling their lands, gave express permission to the United States to use the lands as they saw fit. The tribes retained their rights to reserved lands and retained some specific rights, like hunting and fishing, in ceded lands. As for tribes like the Tee-Hit-Ton, which had not sold their lands, a plausible argument can be made that they actually retained all their rights—political, property, and civil—since they had not ceded any of these away in a treaty.

Reed interjected the third factor in his judicial dismemberment of the aboriginal land rights of the Tee-Hit-Ton when he asserted that the "legal theory" of "discovery"—which he symbiotically linked to conquest—gave the United States complete sovereignty and ownership of the lands so acquired. Here, Reed quoted a long section directly from Marshall's *McIntosh* decision. In actuality, however, "discovery" is not so much a legal theory as it is a legal fiction which was later discredited by the Supreme Court in several cases.[229] Interestingly, Reed, in quoting Marshall, said that discovery gave the discovering nation the exclusive right to either purchase or conquer Indian title. Yet where was the "purchase" of the Tee-Hit-Ton lands and where was the conquest of the Tee-Hit-Ton people? These had not occurred.

Reed, having constructed a set of problematic arguments, completed this section by incorrectly stating, "No case in this Court has ever held that taking of Indian title or use by Congress required compensation."[230] He continued that "the American people [as if the Tee-Hit-Ton, individually, were not Americans] have compassion for the descendants of these Indians who were deprived of their homes and hunting grounds by the drive of civilization. They seek to have the Indians share the benefits of our society as citizens of this Nation. Generous provision has been willingly made to allow tribes to recover for wrongs, as a matter of grace, not because of legality."[231]

Reed was in error when he said that the Supreme Court had never held that a congressional taking of Indian title required compensation. The Court in *United States v. Alcea Band of Tillamooks*[232] had specifically addressed the same question: ". . . whether the Indians have a cause of action for compensation arising out of an involuntary taking of lands held by original Indian title."[233] While recognizing Congress's power to extinguish Indian title, the Court had said this "compels no conclusion that compensation need not be paid."[234] In the Court's opinion, "the Indians have more than a merely moral claim for compensation and [a] contrary decision would ignore the plain import of traditional methods of extinguishing original Indian title."[235] In *Tillamooks*, the Court had also gone to great lengths to show that there was no clear distinction between "original Indian title" and so-called recognized Indian title. In fact, Justice Frederick Vinson, writing for the majority, had said that both the recent and the "older cases explaining and giving substance to the Indian right of occupancy contain no suggestion that only 'recognized' Indian title was being considered. Indeed, *the inference is quite otherwise.*"[236]

Shortly after *Tillamooks* was announced, Felix S. Cohen wrote that with this case "the last large gap in the doctrine of original Indian title [has been] filled. . . ."[237] "The *Alcea* case," Cohen stated, "gives the final coup de grace to what has been called the 'menagerie' theory of Indian title, the theory that Indians are less human and that their relation to their lands is not the human relation of ownership but rather something similar to the relation that animals bear to the areas in which they may be temporarily confined."[238] Justice Reed, joined by Wiley Rutledge and Harold Burton, dissented in *Tillamooks* and emphasized the very menagerie theory that Cohen thought had been displaced. Reed's arguments were similar to those he used in *Tee-Hit-Ton:* the Indians had been discovered and conquered by "Christian nations" which gave them sovereignty over all the discovered lands. Reed went so far in his dissent as to analogize Indians exercising aboriginal rights of occupancy with "paleface squatters on public lands without compensable rights if they are evicted."[239]

Reed's dissenting attitude in 1946 had now become the majority's view nine years later in *Tee-Hit-Ton*. In *Tee-Hit-Ton* Reed was obliged to distinguish the *Tillamooks* decision and the Ninth Circuit Court of Appeals case *Miller v. United States* (1947), which had used the *Tillamooks* precedent to hold that Indian title was indeed compensable under the Fifth Amendment. He did so first by stating that *Tillamooks* had only allowed financial recovery because of a congressional jurisdictional act which had permitted payments.

Second, he noted that under the *Tillamooks* decision, the case was remanded back to the Court of Claims to determine the amount of compensation. The Claims Court held that the Tillamook were entitled to an amount based on the value of the lands at the time of their taking, 1855, plus interest from that date. However, in a per curiam decision in 1951, *United States v. Tillamooks*, the Supreme Court unanimously held that the band was not entitled to interest because the congressional taking was not a Fifth Amendment taking.

Third, Reed drew from yet another Supreme Court decision, *Hynes v. Grimes Packing Company*,[240] where the Court, in a footnote, disagreed with the holding in *Miller* and said that they had wrongly relied on *Tillamooks* as authority. "That opinion," the *Hynes* Court held, "does not hold the Indian right of occupancy compensable without specific legislative direction to make payment."[241]

Demography and Economy

In two telling footnotes to *Tee-Hit-Ton*, Reed showed how demography and financial figures may be used to dismantle Indian rights. First, in describing *Hynes*'s interpretation of *Miller*, Reed said a major reason for the *Hynes* ruling was that the Congress could not have intended to authorize the Department of the Interior to include "an important and valuable fishing area . . . in a permanent reservation for an Indian population of 57 eligible voters."[242] In the next footnote, Reed discussed dollar amounts. He said that in *Tillamooks*, the value of the land was estimated at 3 million dollars, while the interest would have amounted to 14 million dollars. Reed accepted the government's argument that if Indian title were to be compensable without specific authorizing congressional legislation, there would be pending claims "under the jurisdictional act aggregating 9,000,000,000 dollars."[243]

Reed was unable, however, to avoid the fact that the Tillamook were still entitled to recovery based on their aboriginal title. He skirted this and the discussion which focused on the nondistinction between "recognized" and "original" Indian title and instead emphasized that the Tillamook could not recover interest, and that Congress had allowed for recovery under a jurisdictional act. While both of these later statements are undeniably true, they do not diminish the reality that the Tillamook's aboriginal land rights had received judicial approval.

Communal Ownership: An Oxymoron?

In Reed's opinion, aboriginal land title of an unrecognized character was no title whatsoever. "This was true," said Reed, "not because an Indian or an Indian tribe has no standing to sue or because the United States has not consented to be sued . . . but because Indian occupation of land without government recognition of ownership creates no rights against taking or extinction by the United States protected by the Fifth Amendment or any other principle of law." [244] Reed had fabricated such a broad rule that under it, the Alaskan native groups, and by extension all other tribes without explicit treaty guarantees, had no property rights whatsoever. Earlier it had been a Fifth Amendment question; Reed expanded it to an unlimited realm by noting that no "other principle of law" could protect them either.

Not content with this unprecedented assault on Indian property rights, Reed attempted to justify his opinion with a sociocultural assessment of the Tee-Hit-Ton. In Reed's view, the reality that the Tee-Hit-Ton band held the land communally and not individually was enough to doom them. "Tribal" claims to lands, maintained Reed, in contrast to individual property claims, represent more "a claim of sovereignty than of ownership." [245] Using the same rationale he had used to defeat the Shoshone claims, Reed contended that "the Tee-Hit-Ton were in a hunting and fishing stage of civilization, with shelters fitted to their environment, and claims . . . identified territory for these activities as well as the gathering of wild products of the earth." [246] Although the tribe's attorneys had sought to distinguish the Tee-Hit-Ton from tribes in the lower forty-eight states, Reed insisted that the tribe's "use of its lands was like the use of the nomadic tribes of the State's Indians." This is in interesting contrast to his earlier statements that from a legal and political standpoint the Tee-Hit-Ton were entirely different from the tribes of the "lower forty-eight."

Again, the Court was acting less as a court of a law and more as an anthropological assessment team. Somehow, the Tee-Hit-Ton's subsistence lifestyle was interpreted in a way that diminished their legal and property rights. Reed was denying the Tee-Hit-Ton their property rights based on their alleged "stage of evolution."

In an extended footnote, Reed proposed the Pueblo Indians as the lone exception to the general "nomadic" tribal mode he had attributed to Indians in general. He contrasted the Pueblo's so-called "sedentary agricultural and pastoral life" with that of the "nomadic" Alaskan tribal communities.[247] In addition to the Pueblo's allegedly stronger "cultural" claims to property, Reed indicated that their land claims were also based upon "stronger legal and historical basis than the Tlingits."[248] This is an interesting comparison in that Reed employed the same tactic used by his nineteenth-century predecessor Chief Justice Roger Taney, who in the pivotal 1857 *Dred Scott* decision engaged in a selective and distorted comparison of blacks and Indians in a way which used Indian culture and political status as a foil of superiority to justify treating African Americans as inferior beings. It is important to recall that just eleven years before *Dred Scott*, Justice Taney and the Court in *U.S. v. Rogers* had shown virtually no respect for tribal culture and sovereignty when rendering a decision that seriously undermined the rights of Indian tribes. The Court, in other words, is sometimes pleased to use what we will call the mask of selective and distorted comparison in which the justices, both individually and as a collective body, carefully seek to maintain the legitimacy of their rulings by appearing not to denounce all minorities or disempowered peoples, only those who do not, for the purposes of the case at hand, meet the Court's particular standards of what it determines is just and fair.

In closing, Reed inaccurately announced that "the line of cases adjudicating Indian rights on American soil leads to the conclusion that Indian occupancy, not specifically recognized as ownership by action authorized by Congress, may be extinguished by the Government without compensation."[249] It is significant that Reed neglected to name the cases in this "line." In his footnote to this quote, he cited several reports by executive agencies—Interior, Agriculture, and Justice—the same agencies which in the *Shoshone* case had provided solid documentary evidence affirming Shoshone land boundaries. In that case, though, Reed had called the evidence "inferential," "secondary," and "not authoritative." Continuing, and in what has become one of the most repeated passages of any Indian Supreme Court case, Reed made a staggering announcement:

Every American schoolboy knows that the savage tribes of this continent were deprived of their ancestral ranges by force and that, even
when the Indians ceded millions of acres by treaty in return for blan-
kets, food, and trinkets, it was not a sale but the conquerors' will that
deprived them of their land.[250]

Doubtless this statement is one of the most glaring misrepresenta-
tions of fact ever uttered by a Supreme Court justice. There is little in
the historical record to corroborate what Reed said here; federal Indian policy and the history of treatymaking give ample evidence to the
contrary. Reed quoted from Justice Jackson's concurrence in the *Shoshone* case where Jackson had said that while the Shoshone had no *legal*
treaty rights to land, they had certain *moral* rights. But Reed was firmly
in concurrence with the prevailing economic developmental sentiment
in Washington and in the Territory of Alaska, notwithstanding the extant aboriginal interests and property claims of the Alaskan Natives.
Reed believed that indigenous claims to territory, which lacked any substantive merit anyway, could not be allowed to hinder the economic
growth of the nation or the Alaskan Territory, and that the government
was only obliged—but certainly not obligated—to make some "congressional contributions," that is, in kind rather than in dollars, for indigenous lands taken. There was, in Reed's view, no compelling obligation on the part of the government to pay the Alaskan Natives for their
homeland.[251] American expansion in Alaska would not be held up by a
small band of culturally backward, treatyless natives.

"Our conclusion," said Reed, "does not uphold harshness as against
tenderness toward the Indians, but it leaves it with Congress, where it
belongs, the policy of Indian gratuities for the termination of Indian
occupancy of Government-owned land rather than making compensation for its value a rigid constitutional principle."[252] This is a definitive
passage. Reed combined the political question doctrine with American
technical and legal supremacy and moralism, and with Indian tenancy-
at-will, to crush aboriginal property rights. The passage harks back to
Johnson v. McIntosh and continues to represent a viable threat to the
property of all indigenous peoples. The gist of *Tee-Hit-Ton* was stark
and ominous—"Native Americans with treaties held certain privileges
that may or may not be retained over time; tribes without treaties simply had no legal footing. In effect, all tribes, even those with treaties,
were subject to termination."[253] The combination of the *Lone Wolf*

precedent—Indian treaty–defined property rights can be confiscated—and the *Tee-Hit-Ton* precedent—Indian aboriginal (nontreaty) property rights can be confiscated—left tribes contemplating their extraconstitutional standing, even when the members allegedly had constitutional rights as American citizens.

JUSTICE DOUGLAS'S DISSENT

Joined by Chief Justice Earl Warren and Justice Felix Frankfurter, Justice William Douglas authored a dissent. Even the dissent agreed that unrecognized aboriginal title was not protected by the Fifth Amendment; rather, Douglas asserted that the Tee-Hit-Ton held recognized title under the Alaskan Organic Act of 1884. Section 8 of that Act stated that the Indians "shall not be disturbed in the possession of any lands actually in their use or occupation or now claimed by them."[254] This excerpt, along with the congressional debate about the 1884 act, indicates that it was Congress's intention to "protect to the fullest extent all the rights of the Indians in Alaska and of any residents who had settled there," while at the same time allowing for the development of mineral resources by Euro-American miners.

After analyzing congressional intent surrounding Alaska's admission as a territory, Douglas said, "The conclusion seems clear that Congress in the 1884 Act recognized the claims of these Indians to their Alaskan lands."[255] The dissent refused to speculate on precisely what was meant by the Indian right of "use and occupancy." They preferred to let the Court of Claims make that determination. It was obvious, however, to the minority that the 1884 Act entailed a distinct recognition of some sort of title.

THE AFTERMATH

In 1980, Nell J. Newton published a splendid analysis of the *Tee-Hit-Ton* decision pointing out that this opinion had stood for twenty-five years without serious scrutiny. She urged reexamination for three reasons: (1) because it implicitly authorized federal confiscation of Indian lands, including reservation land established by executive order or treaty—which posed a grave threat to many Indians; (2) because it affirmed virtually unlimited congressional power to confiscate Indian land without due process or just compensation, thus creating a fear of reprisal in many tribes who were reluctant to file claims against the United States; and (3) because the case established a construct of law that if left unbridled, could be used to justify other arbitrary congressional actions in "derogation of Indian tribal rights."[256]

This case had sent shock waves throughout Indian country, particularly to the many tribes with claims pending before the ICC, many of which were based on aboriginal title. Implicitly, Reed had said that all cases involving Indian title would first have to be recognized by Congress before they could be submitted to the judicial process. More specifically, if the *Tee-Hit-Ton* precedent were strictly applied to the claims pending before the ICC, it was questioned "whether or not the decision might lead to exclusion of all cases of Indian title from the general jurisdiction of the commission."[257] However, in a case which had begun in the ICC in 1953, *Otoe and Missouria Tribe of Indians v. United States,* the ICC recognized the government's liability under Indian title. That decision was appealed to the Court of Claims in 1955 after *Tee-Hit-Ton* had been decided.[258] The Court of Claims held that Indians could indeed pursue claims in the Indian Claims Commission using original title or aboriginal title. Congress, said the Court of Claims, in enacting the general jurisdictional act—the ICC—had fulfilled provisions apparently lacking in the *Tee-Hit-Ton* case. The Supreme Court subsequently declined to review the case. This was an important, if narrow and constrained victory, however, since tribes basing their claims on aboriginal title still had to meet a number of Court-defined criteria.[259]

Despite the Tee-Hit-Ton attorneys' call for a rehearing on the grounds that "this Court's judgment rests upon an opinion which shows on its face complete misconception of the record, studied avoidance of even the slightest consideration of the chief proposition relied upon—and argued *in extenso*—by petitioner, utter ignoring of basic principles established by many decisions of this Court, and similar ignoring of the recognized principles of international law,"[260] the decision was not reexamined and remains a legal fixture. Finally, aside from rejecting the Fifth Amendment constitutional rights of over 35,000 Alaskan natives to lands they had inhabited for thousands of years, the case effectively placed the issue of final settlement of Alaskan natives' general land claims at the doors of Congress. Congress would not respond until 1971 with the enactment of the Alaskan Native Claims Settlement Act.[261]

CHAPTER 5

The Era of Judicial Backlash and Land Claims

The period from the end of the termination years in the 1960s to the self-determination era of the 1970s represented a pivotal time in tribal-federal relations. It was, by most accounts, an era when tribes and their members won a series of important political and legal victories in their efforts to reclaim a measure of self-determination.[1]

Many of these victories were a result of the legal and political activism exhibited by the tribes—from the Alcatraz occupation in 1969 to the 1972 Trail of Broken Treaties, to the 1973 occupation of Wounded Knee on the Pine Ridge Indian Reservation, to the untold fish-ins, marches, demonstrations, and boycotts. This indigenous activism, however, combined with the political and legal victories tribes had wrested from the Executive Branch,[2] Congress,[3] and the Court,[4] sufficed to provoke a sizable backlash among disaffected non-Indians.

This backlash was spearheaded by several non-Indian organizations, a number of state officials, and some members of Congress from states where tribes were gaining positive legislative and judicial results. These tribal victories included the enactment of federal laws which affirmed long-standing treaty rights, upheld Indian claims to lands which had been illegally purchased or simply appropriated, and extended federal protection of historically disregarded Indian civil rights.[5] The backlash, as it unfolded, gave voice to an almost sinister mood of anger and resentment. It advocated the abrogation of Indian treaties, the abolition of the Bureau of Indian Affairs, the termination of the federal trust relationship, the extinguishment of Indian hunting and treaty rights; and it tried to subject Indians to state and even local fish and game regulations.[6]

The two cases examined in this chapter, *Oliphant v. Suquamish Indian Tribe* (1978) and *United States v. Sioux Nation of Indians* (1980), are powerful cases which affected tribes in very different ways. *Oliphant*, in the words of a pair of scholars,[7] moved definitively "in the direction of tribal termination" by articulating a dramatically diminished definition of tribal sovereignty, while *Sioux Nation* is the only case in this study which can be termed a legal victory for Indians, since it upheld the federal government's obligation to compensate the Sioux Nation for the illegal taking of the Black Hills in 1877. It is not a definitive tribal victory, as the analysis will show, because the decision perpetuates and reinforces a host of legal masks and is steeped in a legal consciousness that can only frustrate tribes in their efforts to secure full justice.

Oliphant v. Suquamish Indian Tribe

THE JUDICIAL SHEARING OF A TRIBAL RIGHT

By the early 1970s, the nominally operative, if infrequently used, concept in federal Indian policy was that of Indian self-determination. Self-determination, for both tribes and individual Indians, was conceived as the linchpin doctrine of a new federal policy aimed at strengthening the concept of tribal self-governance while reinforcing the so-called trust relationship between tribes and the federal government.[8] The concept of self-determination was first articulated by President Nixon when he stressed in his Indian policy statement "self-determination without termination."[9] The term was given legislative substance on January 4, 1975, with the enactment of the Indian Self-Determination and Education Assistance Act.[10] This law authorized the secretary of the interior and the secretary of health, education, and welfare to contract with Indian tribal organizations for tribal operations and the administration of specified federally funded programs administered by these agencies.

The act was designed to provide "an orderly transition from Federal domination of programs for and services to Indians to effective and meaningful participation by the Indian people in the planning, conduct, and administration of those programs and services."[11] To its credit, the act permitted tribes, not the Bureau of Indian Affairs, to decide whether they wished to participate in a given program. Although a number of veteran observers of Indian affairs noted that "the statute was a thinly disguised version of Collier's original program for the tribes in 1934," it was at least a start in a more acceptable direction.[12]

Two days before the act was passed, the Senate had, by Joint Resolution 133 and at the behest of Senator James Abourezk (D., South Dakota), established the American Indian Policy Review Commission. Congress, declaring it both "timely and essential," mandated this two-year, eleven-member commission to reassess the direction of federal Indian policy and to provide legislative recommendations. The commission was to conduct a "comprehensive review of the historical and legal developments underlying the Indians' unique relationship with the Federal Government in order to determine the nature and scope of necessary revisions in the formulation of policies and programs for the benefit of Indians."[13] This was to be a bipartisan and interracial (Indian and non-Indian) commission, with six members from Congress and five slots reserved for Indians.

The commission was directed to appoint investigative task forces to study special problem areas; eleven task forces were formed, staffed mostly by Indians. They worked in areas ranging from trust responsibilities and tribal governments to federal administration and the structure of Indian affairs, issues of intragovernmental development, urban and rural nonreservation Indians, and terminated and nonrecognized tribes. It was hoped that by the end of the two-year period a "blue print for future Indian policy" would be produced.[14] Instead, what emerged were 206 recommendations, "which resembled a bureaucratic shopping list rather than a high-level investigation. No philosophical overview or ideology emerged in spite of a continuous recital of the misdeeds of the federal government and the assertion of the ultimate sovereignty of tribes."[15] The final report was fragmented and highly politicized. As a result, the vice-chairman of the commission, Representative Lloyd Meeds (D., Washington) with the assistance of Frederick Martone and Neil Wake, submitted an animated dissent. They argued that the majority report, "hastily presented and hastily prepared," was the "product of one-sided advocacy in favor of American Indian tribes" and that "the interest of the United States, the States, and non-Indian citizens, if considered at all, were largely ignored."[16]

Meeds's attack on the majority's recommendations covered a wide range of areas: tribal self-government, jurisdiction, the United States' legal obligation to tribes, and sovereign immunity, among others. Meeds's comments regarding tribal sovereignty and the tribe's jurisdictional authority over non-Indians are crucial to a discussion of *Oliphant* because they foreshadow not only *Oliphant* but many subsequent Supreme Court opinions. In Meeds's opinion, tribes were not sovereign in the same sense that the United States or the individual states were. "The blunt fact of the matter," said Meeds, "is that American Indian tribes are not a third set of governments in the American federal system. They are not sovereign. The Congress of the United States has permitted them to be self-governing entities but not entities which would govern others."[17] It then followed, according to Meeds's theory, that if tribes were not sovereign then they could not have and "should not have" power over non-Indians or their property, "except in the narrowest circumstances." [18]

Meeds then discussed the recent Federal Court of Appeals case, *Oliphant v. Schlie*.[19] That decision held that tribes could prosecute non-Indians in tribal Courts for criminal violations occurring in Indian country. The Supreme Court had already granted certiorari, and Meeds was no doubt anxious to send a message to that body urging a more constricted interpretation of tribal sovereignty and the tribes' power of governance over non-Indians. Meeds asserted that the federal court's decision in *Oliphant* "invert[ed] the proper analysis and ignore[d] history." [20] Without explaining what history was ignored, or exactly how the alleged inversion had transpired, Meeds stated that the dissent of District Judge Anthony Kennedy was more correct because it pointed out that tribal jurisdiction over such non-Indian individuals "has generally not been asserted and that the lack of legislation on this point reflects a Congressional assumption that there was no such tribal jurisdiction. . . ." [21] "The *Oliphant* case," insisted Meeds, "does not dispose of the question, and even if it is upheld by the United States Supreme Court, the Congress must still decide whether Indian power over non-Indians is wise." [22] Meeds did not have to wait long to hear the Supreme Court's answer. It was a ruling he must have found particularly comforting.

Factually, *Oliphant* is a most interesting case. The Suquamish were a very small tribe[23] at the time of the decision—their homeland, with about 43 enrolled tribal members (19 adults and 24 minors), constituting less than 1.7 percent of the reservation population, who occupied only 37 percent of the land. The non-Indian population, by contrast, was nearly 3,000, or 98.3 percent, who owned in fee simple the remaining 63 percent of the 7,278 acres in the Suquamish Port Madison Reservation.

The Port Madison Reservation, like most others, had been allotted. Over time, non-Indians secured title to many Indian allotments by purchase through the secretary of the interior, through congressional laws which allowed the sale of Indian allotments in heirship, or through sales by individual Indians after trust restrictions had been lifted. Interestingly, the Suquamish tribe, unlike many others, did not grant their consent to non-Indian homesteading of unallotted or "surplus" lands within their reservation.[24]

HISTORICAL BACKGROUND

The Port Madison Indian Reservation is located in Kitsap County, Washington. The reservation was established through the treaty of Point Elliot[25] in 1855, and the tribe was organized under the Indian Reorganization Act in 1934. Later they established a tribal constitution and a set of bylaws which were approved by the secretary of the interior on July 2, 1966.[26] The tribe holds an annual "Chief Seattle Days" celebration, which is attended by thousands of people. This ceremonial had grown tremendously by the early 1970s, and with this growth there was a sharp increase in crimes associated with these large social events. The tribe had made several requests of state, county, and federal law-enforcement officials for manpower assistance to deal with these massive crowds. "The tribe was told that it would have to provide its own law enforcement out of tribal funds and with tribal personnel."[27] The newly instituted Suquamish Tribal Court, which had been set up in 1973, proceeded to develop a justice and law-enforcement program on the reservation by enacting a comprehensive law and order code. The law and order code covered a variety of offenses, from addiction to weapons. The tribe's right to exercise such governmental authority was recognized by the Department of the Interior, and the Bureau of Indian Affairs.[20]

During the Chief Seattle celebration on August 19, 1973, Mark David Oliphant, a Port Madison resident and non-Indian, was arrested by tribal police and charged with assault and battery. Oliphant was arraigned in Suquamish Tribal Court by tribal judges Grace Duggan and Cecilia M. Hawk and then transported off the reservation to the Bremerton city jail on August 24. By agreement with the Bureau of Indian Affairs, Bremerton serves as a holding facility for the tribal court. Oliphant was later released on his own recognizance.

The other petitioner in the case, Daniel B. Belgarde, also a non-Indian resident of the reservation, was arrested a year later on October 12, 1974, by tribal authorities after a high speed chase on reservation roads. The chase ended when Belgarde's vehicle (in which Oliphant happened to be a passenger) rammed into a tribal police car. Belgarde was charged with reckless driving in violation of section 59, chapter 3 of the Suquamish Tribal Law and Order Code. He was placed in jail in the off-reservation city of Port Angeles, Washington, which, like Bremerton, also had a contract with the tribe and the Bureau of Indian Affairs to hold criminal defendants. After posting bond, Belgarde appeared before the

Suquamish Tribal Court for arraignment and was charged with reckless driving and damaging tribal property.

Both Oliphant and Belgarde applied for a writ of habeas corpus in the United States District Court for the Western District of Washington. They based their application for the writ on the grounds that the Suquamish Indian tribal court lacked criminal jurisdiction over non-Indians committing crimes against Indians on reservation land held in trust by the United States for the benefit of the tribe. In separate proceedings, District Judge Morril E. Sharp denied each of the petitions. Sharp maintained that the tribe's law and order code was a valid expression of Suquamish sovereignty: a sovereignty which had been recognized "at all times" by the Interior Department, the Congress, and the courts. "So long," said Sharp, "as a complete and independent sovereignty of an Indian tribe was recognized, its criminal jurisdiction, no less than its civil jurisdiction was that of any governing power."[29] Judge Sharp stressed that since the Suquamish tribe clearly had jurisdiction over both the person and subject matter, and since Oliphant had "been afforded all the protection available to him under the Indian Civil Rights Act," then the application for a writ had to be denied.[30]

Oliphant appealed to the 9th Circuit Court of Appeals,[31] which on August 24, 1976, affirmed the Suquamish tribe's jurisdiction over non-Indians by a 2–1 margin.[32] Judge Ben C. Duniway, writing for the majority, used elegant and historically, legally, and politically accurate data to show convincingly that American Indian tribes, as governments, had the right to protect the peace and safety of their citizens by prosecuting persons—regardless of their race—who voluntarily entered the territorial jurisdiction of that government and committed punishable offenses. Duniway was well aware that he was dealing with an issue of major importance. "This case," he said, "involves a question of Indian law which has been unresolved since it first arose almost a century ago: what is the jurisdiction of an Indian tribe over non-Indians who commit crimes while on Indian tribal land within the boundaries of the reservation?"[33]

Oliphant's primary argument in his appeal was that the Suquamish lacked such jurisdiction because Congress had never bestowed that power upon the tribe. Duniway, however, shredded that point. Drawing from informed federal Indian policy directives, prior congressional statutes, and Supreme Court Indian case law principles, Duniway said of Oliphant's contention: "This misstates the problem. The proper approach to the question of tribal criminal jurisdiction is to ask 'first, what the original sovereign powers of the tribes were and, then, how far and in what respects these powers have been limited.'"[34] More emphatically, Duniway declared that Judge Kennedy's "dissenting opinion similarly misstates the problem."[35] "The question," noted Duniway, "is not whether Congress has conferred jurisdiction upon the tribe. The tribe, before it was conquered, had jurisdiction, as any independent nation does. The question therefore is, did Congress (or a treaty) take that jurisdiction away? The dissent points to no action by the Congress, and no treaty language, depriving the tribe of jurisdiction."[36]

Duniway was referring to the Reserved Rights doctrine discussed in the previous chapter. This doctrine is a political understanding that has been recognized in federal policies and laws dating back to the 1787 Northwest Ordinance. It is an understanding in which the tribes' preconstitutional existence and extraconstitutional standing directly affirm their sovereign status, and any rights they did not specifically cede in their treaties or agreements with the United States they retain to themselves.

Duniway, citing directly from the foundational cases *Cherokee Nation v. Georgia* (1831), *Worcester v. Georgia* (1832), and more recent cases like *McClanahan v. Arizona State Tax Commission* (1973), said that while it was true that tribes had lost some layers of their preexisting sovereignty through military defeats or direct Congressional action, "[s]urely the power to preserve order on the reservation, when necessary by punishing those who violate tribal law is a sine qua non of the sovereignty that the Suquamish originally possessed."[37] The question then becomes one of trying to ascertain whether any relevant treaties or congressional acts have "withdrawn" from the Suquamish their power to punish non-Indians.

After critical review of both the Suquamish Treaty of Point Elliot[38] and their bilateral agreement with the United States in 1905,[39] of the pertinent federal statutes, and finally of whether the tribe's actions constituted any interference with federal policies, Judge Duniway concluded that nothing in the prevailing law or federal policies denied the Suquamish this power. On the contrary, "[w]ithout the exercise of jurisdiction by the Tribe and its courts, there could have been no law enforcement whatsoever on the Reservation during this major gathering which clearly created a potentially dangerous situation with regard to law enforcement. Public safety is an underpinning of a political entity."[40]

Circuit Judge Anthony Kennedy, who would become a Supreme Court justice in 1988, wrote a dissent that would largely form the contextual framework for the Supreme Court opinion involving criminal jurisdiction. Kennedy's contention focused on what powers had been delegated to tribes by the United States. In Kennedy's view, Congress had never expressly granted to tribes the power to try non-Indians, therefore they clearly lacked such authority. The assumption by Kennedy that tribes were without criminal jurisdiction because it was not one of the delegated rights that he thought tribes were capable of exercising was diametrically opposed by Duniway, who assumed that tribes did have powers such as criminal jurisdiction, because it was one of their reserved rights not ceded away. *Oliphant* represents one of the legal/ideological/political dichotomies—*delegated* versus *reserved*—that precludes any consistently accurate articulation of Indian rights under the western legal paradigm. Other such dichotomous pairs include *implied repeals* versus *explicit repeals, independent/semi-independent tribal status* versus *dependent tribal status*, and *tribes as nonincorporated polities* versus *tribes as incorporated polities.* Since justices, depending on their proclivities, pick and choose among these, it is virtually impossible, notwithstanding the actual historical record and treaty-based relationship, for tribes to receive a consistent interpretation of their actual political legal standing vis-à-vis the states and the federal government.

ORAL ARGUMENTS BEFORE THE SUPREME COURT

Philip P. Malone, attorney for Oliphant and Belgarde, petitioned for a writ of certiorari on November 22, 1976. Malone's major arguments were both racial and demographic. In his petition he emphasized the gross disparity in Indian versus non-Indian population and in the ownership of land on the reservation. As he noted: the 9th Circuit Court's decision "results in sovereign jurisdiction and authority of an Indian tribe on Indian reservations over criminal offenses of non-Indians where the majority of the population and the land is not Indian . . . causing conflict in the application and enforcement of criminal laws and state and local governments as from laws of the Indian tribe in the application to non-Indian."[41]

The tribe's attorneys, in an effort to block the Court's granting of certiorari, argued contrarily that the issue was simply whether a federally recognized "local government" had the right to protect its citizens. As they said: "That the government is an Indian tribe, and the alleged perpetrators are non-Indians, cannot change the nature of the case into one compelling Supreme Court review."[42] They astutely pointed out that Oliphant and Belgarde were not claiming violation of their rights to due process. "Rather," they pointed out, "petitioner [Oliphant] takes the novel position that since his race differs from that of the government controlling the land on which he committed his offense, he is immune from prosecution by that government."[43] Furthermore, the tribe's lawyers tried to distinguish the Suquamish demographic situation from that of other tribes. They argued that the tribe was not claiming exclusive jurisdiction but maintained that the jurisdiction was "concurrent with any other operative criminal jurisdiction—whether federal or state."[44]

Neither of these very pertinent caveats, however, was to be accorded much respect by the Rehnquist-led majority. The Supreme Court granted the writ on June 13, 1977, and by the time the Court heard oral arguments on January 8, 1978,[45] it was evident that a tremendous chasm existed between the Court and the Suquamish. It was also evident by the justices' questioning of both attorneys that even the liberal justices (Thurgood Marshall and Harry Blackmun—William Brennan did not participate) were inclined to support Oliphant's position rather than the tribe's. For example, note the tone of the following interchange between Justice Marshall and Barry D. Ernstoff, lead attorney for the Suquamish:

> [Marshall] The fundamental difference between you and your opponent is, who has the burden of proof with Congress, as I understand it. Your opponents say that unless Congress has conferred jurisdiction on the Indian tribe they do not have it and you say, unless Congress has taken it away, they do have it.[46]
>
> [Ernstoff] I think that is—
>
> [Marshall] And I do not see how this rapport really moves the ball one way or the other.
>
> [Ernstoff] It does not, one hopes that legislation will come for this . . . which takes a great deal of time and a lot of discussion . . . [a political solution, he also said] . . . is a much better solution than this Court having to deal with the problem. . . .
>
> [Marshall] But this case is here and now and not five years from now. . . . That all could have been handled *by not arresting these men.*
>
> [Ernstoff] That brings up the problem of the facts, Mr. Justice Marshall.[47] (emphasis mine)

One senses that Justice Marshall, who usually sided with tribes, felt that the Suquamish may have been too hasty in wanting to flex their newly resuscitated political clout and had taken on more than they could practically deal with. Yet another exchange, this one involving the U.S. Solicitor H. Bartow Farr III, who had filed an amicus in support of the Suquamish position, shows how strong judicial sentiment was against the tribal stance on their reserved criminal jurisdiction:

[Farr] First, at the heart of our submission and directly opposed to the position taken by Petitioners in the State of Washington, is the principle that the Indian tribes do not depend upon the United States for the creation of their powers of government. These powers instead are derived from an inherent sovereignty that antedates the European settlement of the United States and indeed, the formation of the United States itself. We do not depend on those [treaties, statutes, or the Constitution for tribal sovereignty]. We believe that the sovereignty antedates all of that and in fact, the reason that Congress did not pass statutes, for example, creating the sovereignty of the tribes.

[A Justice] And you suggest that we should just assume to recognize that?

[Farr] I believe that the Court has recognized it before and should again, yes sir.

[Justice] Well, even if we buy that position one hundred percent, the question would still remain whether or not that historic sovereignty included the power to try and convict non-tribal members of criminal offenses in violation of tribal law and certainly historically, before the white man got here, it did not, by hypothesis.[48]

This last statement, that "by hypothesis" Indians lacked criminal jurisdiction over whites "before the white man got here," is an excellent example of judiciary probing for a rationale, in this case a hypothetical situation with disputable content, on which to deny tribal jurisdiction over non-Indians.

Farr, under intense questioning, weakened his own and, by extension, the Suquamish standing by positing that tribes, unlike the federal government or the states, had only a limited sovereignty. This meek assertion was immediately confronted by another justice who asserted: "Well, it leaves it open, does it not? I mean, you concede that it is not a full sovereignty—as indeed, you must." Farr agreed: "We do concede that it is not a full sovereignty." The justice then said: "And the question is, then does it include, as I say, the power to try and convict and punish either non-members of the tribe or non-Indians?" Farr lamely retorted, "That is right. I mean, I think that is a question which the Court has to decide in this case."[49]

The tribe's attorney, Barry Ernstoff, also had problems trying to convince the justices of the Suquamish's right to exercise criminal jurisdiction over non-Indians. This was made even more difficult because Ernstoff, like Farr, also surrendered in part on the fundamental issue of tribal sovereignty. After querying by a justice who maintained that while tribes possessed some attributes of sovereignty, they clearly did not possess "all attributes of sovereignty," Ernstoff acquiesced: "That is correct. Most attributes, what we call real sovereignty, have been given up by Indian tribes. There is no question about it." [50] He quickly recovered, though, and asserted that the doctrine of retained sovereignty was nonetheless valid. "I am arguing," said Ernstoff, "that the Court's analysis under those cases that Indian tribes must retain whatever it was they were except that which was expressly taken away by Congress, by treaty, or, in the analysis of this Court, has to be viable because if it is not, then Indian tribes really possess almost no power." [51]

Some of the justices continued to insist, however, that Ernstoff needed to point to some congressional delegation or another direct affirmation of the tribe's right to exercise criminal jurisdiction over non-Indians. The following exchange illustrates the frustrated position the tribe had been placed in of being obliged to prove their case for the exercise of jurisdiction over non-Indians with nonexistent legislation or litigation.

[Justice] Well, what do you have—what do you point to?

[Ernstoff] I point to *Mazurie* [*United States v. Mazurie*] which talks about tribes having independent authority to some extent over these matters.

[Justice] What do you point to other than an opinion of this Court?

[Ernstoff] It is impossible to point—

[Justice] Then actually, you do not have anything.

[Ernstoff] The answer is that Congress has never—

[Justice] The answer is, you do not have anything.

[Ernstoff] That is correct because, your honor, it is very difficult to prove a negative. Congress has never enacted a statute giving a Tribe power and this Court has recognized the power, how can I point to a statute which gave the Tribe that power? All I can point to is this Court's analysis of the fact that one does not need a statute or a treaty in order to determine that there is a power. [52]

By contrast, the questions asked of Oliphant's attorneys, Philip P. Malone and Slade Gordon, centered more on clarification of facts, such as the size and composition of the Suquamish Court system, its jail facilities, etc. Malone then went to the heart of the matter and raised what would be one of the definitive issues—the nonrepresentation of non-Indians in Suquamish political affairs.

> My clients, and a number of non-Indians, I believe, have no immediate interest in voting in the Suquamish General Council. Their immediate interest is to be free from the tribal laws and their enforcement promulgated without their consent. They do not want to be subject to independent tribal powers over which they have no control except with resort to the judiciary but if they may not be left alone, if they are to be subject to the tribal criminal code, then the best choice would be that they would have the right to vote which I believe and argue that they have under the Constitution. This would mean, in effect, if non-Indians were entitled to vote, the very purpose of the claimed powers here of self-determination of tribes would end on such reservations as the Port Madison Indian Reservation. But if a choice had to be made for their freedom, they would desire the choice and power and ability to vote.[53]

A justice then raised a crucial issue: "The effect would be quite different in the Port Madison Reservation on the one hand, which your client came into contact with, and a reservation like the Navajo reservation, which is 20,000 square miles, largely populated with Indians, would it not?"[54] Malone said it would be "startlingly different." The justice then asked Malone "whether whatever principles are forthcoming in this case you feel should apply to all Indian reservations." Malone, sensing he had an opportunity to constrict all tribes in an exercise of sovereignty, unhesitatingly answered, "yes." Neither the Suquamish delegation nor any of the other tribes who had filed amicus curiae briefs could have predicted the scope of the decision that ensued.

MASKING WITHIN THE DECISION: THE OPINION

In a 6–2 decision (Brennan did not participate), the Supreme Court overturned the 9th Circuit Court of Appeals case and held that tribes without an express congressional delegation of power via treaty or congressional act were precluded from trying non-Indians who had committed crimes within their reservations. This result, standing alone, was a crushing, if not altogether surprising, blow to the Suquamish tribe, considering the unique demographic makeup of the reservation. The decision, because of its national impact, effectively disemboweled a sizable portion of tribal sovereignty from all tribes. It was especially troublesome to larger tribes like the Navajo, the Lakota, and the Tohono O'odham who, in terms both of demography and of legal precedent, claimed a stronger right to prosecute non-Indian criminals for minor criminal offenses. But it was the disingenuous methodology, the questionable historical arguments, and the unclear rationale used by Rehnquist to justify this opinion that were especially disquieting. The case left tribes and others interested in the "rule of law" to ponder the method behind the Court's judicial policymaking.

Rehnquist: The Justice

William H. Rehnquist, who has served on the High Court since 1972 and became chief justice in 1986, has consistently placed a heavy emphasis on building and expanding a conservative political agenda. Rehnquist's agenda features a prominent niche for federalism, places a subordinate value on private property, and relegates individual rights "to the bottom of his hierarchy of values," [55] according to Sue Davis.

From his early days as a clerk for Supreme Court Justice Robert Jackson in the early 1950s, when he wrote a memo upholding the infamous "separate but equal doctrine" of *Plessy v. Ferguson*, to his years as a Supreme Court justice where he has often written decisions that have proved pernicious for the enforcement of civil rights, Rehnquist has staked out a position that has often hurt Indian tribes in their efforts to reform and exercise residual sovereign rights. In fact, Rehnquist's opinions have led one pair of scholars to refer to him and other judicial conservatives like Warren Burger and Byron White as "Indian fighters," in contrast to more liberal justices like Thurgood Marshall, William Brennan and Harry Blackmun, whom they described as "Indian lovers." [56] This has been especially true whenever a tribe or an individual Indian has been confronted by either state authority or congressional power. Rehnquist's version of federalism incurs great difficulty when faced with tribal political status, and his political hierarchy invariably places tribes lower than the United States and frequently lower than the states and, in some cases, even county governments.

The Mask of "Affirmative Delegation"

After restating the background of the case, Rehnquist opined that "[r]espondents do not contend that their exercise of criminal jurisdiction over non-Indians stems from affirmative congressional authorization or treaty provision. Instead, respondents urge that such jurisdiction flows automatically from the 'Tribe's retained inherent powers of government over the Port Madison Indian Reservation.'"[57] For Rehnquist, this was the core issue of the case. As he had already shown in his questioning of the tribe's attorneys during oral arguments, he believed that tribes, because their sovereignty differed from that of the states or the federal government, had only those attributes of external sovereignty[58] which had been expressly delegated by Congress or reserved via specific treaty provision. This notion of delegated sovereignty, in contrast to internal and retained sovereignty, directly contradicts the preexisting status of tribes, prior Court precedent in *Worcester v. Georgia* (1832), *Talton v. Mayes* (1896), *Buster v. Wright* (1905), *United States v. Winans* (1905), *McClanahan v. Arizona State Tax Commission* (1973), and federal Indian policies which have historically confirmed the tribes' independence through the negotiation and ratification of treaties and agreements.

In a footnote to his affirmative delegation quote, Rehnquist acknowledged the Suquamish assertion that Congress had "confirmed" the power of tribes to punish non-Indians through federal laws such as the Indian Reorganization Act and the Indian Civil Rights Act. Nevertheless, Rehnquist challenged the tribe's understandings of these acts by stating that "[n]either Act, however, addresses, let alone 'confirms,' tribal criminal jurisdiction over non-Indians." Here, Rehnquist evaded the actual history and legislative intent of both acts and relied solely on his own interpretation of those laws. The Indian Reorganization Act, Rehnquist argued, merely provides Indian tribes with the right to organize and adopt a constitution if they choose to do so. It also recognizes, according to Rehnquist, in each newly organized tribe powers "as are vested 'by existing law.'" It is true that of the powers added to the tribe's preexisting rights—that is, to employ legal council, prevent the sale or lease of tribal land, negotiate with other governments—none dealt specifically with criminal jurisdiction. But the issue he raised—whether the tribe by "existing law" had the power to exercise jurisdiction—appears to have been a diversionary tactic. If a tribe, for example, in acting as a government, has certain inherent rights—of which preserving peace and order is a given for all legitimate governments—it would be unnecessary for Congress to explicitly prescribe this as a power tribes could wield.

Moreover, Rehnquist ignored the crucial solicitor's opinion, "Powers of Indian tribes," which was issued in the fall of 1934 by Commissioner of Indian Affairs John Collier and Solicitor Nathan Margold.[59] This 32-

page opinion was designed to clarify exactly what "powers" were vested in Indian tribes "by existing law." Margold began:

> I have no doubt that the phrase 'powers vested . . . by existing law' *does not* refer merely to those powers which have been specifically granted by the express language of treaties or statutes, but refers rather to the whole body of tribal powers which Courts and Congress alike have recognized as properly wielded by Indian tribes, whether by virtue of specific statutory grants of power or by virtue of the original sovereignty of the tribe insofar as such sovereignty has not been curtailed by restrictive legislation or surrendered by treaties.[60] (emphasis mine)

The opinion further stated that "perhaps the most basic principle of all Indian law, supported by a host of decisions hereafter analyzed, is the principle that those powers which are lawfully vested in an Indian tribe are not, in general, delegated powers granted by express acts of Congress, but rather inherent powers of a limited sovereignty which has never been extinguished."[61] Dramatically opposed to Rehnquist's view, this passage is the most accurate view from a historical and legal perspective. This theory of tribal political powers holds that Indian tribes, which began their relation with the United States as complete sovereigns, have, in linking with the United States via treaties, had some of their sovereign powers altered and in some cases, terminated. The United States, by direct implication, in agreeing to certain cessions during those bilateral negotiations, also had its sovereignty limited. The key point, however, is that both polities, tribes and the United States, retained varying amounts of inherent—not delegated—political powers.[62]

Chief among these inherent powers were: the right to adopt a government; to create various offices and prescribe their duties; to define conditions of enrollment; to provide or withhold the franchise; to regulate domestic relations; to levy fees, dues, and taxes; to remove or exclude nonmembers; to regulate the use of property; and to administer justice.[63] It is the last power—the administration of justice—that necessitates the most discussion. In assessing the continuing power of tribes to exercise criminal jurisdiction over all persons within their reservations, save for certain major crimes (i.e., murder, rape, arson, etc.), Margold emphasized that the question of the judicial powers of an Indian tribe was particularly significant in the field of law and order. "Responsibility for the maintenance of law and order is therefore squarely upon the Indian tribe, unless this field of jurisdiction has been taken over by the States or the Federal Government."[64]

The question of whether tribes had criminal authority over non-Indians was answered in the affirmative when Margold said that tribes could indeed punish nonmembers. This power had been acknowledged as early as 1791 in a Cherokee treaty and "[s]uch jurisdiction continues to this day, save as it has been expressly limited by the acts of a superior government."[65] Margold closed this section of his opinion by forcefully stating that "[w]hat is even more important than these statutory recognitions of tribal criminal authority is the persistent *silence of Congress* [emphasis mine] on the general problem of Indian criminal jurisdiction. There is nothing to justify an alternative to the conclusion that the Indian tribes retain sovereignty and jurisdiction over a vast area of ordinary offenses over which the Federal Government has never presumed to legislate and over which the state governments have not the authority to legislate."[66]

For Margold, congressional silence meant tribes retained their rights. For Rehnquist, and in contradiction of existing statutory and judicial precedent, congressional silence was somehow equated with tribes having lost those rights.

Rehnquist's discussion of the 1968 Indian Civil Rights Act[67] (ICRA) is even more novel. The ICRA was a major law which, for the first time, imposed important segments of federal constitutional law on tribal governments. This act dramatically changed the substance and direction of tribal courts by forcing tribes to enforce a modified version of the United States Bill of Rights which all reservation residents—Indian and non-Indian alike—were entitled to receive.[68]

Rehnquist downplayed the importance of this measure by saying that it "merely" extended to all persons certain enumerated Bill of Rights guarantees. It is unclear what Rehnquist means by the term "merely." In an earlier version of the Indian Civil Rights Act, these constitutional protections were to be afforded only to "American Indians"; however, additional discussion persuaded the Senate Subcommittee on Constitutional Rights, who studied the issue, to extend these protections to all persons, regardless of race. In other words, tribal governments would be constitutionally required to protect the rights of all those in their borders.

After admitting this, Rehnquist did his best to refute the protection this law provided to all reservation residents. Contrary to the actual wording of the legislation and the legislative intent of the law, Rehnquist said that "this change was certainly not intended to give Indian tribes criminal jurisdiction over non-Indians. Nor can it be read to 'confirm' respondents' arguments that Indian tribes have inherent criminal jurisdiction over non-Indians. Instead, the modification merely demonstrates Congress' desire to extend the Act's guarantees to non-Indians if and where they come under a tribe's criminal or civil jurisdiction by either treaty provision or by Act of Congress."[69] This is an incorrect reading of the law and shows Rehnquist's willingness to interject his own personal agenda on an issue Congress had already clearly addressed. His gratuitous tacking on of the expression "by either treaty provision or by Act of Congress" indicates his own bias and is not a reflection of congressional policy.

Rehnquist very selectively employed prior legal doctrines, the treaty process, and history itself to draw a convoluted background on which to construct his questionable case against tribes' retained sovereignty over criminals. He began by erroneously stating that the "effort of Indian tribal courts to exercise criminal jurisdiction over non-Indians, however, is a relatively new phenomenon." Had he asserted that the Suquamish tribe's efforts were new, this would have been accurate. Instead, he chose to make a sweeping generalization which is unsupported by historical fact.

Tribes, dating back to the 1700s, have exercised criminal jurisdiction over non-Indians entering their territory. This was recognized in a number of early treaties. It was acknowledged by the Supreme Court in cases like *Johnson v. McIntosh* (1823), where Justice Marshall said that whites moving into Indian country subjected themselves to tribal power, and in *Worcester v. Georgia* (1832). And it was acknowledged by a House Committee in an 1834 report which stated, "as to those persons not required to reside in the Indian country, who voluntarily go there to reside, they must be considered as voluntarily submitting to the laws of the tribes."[70] Furthermore, as stated in the 1934 solicitor's opinion, it was a power tribes continued to hold inherently even if they had not previously been allowed by federal bureaucrats to practice it.

A dormant power is not a nonexistent power. The only credible evidence Rehnquist mounted in defense of his contention that tribes lacked criminal jurisdiction was a single provision in a single treaty—the 1830 agreement between the Choctaw Nation and the United States.[71] Article 4 reads, "The Choctaws express[ed] a wish that Congress may grant to the Choctaws the right of punishing by their own laws any white man who shall come into their nation, and infringe any of their national regulations."[72] Rehnquist said that such a request "for affirmative congressional authority was inconsistent with respondents' [Suquamish tribe's] belief that criminal jurisdiction over non-Indians is inherent in tribal sovereignty."[73]

The pitfalls, however, of trying to extrapolate from a single treaty provision to all tribes are manifest. Barsh and Henderson have shown in a critique of the *Oliphant* case that the 1830 Choctaw treaty is "the *only* treaty [out of 366] to use this specific language."[74] Equally important, they noted that the Choctaw treaty, like those of the other tribes facing relocation from the Southeast, had been negotiated under unique circumstances. The relocating tribes were receiving their new lands in the Indian territory in fee-simple title, in exchange for the lands in the Southeast that they were ceding. According to Barsh and Henderson, "since these tribes held their territory as land owners rather than as sovereigns, it is not surprising that their treaties would include provisions delegating to them limited powers of self-government."[75] In the federal government's treaties with over 100 nonrelocated tribes, none of their agreements contained such delegatory language.[76]

In his extended footnote accompanying his Choctaw treaty discussion, Rehnquist averred that the Indian treaty process was consistent with the theory that Indian tribes lacked criminal jurisdiction over non-Indians, unless Congress had granted "permission." Rehnquist was hard-pressed to support this radical and incorrect view of tribal-federal relations. In fact, he was compelled to admit that several other early treaties contained language which specifically said that any American citizens settling on Indian land would thereby forfeit the protection of the United States and could be punished by the tribe "as they please." Rather than accept this statement for what it was, a stark reminder that tribal lands were separate countries, jurisdictionally speaking, Rehnquist maintained that "[f]ar from representing a recognition of any inherent Indian criminal jurisdiction over non-Indians settling on tribal lands, these provisions were instead intended as a means of discouraging non-Indian settlements on Indian territory, in contravention of treaty provisions to the contrary." These treaty provisions, however, were definite affirmations of Indian territorial sovereignty. Rehnquist's manipulation of language could not change the clear language of the treaty provisions.

At the end of his footnote, Rehnquist falsely maintained that "only one treaty" with a tribe (the Delaware Treaty of 1778) ever provided for tribal criminal jurisdiction over non-Indians. As the solicitor's opinion noted to the contrary, the 1791 Choctaw treaty also directly addressed tribal criminal jurisdiction. But even in the Delaware Treaty, Rehnquist cited additional language which he interpreted to show that the tribe could still not try whites except "under the auspices of the United States. . . ."[77] Rehnquist was, again, editing the actual language of the treaty. He deleted a crucial phrase from the last line of the treaty provision which prominently required the mutual consent of the parties.[78]

In sum, Rehnquist drew his information from six carefully selected and edited treaties out of a possible 366. More important, "none of the articles he quoted appear on examination to have been representative; one treaty he relied on is unique, while another has been materially misquoted. From this insubstantial foundation, Justice Rehnquist concluded that tribal treaties acquiesced in a historical federal policy against tribal criminal jurisdiction over non-Indians."[79]

In search of judicial support to buffer his fragile legal position, Rehnquist could cite only a single 1878 federal district case, *Ex Parte Kenyon*,[80] which was written by the infamous western "hanging judge," Isaac C. Parker. In *Kenyon*, Parker had said that tribal courts only had jurisdiction over Indians. Rehnquist was perhaps unaware that a few years after *Kenyon*, the Supreme Court in *Elk v. Wilkins* had commented on *Kenyon*, noting that the decision had depended on the fact that both parties were white and that, more importantly, "the crime occurred outside the boundaries of the reservation."[81] In *Oliphant*, the crimes had occurred inside a reservation's borders.

Rehnquist asserted that Parker's opinion had been reaffirmed as recently as 1970 in a solicitor's opinion but acknowledged that the "1970 opinion of the Solicitor was withdrawn in 1974 but has not been replaced."[82] "No reason," he said, "was given for the withdrawal."[83]

The Mask of "Invented Congressional Intent"

Justice Rehnquist opened this section of his opinion with a statement that must rank among the most egregious for its mischaracterization of history:

> While Congress was concerned almost from its beginning with the special problems of law enforcement on the Indian reservations, it did not initially address itself to the problem of tribal jurisdiction over non-Indians. For the reason previously stated, there was little reason to be concerned with assertions of tribal court jurisdiction over non-Indians because of the absence of formal tribal judicial systems.[84]

The text is riddled with errors, beginning with Rehnquist's opening line, which reveals his unfamiliarity with basic federal Indian policy. He said that Congress "almost from its beginning" was concerned about reservation law enforcement. The Continental Congress was established in 1774, and, although the reservation concept was known during these early years, reservation establishment as a general federal policy did not materialize until the 1860s.[85] This is because in between the formation of the federal government and the reservation years there was a traumatic period of Indian removal—1830s–1850s—in which dozens of tribes were removed and resettled to what was then ill-defined as Indian territory. Theoretically, this Indian territory was tribal land that was to be protected from white intrusion.

It logically follows that if there were no reservations and virtually no white presence in Indian territory, there could be no "special problems of law enforcement." Rehnquist wrongly concluded that the absence of "formal tribal judicial systems" justified a lack of concern over tribal court jurisdiction. A strange, convoluted logic seems to be at work here: if Congress were genuinely concerned about tribes exercising power over non-Indians, it would seem that a primary concern would be the tribes' lack of judicial systems comparable to those of the United States.

Wandering briefly into the realm of historical accuracy, Rehnquist remarked that Congress, since its inception, had been interested in protecting Indians and their territory from the lawless advances of whites into their country. He cited as an example the Seventh Annual Message of President George Washington, who was acutely aware of the intergovernmental problems generated by whites who were illegally trespassing in Indian country.[86] But after citing supporting historical and legal evidence (e.g., the Trade and Intercourse Act of 1790 and an 1817 law, "An Act to Provide for the Punishment of Crimes and Offences Committed within the Indian Boundaries," which extended federal jurisdiction over certain crimes except for Indian-on-Indian offenses), Rehnquist brought forth an 1834 congressional bill *which had never been enacted*— the Western Territory Bill—in an attempt to argue that Congress had never intended to allow Indian tribes to exercise criminal jurisdiction over whites.

Throughout its discussion of this unenacted bill, Congress had "proposed" to establish an Indian territory in the western regions of the frontier, which would have entailed a confederation of Indian tribes, with the ultimate goal of the territory's becoming a state. In describing this bill, Rehnquist noted, "[w]hile the bill would have created a political territory with broad governing powers, Congress was careful not to give the tribes of the territory criminal jurisdiction over United States officials

and citizens traveling through the area."[87] This is an interesting statement, as much for what it says as for what it ignores. In a footnote accompanying this excerpt, Rehnquist added, remarkably, that "[t]he Western
Territory bill, like the early Indian treaties, . . . did not extend the protection of the United States to non-Indians who *settled* without Government business in Indian territory"[88] (emphasis original).

Two things stand out in these two extracts. First, Rehnquist seemed
unable or unwilling to distinguish an unenacted measure from constitutionally sanctioned Indian treaties. Second, he conceded by implication that nongovernmental officials were to be subject to tribal jurisdiction. That this admission is problematic for him becomes evident when
he continues, "This exception, like that in the early treaties, was presumably meant to discourage settlement on land that was reserved exclusively
for the use of the various Indian tribes." But whatever was "presumably
meant" by the passage, and however invalid it may be in its unratified
state, the statement was an implicit recognition of tribal sovereignty over
whites who "settled" in Indian territory.

Rehnquist closed out his footnote by moving from his discussion of
that section of the 1834 bill which recognized tribal sovereignty over
resident whites to a contemporary description of the Port Madison Indian Reservation. Rehnquist's phraseology warrants yet another direct
quote:

> Today, many reservations, including the Port Madison Reservation,
> have extensive non-Indian populations. The percentage of non-Indian
> residents grew as a direct and intended result of congressional poli-
> cies in the late 19th and 20th centuries promoting the assimilation
> of the Indians into the non-Indian culture. Respondents point to no
> statute, in comparison to the Western Territory bill, where Congress
> has intended to give tribes jurisdiction today over non-Indians resid-
> ing within reservations.[89]

Rehnquist would have one believe that a nonenacted bill, even one containing a statement expressly acknowledging tribal sovereignty over all
permanent "settlers," was more important than the established doctrine
of tribal sovereignty. Furthermore, after having affirmatively used the
proposed 1834 Western Territory bill as "proof" that tribes lacked jurisdiction over non-Indians, Rehnquist was required to concede that the
bill was considered too "radical" and was ultimately tabled. This is a revealing statement showing that Rehnquist had not strayed inadvertently
into citing a bill that he thought had become law. He was clearly aware

that this measure had no legal weight whatsoever, yet he insisted on treating it as if it were legal precedent.

While Rehnquist focused his attention on a bill with no legal identity, he ignored the 1834 House Report (H. R. No. 474) which had been issued by the Committee on Indian Affairs. The Committee's report examined two other bills: "a Bill to provide for the organization of the Department of Indian Affairs," and "a Bill to Regulate Trade and Intercourse with the Indian tribes." Both were enacted into law in 1834. In his selective use of only that language which he believed supported his position that tribes lacked criminal jurisdiction, Rehnquist deliberately overlooked a more pertinent and lawful measure which directly addressed the subject of jurisdiction and openly discussed the actual bilateral relationship between the tribes and the United States:

> In consequence of the change in our Indian relations, the laws related to crimes committed in the Indian Country, and to the tribunals before whom offenders are to be tried, require revision. By the Act of 3d March, 1817, the criminal laws of the United States were extended to all persons in the Indian Country, without exception, and by that Act, as well as that of 30 March 1802, they might be tried wherever apprehended. It will be seen that we cannot, consistently with the provisions of some of our treaties, and of the territorial act, extend our criminal laws to offenses committed by or against Indians, of which the tribes have exclusive jurisdiction; *and it is rather of courtesy than of right that we undertake to punish crimes in that territory by and against our own citizens.* And this provision is retained principally on the ground that it may be unsafe to trust to Indian law in the early stages of their Governments.[90] (emphasis mine)

This is not the language of a dominant, coercive federal force dictating to tribes over whom it may or may not exercise jurisdiction. It is more the voice of a nation that had been granted a "courtesy" by some tribes to punish interracial crimes since those tribes apparently did not want to deal with the subject. It allowed for a future time in which tribes, when they felt they had developed legal systems comparable to the United States', would be able to reclaim their inherent authority to try and punish non-Indians. On the other hand, Indian-on-Indian crimes were recognized as being solely within the province of tribes "at any place within their own limits."[91] This excerpt and the overall thrust of the House Report contradict Rehnquist's assertion that "Congress shared the view of the Executive Branch and lower federal courts that Indian tribal courts were without jurisdiction to try non-Indians."[92]

Rehnquist cited three more examples (the 1834 Trade and Intercourse Act, the 1885 Major Crimes Act, and an 1891 Supreme Court decision, *In re Mayfield*) which, in his opinion, supported his "unspoken assumption" that tribes lacked internal sovereignty over non-Indians. Each of these examples contributed to his formulation of a novel and logically insupportable principle of federal Indian law—implicit divestiture. "While Congress never expressly forbade Indian tribes to impose criminal penalties on non-Indians, we now may express our implicit conclusion of nearly a century ago that Congress consistently believed this to be the necessary result of its repeated legislative actions."[93] The Supreme Court, in this single statement, judicially usurped an inherent tribal power that had existed since time immemorial or, certainly, since the first whites settled in Indian country. This line of thought raises a series of unanswered and troubling issues. Is it possible that the Supreme Court can implicitly take away a power which, it has just alleged, had never explicitly been recognized to exist? How does a Supreme Court legitimately usurp tribal powers (assuming, as I do and as history and politics attest, that such powers exist), something which historically has not been accomplished except by direct Congressional action?

The Mask of "Undefined Treaty Rights"

In the second part of his opinion, Rehnquist opens his discussion with a minimalist definition of "Indian law." According to Rehnquist, Indian law draws principally upon treaties drawn and executed by the Executive Branch and legislation passed by Congress.[94] This abbreviated definition conveniently ignores other critical documents—agreements, judicial opinions, and administrative rulings—which have also been held to constitute Indian law.[95] Rehnquist did mention that Indian treaties and statutes must be understood "in light of the common notions of the day and the assumption of those who drafted them."[96] This caveat would seem to bode well for tribes, especially when we consider that under the earlier constructed judicial canons, treaties were to be interpreted as the Indians would have understood them.

Justice Rehnquist focused on the Suquamish treaty of 1855, which, he had already indicated, had not explicitly affirmed Suquamish criminal jurisdiction over non-Indians. While admitting that it appeared to be "silent as to criminal jurisdiction over non-Indians," he found that the perspective afforded by history cast "substantial doubt upon the existence of such jurisdiction."[97] Rather than engage in a searching analysis of all existing Indian treaties, or the process of criminal jurisdiction over an extended period of time, Rehnquist, in footnote sixteen, simply described how treaty negotiators examined two other treaties—one with the Omaha, the other with the Otoe and Missouria—to get some idea as to how to draft the Suquamish treaty. Rehnquist conceded that neither of these treaties specifically addressed the issue of Indian criminal jurisdiction over non-Indians. The only evidence he could marshall was article 9 of the Suquamish treaty which stated: "The said tribes and bands acknowledge their dependence on the government of the United States, and promise to be friendly to all citizens thereof, and they pledge themselves to commit no depredation of the property of such citizens. . . . And the said tribes agree not to shelter or conceal offenders against the laws of the United States, but to deliver them up to the authorities for trial."[98] For Rehnquist, the crux of this article lay in "dependence" and "deliver them up to the authorities." Admitting that "[b]y themselves, these treaty provisions would probably not be sufficient to remove criminal jurisdiction over non-Indians if the Tribe otherwise retained such jurisdiction,"[99] Rehnquist persisted that the Suquamish were "in all probability recognizing that the United States would arrest and try non-Indian intruders who came within their Reservation."[100]

A nation, however, does not surrender rights in a "probabilistic" manner. As the 9th Circuit Court had shown, and as Rehnquist had admitted, the Suquamish treaty was "silent" on the specific subject of criminal jurisdiction. District Judge Duniway had stated in his decision that the only "significant surrender of inherent autonomy" by the Suquamish was the extradition section of article 9 where the Suquamish were asked to "deliver up offenders."[101] This appears to be only an extradition statement and is silent about the power of the Suquamish to try non-Indians. The absence of express treaty or statutory language taking away Suquamish power over non-Indians, combined with the rule that treaties and laws affecting Indians were to be construed in their interest, should have protected the tribe's right to pursue, arrest, detain, try, and convict criminal non-Indian offenders. Rehnquist maintained, however, that "an examination of our earlier precedents satisfies us that, even ignoring treaty provisions and congressional policy," Indians lacked such power over non-Indians "absent affirmative delegation of such power by Congress."[102] Intoxication with the extraordinary power he was wielding may be the best explanation for Rehnquist's comment that although neither treaty nor statute had taken away this inherent authority of the tribe, "earlier precedent" had done so. By his own definition, "Indian law" entailed treaties and statutes; therefore, if there was no bilateral or legislative support for such a usurpation of tribal power, whence did such power derive?

At this point, Rehnquist refurbished the old "dependent" and "incorporated" status of tribes, first defined in *Kagama* and expanded in *Lone Wolf,* and quietly slipped it past all existing historical, political, economic, and cultural evidence to the contrary, to enunciate yet another novel principle. While acknowledging that tribes did retain some elements of "quasi-authority," Rehnquist protested that these particular retained powers—which he did not articulate—were "not such that they [were] limited only by specific restrictions in treaties or congressional enactments."[103] In other words, tribes had certain inherent, fundamental, and apparently organic limitations on their efforts to practice their retained sovereignty. Here, Rehnquist managed to find a quote from Judge Duniway's lower court ruling that he concurred with. Duniway had cited from the 1973 Supreme Court decision *McClanahan v. Arizona State Tax Commission,*[104] in which the Court had held that a state could not impose an income tax on revenue earned by Indians from reservation sources. In Rehnquist's recitation of the pivotal section of that generally pro-Indian case, "Indian tribes are prohibited from exercising both those powers of autonomous States that are expressly terminated by Congress and those powers inconsistent with their status."[105] Rehnquist did not attempt an explanation of a "tribal status" in which a recognized sovereign or even a semisovereign could be denied a basic and clearly essential law-and-order power. Moreover, he carefully referred to only the first part of Duniway's statement while ignoring an important second part. Duniway, after quoting the "inconsistent with their status" passage, immediately followed up by stating that "surely the power to preserve order on the reservation, where necessary, by punishing those who violate tribal law, is a sine qua non of the sovereignty that the Suquamish originally possessed."[106] In other words, there was nothing "inconsistent" with Suquamish efforts to punish criminal offenders, despite the fact that they were an Indian tribe. In fact, just the opposite was true; this was a perfectly consistent course of action, necessary to their community's safety and order.

In Rehnquist's view, however, tribes were disallowed from such an exercise of authority because, as they were "incorporated into the territory of the United States," they automatically came under the "territorial sovereignty of the United States."[107] This *Rogers* argument fits Rehnquist's nationalist/federalist view; his refusal to concede the legitimacy of tribal sovereignty echoes his earlier responses to state and federal sovereignty. One of Rehnquist's avowed concerns, and a justifiable one, was that the civil rights of American citizens be protected, regardless of their geographic location in the United States, "from unwarranted intrusions on their personal liberty."[108] Rehnquist was, in effect, elevating the rights of non-Indian American citizens above those of the extraconstitutional sovereign tribal governments which are governed and populated by individuals who are also American citizens. In Rehnquist's words:

> By submitting to the overriding sovereignty of the United States, Indian tribes therefore necessarily give up their power to try non-Indian citizens of the United States except in a manner acceptable to Congress. This principle would have been obvious a century ago when most Indian tribes were characterized by a "want of fixed laws [and] of competent tribunals of justice. . . ." It should be no less obvious today, even though present-day Indian tribal courts embody dramatic advances over their historical antecedents.[109]

The statement that the principle of tribal nonsovereignty over non-Indians "would have been obvious a century ago" is even more puzzling than his general power statement on "overriding sovereignty." Rehnquist was obviously reading contemporary views of the law back onto tribal-federal actions that took place over one hundred years ago. The Court was also downplaying the "dramatic advances" taking place in tribal judicial systems which had been compelled to modernize when Congress enacted the Indian Civil Rights Act of 1968.

Moreover, Rehnquist's position on the potentiality or probability of civil rights of American citizens being "violated" by tribal governments fails to consider the obvious fact that Indian reservation residents also happen to be American citizens. Therefore, following his logic that tribal governments lack jurisdiction over non-Indian citizens on the reservation, then Rehnquist should explain why tribal governments are allowed to exercise jurisdiction over their own members who are also American citizens. Likewise, to extend this racialized argument, "if tribes cannot prosecute non-Indians on reservations because Indian law is alien to whites, then it would follow that state Courts cannot try tribal Indians off reservations."[110]

Rehnquist pushed the racial theme even further when he quoted from the *Ex parte Crow Dog* (1883)[111] decision where the Supreme Court held that the federal government was without criminal jurisdiction to try Indian-on-Indian crimes because the Lakota tribe was an inherent sovereign with the retained right to administer their laws.[112] Rehnquist's treatment of *Crow Dog* ignored the inherent sovereignty and retained rights of the Lakota Nation acknowledged in the case. Instead, he narrowly focused on an overtly ethnocentric section in the opinion by Justice Stanley Matthews who said that the United States was wrong in seeking to extend its law over Indian-on-Indian crimes. The government was trying to do this, said Matthews,

> . . . over aliens and strangers; over the members of a community separated by race, by tradition, by the instincts of a free though savage life, from the authority and power which seeks to impose upon them the restraints of an external and unknown code . . . which judges them by a standard made by others and not for them. . . . It [the U.S.] tries them, not by their peers, nor by the customs of their people, nor the law of the land, but by superiors of a different race, according to the law of a social state of which they have an imperfect conception. . . .[113]

This excerpt from *Crow Dog*, while affirming Sioux traditional law, suffers from overtones of racism and ethnocentrism. While upholding respect for tribal sovereignty in a jaundiced way, the Court was philosophically supporting the federal government's goal of assimilating Indians.

Rehnquist, in citing this particular statement, was speaking as if little had changed in the field of Indian policy and law from the 1880s to the 1970s. Although *Crow Dog* was an internal sovereignty issue not involving outsiders, and while it dealt with a major crime—a murder—and not a minor offense, Rehnquist spoke as if the facts of *Crow Dog* were perfectly comparable to the interracial situation of *Oliphant*. He said, in response to the *Crow Dog* quote, that "[t]hese considerations, applied here to the non-Indian rather than Indian offender, speak equally strongly against the validity of respondents' contention that Indian tribes . . . retain the power to try non-Indians according to their own customs and procedure."[114] The comparison is weak, and Rehnquist admitted as much in his concluding comments, where he acknowledged that (1) some tribes have judicial systems which are "sophisticated and resemble in many respects their state counterparts"; (2) the ICRA of 1968 extended certain basic procedural rights to all persons on Indian reservations, an action which has caused "many of the dangers" that might have arisen when tribes tried to prosecute non-Indians "to have disappeared"; and (3) the increasing violence on Indian reservations, as elsewhere, enables tribes to fashion a forceful argument that they have the "ability to try non-Indians." Despite the cumulative merit of these three points, Rehnquist dismissed them as having "little relevance."[115] In his opinion, such facts were irrelevant to the unusual position that he was imprinting onto the legal landscape: that tribes—all tribes—were without inherent authority to try and punish non-Indians. Rehnquist gratuitously remarked in conclusion that Congress was certainly empowered to authorize tribes to exercise such jurisdiction. Until and unless this transpired, however, tribes were informed that their power to preserve order on their reservations was effectively limited to handling minor Indian-on-Indian crimes.

THE DISSENT OF JUSTICE MARSHALL AND CHIEF JUSTICE BURGER

Justice Thurgood Marshall adopted the view of the lower federal court that the power to preserve order was a "sine qua non of the sovereignty that the Suquamish originally possessed."[116] Marshall and Chief Justice Warren Burger espoused the view that since neither Congress nor the executive branch had ever deliberately dispossessed tribes of this power, it remained a part of their sovereign arsenal.

CONCLUSION

It is certainly debatable whether a tribal nation of fifty Indian individuals inhabiting checkerboarded reservation land in which they are outnumbered forty-to-one could pragmatically wield the type of criminal jurisdiction the Suquamish sought to exercise in *Oliphant*. Equally puzzling is why this case with such an anomalous demographic situation was ever taken before the Supreme Court. But even more important is the question of why the Supreme Court, rather than recognizing the uniqueness of this case as proposed by the Suquamish tribe's attorneys in oral arguments, used it as an excuse to carefully set about the task of dismantling the right of all tribes to criminally punish non-Indian offenders. Unable to find constitutional, treaty, or statutory justification for this dismemberment of a critical tribal right, Justice Rehnquist and five colleagues engaged in sophistry of the highest order to deny tribes with the requisite judicial system the essential right to administer justice for all.

THE AFTERMATH — A TRIBAL RESURGENCE OF SORTS

Within two months after *Oliphant*, the Supreme Court handed down two other important decisions—*United States v. Wheeler*,[117] decided March 22, 1978, six days after *Oliphant;* and *Santa Clara Pueblo v. Martinez*,[118] decided May 15. These two rulings, in certain fundamental respects, represented the virtual antithesis of the *Oliphant* rule that tribes possess only those powers which have been "delegated" by treaty or statute. *Wheeler* upheld successive tribal and federal prosecutions of an Indian for crimes arising out of the same offense committed on a reservation. Wheeler, a Navajo, had pleaded guilty in tribal court to a charge of contributing to the delinquency of a minor. He was later indicted by a federal grand jury for statutory rape based on the same charge.

Wheeler sought to have the federal charge dismissed on the premise that the tribal charge was actually a "lesser included offense" of statutory rape.[119] Justice Potter Stewart, however, speaking for a unanimous Court (again, except for Brennan), held that successive prosecutions of Indians in federal and tribal courts were not barred by the double jeopardy clause of the Fifth Amendment. More important from Stewart's perspective was the source of the tribe's power under which the respective prosecutions had been undertaken. The crucial question, then, especially in light of the week-old *Oliphant* decision, was whether the tribe's conceded power to enforce criminal laws against its own members was based on "inherent tribal sovereignty" or a sovereignty "which has been delegated to the tribe by Congress. . . ."[120]

Citing Felix Cohen's Indian law book and John Marshall's *Worcester* decision, Stewart said that the powers of tribes were inherent. Tribes, in effect, retained all those powers not explicitly removed by Congress.[121] This description of inherent and retained tribal sovereignty was not quite the "ringing" endorsement Wilkinson[122] has suggested it was, since Stewart also adopted the *Oliphant* rule that tribes have lost powers based on their "dependent status." Nevertheless, it was an important recognition of the doctrine of inherent, not delegated, power.

In the *Santa Clara Pueblo* case, the Court was asked to decide whether a federal court could determine the validity of the Santa Clara Pueblo's ordinance denying membership to the children of Julia Martinez, a recognized member of the tribe who had married a non-Pueblo. The Court, through Justice Marshall, ruled that Martinez's sexual discrimination claim against the tribe could not be brought into federal court because the provisions of the ICRA did not entail an unequivocal expression to abrogate tribal sovereign immunity by subjecting the tribe to civil suits in Federal Court. Importantly, this decision was reached notwithstanding the extension of the equal protection guarantee to tribes laid out in the Indian Civil Rights Act, and despite a federal law extending federal courts' jurisdiction over lawsuits filed "under any act of Congress providing for the protection of civil rights."[123] Interestingly, while Justice Byron White filed a dissent, arguing that the ICRA did entitle an aggrieved individual to sue in federal court against tribal officials, Rehnquist, who had so vigorously railed about the civil rights of non-Indians in *Oliphant*, quietly concurred in this decision.

This triumvirate of cases prompted Indian leaders throughout the country to sponsor a conference in Washington, D.C., in June 1978, focusing on the administration of justice on Indian reservations. Senator Edward M. Kennedy (D., Massachusetts) gave the keynote address entitled "Justice on Indian Reservations." After describing the three cases, Kennedy accurately noted that as different as the cases were they shared one common element: "They all helped draw the boundaries of tribal self-determination which will guide the cause of Indian and non-Indian relationships in the decades to come."[124] Unfortunately for tribes, however, their growing efforts to practice genuine self-determination would have to take place without the fundamental authority to punish non-Indians who violated tribal criminal laws.

United States v. Sioux Nation of Indians

LAND CLAIMS IN THE EIGHTIES

Land is at the heart of indigenous identity and it is the definitive factor which has animated indigenous/nonindigenous affairs since that first contact. By the late 1970s, tribes had an ongoing, but uneven, three-pronged land-claims attack aimed against both the states and the federal government. The first, and by far the oldest, land-claims initiative dated back to the 1920s when tribes, through various jurisdictional acts, were finally allowed to bring suits against the federal government for claims relating to lands they had lost. In these suits, tribes could not sue for the return of land but were limited to seeking compensation (i.e., *Northwestern Bands of Shoshone v. United States*).

The second effort entailed cases brought by tribes under the Indian Claims Commission Act of 1946. These were land claims arising before 1946 which were based, from the tribes' viewpoint, on either unfair federal takings or inadequate compensation for takings of Indian land by the United States. Consideration was not given through the implementing legislation as to the possibility of claims against states, cities, or private parties, and tribes, again, were limited to monetary damages only: no land could be recovered.

The third and most recent flank of this attack, which had begun unofficially in 1975 with *Passamaquoddy*,[125] centered around land claims by eastern Indian tribes like the Narragansett of Rhode Island, the Wampanoag of Gay Head, Massachusetts, the Schaghticoke and Western Pequot of Connecticut, the Oneida, St. Regis Mohawk, and Cayuga Nation of New York, the Catawba of South Carolina, the Chitimacha tribe of Louisiana, and, most prominently, the Maine-based Passamaquoddy, the Penobscot, and the Houlton band of Maliseet. The claims of these indigenous groups had not been served by the Indian Claims Commission because their land losses had occurred as a result of actions by individual states, not the federal government.

These cases, with exception of the Chitimacha's, all arose in the original thirteen colonies, "whose state government dealt directly—and, it is asserted, illegally—with Indian nations during the early history of the Republic."[126] The tribes in these cases had argued, and continued to insist, that the states had unlawfully purchased or otherwise secured title to much of their aboriginal territory in direct violation of the Indian Trade and Intercourse Act of 1790. This act had stated that any land transactions involving Indians and other parties had to be supervised and approved by the federal government. Furthermore, this law, as the Court had held in *Passamaquoddy*, protected all tribes, both federally recognized and state- or even nonrecognized tribes.

There are a number of differences between these eastern land-claims cases and the first two sets of cases, which were heard in the Court of Claims and the Indian Claims Commission. The most definitive one is that under the Trade and Intercourse Act, tribes could sue, negotiate, or seek direct presidential action to have their actual land restored. The eastern Indians' most substantial victory to date is that of three Maine tribes, the Passamaquoddy, Penobscot, and Maliseet. Their valid claims to 12.5 million acres in the state were eventually settled among the state, the tribes, and both corporate and private landholders on October 10, 1980, with the mediation of a federally appointed official.[127] Under the agreement, the secretary of the treasury established a 27-million-dollar trust fund; the secretary of the interior was directed to purchase 300,000 acres of forest land for the Indians; and the three groups were acknowledged as federally recognized tribes. Into this teeming claims milieu stepped the United States Supreme Court to announce a verdict—just four months before the negotiated settlement in the Maine case was approved by Congress—on one of the oldest Court of Claims cases, dating back to 1920. This decision was originally perceived as an impressive legal victory in some circles of the Great Lakota Nation because eight Sioux bands had been able to elicit an admission by the Supreme Court that the federal government had indeed illegally appropriated seven million acres of the Great Sioux Reservation, which included the Black Hills. The Lakota bands were also awarded 17.5 million dollars (the cost of the Black Hills at the time of their taking), plus an additional 105 million (representing the government's liability for interest on the judgment, calculated at five percent annually for 103 years). This financial award was touted as the largest ever made by the Court of Claims.[128]

This particular case, however, the culmination of more than a half-century of persistent effort by the Lakota to secure a measure of justice, is not so easily categorized as an overwhelming tribal victory. The language used by Justice Harry Blackmun, who wrote for the eight-to-one majority, included troubling phraseology regarding what constitutes a legal "taking" of Indian land, the nature of the trust relationship, and the nature of law itself. As Vine Deloria Jr. stated with regard to the Black Hills claim, "In my opinion, [the claim] represents a much deeper problem than a simple land transaction." He predicted that the claim would not be fully resolved as long as the Court persisted in regarding it simply as a real estate deal.[129]

HISTORICAL BACKGROUND

The Indian Peace Commission was established on July 20, 1867.[130] The Commission's primary goal was to secure peace with the major Indian nations of the West, who had considerable military power and were exercising it efficiently to prevent settlement of the Great Plains and Rocky Mountain areas. The commission made some treaties in western Kansas in 1867 but failed to secure treaties with the northern plains tribes, the tribes of the Southwest, and the tribes of the Western Indian Territory in that year. Thus efforts were concentrated the following year—1868—the last year treaties were negotiated before Congress terminated the process in 1871.

The commission issued its first report January 7, 1868. It had reviewed the causes of hostility between the races and placed the blame squarely on the shoulders of white Americans. "Have we been uniformly unjust?" the commissioners asked; "We answer, unhesitatingly, yes!"[131] They acknowledged, however, that making good treaties would be no easy task, considering the amount of injustice the federal government had heaped on the tribes. Besides, the commissioners stated, "nobody pays any attention to Indian matters. . . . The only question considered is, 'how best to get his land.'"[132]

The Fort Laramie treaty between various Sioux bands, the Arapaho, and the United States, while completed on April 29, 1868,[133] had actually been under negotiation since late August of 1867 and had been one of the most difficult for the federal government to secure because the Sioux, especially their esteemed leader, Red Cloud, were an imposing military force the likes of which the United States had rarely encountered. Essentially, the treaty accomplished four major objectives: (1) It guaranteed peace between the Lakota and the United States (article I); (2) It established "for the absolute and undisturbed use and occupation of the Indians" the boundaries of the Great Sioux Nation Reservation (article II); (3) It guaranteed that there would be no unauthorized whites allowed within the boundaries of the reservation (article III); and (4) It guaranteed that the recognized Sioux land would never be subject to purchase by treaty with the United States "unless [said treaty was] executed and signed by at least three-fourths of all the adult male Indians, occupying or interested in the same . . . (article XII)." This last treaty provision is virtually identical to a similar provision in the Kiowa, Comanche, and Apache agreement discussed in the *Lone Wolf* case. It was a common provision in the latter treaties negotiated by the commission.

However, unlike the KCA Indians, whose "guaranteed" land rights were generally protected until the 1890s, the Lakota, within less than a decade, would witness their lands being invaded by gold diggers, silver miners, and unauthorized United States military personnel. Lt. Col. George A. Custer, in direct violation of the 1868 treaty, led an exploratory gold-seeking and fort-building expedition of nearly 1,000 men into the Black Hills of South Dakota in the summer of 1874. By mid-August their search for gold, unfortunately for the Lakota, proved a success. The Black Hills area was soon flooded with miners, speculators, and settlers, all seeking their fortunes in territory that they were illegally trespassing on.

Initially, the federal government tried to fulfill its treaty obligation by having the Army prevent non-Indians from entering the Great Sioux

Nation Reservation. But yielding both to the pressure of individual entrepreneurs and to the undercurrent of economic "manifest destiny" that has characterized most government decisions with regard to Indian lands, the United States decided to attempt a purchase of the Black Hills from the Lakota Nation.[134] The government sent in a commission, headed by William B. Allison, in an effort to negotiate this cession. The commissioners failed; the Lakota had no interest in ceding an area considered particularly sacred.

In the fall of 1875, a covert and collusive decision was made by President Grant, the secretary of the interior, and the Army's commanding generals to violate the United States' treaty promise to protect the Sioux from unauthorized non-Indian interference in their territory. The collusion between the federal officials is plainly revealed in three confidential letters which were finally released to the public in 1974. I cite each letter in full:

> [Confidential]   Nov. 9th (1875)
> My dear Gen. Terry: At a meeting which occurred in Washington on the 3rd of November, at which were present the President of the United States, Secretary of the Interior, the Secretary of War and myself, the President decided that while the orders heretofore issued forbidding the occupation of the Black Hills country by miners, should not be rescinded, still no further resistance by the military should be made to the miners going in; it being his belief that such resistance only increased their desire and complicated the troubles. Will you therefore *quietly* cause the troops in your Department to assume such attitudes as will meet the views of the President in this respect. Yours truly,
>
> P. H. Sheridan, Lieut. General (emphasis mine)

> Chicago, November 13, 1875
> My dear Genl Sherman: After my return from the Pacific, I was obliged to go East to see Mr. Chandler about the Black Hills and my report has thus been delayed.
>
> Terry has been sick, but is now better and I am expecting his report daily.
>
> The enclosed copy of Confidential letter to Terry will best explain the present status of the Black Hills. The whole thing has gone along about as I had expected. *The Terry letter had best be kept confidential.*
>
> Yours truly, P H Sheridan. (emphasis original)

[Headquarter Army of the United States]
St. Louis, Mo., November 20, 1875.
Gen. P. H. Sheridan,
Chicago, Ill.
Dear General: Your letter of Nov. 13 with enclosure was duly received, and would have been answered immediately. Only I know that the matter of the Black Hills was settled in all events for this year. In the spring it may result in Collision and trouble. *But I think the Sioux Indians are all now so dependent on their rations, that they will have to do whatever they are required to do.* My own idea of their Treaty is that settlements may now be made all along up the Western Boundary. And if some go over the Boundary into the Black Hills, *I understand that the President and the Interior Department will wink at it for the present.* Truly your friend,

W. T. Sherman.[135] (emphasis original)

These letters show that the Grant administration was knowingly and secretly violating Article II of the 1868 treaty which had said that the United States would never allow unauthorized persons to "pass over, settle upon, or reside in the territory described. . . ." In fact, the President, his generals, and the secretary of the interior intentionally kept this decision from the Senate and from the House of Representatives.[136] By quietly withdrawing the Army from the Black Hills, the government was signaling to interested whites that the Black Hills were open territory. Soon thereafter, the Black Hills were overrun with miners and others anxious to establish their claims in Lakota Territory.

The commissioner of Indian affairs, in an overt effort to challenge and incite the Sioux to a military response, issued a controversial directive in January 1876 which declared that any Sioux found away from their agencies were to be considered "hostile." Such a declaration meant that the United States military were authorized to use all available means to "suppress" the Indians. It apparently did not matter that the Sioux, who were not even assigned to agencies, were engaged in essential and treaty-recognized hunting activities within their own territory, or that without the ability to hunt they would, in all likelihood, starve to death, since the winter of 1875–1876 was particularly severe. At this point, Lt. Col. Custer was sent with the decorated Seventh Cavalry to engage the allegedly "hostile" Sioux. When Custer located the Indians on the Little Big Horn River on June 26, 1876, he and his command were overwhelmingly defeated by a sizable force of Lakota, led by Sitting Bull.

Congress was incensed and embarrassed at this shattering defeat and attached a rider to the 1876 Appropriation Act which illegally denied the Sioux all further appropriations and treaty-guaranteed annuities (a violation in itself) until and unless they agreed to sell the Black Hills to the United States. This remarkable act has come to be known as the "sell or starve" rider.[137] The United States then sent out another treaty commission, this time led by George W. Manypenny and Henry Whipple. They brought with them a proposed agreement for the Lakota to consider.

The commission hoped to obtain the requisite number of signatures—three-fourths of adult males—as required by the 1868 treaty. Although a number of Sioux were starving, because of the fighting and the annuity and appropriation freeze, they still refused to sell their beloved Black Hills.[138] The commissioners were able to muster the signatures of only ten percent of the adult Sioux males. The fact that the Congress would go so far as to enact a "sell or starve" provision may have alerted the Sioux that regardless of their commitment to the treaty agreement or refusal to sign the current document, the United States had every intention of securing the Black Hills, notwithstanding the 1868 treaty and the prior agreements (the various Sioux tribes had negotiated seven other treaties with the United States) which had been negotiated between the parties.

The commission returned to Washington with the agreement containing the signatures of only ten percent of the adult Sioux males but "claimed that since their [Lakota] Chiefs sometimes represented their bands politically," that they in fact "represented" three-quarters of the adult males. Congress, on February 28, 1877,[139] simply attached a preamble to this alleged "agreement" and declared it law. It was, in fact, a unilateral, illegal taking of 7.7 million acres of Lakota territory in direct violation of the treaty provision requiring the consent of three-fourths of all adult Sioux males.[140]

The Sioux, under the agreement, received no monetary settlement. Their only "compensation" for the loss of over 7 million acres of land, interestingly enough, was a continuation of the previously secured annuities, and the promise of schools and instruction in mechanical and agricultural arts. The government also promised to provide heads of households with additional "subsistence" in the form of small amounts of beef, flour, corn, coffee, sugar, and beans. These rations were to continue until the Indians could "support themselves." The only lasting benefit secured through the agreement was that the head of a family was entitled "to a comfortable house" after he or she had selected an allotment of land. This was an amazing deal for the United States. The federal government had just "legally" sanctioned an illegal agreement which gave the United States title to nearly 7.7 million acres of Sioux land in exchange for (1) another promise to meet its 1868 treaty pledge to provide annuities; (2) a meager amount of subsistence rations (beef, flour, and corn); and (3) the promise of a home once an allotment was selected. But, as Deloria has argued:

> Even if one were to follow the argument of the United States and argue that the 1876 agreement was legal (and this sentence is in no way to be construed as indicating that the agreement was a legal act) even then the United States did not fulfill its promises. The 1876 agreement promised that the government would build comfortable houses for every Indian who would agree to take an allotment. Needless to say the government never did anything of the kind. Rather, the 1876 agreement's terms were forgotten as soon as the area was secured to the United States.[141]

The succeeding five decades—the 1880s through the 1920s—were arguably the darkest years for the Lakota people. Under the so-called Crook Treaty in 1889, the Sioux lost an additional 11 million acres of land in the breakup of the Great Sioux Reservation and had the remainder subdivided into six smaller reservations. And Bureau of Indian Affairs policies aimed at dominating virtually every phase of the lives of the Lakota resulted in the effective disempowerment of traditional tribal leadership.[142]

GENESIS OF THE SIOUX NATION'S JUDICIAL EFFORTS

By 1915 a number of business councils had formed on the separate Sioux reservations. While not vested with substantive political authority, since they were largely controlled by Indian agents and superintendents and were usually convened only by the government agent, they nevertheless began to give voice to the Lakota feeling of betrayal by the federal government regarding their lands.[143] These Sioux had never accepted the loss of the Black Hills, but although they were vocal in their protestations, for many years they had virtually no legal or even political means of seeking redress.

Their first opportunity for a measure of justice arrived in 1920 when Congress authorized the Sioux to bring their claim against the United States before the Court of Claims.[144] The eight bands of the Great Sioux

Nation,[145] through their lead attorney, Ralph Case, on May 7, 1923, filed the Black Hills claim, Sioux C-531. This petition was actually divided into twenty-four separate claim petitions, which contained all the allegations set forth in the original petition,[146] asserting that the United States had illegally taken the Black Hills and had generally failed to fulfill its treaty and trust obligations to the Sioux bands, which they maintained was a violation of the Fifth Amendment to the United States Constitution. On May 7, 1934, on the eleventh anniversary of Case's original filing, the Sioux lawyers submitted twenty-four "Separate Amended Petitions" to the Claims Court on behalf of the Sioux Tribe.

> Bound in a single volume of more than three hundred pages, each amended petition detailed a single Sioux claim, for the first time defining in legal terms the many grievances vaguely alluded to back in 1923. The Indians brought suit for nearly $1 billion. This included $40 million plus 5 percent interest for the misappropriation of funds pursuant to the 1889 land cession, $14 million for undelivered annuities, $12 million for deficient education programs, and $8 million for insufficient rations and clothing.[147]

The Sioux's major claim was the Black Hills claim, C-531-7, which entailed the value of over 73 million acres of land that the Sioux alleged had been illegally taken under the 1851 and 1868 treaties. They sought compensation in the amount of $189,368,531.05 for their land loss, since by law they were not entitled to seek the actual return of land.

The overwhelming majority of lesser Sioux claims were dismissed by the Court of Claims. Although in several cases the Sioux were awarded judgments, the Court of Claims determined after an accounting that the amount of allowable offsets exceeded the amount of the award and the petitions were dismissed.[148]

On June 1, 1942, the Court of Claims rendered its harshest blow to the Sioux in the Black Hills claim, the largest of the twenty-four suits. In *Sioux Tribe of Indians v. United States*, the Court dismissed the Sioux petition on the grounds that the Black Hills claim was essentially a moral claim not protected by the Fifth Amendment and therefore fell outside the jurisdiction conferred by the 1920 act.[149] This decision prompted a plethora of litigation that would culminate in the decision under discussion.[150]

When Congress established the Indian Claims Commission (ICC) in 1946, the Sioux received another opportunity to file their claim. On August 15, 1950, the Sioux counsel resubmitted the tribes' claim. In 1954, the ICC entered what it termed a "final judgment" and dismissed the tribes' plea on the basis that the Sioux had "failed to prove their case."[151] Interestingly, the commission "disposed of this large and complex litigation after a hearing which lasted two hours and twenty minutes."[152] The Sioux appealed to the Court of Claims, which affirmed the dismissal.[153] The Sioux Nation then hired new attorneys and petitioned the Court of Claims with a motion to vacate their affirmation because the ICC's decision had been reached "on the basis of an incomplete record due to inadequate representation by former Sioux counsel and that respondents' [Sioux Tribe] rights should not be prejudiced by his erroneous factual concessions."[154] The Claims Court granted this motion and in 1958 ordered the ICC to reconsider its judgment.

Some sixteen years after the initial refiling, and after a complicated and time-consuming series of hearings, pleadings, and petitions, the ICC rendered its "principal decision," which totaled 212 pages. The Commission held (1) that the Black Hills land and precious minerals, mainly gold, had a fair market value on February 28, 1877, of 17.1 million dollars; (2) that the 1877 agreement did, in fact, constitute a "taking" of Sioux land and rights for which just compensation was due under the Fifth Amendment; (3) that the United States had effectively waived the res judicata defense; (4) that 2,250,000 dollars in gold had been illegally removed from the Black Hills by trespassing miners before the 1877 agreement, and that this gold had an in-ground value of 450,000 dollars, for which the United States was liable; and (5) that the United States should be credited for the food and other rations (the amount to be later determined) it had furnished to the Sioux under the 1877 agreement.[155]

The federal government immediately appealed this decision, arguing that the Sioux's Fifth Amendment claim should have been barred by res judicata[156] or, in the alternative, that the 1877 act did not constitute a "taking" for which just compensation was due. Even as the government's appeal was pending, Congress enacted a law[157] in 1974 aimed at addressing the ICC's determination of offset costs that the United States had paid out to the Sioux. The Senate Committee on Interior and Insular Affairs was flabbergasted that the government would attempt to offset the cost of supplies and rations it had expended on behalf of the Sioux against whatever settlement was reached. As the Senate report stated:

> Having violated the 1868 Treaty and having reduced the Indians to starvation, the United States should not now be in the position of saying that the rations it furnished constituted payment for the land which

it took. In short, the Government committed two wrongs: First, it deprived the Sioux of their livelihood; secondly, it deprived the Sioux of their land. What the United States gave back in rations should not be stretched to cover both wrongs.[158]

In 1975, the Court of Claims, in a majority ruling but without reaching the merits of the case, held that its 1942 opinion, whether "rightly or wrongly" decided, gave rise to a valid res judicata defense to the Sioux's claim for just compensation under the Fifth Amendment.[159] The Supreme Court again denied certiorari.[160] What the Claims Court decision meant was that the Sioux's 17.5 million award, plus interest, had been lost. However, the ICC had also stated that the federal government had taken the Black Hills using dishonorable and unfair procedures. The Lakota, therefore, were entitled to damages of at least 17.5 million, without interest, under section 2 of the ICC Act, and for the value of the gold taken by trespassing prospectors before the 1877 act.

When the case returned to the ICC from the Court of Claims, the value of the rights-of-way obtained by the United States under the 1877 act was determined to be $3,484 dollars. In addition, the ICC ruled that the government had not made any payments that could be considered offsets. Then, on October 15, 1976, the government moved for the commission to enter a final award in favor of the Sioux Nation for the amount of $17,553,484. They concluded, however, that the final judgment should be deferred because of pending congressional legislation. The matter lay in abeyance until Congress enacted legislation on March 13, 1978,[161] authorizing the Court of Claims to review the merits of the case.

The Court of Claims in 1979, by a six-to-two decision, affirmed the ICC's 1974 decision that the 1877 treaty had effected a "taking" of the Sioux's Black Hills and of the rights-of-way across the Great Sioux Nation Reservation in violation of the Fifth Amendment. The Court, in acordance with the ICC opinion, entered a final judgment for the Lakota Nation of over 17 million dollars, with interest at 5 percent from February 28, 1877. The United States petitioned for a writ of certiorari on October 19, 1979, and the writ was granted in December of that year.

MASKING WITHIN THE DECISION: THE OPINION

On June 30, the Supreme Court, in an 8–1 decision, affirmed the lower court's ruling that the federal government, in exercising its powers of eminent domain, had indeed unconstitutionally taken the Black Hills from the Lakota people in violation of the Fifth Amendment and had not paid adequate compensation for the land. In an example of the Supreme Court's oft-exercised constitutional/treaty legal consciousness, the Court relied, accurately this time, on the 1868 treaty and the Constitution to reach a conclusion that favored the Lakota. There were two major issues to be addressed by the Blackmun-led majority. The first was whether Congress, in enacting the 1978 amendment which voided the res judicata defense, thus directing the Court of Claims to review the merits of the case, had inadvertently violated the separation of powers doctrine which partitions the three branches of government. The Court devoted nearly sixteen pages to this issue, and while the theory of separation of powers is certainly an important constitutional matter, it is sufficient to say that Blackmun expressed the view that Congress's waiver of res judicata did not violate the doctrine.

Plenary Power, Eminent Domain, or Treaty Rights?

An issue that has been at the forefront of Lakota-United States political and litigious activity for over one hundred years is that of Congress's power vis-à-vis tribal property. It is important in the issue of whether Congress in "taking" the Black Hills was following (1) the line of *plenary power*, or (2) the line of *eminent domain*. The line of plenary power, enunciated fully in *Lone Wolf*, established Congress's preeminent authority over tribal property "by reason of its exercise of guardianship over their interest, and that such authority might be implied, even though opposed to the strict letter of a treaty with the Indians."

The line of eminent domain, described in the 1937 case *Shoshone Tribe of Indians v. United States*,[162] while conceding Congress's "paramount power over Indian property," did hold that such power did not enable the government to "give the tribal lands to others, or to appropriate them to its own purposes, without rendering or assuming an obligation to render just compensation."[163] The power of eminent domain recognizes a government's right to take private property for public purpose so long as just compensation is paid. The fundamental problem for tribes, however, is that both of these lines presume that Congress retains a vast, unarticulated power over tribal nations without a constitutional mooring and without tribal consent. Furthermore, both of these lines ignore or subsume the more correct line of *treaty rights*, which guaranteed to tribes respect for their sovereignty and their property and which were to be inviolate unless tribal consent was first obtained.

Nevertheless, the lines of plenary power and eminent domain were the parameters that would instruct Blackmun's decision. Both of these lines are steeped with an implicit belief in congressional supremacy over tribal nations. Blackmun moved to a discussion of a recent Court of Claims case, *Three Affiliated Tribes of Fort Berthold Reservation v. United States*,[164] in which the "good faith" test was articulated. This was ostensibly designed to reconcile the plenary power and eminent domain lines. *Three Tribes* held that while Congress could act in either capacity—as a plenary power or as a sovereign exercising eminent domain—it could not act in both ways simultaneously. "Congress," the Court said, "can own two hats, but it cannot wear them both at the same time."[165]

The problem, however, is that the good faith test is not really a test. It is merely a manipulation of the so-called trustee/guardian theory, which, earlier courts had maintained, "is a relationship that has already been disclaimed unless a treaty, agreement, or statute specifically states that the Federal Government is assuming such an obligation. The test further waits until Congress has acted and then suggests a means by which such action can be interpreted as a legal and authorized act."[166]

Blackmun said that the Court of Claims had applied the *Three Tribes* test to the facts of the Sioux claims case and had concluded that when Congress enacted the 1877 act, that body had failed to make a good faith effort to give the Sioux full value for the Black Hills. Therefore, the major issue before the Court, Blackmun now stated, was "whether the legal standard applied by the Court of Claims was erroneous."[167]

Who Is Representing the Lakota?

The attorneys for both parties had each adopted one of the lines as their primary argument. The United States attorney, Deputy Solicitor General Louis F. Claiborne, maintained that the United States had committed no discernible wrong when it unilaterally took the Sioux lands and violated the 1868 treaty. In oral arguments, when asked to explain the so-called trust relationship between the federal government and tribes, Claiborne averred, "[The] trustee relationship, Mr. Chief Justice, carries both obligations but also unusual powers, the power to dispose against the will and without exercising the power of eminent domain."[168] In response to a justice's query, "[The] Constitution itself recognizes Indian tribes as sovereigns, does it not?" Solicitor Claiborne casually remarked, "yes, but the Constitution *perhaps* also recognizes the dependent status of Indian tribes, their inability to alienate their land which accordingly, if it must be done in their interest, may occasionally have to be done against their will by their guardian"[169] (emphasis mine).

Apart from the fact that there has never been a congressionally mandated "guardian-ward" relationship between tribes and the United States, Claiborne was reading into the Commerce Clause a nonexistent "dependent status" for tribes. The Constitution's most pertinent clause, the Indian Commerce Clause, simply states that Congress will manage the government's commercial trade affairs with tribal nations. Nothing in the Constitution can be read as "perhaps" recognizing Indian "dependent status."

The Lakota's lead attorney, Arthur Lazarus Jr., also remarkably conceded not only that the government had the power to break treaties but that this could happen without tribal consent. "*Lone Wolf*," said Lazarus, "tells us that Congress—if Congress determines that the reservation should be cut in half, Congress can come in and do it; it can do it without the consent of the Indians and they can do it in violation of the treaty."[170] The only substantive difference, then, between the arguments of Lazarus and Claiborne was that the former believed that Congress's enactment of the 1877 law effected a "taking" and therefore the United States was liable under the Fifth Amendment to pay for the taken property. "The Constitution," Lazarus maintained, "was not only color blind, it is dollar blind and we are entitled to just compensation under every single ruling of this Court. . . ."[171] In response, a majority of the justices refused to confront Congress and say that something more substantial than "just compensation" was at stake. Blackmun seemed to sense the inadequacy of his theory since he dumped the question before the Court into a footnote. The most the Court could do, said Blackmun, would be to consider whether "Congress was acting under circumstances in which that 'taking' implied an obligation to pay just compensation, or whether it was acting pursuant to its unique powers to manage and control tribal property as the guardian of Indian welfare, in which event the Just Compensation Clause would not apply."[172] However, as one leading scholar observed, "an action like this taking judged 'unconstitutional' in an Indian setting seems to mean that something horribly distasteful has occurred, but that it is nevertheless permanent and irreversible."[173]

While an affirmation of the Court of Claims case would constitute a financial victory of sorts for the Lakota, and especially their attorneys, it in no way provided any of the much needed clarification as to the actual basis of the Lakota/United States political relationship. The majority, by refusing to question whether the Congress could take the land; by refusing to consider any return of the stolen land; and by refusing to disavow the *Lone Wolf* holding that Congress may unilaterally abrogate Indian treaties based on its own perception of what it considers the maintenance of "perfect good faith" toward Indians, failed to inspire much hope for justice among the Lakota or other tribes with treaty-based claims before the Supreme Court.

The "Timely" Demise of the Mask of the Political Question Doctrine

Although Blackmun refused to renounce the extraconstitutional plenary power doctrine, his opinion in *Sioux Nation*, coming on the heels of another Supreme Court case, *Delaware Tribal Business Committee v. Weeks*,[174] finally buried the infamous "political question" doctrine, which had for years been employed to deny tribes even a judicial hearing on various issues. The government had argued in *Sioux Nation* that under the political question doctrine, the Court had to accept Congress's taking of the Black Hills as the action of a "trustee" working for the good of "dependent wards." Blackmun, however, citing *Delaware Tribe*, said that the prescription of congressional good faith, which was historically based on the view that the tribes/U.S. government relationship entailed political matters not subject to judicial review, had "long since been discredited in takings cases, and was expressly laid to rest in *Delaware....*"[175]

Blackmun terminated his discussion of the now doubly discredited political question doctrine by observing that the "presumption of congressional good faith has little to commend it as an enduring principle for deciding questions of the kind presented here.[176] He then made two statements which illustrate that even a liberal justice may accept the plenary (absolute) power of Congress over Indian tribes, despite its dubious constitutional basis. Blackmun said, "In every case where a taking of treaty-protected property is alleged, a reviewing court must recognize that tribal lands are subject to Congress' power to control and manage the tribes' affairs."[177]

The important phrases in this quote are "treaty-protected," "control," and "manage." In a footnote, Blackmun emphatically reinforced the disastrous *Tee-Hit-Ton* principle that so-called unrecognized or aboriginal title was not compensable under the Fifth Amendment. Second,

Blackmun's statement that Congress retains power to "control and manage" Indian tribal affairs is presumptuous—this self-generated congressional power lacks constitutional or treaty support. Blackmun went on to note, however, that this congressional power "is not absolute." It was limited, he said, by the guardianship doctrine and "pertinent constitutional restrictions." But he had already stated that this power was unlimited if the tribal lands in question (like those of Alaskan natives) had not been expressly set aside by treaty or agreement. And some courts maintain that the constraints seemingly inherent in the "guardianship" idea are not applicable unless a tribe has been specifically determined to be in a guardianship relationship with the United States based on a prior treaty, statute, or court case.

Blackmun turned to the question of whether the Court of Claims' assessment of the case had been guided by an appropriate legal standard. He recited a long quote from the Claims Court case in which the judges affirmed and expanded the *Three Tribes* test regarding the adequacy of the consideration provided by the government for the lands it had taken in 1877. That court had held that the government's basic assertion of "good faith" was insufficient reason precluding the court from examining the merits of the tribes' claims. In yet another interesting footnote, Justice Blackmun, in interpreting the Court of Claims' discussion on congressional takings, based on the test of "good faith," indicated that it was still possible for this test to serve as the basis for a future taking. He noted that "in an appropriate case" the test would still be valid if supported by "objective indicia" and that there might be instances where "the consideration provided the Indian for surrendered treaty lands was so patently adequate and fair that Congress' failure to state the obvious would not result in the finding of the compensable taking."[178] Who has the power to make the determination of "good faith" or "patently adequate" is the problematic issue from the tribal perspective. There is not even a hint here that Congress would curtail its activities in the face of tribal protest. On the contrary, one is left with the understanding that takings are solely at the discretion of Congress.

Finally, in a footnote that must have elicited a collective smile from the Lakota, Blackmun reacted forcefully to the central arguments of Justice Rehnquist's dissent. Rehnquist had asserted that the factual findings of the ICC, the Court of Claims' determination, and Blackmun's majority opinion were based on what he called a "revisionist" view of history. Blackmun vigorously refuted those charges by noting that Rehnquist was unable to "identify a single author, non-revisionist, neo-revisionist, or otherwise," who subscribed to the view of history that Rehnquist had offered. In reality, Rehnquist was the "revisionist."

"The primary sources for the story told in this opinion," said Blackmun in reference to the majority opinion, "are the factual findings of the Indian Claims Commission and the Court of Claims. A reviewing Court generally will not discard such findings because they raise the specter of creeping revisionism, as the dissent would have it, but will do so only when they are erroneous and unsupported by the record."[179] None of the affected parties, including the federal government, had even hinted that the lower court's factual findings could not withstand close scrutiny.

Finally, Blackmun chided Rehnquist for his reliance on the original 1942 Court of Claims decision. He reminded Rehnquist that that decision was not at issue and, more significantly, brought out—no doubt to Rehnquist's chagrin—that the 1942 court's reliance on the presumption of good faith was actually based on "an erroneous *legal* interpretation" (emphasis original) of the *Lone Wolf* precedent.[180] Blackmun's admonition of Rehnquist in this case makes one pause to wonder why such a rebuke did not arise with *Oliphant*.

JUSTICE REHNQUIST'S DISSENT

Unfolding in the wake of his *Oliphant* ruling, Rehnquist's dissent failed to surprise most informed people. He had displayed a willingness to recreate and, in some cases, to fabricate historical scenarios that would enable him to reach the legal conclusions he sought. He had also shown adroitness at selectively using documentary sources to prove his often constitutionally unsupported points. Although Justice Blackmun succeeded in refuting Rehnquist's multiple faulty arguments, the dissent is a fascinating document that bears examination. The following quotation from it serves to illustrate Rehnquist's garbled view of the tribal world and the tribal-federal political relationship:

> There were undoubtedly greed, cupidity, and other less-than-admirable tactics employed by the Government during the Black Hills episode in the settlement of the West, but the Indians did not lack their share of villainy either. It seems to me quite unfair to judge by the light of "revisionist" histories or the mores of another era actions that were taken under pressure of time more than a century ago.[181]

This is an extraordinary statement. Rehnquist was saying that Congress's unconstitutional and unilateral confiscation of the Black Hills in direct

AMERICAN INDIAN SOVEREIGNTY AND THE SUPREME COURT

violation of the 1868 treaty was counterbalanced by the Sioux's being a less-than-perfect people who had their share of behavioral problems. "Different historians," he claimed, "not writing for the purpose of having their conclusions or observations inserted in the reports of congressional committees, have taken different positions than those expressed in some of the materials referred to in the Court's opinion." [182] However, in response to Blackmun's inquiry as to the identity of these phantom historians, Rehnquist neglected to cite a single name or source to support his remarks. He then excused his inability to produce a source on the grounds that "history, no more than law is not an exact (or for that matter, an inexact) science." [183] It is inarguable that neither history nor law is a scientific enterprise. The historical record of the United States' "greed, cupidity, and other less-than-admirable tactics" that Rehnquist acknowledged, however, is obvious to those students of history who are not already wedded to any particular doctrinal or ideological conclusions of their own creation. Note the tone of this statement:

> But the inferences which the Court itself draws from the letter from General Sheridan to General Sherman . . . as well as other passages in the Court's opinion, leave a stereotyped and one-sided impression both of the settlement regarding the Black Hills portion of the Great Sioux Reservation and of the gradual expansion of the National Government from the Proclamation Line of King George III in 1763 to the Pacific Ocean.[184]

The majority, however, was not drawing "inferences." It is, as the documentary record shows, a fact that, subsequent to that correspondence, the Grant administration pulled the U.S. cavalry out and allowed the Black Hills to be overrun with non-Indians. These and other episodes were, therefore, open violations, not inferential interpretations.

Rehnquist ended his revisionist history by citing from two dated and biased sources—a statement by Ray Billington in a 1963 work, *Soldier and Brave*, and a quote from Samuel E. Morrison in his 1965 study, *The Oxford History of the American People*. Both statements are laced with stereotypes and errors. They had been selected by Rehnquist, apparently to show that it was really the Indians' "cultural differences" which had forced the United States into open conflict with tribes. Rehnquist's selection of the following Morrison quote is particularly telling:

> The Plains Indians seldom practiced agriculture or other primitive arts, but they were fine physical specimens; . . . They lived only for the

day, recognized no rights of property, robbed or killed anyone if they thought they could get away with it, inflicted cruelty without a qualm, and endured torture without flinching.[185]

This ethnocentric statement points out that Rehnquist had no inclination whatsoever to grapple with the valid constitutional and treaty issues raised through the Black Hills claim. More evidence for Rehnquist's ethnocentricity is found in his closing paragraph:

> That there was tragedy, deception, barbarity, and virtually every other vice known to man in the 300-year history of the expansion of the original 13 Colonies into a Nation which now embraces more than three million square miles and 50 States cannot be denied. But in a court opinion, as a historical and not a legal matter, both settler and Indian are entitled to the benefit of the Biblical adjuration: "Judge not, that ye be not judged."[186]

CONCLUSION

Despite an apparently impressive monetary award in the amount of 105 million dollars, plus the earlier approved 17.5 million, today's 60,000 constituted Lakota people, congregated into eight relatively autonomous tribes, have thus far refused to accept any payment. They generally believe that the claim entails issues that go far beyond a mere land transaction. This has been best summarized by a statement made by Court of Claims Judge Fred Nichols in the 1975 opinion involving the Sioux claim. In that case, the court ruled that the Indians Claims Commission was barred by the doctrine of res judicata from reaching the merits of the Sioux's Fifth Amendment claim, although Nichols did affirm that the Sioux were entitled to payment with a value of the Black Hills at the time of their taking in 1877 because the United States had used unfair and dishonorable dealings with the Sioux. Nichols candidly said:

> A Treaty was tendered the Sioux for adhesion in 1876. However, breach of the obligation to protect the Indians' lands from unwanted intruders, as promised in the 1868 treaty, reneged on another special relationship. The duplicity of President Grant's course and the duress practiced on the starving Sioux, speak for themselves. *A more ripe and rank case of dishonorable dealings will never, in all probability, be found in our history, which is not, taken as a whole, the disgrace it now pleases some persons to believe.*[187] (emphasis mine)

Meanwhile, the award for the taking of the Black Hills rests in the Federal Treasury where interest continues to accrue. It is now estimated at 350 million dollars.[188] The fact that each of the participating Sioux bands enacted tribal resolutions opposing any distribution of the award is a powerful testament to the tribe's principled position—land is more precious, and certainly more enduring than money. In the ensuing years, because of the Lakota resistance to a dollar settlement, and because of a small but vocal congressional support, several legislative proposals have been broached that would have entailed the return of some "federal" land in the Black Hills, financial recompense, and other items to the Lakota. To date, none of these has succeeded because of state and business opposition, congressional roadblocks, and some Indian resistance. The process remains complex and cumbersome.[189] No resolution is in sight, but at least, for now, it is out of the hands of the United States Supreme Court.

Since the late 1980s, the federal government's executive, legislative, and judicial branches—along with that unwieldy and unyielding mass known simply as the "bureaucracy"—have produced a dizzying crop of laws, policies, proclamations, regulations, and court decisions which have served, ironically, to (1) reaffirm tribal sovereignty; (2) permit and encourage greater state interference within Indian country; (3) enhance federal legislative authority over tribes; and (4) deny constitutional "free exercise" religious protections both to individual Indians and tribal nations.

In 1988, Congress established the experimental Tribal Self-Governance Demonstration Project (TSGDP),[1] which was made permanent on October 25, 1994.[2] Potentially, this was an important step towards the restoration of the tribal right to self-determination. The TSGDP and accompanying policy discussions had been preceded by two 1987 congressional resolutions—one joint, the other a Senate concurrent resolution—which reaffirmed the political nature of the tribal-federal relationship.

Public Law 100-67,[3] enacted July 10, 1987, was a joint resolution commemorating the bicentennial of the Northwest Ordinance of 1787 and reaffirming the ordinance as one of the fundamental legal documents of the United States. The ordinance, the articles of which were to "forever remain unalterable, unless by common consent,"[4] provided a civil government for the Northwest Territory and included a declaration by the federal government that it would adhere to "democratic principles, religious freedom, and individual rights."[5] Moreover, the ordinance enunciated the fundamental political premise—consent—on which subsequent federal Indian policy was to be based:

> The utmost good faith shall always be observed toward the Indians, their lands and their property shall never be taken from them without their consent; and in their property, rights and liberty, they never shall

be invaded or disturbed, unless in just and lawful wars authorized by Congress; but laws founded in justice and humanity shall from time to time be made, for preventing wrongs being done to them and for preserving peace and friendship with them. . . .[6]

About two months later, Senator Daniel Inouye (D., Hawaii), along with eighteen of his colleagues, introduced Senate Concurrent Resolution 75, which acknowledged (1) the democratic traditions of the Iroquois Confederacy and other tribal nations and the role that these nations played in the formation of the United States Constitution; (2) the "government-to-government" relationship between tribes and the federal government; (3) the federal government's continuing legal obligations to tribal nations in the areas of health, education, economic assistance, and cultural identity; and (4) a statement reaffirming the government's goal to exercise "utmost good faith" in upholding its treaties with tribal nations, as stated in the provisions of the Northwest Ordinance.

The year 1987 was also noteworthy in that it signaled the start of yet another congressional investigation[7] of the alleged corruption, fraud, incompetence, and mismanagement lacing the Bureau of Indian Affairs (BIA) and other federal agencies that deal with tribes and individual Indians in several areas. Included in the survey and analysis were issues relating to tribal economic development, Indian preference contracting, Indian child sexual abuse, natural resource issues, health issues, housing concerns, and tribal elite corruption.

Not surprisingly, the Special Committee on Investigations, cochaired by Arizona Senators DeConcini and McCain of the Senate Select Committee on Indian Affairs, which conducted the study, was not directed as part of its congressional mandate to investigate the impact of Supreme Court decisions on Indian tribes. The government's three branches have historically, if not always consistently, operated from a common set of intellectual, political, and cultural premises when it came to developing, implementing, and evaluating programs and policies for America's tribal nations. This is not at all surprising, considering that national politics, according to Robert Dahl, is dominated by fairly enduring, cohesive alliances among the branches. And the Supreme Court, like other political institutions, Dahl notes, "is a member of such ruling coalitions," and its decisions are therefore "typically supportive of the policies emerging from other political institutions."[8]

In 1988, however, the political and judicial branches began moving in radically divergent directions on several important issue areas, most dramatically in the sensitive areas of religious freedom for tribal peoples and local taxation on Indian-owned land. In *Lyng v. Northwest Indian Cemetery Protective Association* (the first of three decisions to be reviewed in this chapter), the Supreme Court held in a majority opinion that the Constitution's Free Exercise clause did not prevent governmental destruction of the most sacred sites of three small tribes in northern California. The majority made this ruling in full realization that an activity of the United States Forest Service—the construction of a six-mile road—would virtually destroy the Indians' ability to practice their religion.

That April, just eight days after *Lyng*, the Supreme Court in *Employment Division, Department of Human Resources v. Smith* (also known as *Smith I*) granted certiorari and remanded the case back to the Oregon Supreme Court for determination of whether an Oregon statute criminalizing peyote provided an exception for Indian religious use. The High Court suggested that "if Oregon does prohibit the religious use of peyote, and if that prohibition is consistent with the federal Constitution, there is no federal right to engage in that conduct in Oregon."[9] The Supreme Court later reheard the case and rendered final judgment on April 17, 1990. In *Smith II*, which will be examined in this chapter, the Court flatly denied that the First Amendment protected the religious rights of Native American Church (NAC) members and unceremoniously discarded the "compelling interest" test.

On the day after *Smith II* was decided, however, Congress struck a blow for Indian rights by enacting a Comprehensive Elementary and Secondary Education law[10] which contained a provision of largely symbolic but still considerable significance: "The Congress," it was declared, "hereby repudiates and rejects House Concurrent Resolution 108 of the 83rd Congress and any policy of unilateral termination of federal relations with any Indian nation." The essence of unilateral termination, an aberrant and short-lived federal policy arising in the wake of World War II, was that the federal government was intent on abolishing federal supervision and protection of tribes and their resources and making the "terminated" Indians subject to state law. This policy aroused strong tribal resentment, and in 1958 Secretary of the Interior Fred A. Seaton stated that termination acts would not be passed without the full consent of the Indians concerned.[11] In addition, unilateral termination was later verbally discredited by Presidents Nixon (1970) and Reagan (1983) in their Indian policy statements. It was not, however, officially rejected by the body which had created it until 1988.

Besides this belated expulsion of the termination resolution, 1988 witnessed amendments to several existing laws,[12] the enactment of several laws to settle claims and expand, protect, or create Indian reservations,[13] and, finally, the enactment of new legislation on important issues such as political recognition,[14] economic development,[15] gambling,[16] and water rights.[17] Laws passed in subsequent years have also played an important role in underscoring the growing viability of American Indian tribes as peoples and as governments. A partial list includes the 1989 National Museum of the American Indian Act,[18] the Indian Law Enforcement Reform Act of 1990,[19] the Indian Environmental Regulatory Enhancement Act of 1990,[20] the Seneca Nation Settlement Act of 1990,[21] the Native American Graves Protection and Repatriation Act of 1990,[22] and a 1991 act to restore to tribal governments criminal jurisdiction over nonmember Indians,[23] a right which had been nullified by a Supreme Court decision (*Duro v. Reina*) the year before.

The congressional enactments cited above are of variable importance and substance. Several were, in fact, mere minor modifications of existing laws which have had negligible influence in improving either tribal socioeconomic conditions or in repairing the structural inequities evident in the relationship between tribes and the United States. Others, however, came to be considered by many tribal citizens and their governments as nothing less than fresh breaches of sovereign tribal rights (e.g., the Indian Gaming Act). Nevertheless, when compared with the Supreme Court's two decisions on matters of Indian religion—*Lyng* and *Smith II*—and the third case we will examine, *County of Yakima v. Confederated Tribes and Bands of the Yakima Indian Nation* (1992), it is evident that the Congress was at least attempting to address and resolve certain issues of importance to the tribes and to improve intergovernmental relations, while the Supreme Court seemed to focus on battering the ever-fragile existence not only of tribal sovereign rights but also of the constitutional rights of American citizenship to which American Indian individuals are entitled.

THE BELATED FEDERAL PROTECTION
OF INDIAN RELIGIOUS FREEDOM

General legislative support for a degree of genuine tribal autonomy has been evident since a spate of federal activity and legislation in the 1970s focused on the disavowal, but not the official renunciation, of the unilateral termination policy. Termination was replaced by a more enlightened, though still flawed, policy of tribal self-determination. A crucial dimension in the congressional quest to improve relations with tribes centered on the problems that tribal people faced in attempting to access sacred sites, utilize sacred objects, and practice their traditional religions. Each of these problems came as a direct result of the inconsistent and sometimes insensitive federal administrative policies and practices which hampered Indian religious rights.

The history of the federal government's ultimate goal of the destruction of American Indian cultural identity, especially aboriginal religions, from the early treaty period through the 1920s is well documented.[24] Once tribal identity and all vestiges of aboriginal culture had been eradicated, Judeo-Christian values, beliefs, and institutions were to be the vehicle through which the assimilation and Americanization of Indians was to take place. That this plan of indoctrination was officially sanctioned by the federal government and supported by federal tax dollars, not to mention Indian treaty funds, was, of course, a clear violation of the separation of church and state doctrine.

For much of this period, beginning most systematically with Grant's Peace Policy in the late 1860s,[25] various Christian denominations strove mightily to impart their religion to tribal people. Although they talked about freedom of religion, their concept completely disregarded the religious rights of Indians and belittled indigenous spiritual beliefs. "By religious freedom," notes Prucha, "they [Christians] meant liberty of actions on the reservations for their own missionary activities. 'The Indians have a right, under the Constitution, as much as any other person in the Republic . . . to the full enjoyment of liberty of conscience; accordingly they have *a right to choose whatever Christian belief they wish* [emphasis mine], without interference from the government.'"[26]

Despite a gradual extension of the federal franchise to a majority of Indians who had received allotments under the 1887 General Allotment Act,[27] with the remainder receiving citizenship in 1924,[28] the fundamental questions of constitutional protection for aboriginal tribal religions and a constitutional prohibition against establishment of religion among the tribes were nonissues until the late 1970s.[29]

Congress finally responded to the lobbying efforts of tribal people and non-Indian advocates of Indian rights by enacting the American Indian Religious Freedom Act[30] (AIRFA) in 1978. This joint resolution declared that from that time on, it would be the policy of the United

States "to protect and preserve for American Indians their inherent right of freedom to believe, express, and exercise the traditional religions of the American Indian, Eskimo, Aleut, and Native Hawaiians, including but not limited to, access to sales, use and possession of sacred objects, and the freedom to worship through ceremonial and traditional rights."

The resolution's enactment was a clear admission on the part of Congress that traditional tribal religious rights had not been protected, in part because of the anomalous status of Indians as both citizens and subjects. Hence, Congress, exercising its plenary legislative authority, recognized the need to legislatively extend federal protection for religious rights to tribes and their members because the First Amendment of the Constitution had failed to protect those rights.[31]

Tribal governments and their citizens assumed that this belated congressional acknowledgment regarding the distinctive status of traditional Indian religious rights was a clarification of the federal government's attitude toward traditional religions. However, it was, in reality, a largely symbolic measure. Notwithstanding laudatory comments from conservative North American historians like Wilcomb Washburn, who stated in a 1984 article that "there is no question that the religious rights of American Indians, after hundreds of years of assault, are more fully protected than ever before,"[32] virtually all of the data emanating from the federal courts from the passage of AIRFA to 1984 show that such was not the case. The religious rights of tribal citizens recognized by Congress in the enactment of AIRFA were subsequently devastated by federal court activity; indeed, a majority of such cases have been decided *since* the religious freedom policy directive. Even AIRFA's author, Morris Udall (D., Arizona), said that the bill conferred no "special religious rights on Indians; changes no existing state or federal law, and has no teeth in it."[33] The "lack of teeth" statement, importantly, meant that "nowhere in the law is there so much as a hint of any intent to create a course of action or any judicially enforceable individual rights."[34]

The accompanying table details the most important federal court cases involving questions of Indian individual and tribal religious freedom. Of these, only *Native American Church v. Navajo Tribal Council* (1959) was a substantial victory for tribal nations. This case, however, did not involve a federal, state, or private activity in direct conflict with the rights of American Indians to protect their religion or access to sacred sites. Instead, it affirmed the inapplicability of the Constitution's First Amendment to tribal governments.

Lyng v. Northwest Indian Cemetery Protective Association

HOW LONG IS THE ROAD TO THE DESTRUCTION OF A RELIGION? SIX MILES BY THE COURT'S ODOMETER

> The Secretary [of War John C. Calhoun] directs that the condition of building the mill for the Caddoes and the Quapaws . . . to cost not more than $400.00, will be, that they bury the hatchet, and make peace in regard to the late murder of one of their people. *Tell them their great father hears with surprise that they believe in wizards and witches; that there are no such things; and that he is angry with them for killing the man under such a foolish belief.* (emphasis mine)
>
> Thomas L. McKenney, Bureau of Indian Affairs[35]

> The First Amendment declares that Congress shall make no law respecting an establishment of religion or prohibiting the free exercise thereof. The Fourteenth Amendment has rendered the legislatures of the states as incompetent as Congress to enact such laws. The constitutional inhibition of legislation on the subject of religion has a double aspect. On the one hand, it forestalls compulsion by law of the acceptance of any creed or the practice of any form of worship. Freedom of conscience and freedom to adhere to such religious organization or form of worship as the individual may choose cannot be restricted by law. *On the other hand, it safeguards the free exercise of the chosen form of religion. Thus the Amendment[s] embrace two concepts — freedom to believe, and freedom to act.* (emphasis mine)
>
> *Cantwell v. Connecticut* (1939)[36]

These quotes from Commissoner McKenney and the *Cantwell* decision of 1939 enunciate, respectively, the ethnocentric arrogance that historically has been displayed by Euro-Americans in their attitudes toward tribal beliefs and practices, and the beauty, tolerance, and equality inherent in the Constitution's doctrine on religious freedom. A close examination of *Lyng* and *Smith II* will reveal that the attitudes expressed in 1826 by Commissioner McKenney are still present in a modern-day Supreme Court. The constitutional force of the *Cantwell* excerpt, on the other hand, has rarely been sufficient to protect Indian religious practices.

The free-exercise component of the First Amendment is not an absolute guarantee that Congress cannot act to hinder a person's exercise of

TABLE I *Federal Court Activity Pertaining to Religious Freedom of American Indians*

Case	Issue(s)
Quick Bear v. Leupp, 210 U.S. (1908)	Treaty funds; First Amendment Establishment Clause
Native American Church v. Navajo Tribal Council, 272 F.2d 131 (1959)	Applicability of First Amendment to tribal nations; peyote
Sequoyah v. Tennessee Valley Authority, 620 F.2d 1159 (6th Cir., 1980), cert. denied, 449 U.S. 953 (1980)	First Amendment Free Exercise Clause; sacred Indian sites: Chota, Tennessee
Badoni v. Higginson, 638 F.2d 172 (10th Cir., 1980), cert. denied, 452 U.S. 954 (1981)	First Amendment Free Exercise Clause; sacred Indian sites on "public" lands: Rainbow Bridge, Arizona
Fools Crow v. Gullet, 541 F. Supp. 785 (D.S.D. 1982), aff'd., 706 F.2d 856 (8th Cir., 1983), cert. denied, 464 U.S. 977 (1984)	First Amendment Free Exercise Clause; sacred Indian sites on "public" lands: Bear Butte, South Dakota
Wilson v. Block, 708 F.2d 735 (D.C. Cir., 1983), cert. denied, 464 U.S. 956 (1984)	Free Exercise and Establishment Clauses of First Amendment; sacred Indian sites on "public" lands: San Francisco Peaks, Ariz.
Inupiat Community of the Arctic Slope v. United States, 548 F. Supp. 182 (D. Alaska, 1982), aff'd., 746 F.2d 570 (9th Cir., 1985), cert. denied, 474 U.S. 820 (1985)	First Amendment Free Exercise Clause; sacred area: Arctic Sea
Bowen v. Roy, 476 U.S. 693 (1986)	First Amendment Free Exercise Clause; administrative policy
Lyng v. Northwest Indian Cemetery Protective Association, 485 U.S. 439 (1988)	First Amendment Free Exercise Clause; sacred Indian sites: Chimney Rock area of northern California
U.S. v. Means, 858 F.2d 404 (8th Cir., 1988)	First Amendment Free Exercise Clause; public lands: Black Hills, South Dakota
Employment Division v. Smith, 494 U.S. 872 (1990)	First Amendment Free Exercise Clause; peyote; state criminal law

Tribe	Holding
Lakota	Federal statute prohibiting appropriations to sectarian schools is only applied to gratuitous appropriations and public moneys, not Indian treaty funds, which were paid by the government to fulfill treaty provisions.
Navajo	First Amendment does not restrict actions of tribal governments on question of religious freedom.
Cherokee	Cherokees' interest in protecting land was not sufficiently "religious" to invoke First Amendment protection.
Navajo	Navajo religious use of Rainbow Bridge, however indispensable to Navajo life, could not outweigh the economic benefits (electricity and tourism) generated by the Glen Canyon Dam.
Lakota, Cheyenne, and others	Tourism and other developments do not pose a "substantial burden" to the Indians' free exercise of religion. Promotion of tourism is a "compelling" state interest.
Navajo and Hopi	U.S. Forest Service may expand ski resort area on federal land despite Indian arguments that the expansion would desolate the area and violate their religious rights.
Inupiat	Federal government may grant petroleum leases despite Inupiat assertions of religious use and aboriginal title.
Abenaki	Free exercise does not require the government to conduct its internal affairs (requiring an Indian child to have a Social Security number) in ways that comport with the religious beliefs of citizens.
Yurok, Karok, and Tolowa tribes	Denied free exercise challenge to federal highway project that will destroy Indian religious sites.
Lakota	U.S. Forest Service did not violate Free Exercise Clause in denying Sioux Indians a special permit to use eight hundred acres of national forest as a religious, cultural, and educational community.
Klamath	The Free Exercise Clause permits the state to prohibit sacramental peyote use and thus to deny unemployment benefits to persons discharged for such use.

such rights. While religious beliefs are theoretically immune from governmental sanctions, religious practices may be regulated by the government. Historically, before allowing any burden on an individual's free exercise of religion, the courts required that the government show its actions to constitute the least restrictive means of accomplishing a compelling government objective.[37] The operative word here is *compelling*. For example, the government could prevent a group from conducting human sacrifices even if it was claimed that this was a necessary part of a religious ceremony. From the federal government's perspective, the "protection of human life is not only a valid secular purpose but also a subject in which the State has a compelling interest."[38]

HISTORICAL BACKGROUND

For untold generations the Yurok, Karok, and Tolowa tribes have lived in Northwestern California. Since 1876 they have lived on the Hoopa Valley Indian Reservation, which is adjacent to the Six Rivers National Forest. Created in 1947, the Six Rivers National Forest encompasses about 956,000 acres of rugged mountain terrain. Over time, certain members of these tribes have traveled to a remote, undeveloped area in the northeastern corner of the forest, known to the United States Forest Service as the Blue Creek Unit, to perform what they consider essential "rituals, and to prepare for specific religious and medicinal ceremonies."[39] Among Indian practitioners, this area is known simply as "High Country." This unadorned phrase understates the importance of this particular area for the tribes. It is considered "sacred and constitutes the center of the spiritual worlds for these tribes." In fact, "no other geographic areas or sites hold equivalent religious significance."[40] The High Country is the core of the tribe's religious complex known as "World Renewal." The following excerpt succinctly conveys the sacredness of this area to the Indians:

> World Renewal ceremonies, such as the major ceremonies known as the White Deerskin Dance and the Jump Dance, involve a number of specific functionaries and possess particular characteristics of form and setting; they are performed at the sites where the pre-human spirits are said to have first brought certain gifts to man.[41]

Furthermore, the spiritual leaders who conduct these ceremonies are initially trained in this area and must return periodically for renewal of their spiritual power in order to continue to preside. The area is also necessary for the carrying out of certain healing ceremonies. Medicine women are trained in the High Country for their healing tasks; they, too, are required to return periodically for prayers, to refurbish or acquire new power, and to gather essential medicines.

Finally, this sacred area served as "the training ground for the young people of the tribes to learn their tribe's traditional and religious beliefs and ceremonies. This training is necessary to preserve and convey such practices to future generations."[42] Until 1972, the Forest Service managed the area basically as a wilderness area. It was, in other words, left in its natural state for the protection of wildlife, fish habitat, scenic appeal, and opportunities for individuals interested in "primitive" recreational experiences.

In 1972, however, the Forest Service began preparations for a "multiple use management plan" for the Blue Creek unit, which encompassed the High Country. The principal impetus for the plan was the presence of more than 700 million board feet of Douglas fir. According to Charles Fried, an attorney for the secretary of agriculture, the timber industry, which is a key component in the economies of Del Norte and Humboldt counties, had been adversely impacted by congressional action directed at expanding the Redwood National Park. Such an expansion would reduce the amount of harvestable timber available to the timber companies; thus, the Forest Service was prompted by timber officials to seek an improved road network in the Six River National Forest to offset this alleged loss.[43] The Forest Service plan called for logging to be carried out over an eighty-year period and for the completion—by paving an existing dirt road—of a six-mile section of road to connect two northwestern California towns, Gasquet and Orleans (G-O Road). The road's major purpose was to make it easier to haul away timber, but it was also touted as necessary to increase public access to the National Forest and to facilitate fire control.[44]

In 1977, the Forest Service dispersed the draft of an Environmental Impact Statement which had evaluated ten different road proposals, several of which bypassed the High Country area deemed sacred by the Indians. Ultimately, the agency had selected a route which ran along the Chimney Rock and directly cut through the High Country. It was estimated that this Chimney Rock corridor road would bring "an average of 168 vehicles a day, including 76 logging vehicles, 84 administrative vehicles and 8 recreational vehicles," into the High Country.[45]

While the Forest Service pondered their choice, Congress, on August 11, 1978, enacted the AIRFA, which President Carter signed into law the next day. In section 2, the President directed the "various Federal departments, agencies, and other instrumentalities whose duties impact on Native American religious practices to evaluate their policies and procedures in consultation with Native religious leaders in order to determine and implement changes which may be necessary to protect and preserve Native American religious cultural rights and practices."[46] Every federal entity was to report back to the President in a year on how their program could be better administered so as to accommodate and be more sensitive to traditional Indian needs. Secretary of Agriculture Bob Bergland assured Senator James Abourezk, chairman of the Senate Select Committee on Indian Affairs, that he was well aware of how vital the protection and preservation of religious freedom for American Indians was for the continuation of their "cultural traditions" and to the "democratic traditions of this country." He said that he had, therefore, established a Native American task force "to improve the effectiveness of the United States Department of Agriculture's programs as they apply to Native Americans."[47]

Meanwhile, the Forest Service, after having received comments on its road proposals from the California tribes, the Advisory Council on Historic Preservation, and others, commissioned a comprehensive ecological, historical, and archaeological study of the Chimney Rock area to gauge the effect the proposed road would have. The research team, which consisted of twenty people, was headed by Dr. Dorothea Theodoratus. The investigation lasted a year and was completed in 1979. Theodoratus and her investigators combed the literature, carried out field investigations, and conducted 166 interviews with Yurok, Karok, and Tolowa Indians. The report confirmed that the entire area was "significant as an integral and indispensable part of Indian religious conceptualization and practice."[48] The study concluded by emphatically stating that the construction of a road along any of the proposed routes "would cause serious and irreparable damage to the sacred areas which are an integral and necessary part of the belief systems and lifeway of Northwest Californian Indian peoples."[49] Theodoratus and her colleagues recommended that the G-O road not be completed.

The Theodoratus report's findings were made public as the Forest Service and the Department of Agriculture were responding to the AIRFA policy request. The Forest Service, in particular, maintained in its August 1979 report to the President that "[r]eview by field offices has not identified any policies or procedures which have a negative effect on or will result in [abridgment] of the religious freedom of Native Americans." The agency declared that it would "continue to review these potential conflict areas in close cooperation with traditional religious leaders or their representatives to assure the protection and preservation of Native American religious rights and practices."[50]

Little did the tribes or President Carter realize how short-lived this commitment would be. Despite acting in 1981 to place over 13,000 acres of the High Country on the National Register of Historic Places, the Forest Service proceeded on March 2, 1982, the following year, to disregard not only the findings of the Theodoratus report, but even its own statement that it would respect the traditional religious rights of the three tribes. Instead, the Forest Service, under the direction of R. Max Peterson, proceeded to select the road proposal deemed potentially the most disruptive to the High Country. The other routes under consideration were apparently rejected because (1) they were longer and would exact higher construction and timber-hauling costs; (2) they would require the purchase of private land; and (3) they would still have an adverse effect on lands considered sacred to the indigenous people.[51]

This reversal left the Indians in a state of shock. The Forest Service proceeded to prepare a final Environmental Impact Statement for the construction of the G-O road. The head of the Regional Forest Office had devised a modified route that avoided archaeological sites and was situated "as far as possible from the sites used by contemporary Indians for specific spiritual activities."[52] Simultaneously, the Forest Service developed a management plan which called for the harvesting of "significant amounts of timber." As a demonstration to the Indians that the government had an awareness of the area's importance, the plan called for "half-mile protective zones" around "all religious sites identified in the report."[53] They could not, or would not, comprehend that tribal members considered the entire region sacred, and that the planned road would, by bisecting the area, sever the interconnectedness of the entire zone and cause massive disruption to tribal religious activity because of the cutting, trucking, and associated side-effects of timbering activity.

Having exhausted all administrative remedies, six Indians, joined by an Indian cultural and religious organization, several conservation organizations, and the State of California, filed two separate suits challenging the Forest Service's decision to implement the Blue Creek land use plan and construct the road.[54] Their arguments, simply stated, were that the planned activity (1) would constitute a gross interference with tribal religious practices in violation of the Free Exercise Clause of the First Amendment; (2) would violate the Federal Water Pollution Control Act and the National Environmental Policy Act, as well as other statutes; and (3) would contravene the federal government's trust responsibilities to the Indians of the Hoopa Valley Indian Reservation.[55]

After a ten-day trial in 1983, the district court agreed with the Indians and the other respondents and granted a permanent injunction prohibiting the Forest Service from implementing the plan.[56] The court, in a powerfully worded opinion, agreed with virtually every point argued by the Indians. Most importantly, it held that the construction of the road would "seriously impair the Indian plaintiffs [*sic*] use of the High Country for religious practices. This would be a violation of their First Amendment rights and also entailed a breach of the government's trust responsibilities to the Indians." The Indians' position was strengthened by the frailty of the Forest Service's arguments. At trial, the agency conceded that the road construction would not vastly improve access to the timber; that the road would not increase jobs in the timber industry; and that the accompanying recreational use of the region would create major environmental problems. The factors that the Forest Service had developed as compelling justifications for the road "devolved to the simple proposition that the agency wanted to build a road period. Period."[57]

The Forest Service and the Department of Agriculture, despite a paucity of critically important reasons to build the road, nevertheless appealed this rare court victory for Indian religion to the 9th Circuit Court of Appeals. While the case was pending, Congress enacted the California Wilderness Act of 1984,[58] which designated as part of the new Siskiyou Wilderness much of the Blue Creek and Eight Mile Creek Units, including most of the High Country. A "wilderness" designation prohibits commercial timber harvesting and other commercial enterprises such as permanent roads, etc. This congressional action alone was a clear signal that the lands in question were of a special character and Congress had indicated as much when it said the area was of "critical importance to Native Americans for cultural and religious purposes."[59]

Despite this favorable statement, the acknowledged trust responsibility, and the lower court decision supporting the Indians, Congress compromised the religious rights of the Indians by exempting a 1,200-foot-wide corridor through the newly designated wilderness area, which coincided with the Forest Service's proposed road route. This equivocal congressional position—that a recognized wilderness area should be bisected by a paved road with projected heavy traffic flow—was most strange. "The most obvious interpretation of the situation," observed one scholar, "was that Congress did not want to deal with the politics of the road and hoped that things would be resolved locally without any further direction or involvement at the Washington level."[60]

The 9th Circuit Court in 1986[61] affirmed the District Court's findings that the construction would indeed virtually destroy the Indians' ability to practice their religion. The majority also held that the Forest Service had failed to show any compelling reasons why the road needed to be built. The government's interests in road construction, the court concluded, were not sufficient to justify the damage to the Indians' exercise of their religious beliefs.

The Court of Appeals, however, refused to consider the Indians' and the conservation groups' argument that the California Wilderness Act should be considered an intervening statement in which Congress, by designating the area as a "wilderness," was expressing its intention to set the land apart. Second, and more damaging from the Indians' view, the court unanimously rejected the district court's conclusion that the government's proposed actions would constitute a breach of its trust responsibilities to the Indians.

The Forest Service and Secretary of Agriculture Richard E. Lyng appealed to the Supreme Court for relief. The High Court granted certiorari on the curious ground that "the courts below did not articulate the bases of their decision with perfect clarity."[62] Whether "perfect clarity" is ever possible when human actors, institutions, and language are involved is debatable, but a thorough reading of both lower court cases reveals a fairly explicit understanding of the consequences of the road's construction to Indian religious practices. The fact that the Forest Service had not shown any compelling reasons to justify its desire to develop the road was also very important to the trial and appellate courts.

The Supreme Court noted that it had agreed to review the case because the lower courts had apparently violated the principle of judicial restraint which holds that courts should not decide constitutional questions "until it is necessary to decide them."[63] In the Court's ambiguous language: "This principle required the courts below to determine, before addressing the constitutional issue, whether a decision on that question could have entitled respondents to relief beyond that to which they were entitled on their statutory claims. If no additional relief would have been warranted, a constitutional decision would have been unnecessary and therefore inappropriate."[64] Justice Sandra Day O'Connor claimed that neither of the courts below had "explained or expressly articulated the necessity for their constitutional holdings."[65] This rationale for granting certiorari, in effect, placed minor statutory relief on a higher plain than the protections—such as freedom of religion—guaranteed by the Bill of Rights. Having chided the lower courts for deciding the constitutional questions, the Court conceded that the First Amendment issue "was necessary" to the lower court's decision. The Forest Service, in fact, which had petitioned for certiorari "on the constitutional issue alone," had informed the justices that it could "cure the statutory defects below [i.e., the violations of the environmental statutes], intends to do so, and will not challenge the adverse statutory rulings."[66] This almost apologetic "willingness" on the part of the Forest Service to fix the environmental degradation its plans would entail, although it said nothing about the adverse affects on the Indian religious rights, seemed to disarm the Court and set the tone for the decision.

MASKING WITHIN THE DECISION:
THE MAJORITY OPINION AND THE DISSENT

Sandra Day O'Connor, the first female member of the Supreme Court, wrote the majority opinion with concurring justices William Rehnquist, Byron White, John Paul Stevens, and Antonin Scalia. Justice William Brennan, joined by his brothers Thurgood Marshall and Harry Blackmun, filed an energetic dissent. In answer to her overarching question, whether the Court is precluded by the Free Exercise Clause of the First Amendment from constructing the road and harvesting timber through a national forest that has historically been used for the religious purposes of three Indian tribes, O'Connor concluded that although the government "does not dispute, and we have no reason to doubt, that the logging and road-building projects at issue in this case could have devastating effects on traditional Indian religious practices, . . . the Constitution simply does not provide a principle that could justify upholding respondents' [Indians et al.] legal claims."[67] This was because, and she quoted *Sherbert v. Verner*,[68] the First Amendment's Free Exercise Clause had been written "in terms of what the government cannot do to the individual, not in terms of what the individual can exact from the government."[69]

The majority and dissenting opinions are so diametrically opposed that it behooves us to consider their rationales and arguments in parallel fashion. Only then is it possible to begin to gauge the depth and texture of the conflict and confusion within the Court insofar as Indian religious issues and the tribal-federal relationship are involved. In the section that follows, the conflicting opinions will be presented in "tennis-match" format under headings which define the themes of the exchanges: reading of precedent, defining tribal religions, the threat posed to the U.S. as land-owner, Indians' central focus on religion, the American Indian Religious Freedom Act, and government coercion of tribal religious practices.

On Precedent

In *Bowen v. Roy*[70] the Supreme Court had considered an Indian family's challenge to a federal law that required the states to use social security numbers in administering particular welfare programs. The Indian family argued that their religious beliefs would be violated if they allowed the government to assign a social security number for their two-year-old daughter because the use of such a number would "rob the spirit of their child and prevent her from achieving greater spiritual power."[71] The Supreme Court rejected that argument. O'Connor in *Lyng* read *Roy* as follows:

> The building of a road or the harvesting of timber on publicly owned land cannot meaningfully be distinguished from the use of a Social Security number in *Roy*. In both cases, the challenged Government action would interfere significantly with private persons' ability to pursue spiritual fulfillment according to their own religious beliefs. In neither case, however, would the affected individuals be coerced by the Government's action into violating their religious beliefs; nor would either governmental action penalize religious activity by denying any person an equal share of the rights, benefits, and privileges enjoyed by other citizens.[72]

Brennan:

> Today the Court professes an inability to differentiate *Roy* from the present case, suggesting that "[t]he building of a road or the harvesting of timber on publicly owned land cannot meaningfully be distinguished from the use of a Social Security number. . . ." I find this inability altogether remarkable. In *Roy*, we repeatedly stressed the "internal" nature of the Government practice at issue: noting that *Roy* objected to "the widespread use of the Social Security number by the federal or state governments in their computer systems. . . ." (emphasis original)[73]

> Federal land-use decisions, by contrast, are likely to have substantial external effects that government decisions concerning office furniture and information storage obviously will not, and they are correspond-

ingly subject to public scrutiny and public challenge in a host of ways that office equipment purposes are not. . . .[74]

The Court today, however, ignores *Roy's* emphasis on the internal nature of the Government practice at issue there, and instead construes that case as further support for the proposition that governmental action that does not coerce conduct inconsistent with religious faith simply does not implicate the concern of the Free Exercise Clause. That such a reading is wholly untenable, however, is demonstrated by the cruelly surreal result it produces here: governmental action that will virtually destroy a religion is nevertheless deemed not to "burden" that religion.[75]

On Governmental Coercion of Religions and the "Incidental Effects" of Government Programs

O'Connor:

It is true that this Court has repeatedly held that indirect coercion or penalties on the free exercise of religion, not just outright prohibitions, are subject to scrutiny under the First Amendment. Thus, for example, ineligibility for unemployment benefits, based solely on a refusal to violate the Sabbath, has been analogized to a fine imposed on Sabbath worship . . . This does not and cannot imply that incidental effects of government programs, which may make it more difficult to practice certain religions but which have no tendency to coerce individuals into acting contrary to their religious beliefs, require government to bring forward a compelling justification for its otherwise lawful actions. The crucial word in the constitutional text is "prohibit": "For the Free Exercise Clause is written in terms of what the government cannot do to the individual, not in terms of what the individual can exact from the government."[76]

Brennan:

The Court does not for a moment suggest that the interests served by the G-O road are in any way compelling, or that they outweigh the destructive effect construction of the road will have on respondents' religious practices. Instead, the Court embraces the Government's contention that its prerogative as landowner should always take precedence over a claim that a particular use of federal property infringes religious practices. Attempting to justify this rule, the Court argues that the First Amendment bars only outright prohibitions, indirect coercion, and penalties on the free exercise of religion. . . .[77]

Since our recognition nearly half a century ago that restraints on religious conduct implicate the concern of the Free Exercise Clause . . . , we have never suggested that the protections of the guarantee are limited to so narrow a range of governmental burdens. The land-use decision challenged here will restrain respondents from practicing their religion as surely and as completely as any of the governmental actions we have struck down in the past, and the Court's efforts simply to define away respondents' injury as nonconstitutional are both unjustified and ultimately unpersuasive.[78]

　　Ultimately, the Court's coercion test turns on a distinction between governmental actions that compel affirmative conduct inconsistent with religious belief, and those governmental actions that prevent conduct consistent with religious belief. In my view, such distinction is without constitutional significance. The crucial word in the constitutional text, as the Court itself acknowledges, is "prohibit" . . . a comprehensive term that in no way suggests that the intended protection is aimed only at governmental actions that coerce affirmative conduct.[79]

　　. . . Here, respondents have demonstrated that the Government's proposed activities will completely prevent them from practicing their religion, and such a showing, no less than those made out in *Hobbie*, *Thomas*, *Sherbert*, and *Yoder*, entitles them to the protections of the Free Exercise Clause.[80]

On the "Centrality" of Tribal Religions

O'Connor:

To be sure, the Indians themselves were far from unanimous in opposing the G-O road . . . and it seems less than certain that construction of the road will be so disruptive that it will doom their religion. Nevertheless, we can assume that the threat to the efficacy of at least some religious practices is extremely grave.[81]

Brennan:

The Court today suggests that such an approach would place courts in the untenable position of deciding which practices and beliefs are "central" to a given faith and which are not, and invites the prospect of judges advising some religious adherents that they "misunderstand their own religious beliefs." . . . In fact, however, courts need not undertake any such inquiries: like all other religious adherents, Native Americans would be the arbiters of which practices are essential to their faith, subject only to the normal requirement that their claims be genuine and sincere. The question for the courts, then, is not whether the Native American claimants understand their own religion, but rather whether they have discharged their burden of demonstrating, as the Amish did with respect to the compulsory school law in *Yoder*, that the land-use decision poses a substantial and realistic threat of undermining or frustrating their religious practices. Ironically, the Court's apparent solicitude for the integrity of religious belief and its desire to forestall the possibility that courts might second-guess the claims of religious adherents leads to far greater inequities than those the Court postulates: today's ruling sacrifices a religion at least as old as the Nation itself, along with the spiritual well-being of its approximately 5,000 adherents, so that the Forest Service can build a 6-mile segment of road that two lower courts found had only the most marginal and speculative utility, both to the Government itself and to the private lumber interests that might conceivably use it.[82]

On the "Threat" to the United States as Landowner

O'Connor:

. . . Nothing in the principle for which they contend, however, would distinguish this case from another lawsuit in which they (or similarly situated religious objectors) might seek to exclude all human activity but their own from sacred areas of public lands. The Indian respondents insist that "[p]rivacy during the power quests is required for the practitioners to maintain the purity needed for a successful journey." . . . No disrespect for these practices is implied when one notes that such beliefs could easily require *de facto* beneficial ownership of some rather spacious tracts of public property . . . The Constitution does not permit government to discriminate against religions that treat particular physical sites as sacred, and a law prohibiting the Indian respondents from visiting the Chimney Rock area would raise a different set of constitutional questions. Whatever rights the Indians may have to the use of the area, however, those rights do not divest the government of its right to use what is, after all law *its* land.[83] (emphasis original)

Brennan:

> . . . [T]he Court's concern that the claims of Native Americans will place "religious servitudes" upon vast tracts of federal property cannot justify its refusal to recognize the constitutional injury respondents will suffer here. It is true, as the Court notes, that respondents' religious use of the high country requires privacy and solitude. The fact remains, however, that respondents have never asked the Forest Service to exclude others from the area. Should respondents or any other group seek to force the Government to protect their religious practices from the interference of private parties, such a demand would implicate not only the concern of the Free Exercise Clause, but also those of the Establishment Clause as well. That case, however, is most assuredly not before us today, and in any event cannot justify the Court's refusal to acknowledge that the injuries respondents will suffer as a result of the Government's proposed activities are sufficient to state a constitutional cause of action.[84]

On the American Indian Religious Freedom Act

O'Connor:

> Except for abandoning its project entirely, and thereby leaving the two existing segments of road to dead-end in the middle of a National Forest, it is difficult to see how the government could have been more solicitous.[85] . . . Respondents, however, suggest that AIRFA goes further and in effect enacts their interpretation of the First Amendment into statutory law. Although this contention was rejected by the District Court, they seek to defend the judgment below by arguing that AIRFA authorizes the injunction against completion of the G-O road . . . Nowhere in the law is there so much as a hint of any intent to create a cause of action or any judicially enforceable individual rights.[86]

Brennan:

> Indeed, in the American Indian Religious Freedom Act (AIRFA) . . . Congress expressly recognized the adverse impact land-use decisions

and other governmental actions frequently have on the site-specific religious practices of Native Americans, and the Act accordingly directs agencies to consult with Native American religious leaders before taking actions that might impair those practices. Although I agree that the Act does not create any judicially enforceable rights . . . the absence of any private right of action in no way undermines the statute's significance as an expressed congressional determination that federal land management decisions are not "internal" Government "procedures," but are instead governmental actions that can and indeed are likely to burden Native American religious practices. That such decisions should be subject to constitutional challenge, and potential constitutional limitations, should hardly come as a surprise.[87]

On Defining Tribal Religions As against Judeo-Christian Religions

O'Connor (tribes as private citizens with nondistinctive rights):

However much we might wish it were otherwise, government simply could not operate if it were required to satisfy every citizen's religious needs and desires. A broad range of governmental activities—from social welfare programs to foreign aid to conservation projects—will always be considered essential to the spiritual well-being of some citizens, often on the basis of sincerely held religious beliefs. Others will find the very same activities deeply offensive, and perhaps incompatible with their own search for spiritual fulfillment and with the tenets of their religion. The First Amendment must apply to all citizens alike, and it can give to none of them a veto over public programs that do not prohibit the free exercise of religion. The Constitution does not, and courts cannot, offer to reconcile the various competing demands on government, many of them rooted in sincere religious belief, that inevitably arise in so diverse a society as ours. That task, to the extent that it is feasible, is for the legislatures and other institutions.[88]

Brennan (tribes as separate and distinct peoples with unique rights):

A pervasive feature of this lifestyle is the individual's relationship with the natural world; this relationship, which can accurately though somewhat incompletely be characterized as one of stewardship, forms a core of what might be called, for want of a better nomenclature, the Indian religious experience. While traditional Western religions view creation as the work of a deity, "who institutes natural laws which then govern the operation of a physical nature," tribal religions regard creation as an on-going process in which they are morally and religiously obligated to participate ... Native Americans fulfill this duty through ceremonies and rituals designed to preserve and stabilize the earth and to protect humankind from disease and other catastrophes. Failure to conduct these ceremonies in the manner and place specified, adherents believe, will result in great harm to the earth and to the people whose welfare depends upon it.[89] ... Where dogma lies at the heart of Western religions, Native American faith is inextricably bound to the use of land. The site-specific nature of Indian religious practice derives from the Native American perception that land is itself a sacred, living being.[90]

THE MASKS OF TRUSTEESHIP, "PUBLIC" OWNERSHIP OF PUBLIC LANDS, AND INCIDENTAL EFFECTS

The preceding presentation of the virtually polarized opinions of Justices O'Connor and Brennan on a wide range of issues and topics is convincing evidence that the religious concerns of tribes, as perceived by the Supreme Court, are not about to be resolved in the near future. Of obvious importance to tribes, however, are O'Connor's majority views which essentially disavowed the long-standing trust responsibility to tribes insofar as this responsibility involved access to and use of sacred lands.[91] As one leading law expert put it: "Stripped of peripheral issues, the matter before the High Court was to weigh the government's trust responsibility toward Indians against its own right to manage its affairs. Undeniably, part of those affairs, a very important part, was execution of the trust responsibility itself. Hence, the question should have been academic."[92] This casting aside of the trust responsibility was accomplished when the Court chose to ignore the distinctive sovereign rights of the tribes as polities. The Court focused, instead, on treating Indians simply as individual American citizens.

A second, and equally pivotal, theme emerging from this decision is that of the power of even mid-level federal bureaucrats to interpret "public lands" of the United States in a way that elevates a federal agency to a superior position over the rights not only of tribal nations but of American citizens as well. National Forests are public lands and belong to the American people, of which tribal nations and their citizens constitute a small but historically and legally unique component. This decision, however, enables government bureaucrats to make critically important decisions over the spiritual/property rights of tribal nations and American citizens also.

For example, in oral arguments before the Supreme Court, United States Attorney General Andrew J. Pincus was asked by a justice: "Is it your position, Mr. Pincus, that the Government need not make any concessions whatever to the interest of the Indians in this case?" Pincus's response: "Yes, your Honor, it is our position that under the Constitution, because the Constitution does not require the government to do anything, we think that it's certainly appropriate to do exactly what the Forest Service did in this case. . . ."[93] A little later Pincus was asked who in the Forest Service ultimately made the final decision to construct the road over the vigorous protests. Pincus named the chief of the Forest Service. Surprised, the chief justice reacted: "It hasn't even gone to the Secretary [of Agriculture]?"[94] "The Secretary," said Pincus, "intends to review that decision."[95]

Finally, a malevolent test emerged in this case—the "incidental effects" test, which, in effect, holds that nonmajoritarian religions no longer "have the freedom to engage in religious practices that conflict with generally applicable laws, no matter how insignificant the law or how important the particular religious practice."[96] Armed with this, future administrations, backed by the Court, may be able to deliberately harm minority religions. Furthermore, using this test allows the court to avoid having to show a compelling interest if its action are otherwise lawful. The incidental effects test figures prominently in the blockbuster *Smith II* case, which, as will presently be seen, refined and expanded the principle.

CONCLUSION

The G-O road was never constructed. The project was abandoned, due, in large part, to the "wilderness" designation, which effectively closed the area to logging and to the general traffic. One can speculate on why, then, the Supreme Court agreed to hear this case, since the "wilderness" designation had occurred several years before the case reached the High Court. Perhaps the majority desired to make a statement about tribal religious beliefs and practices. The essence of that statement may be that the Supreme Court "cannot or will not conceive of traditional tribal religions as different in form, substance and orientation from the mainstream Christian and Jewish denominations. Consequently when it applies Constitutional doctrines and tests to cases involving American Indian religious freedom the results are disastrous—they do not protect traditional Indian practitioners and they disrupt long-standing doctrines in the First Amendment field in the fundamental way."[97]

The next case to be reviewed, *Smith II*, corroborates this statement fully and shows that even individual Indians remain outside the protection of the Constitution and only have minimal protections of their basic religious rights as American citizens.

Employment Division, Department of Human Resources v. Smith (Smith II)

UP AND DOWN THE JUDICIAL STAIRCASE

Contrasted with our earlier cases, which ascended to the Supreme Court in typical linear fashion—from lower courts (either state or federal trial courts to federal appellate courts or state supreme courts)—and were settled, the route *Smith* took more closely resembles a judicial yo-yo. Let us quickly capsulize the major events leading to Justice Antonin Scalia's decision.

HISTORICAL BACKGROUND

Alfred Smith (a Klamath Indian) and Galen Black (a non-Indian) were both members of the Native American Church (NAC), the largest and only formally chartered American Indian religious institution, with an estimated 250,000 to 500,000 members (definitions vary as to who may be a member).[98] The core element of the NAC service is the sacramental use of peyote, which is a small cactus found in southern Texas and in northern Mexico. While it can be harvested by registered individuals who may be non-Indian, actual use of peyote is restricted to those who are "bona fide" members of the NAC.[99] Peyote, according to its adherents, is a living deity and, as such, it is the foundation of the NAC members' faith. The traditional ceremonial use by Indians of the peyote cactus, dating back thousands of years, is integral to the perpetuation and enhancement of a unique way of life.[100] This ceremonial usage is essential for sacramental purposes, and for healing and curing, especially of alcoholism and drug addiction. In some NAC bodies, elements of Christianity have been introduced into the service, although many other branches avoid the integration of Christian elements or symbols into their ceremonies.

From a western scientific perspective, peyote contains several alkaloids, the most important of which is mescaline, which, when ingested, tends to produce a hallucinatory effect in the user. The federal government has defined peyote as a "controlled substance," classified it as a "drug," and listed it on Schedule I of the Federal Controlled Substance Act. The tension between these two diametrically opposite views of peyote—a sacred deity (Indian) and a hallucinogenic drug (western)—is an excellent microcosm in which to view the ongoing religious contentions between tribal peoples and some state and federal policymakers. In this case, as in *Lyng*, the organic tribal understanding and use of peyote were completely overwhelmed by the Court's secular/scientific understanding. Furthermore, the evidence that both Smith and Black had prior histories of drug and alcohol abuse that had been corrected by the religious use of peyote and membership in the NAC seemed to be of no consequence to the Court.

Both men had become substance abuse counselors for a private, nonprofit drug rehabilitation organization, Alchohol and Drug Abuse Prevention and Treatment (ADAPT) in the early 1980s. ADAPT had a zero-tolerance philosophy toward drug and alcohol use that it expected its employees to follow. It was inevitable that a conflict would arise, since ADAPT at the time had classified peyote as a "drug," whereas Smith and Black recognized it as a holy sacrament. Conflict erupted in the mid-1980s when the rehabilitation firm discovered that Smith and Black had participated, on their own time, in an NAC meeting. They were summarily fired, though on different dates; Black was released on October 3, 1983, Smith on March 5, 1984. The two men applied to the Employment Division of the State of Oregon for unemployment benefits. The agency, however, declared them ineligible because they had been fired for "misconduct." This was based on the agency's perception that Smith and Black had willfully violated ADAPT's standards of behavior, entailing a disregard of the employer's interests, which were held to be sacrosanct while Smith and Black's religiously motivated arguments were rebuffed.

The discharged counselors challenged the state's denial of unemployment compensation as an unconstitutional infringement on their religious rights. In 1985, the Oregon Court of Appeals reversed the Employment Division's decision and held that the denial was a violation of the claimants' free exercise rights.[101] The Oregon Supreme Court affirmed this decision the following year.[102] The Oregon High Court rejected the agency's argument that the state's law enforcement interest in proscribing peyote was relevant in unemployment proceedings. The court relied heavily on the "balancing test" developed by the Supreme Court in an earlier case, *Sherbert v. Verner*,[103] and reinforced in *Thomas v. Review Board, Indiana Employment Security Division*.[104]

The balancing test requires the state to show that any law imposing a heavy burden on a person's free exercise of religion is the "least restrictive means of achieving a 'compelling' state interest."[105] The Oregon Supreme Court held that the state's interest in preserving the unemployment insurance fund for "deserving" individuals was not compelling enough to allow the state to restrict the claimants' right to practice their religion.

The Employment Division of the Department of Human Resources appealed to the United States Supreme Court. The Court granted certiorari on the grounds that the Oregon Supreme Court had ignored the state's law-enforcement interests. In *Smith I*, decided in 1988, the Court remanded the case back to the Oregon Supreme Court and forced the Oregon High Court to determine whether the Oregon statute criminalizing peyote provided an exception for religious use.[106] But Oregon's Supreme Court, said Brennan in dissent, had already disavowed "any State interest in enforcing its criminal laws through the denial of unemployment benefits. . . ."[107] "Perhaps more puzzling," said Brennan, "than the imagined ambiguity is the Court's silence as to its relevance. The Court merely remands these cases to the Oregon Supreme Court for further proceedings after concluding that a 'necessary predicate' to its analysis is a pronouncement by the state court on whether respondents' conduct was criminal."[108] Brennan, joined by Marshall and Blackmun, concluded: "Today's foray into the realm of the hypothetical will surely cost us the respect of the State Supreme Court whose words we misconstrue. That price is particularly exorbitant where, as here, the state court is most likely to respond to our efforts by merely reiterating what it has already stated with unmistakable clarity."[109]

As Justice Brennan had predicted, on remand the Oregon Supreme Court was constrained to answer the Supreme Court's question regarding the legality of peyote under Oregon law: no, the Oregon statutes did not make any exceptions for the use of peyote, but the court affirmed its earlier ruling that "outright prohibition of good faith religious use of peyote by adult members of the NAC would violate the First Amendment directly and as interpreted by Congress. We therefore reaffirm our holding that the First Amendment entitles petitioners to unemployment compensation."[110]

This plain statement was the rough equivalent of Justice Brennan's prediction. As Brennan put it: "I must assume that the [Supreme] Court has tacitly left the Oregon Supreme Court the option to dispose of these cases by simply reiterating its initial opinion and appending, 'and we really mean it,' or words to that effect."[111]

Despite the reiterated state court ruling, it was clear that the Supreme Court still intended to have the final say. When it again granted certiorari to the persistent state employment agency, the table was set for Scalia's First Amendment revolution.

THE "MOOTNESS" OF SMITH

This case, which like *Lyng* should have been considered moot because the issue involved sacramental use of peyote, had already been resolved between the actual parties long before it was decided by the Supreme Court. On March 5, 1986, Smith and Black entered into a federal consent decree with ADAPT. In this federally sponsored agreement, known as *Equal Employment Opportunity Commission v. ADAPT*, ADAPT agreed that religious use of peyote by NAC members would no longer be considered work-related misconduct and Smith and Black agreed to withdraw their suit. This arrangement affirmed that individuals in similar situations would never again be fired for engaging in the same kind of "alleged misconduct"[112] that occurred in this case.[113]

On September 25, 1987, the Oregon State Board of Pharmacy adopted a permanent rule exempting the nondrug use of peyote in "bona fide ceremonies" of the NAC. The exemption was necessary since possession of peyote is considered a class B felony on schedule I of Oregon's Controlled Substances Act. However, a few weeks later, at the urging of the state attorney general's office, a temporary rule was issued to suspend the permanent exemption. The attorney general asserted that the exemption might be unconstitutional on the grounds that it gave exemption to a particular church. Ruth Vandever, executive director of the Pharmacy Board, concluded that the Board should seek further advice on the constitutionality of the rule before it became effective.[114]

Such "advice" issued from both the Oregon Court of Appeals and two Oregon Supreme Court opinions which, in analyzing the constitutional question, found that although peyote was "illegal" under state law as worded, such prohibition was invalid and violated the free exercise rights of Smith and Black.

MASKING WITHIN THE DECISION: THE OPINION

Justice Antonin Scalia, a 1986 Reagan appointee, filled the seat vacated by newly appointed Chief Justice William Rehnquist. And while Rehnquist had long been considered the most doctrinaire conservative, by the end of his first term, Scalia had assumed that mantle.[115] Considered by many an intellect of probing logic, Scalia is regarded in other circles as one willing to make imaginative use of the hypothetical in making his points. He has strongly supported starkly conservative ideological positions on the policymaking discretion of the executive, on questions of criminal law, on the rights of property owners, and on the scope of personal and minority rights. Scalia's raw intellectual prowess, moreover, has led some to refer to him as the "Great Right Hope."[116] His decisions have a particular clarity and consistency because he deifies the legal text or legal statute, avoiding, wherever possible, balancing tests or compromises. Such a focus, however, on legal text alone often means avoiding or denying the real-world impact of the Court's decisions.

Scalia began the decision by discounting the Court's earlier free exercise cases on the basis that the conduct at issue in those cases was not "prohibited by law." In other words, from Scalia's viewpoint, peyote had been confirmed to be "illegal," and it was now the task of the Court to determine whether that prohibition was lawful under the Free Exercise Clause. But, as brought out in Smith and Black's briefs, in the Oregon Court's opinion, and in the dissent by Blackmun, the state had never prosecuted Indians for religious use of peyote. Blackmun noted:

> I have grave doubts, however, as to the wisdom or propriety of deciding the constitutionality of a criminal prohibition which the state has not sought to enforce, which the state did not rely on in defending its denial of unemployment benefits before the state courts, and which the Oregon courts could, on remand, either invalidate on state constitutional grounds, or conclude that it remains irrelevant to Oregon's interest in administering its unemployment program.[117]

For Scalia, this reality was irrelevant. He moved to separate and distinguish the right to "believe and profess" religious doctrines from the right to "exercise" religion. Building upon the language of *Lyng* and citing *Sherbert*, Scalia agreed that the First Amendment absolutely excluded any governmental regulation of "beliefs as such." However, he declared that the "exercise of religion," on the other hand, as carried out by Smith and Black, was a different matter because they sought to go "beyond the reach of a criminal law that is not specifically directed at their religious practice, and that is concededly constitutional as applied to those who use the drug for other reasons."[118] In Scalia's opinion, "[i]t would doubtless be unconstitutional, for example, to ban the casting of 'statues that are to be used for worship purposes,' or to prohibit bowing down before a golden calf." Scalia maintained that governments are justified in enacting "concededly constitutional" laws which in this case only "incidentally" affected the religious practices of NAC members. "We have," said Scalia, "never held that an individual's religious beliefs excuse him from compliance with an otherwise valid law prohibiting conduct that the State is free to regulate."[119]

Justice O'Connor vigorously argued against this interpretation of the First Amendment and the effects of generally applicable laws on religious beliefs. As she noted, the First Amendment makes no distinction between religious belief and religious practice. "Conduct motivated by sincere religious belief," said O'Connor, "like the belief itself, must therefore be at least presumptively protected by the Free Exercise Clause."[120] It is curious that O'Connor chose not to make this point in connection with the *Lyng* case, in which the exercise of religion was especially important since practitioners of traditional Indian beliefs must travel to religious sites, whereas the NAC ceremony is transportable.

Moreover, O'Connor attacked Scalia's allowance of government conduct which manifestly prohibited respondents' religious practices—without justification—as long as the prohibition was generally applicable. O'Connor asserted, "[A] law that prohibits certain conduct—conduct that happens to be an act of worship for someone—manifestly does prohibit that person's free exercise of his religion. A person who is barred from engaging in religiously motivated conduct is barred from freely exercising his religion."[121] Finally, O'Connor opined that the clause makes no distinction between laws "that are generally applicable" and laws that specifically target certain religious practices. "Indeed," she observed, "few States would be so naive as to enact a law directly prohibiting or burdening a religious practice as such."[122]

Scalia, confronted by the precedents in *Cantwell* and *Yoder* in which the Supreme Court held that the First Amendment categorically forbade governmental regulation of religious beliefs and that religious beliefs and actions cannot be easily compartmentalized, declared them "hybrid" cases that involved not only the Free Exercise Clause but other constitutional provisions as well. "The present case," said Scalia, "does

not present such a hybrid situation, but a free exercise claim unconnected with any communicative activity or parental right." [123] But there
is little denying upon a close reading that those "hybrid" opinions
clearly relied on the Free Exercise Clause. And despite Scalia's effort
to marginalize those decisions, O'Connor stated, ". . . we have consistently regarded those cases as part of the mainstream of our free exercise
jurisprudence." [124]

Justice Scalia's primary legal support for this denial of the Indians'
right to practice their religion was the century-old decision *Reynolds v.
United States*.[125] In that case, the constitutionality of a congressional law
which had outlawed polygamy in the Mormon church, even though
the Mormons believed the practice was divinely inspired, was upheld.
Apart from the inherently prejudicial nature of the *Reynolds* decision—
why, after all, is polygamy necessarily wrong and monogamy necessarily
right?—and the inconsistent reasoning used by Justice Morrison Waite,
who argued that if polygamy were allowed on religious grounds, Congress would ultimately be asked to sanction "human sacrifice" or to allow
a wife to burn herself upon the funeral pyre of her deceased husband, this
decision was inappropriate for two fundamental reasons. First, polygamy, while it had historically been a basic tenet of Mormonism, was not
essential to the practice of their religion. Peyote, by contrast, is the "sine
qua non" of the NAC members' faith.[126] Second, the *Reynolds* Court perceived polygamy as a real threat to "democratic institutions and injurious
to the morals and well-being of its practitioners." [127] With the exception
of one unsuccessful attempt to outlaw it in the early 1900s, peyote has
not been perceived in such a threatening light. Nevertheless, *Reynolds*,
not the intervening and more pertinent cases of *Cantwell* and *Yoder*, new
federal policy directives like the AIRFA, or the exempt status of peyote
under federal law and that of more than half the states, was the principal
case Scalia relied upon.

*The Mask of Neutrality:
A "Compelling" Ouster of the Free Exercise Clause*

The right of individuals to freely exercise their religion, unlike their right
to religious beliefs, is not an absolute right with no bounds. Before a state
can establish boundaries on the free exercise of religion, the Court has
held in a line of cases, but especially in *Sherbert v. Verner*,[128] that the government must "justify any substantial burden on religiously motivated
conduct by a 'compelling state interest' and by means narrowly tailored

to achieve that interest."[129] This test meets the First Amendment guarantee that "religious liberty is an independent liberty, that it occupies a preferred position, and that the Court will not permit encroachments upon this liberty, whether direct or indirect, unless required by clear and compelling governmental interests. . . ."[130]

Scalia, however, drawing heavily from two other decisions which also involved Indians, *Bowen v. Roy* and *Lyng*, began by incorrectly asserting, "We have never invalidated any governmental action on the basis of the *Sherbert* test except the denial of unemployment compensation."[131] He was forced to acknowledge, however, that "we have sometimes purported to apply the *Sherbert* test in contexts other than that. . . ."[132] And, as O'Connor and Blackmun would note in their dissents, *Cantwell* and *Yoder* are obvious free exercise cases that explicitly apply the compelling interest test in areas other than unemployment compensation cases.

Amazingly, after a brief synopsis of cases—*United States v. Lee*,[133] *Gillette v. United States*,[134] *Bowen v. Roy*,[135] *Goldman v. Weinberger*,[136] and *Lyng*—Scalia spoke as if the compelling interest test had been regarded as largely irrelevant in all cases except unemployment cases. "Even if we were inclined to breathe into *Sherbert* some life beyond the unemployment compensation field, we would not apply it to require exemptions from a generally applicable criminal law."[137] Scalia attempted to downplay the relevance of the *Sherbert* compelling interest test in this decision by stating that it had been developed "in a context that lent itself to individualized governmental assessment of the reasons for the relevant conduct."[138]

O'Connor noted in her dissent that the Court had never distinguished between cases where a state conditions receipt of benefits [whether individual or group] on conduct that is prohibited by religious beliefs and cases where a state affirmatively denies such conduct.[139] As O'Connor stated: "A neutral criminal law prohibiting conduct that a state may legitimately regulate is, if anything, *more* burdensome than a neutral civil statute placing legitimate conditions on the award of a state benefit"[140] (emphasis original).

Scalia, despite a preponderance of scientific, religious, and cultural data to the contrary, was unwilling to conceive of peyote as anything but a "drug," and he cast aside the compelling interest test. "The Government's ability to enforce generally applicable prohibitions of socially harmful conduct, like its ability to carry out other aspects of public policy, 'cannot depend on measuring the effect of a governmental action on a religious objector's spiritual development.'"[141] Citing *Reynolds*, Scalia said that if the government had to countenance every person's religious beliefs by having to show a "compelling" reason for its interference with such, this would contradict both "constitutional tradition and common sense."[142]

A strong argument can be made that it was Scalia's logic that ran counter to constitutional tradition and even common sense. As Blackmun asserted in dissent, "This Court over the years painstakingly has developed a consistent and exacting standard to test the constitutionality of a state statute that burdens the free exercise of religion . . . [and] until today, I thought this was a settled and inviolate principle of this Court's First Amendment jurisprudence."[143]

In a footnote to his "common sense" quote, Scalia justifiably attacked O'Connor's tepid efforts to distinguish *Lyng* and *Bowen* on the basis that they involved the government's conduct of "its own internal affairs." The rule, Scalia noted, should apply to both the state and federal government if the Constitution's principles are enforced throughout the United States. In pursuit of his rationale for discarding the compelling interest test, Scalia asserted that while the test still had ongoing relevance in areas involving racial discrimination and free speech, this was in no way comparable to freedom of religion:

> What it produces in those other fields—equality of treatment and an unrestricted flow of contending speech—are *constitutional norms;* what it would produce here—a private right to ignore generally applicable laws—is a *constitutional anomaly.*[144] (emphasis mine)

How and when freedom of religion became an "anomaly" for five Supreme Court justices, rather than a constitutional "given," Scalia refused to say. His statement clashed directly with constitutional theory and a significant body of judicial precedent, as was reflected in the dissents. O'Connor observed (with the concurrence of three other justices):

> The Court today gives no convincing reason to depart from settled First Amendment jurisprudence. There is nothing talismanic about neutral laws of general applicability or general criminal prohibitions, for laws neutral toward religion can coerce a person to violate his religious conscience or intrude upon his religious duties just as effectively as laws aimed at religion. Although the Court suggests that the compelling interest test, as applied to general applicable laws, would

result in a "constitutional anomaly," . . . the First Amendment un-equivocally makes freedom of religion, like freedom from race discrimination and freedom of speech, a "constitutional nor[m]," not an "anomaly." [145] (brackets in original)

Scalia scoffed at O'Connor's comment and asserted that O'Connor's comparison of the freedom of religion with the freedoms of speech and freedom from discrimination actually supported the majority's conclusion because the Court subjects classifications based on religion to the same exacting scrutiny it uses to examine classifications based on race or content of speech. Blackmun, by contrast, showed that although twenty-eight states and the federal government exempt the religious use of peyote, they "have not found themselves overwhelmed by claims to other religious exemptions. Allowing an exemption for religious peyote use would not necessary oblige the State to grant a similar exemption to other religious groups." [146] Nor would an exemption for peyote use violate the Constitution's Establishment Clause, because while the state "must treat all the religions equally, and not favor one over another, this obligation is fulfilled by the uniform application of the 'compelling interest' *test* to all free exercise claims, not by reaching uniform *results* as to all claims" [147] (emphases original).

Additionally, a factor ignored by Scalia and the two dissents is that Indian religious rights could be shielded by an acknowledgment that since Indians belong to separately recognized sovereign governments which are not generally subject to or beneficiaries of the federal Constitution, their rights are more easily understood as being recognized under treaties or under the domestic and international trust doctrine. And although Indians are also bearers of state and federal citizenship, those who choose to practice a religion that is tribally recognized should have that right so long as their religious activity poses no direct threat to other individuals or government activities.

Next, Scalia blasted the "centrality" statements made by Smith and Black, whose substantiated argument was that peyote use was absolutely central to the perpetuation of NAC religion. The majority brushed this aside by equating the sacramental use of peyote with "the practice of throwing rice at church weddings," and said that justices were not in the position to determine what was essential to various religious beliefs.[148] Blackmun, however, while agreeing that the Court was not in a position to determine which practices were central and which were peripheral to religion, remarked that the Court, nevertheless, should not "turn a blind eye to the severe impact of a State's restrictions on the adherents of a minority religion."[149]

Scalia then delivered his final blow to the compelling interest test:

> If the "compelling interest" test is to be applied at all, then, it must be applied across the board, to all actions thought to be religiously commanded. Moreover, if "compelling interest" really means what it says (and watering it down here would subvert its rigor in other fields where it is applied), many laws will not meet the test. Any society adopting such a system would be courting anarchy, but that danger increases in direct proportion to the society's diversity of religious beliefs, and its determination to coerce or suppress none of them. Precisely because "we are a cosmopolitan nation made up of people of almost every conceivable religious preference," . . . and precisely because we value and protect that religious divergence, we cannot afford the luxury of deeming *presumptively invalid*, as applied to the religious objector, every regulation of conduct that does not protect an interest of the highest order.[150] (emphasis original)

The important terms in this quotation are "anarchy" and "luxury." Historically, the construction of "what if" scenarios has not been widely regarded as a proper role for the judiciary; and the majority's specter of hordes of religious fanatics overwhelming the judicial system with religious claims has, of course, never materialized in areas where religious use of peyote has been sanctioned. As O'Connor pointed out: "The Court's parade of horribles . . . not only fails as a reason for discarding the compelling interest test, it instead demonstrates just the opposite: that courts have been quite capable of applying our free exercise jurisprudence to strike sensible balances between religious liberty and competing state interests."[151]

Scalia's assertion that the Supreme Court could ill afford the "luxury" of granting such religious exemptions is even more troubling, from a perspective of pragmatic and democratic theory. As Blackmun stressed in dissent, "I do not believe the Founders thought their dearly bought freedom from religious persecution a 'luxury,' but an essential element of liberty. . . ."[152]

Finally, the Supreme Court, in contradicting earlier precedent, informed Smith and Black—and by extension all minority religious proponents—that their religious values, although enshrined in the Constitution's Bill of Rights, were still subject to the political process. In an attempt to justify this staggering statement—particularly crushing for Indians, who have not generally received constitutional protections and who lack necessary clout to be active in the political world—Scalia said "[i]t may fairly be said that leaving accommodation to the political process will place at a relative disadvantage those religious practices that are not widely engaged in; but that unavoidable consequence of democratic government must be preferred to a system in which each conscience is a law unto itself or in which judges weigh the social importance of all laws against the centrality of all religious beliefs."[153]

This excerpt means that the Supreme Court has abdicated its role of protecting religious minorities and has thrown these groups on the mercy of the legislature and the principle of majority rule. O'Connor, in her dissent, seemed genuinely stunned by this development. She maintained, on the contrary, that the First Amendment had been enacted "precisely to protect the rights of those whose religious practices are not shared by the majority and may be viewed with hostility."[154] She pointed out instances of majority rule's wreaking havoc on the Amish and Jehovah's Witnesses. And she quoted from *Barnette*, wherein Justice Robert Jackson declared that the very purpose of the Bill of Rights was to place certain subjects—life, liberty, property, free speech, freedom of worship—outside the reach of legislative majorities. These rights, Jackson maintained, were not to be submitted to vote. For although voting may be a good way to select leaders, it is a wholly inadequate way to define rights, especially fundamental political and civil rights.[155]

Justice O'Connor: Concurrence in the Result,
Dissent in the Method

O'Connor agreed, finally, with the result of the majority but decried the methods and arguments used to reach the decision. She asserted that the decision "not only misreads settled First Amendment precedent; it appears to be unnecessary to this case." O'Connor, despite her vigorous denunciation of Scalia's rationale, nevertheless agreed that the First Amendment did not compel an exemption from Oregon law for the Indians' religious use of peyote. In her estimation, the state did indeed have a "compelling interest" in prohibiting the possession and use of peyote.[156] Thus, although the question was "close," she claimed that an exemption for peyote use from the state's general criminal prohibition would interfere with the government's uniform application of its drug laws. This is an interesting interpretation, particularly in light of the fact that O'Connor had earlier chided Scalia for not using a case-by-case approach.

JUSTICE BLACKMUN'S DISSENT

Blackmun, joined as in *Lyng* by the remaining liberal justices, Brennan and Marshall, concurred with the first two parts of O'Connor's opinion, but strongly disagreed with her answer to the question. Blackmun appeared baffled at the way the majority had "perfunctorily dismissed" the compelling interest test. He argued that Scalia's refusal to apply the strict scrutiny test in this case, which was replaced by the "incidental effects" rule, "effectuates a wholesale overturning of settled law concerning the Religion Clauses of our Constitution. One hopes the Court is aware of the consequences, and that its result is not a product of overreaction to the serious problems the country's drug crisis has generated."[157]

The pivotal points in Blackmun's dissent were these. First, for Blackmun, the question to be answered was not the state's broad interest in fighting drugs versus the Indian's right to practice religion, but the state's narrow interest in refusing to make a religious exemption to its drug laws. Second, the state, as the lower courts had shown, lacked any semblance of a "compelling interest" because the state had never sought to criminally prosecute the Indians and had made virtually no effort against other peyote users. Third, even accepting the "illegality" of peyote, many states and the federal government exempt its ceremonial use, and there is "practically no illegal traffic in peyote." Finally, the state's symbolic preservation of an unenforced prohibition was an insufficient reason to violate the constitutionally articulated religious rights of these individuals, especially when the government relied on "mere speculation and potential harm" of a proscribed activity without providing "evidentiary support" that peyote was harmful.

On the contrary, Blackmun showed that there was virtually no scientific evidence that peyote caused any physical harm. He cited several lower court cases, especially *People v. Woody*, and mentioned that a majority of states and the federal government exempted its religious use. He also pointed out that the state had "never asserted this health and safety interest before the Oregon courts."[158] The federal government's policy of protecting traditional Indian religions, as enunciated in the AIRFA, Blackmun stated, while not creating enforceable rights, was a clear signal to the courts that they should carefully assess the religious claims of Indians. These sound historical, legal, constitutional, and policy arguments were dismissed by the majority.

THE AFTERMATH: WHAT TO DO ABOUT SMITH

Scalia's excising of the Free Exercise Clause meant that the exercise of religion, notwithstanding what the Constitution said, deserved no special protection, and American Indians and tribes had another defeat to add to their scrap heap of trampled rights. Scalia's reasoning in this decision harks back to Felix S. Cohen's oft-quoted statement of 1949 that "for us [Euro-Americans], the Indian tribe is the miners' canary and when it flutters and droops we know that the poison gases of intolerance threaten all of the minorities in our land. And who of us is not a member of some minority?"[159]

In the wake of *Smith*, a diverse coalition of religious groups and constitutional scholars, after carefully assessing the revolutionary impact of this case, confronted the Supreme Court and asked it to reconsider its decision. The petition said that "every religious group in the country will be profoundly disadvantaged" by this "far-reaching holding."[160] Among the fifteen or so organizations jointly involved in the petition for the rehearing, only a few represented religious minorities, and no Indian groups were included. The American Jewish Congress, the National Association of Evangelicals, the American Friends Service Committee, and the General Conference of Seventh Day Adventists teamed up with the National Council of Churches and nonreligious public interest groups including the American Civil Liberties Union and People for the American Way on the liberal side, and the Rutherford Institute on the conservative side. Moreover, fifty-five constitutional scholars signed the petition. This rehearing request, like all others since the early 1960s, was rejected. The anti-*Smith* coalition persisted, however, turning their focus to Congress where they found leaders willing to introduce legislation that would reestablish the compelling governmental interest standard.

Tribal individuals and their governments also reacted swiftly to *Smith*. In the early eighties, they had formed an organization called the American Indian Religious Freedom Coalition (AIRFC), which had sought amendments to the weak American Indian Religious Freedom Act. Supported by concerned congressional representatives, various Christian denominations, and a number of Indian and non-Indian lobbying interest groups and organizations,[161] they vigorously sought legislative action to counter the destructive effects of both *Lyng* and *Smith*. Tribes and their supporters were buoyed by their success in securing enactment of a 1991 law[162] which overturned a major criminal law case, *Duro v. Reina* (1990). *Duro* had deprived tribal governments of the right to exercise misdemeanor criminal jurisdiction over nonmember Indians.

Broad legislation to reconstruct the compelling interest test, called the "Religious Freedom Reformation Act of 1993," was enacted on November 16, 1993.[163] It explicitly restored the compelling interest test as originally set forth in *Sherbert v. Verner* and *Wisconsin v. Yoder*. It also guaranteed application of the test in all cases where free exercise of religion is substantially burdened, and it provided a claim or defense to persons whose religious exercise is substantially burdened by government. Section 3 of the law says, "[G]overnment shall not substantially burden a person's exercise of religion even if the burden results from a rule of general applicability, except as provided in Subsection B." The exception is when the government is acting "in furtherance of a compelling governmental interest" and where the government's action "is the least restrictive means of furthering that compelling governmental interest."

The focus of the AIRFC became dramatically intensified and sharpened after *Lyng* and *Smith*. An omnibus Indian religious freedom bill was introduced July 1, 1994, by Senator Daniel Inouye (D., Hawaii). Entitled the "Native American Cultural Protection and Free Exercise of Religions Act" (S. 2269), it would not only address the Court's anti-peyote *Smith* precedent, it would also, and more importantly, charter new federal policy designed to provide religious protection for tribal people in three other areas: sacred sites, Indian prisoners' rights, and religious use of eagles and animal parts. Moreover, the bill contained enforcement mechanisms which the original 1978 resolution had lacked. Such legislation would have provided American Indians with substantial religious rights.[164] Although this omnibus legislation failed, a separate bill, H.R. 4230, which focused solely on peyote, was enacted into law on October 6, 1994. Entitled the "American Indian Religious Freedom Act Amendments of 1994,"[165] this measure rebuffed *Smith* and legalized the use of peyote so long as it was connected with the practice of traditional Indian religions.

In effect, two related but distinctive legislative thrusts were underway—the legislation being pushed by the largely non-Indian movement seeking restoration of the compelling interest test; and the AIRFC-inspired legislation which had a broader goal of recognizing traditional Indian religious rights. While some members of Congress questioned the need for separate bills, one for Native Americans and another for all other religions, Senator Paul Wellstone (D., Minnesota), a cosponsor of the 1993 version of the Indian religion bill, put it best in addressing this issue:

> Throughout the series of hearings held around the country on NA-FERA [Native American Free Exercise Religious Act] one theme repeated itself over and over again: our traditional understanding of how to protect religious freedom, based on a European understanding of religion, is insufficient to protect the rights of the first Americans. . . . The question is not, should we protect Indian religious freedom? Instead, we must ask, how can we best live up to our obligation to protect that freedom? This is an important question, because one might legitimately want to ask why we need a bill to address specifically the religious freedom of Native Americans, instead of a bill that addresses all religions at one time. There is, of course, such a bill, the Religious Freedom Restoration Act (RFRA), which has recently been introduced by my colleague from Massachusetts, Senator Kennedy, and of which I am an original co-sponsor. I believe that there is a strong argument to be made that both of these bills ought to be made into law. RFRA is designed to respond in a very general way to judicial decisions that have been made in recent years restricting the right to free practice of religion. . . . But leaving the definition of such standards up to the judiciary has not proven very effective for Native American religions. In NAFERA, on the other hand, we provide language that makes clear the particularities of Native religious practices we intend to address.[166]

CONCLUSION

The more comprehensive Indian religious bill, excluding the peyote aspect, which was directly aimed at the protection of all traditional Indian religions, was never enacted, while the Religious Freedom Restoration Act (RFRA), which was supported by western religions, did become law. This failure is yet another stark testimony to the difficulty tribal nations have experienced in their quest for permanent recognition of their unique religious and cultural traditions.

Though Indian tribes and individuals were on the receiving end of three disastrous Supreme Court decisions involving religion—*Bowen*, *Lyng*, and *Smith*—which sparked a successful counterrevolution of religious organizations and constitutional scholars, American Indian tribal nations who practice traditional religions that do not involve the use of peyote have yet to receive the basic constitutional protection which has been legislatively "restored" for other Americans under the RFRA and for the use of peyote under the AIRFA.

County of Yakima v. Confederated Tribes and Bands of the Yakima Indian Nation

THE RETURN OF OLD MASKS: THE RESURRECTION OF DISAVOWED NINETEENTH-CENTURY POLICIES

In the celebrated *Worcester v. Georgia* (1832), the United States Supreme Court acknowledged that tribes were sovereign nations with broad, inherent powers of self-government. Moreover, Indian Country, Chief Justice Marshall said, was excluded from the application of state law because of the extraterritorial status of tribes, their preexisting sovereignty, and the supremacy of Indian treaties which affirmed the independent status of tribes and the plenary power of Congress over the federal government's trade relations with Indian tribes as identified in the Commerce Clause of the Constitution. Over the past 150 years, however, the *Worcester* ruling has been modified and the once-impregnable wall shielding tribes from state jurisdictional authority may now be breached, according to the United States, by federal legislation or with Supreme Court authorization, if one of two conditions is met. In Cohen's words: ". . . either that Congress has expressly delegated back to the State, or recognized in the State, some power of government respecting Indians; or that a question involving Indians involved non-Indians to a degree which calls into play the jurisdiction of a State government. Of these two situations, the former is undoubtedly more definite and therefore simpler to analyze. Such an analysis requires a listing of the acts of Congress which confer upon the States, or recognize in the States, specific powers of government with respect to Indians."[167]

Examples of the first condition include the General Allotment Act of 1887, which applied the states' inheritance laws over allotted lands in reservations;[168] state laws regarding inspection of health and educational conditions;[169] state criminal laws which apply where the offense involves non-Indians against Indians or Indians against non-Indians;[170] and specific tribal termination statutes enacted in the 1950s and 1960s and Public Law 280, which gave certain states partial civil and criminal jurisdiction over specific parts of Indian country.[171]

Examples of the second situation include *United States v. Bailey*,[172] *United States v. Ward*,[173] and *United States v. McBratney*.[174] These cases involved crimes by non-Indians committed in Indian country. In each decision, the Supreme Court held that state courts had exclusive jurisdiction over the crime, although the Court's decision in *McBratney* is particularly problematic.[175] These cases illustrate a central dynamic: "The rights of the States within Indian country are based ultimately on the presence of non-Indian citizens within Indian country. As non-Indians moved in, so too did State law."[176]

THE ASCENDANCY OF STATE POWER

Importantly, each of the cases just cited involved only non-Indians. And, notwithstanding the few statutes previously cited, until the advent of the Rehnquist Court the general principle guiding tribal-state affairs remained as follows: "That State laws have no force within the territory of an Indian tribe in matters affecting Indians. . . ."[177] Although this principle emerged clearly from *Worcester* and is imbedded in tribal sovereignty, three major Supreme Court decisions, *Williams v. Lee*,[178] *Warren Trading Post Co. v. Arizona State Tax Commission*,[179] and *McClanahan v. Arizona State Tax Commission*,[180] set the stage for what has become a dramatically altered tribal-state relationship. All of these involved Navajo individuals or private businesses doing business on Navajo lands and all produced important precedential modifications to *Worcester*.[181]

Williams involved the Arizona Supreme Court's effort to wield civil jurisdiction over a case in which a non-Indian had sought to collect on an overdue debt for goods he had sold to a Navajo couple on the reservation. The Supreme Court held that the case should have been heard in tribal court. While Navajo sovereignty was reaffirmed, the Supreme Court departed from the *Worcester* ruling of complete state exclusion from Indian country by holding that the states might be allowed to extend their jurisdiction into tribal trust land, unless their action "infringed on the right of the reservation Indians to make and enforce their own laws and be ruled by them."[182] Justice Hugo Black dulled the emphatic *Worcester* holding by noting that "over the years this Court has modified these principles in cases where essential tribal relations were not involved and where the rights of Indians would not be jeopardized. . . ."[183]

Six years later, Arizona once again tried to extend its regulatory authority into Navajo country. The state levied a two percent tax on the gross proceeds of the Warren Trading Post Company, which conducted a retail trading business on the Navajo reservation. The Supreme Court in *Warren Trading Post Co. v. Arizona State Tax Commission* overturned the State Supreme Court's ruling and held that the state could not tax the income of a federally licensed trader that had been earned through trade with Navajos within the Navajo Nation. The Court based its decision on federal preemption grounds, and also emphasized the lack of benefits afforded by the states to the Navajo Indians. The preemption test posits that Congress has the legislative authority to control any subject matter. If the *federal* government has acted affirmatively in a field, then the state is effectively "preempted" and cannot claim any jurisdictional authority over the same subject matter. The Court further noted that the federal policy of letting the tribes "run the reservation and its affairs without state control . . . [had] . . . automatically relieved [the State] of all burdens of carrying on those same responsibilities."[184]

In 1973, Arizona's Tax Commission once again sought to extend state law into Navajo country. In *McClanahan v. Arizona State Tax Commission*, Rosalind McClanahan, an enrolled citizen of the Navajo Nation, contended that Arizona's state income tax on wages was unlawful as applied to reservation Indians. The State Supreme Court dismissed McClanahan's claim. On appeal to the United States Supreme Court, Justice Thurgood Marshall, speaking for a unanimous Court, held that Indians and Indian property on an Indian reservation were not subject to state taxation "except by virtue of express authority conferred upon the State by Act of Congress, and that the Navajo treaty precludes extension of state law, including state tax law, to Indians on the Navajo reservation."[185]

While the Court's decision to strike down Arizona's personal income tax on Indians who earned their income in Indian Country was certainly important for tribal self-government, additional language employed by the Court signified the reduced viability of the tribal sovereignty concept. Sovereignty, the Court said, was to be used only as a "backdrop" against which the applicable treaties and statutes must be read. The question was not so much that of tribal sovereignty, but whether the treaties, statutes, and tribal laws had given rise to a preemption of the subject field so as to preclude state intrusion. In other words, Arizona's tax law was excluded because of the doctrine of preemption, not because of the Navajo Nation's inherent sovereignty.

In 1980, in *White Mountain Apache Tribe v. Bracker*,[186] departing even further from tribal sovereignty as an independent defense against intrusive state law, the Supreme Court asserted that "there is no rigid rule" available to the Court to determine whether a state law may be applied in Indian country.[187] Here the High Court combined the preemption and infringement doctrines into a two-part test to determine which state laws could be enforced in Indian Country without congressional or tribal consent. A state law, Justice Marshall insisted, must pass both tests before it can be applied. "The two barriers," the Court maintained, "are independent because either, standing alone, can be a sufficient basis for holding state law inapplicable to activity undertaken on the reservation or by tribal members." [188] Marshall then added that the two were related and that tribal government was "dependent on and subject to the broad power of Congress," while the idea of Indian self-governance remained important merely as a "backdrop." [189] This so-called tradition of Indian sovereignty, Marshall concluded, "must inform the determination" of whether a state's exercise of authority has been preempted by federal law or whether it infringed on tribal self-government. [190]

In a fairly substantial follow-up case, *California v. Cabazon Band of Mission Indians*, [191] the Supreme Court in 1987 upheld the right of tribal governments to regulate gaming in Indian Country free from state and local government interference. California had sought to impose its bingo laws, limiting the profits from the operation of bingo games to charitable purposes, placing a ceiling of 250 dollars per pot, and requiring that the people who operated the games do so without compensation. In addition, the county wanted to impose a local ordinance to prohibit the operations of a card parlor.

The Supreme Court rebuffed the state and reaffirmed in a majority opinion written by Justice Byron White that in the area of a state's efforts to tax Indian tribes and their members, the "*per se* rule" held sway. This rule, laid out in *Montana v. Blackfeet Tribe*, [192] holds that while Congress, in its exercise of exclusive plenary authority, may authorize a state to tax a tribe or its members, "[i]t has not done so often, and the Court consistently has held that it will find the Indians' exemption from state taxes lifted only when Congress has made its intention to do so unmistakably clear." [193] Justice White continued, "We have repeatedly addressed the issue of state taxation of tribes and tribal members and the state, federal, and tribal interests which it implicates. *We have recognized that the federal tradition of Indian immunity from state taxation is very strong and that the state interest in taxation is correspondingly weak* [emphasis mine]." [194]

The "tradition of sovereignty" and Indian immunity from state taxation are, of course, very much subject to interpretation and may or may not be adhered to. And, as the Rehnquist Court gained new members, a conservative ideology became predominant and these two "traditions" were less and less respected. In 1989, the Supreme Court was asked to decide in *Cotton Petroleum Corporation v. New Mexico* [195] whether the State of New Mexico could impose a severance tax on oil and gas produced on tribal land by a non-Indian company which was already paying a similar tribal tax. The Supreme Court held that the federal government's extensive regulation of reservation oil and gas development and the tribe's preexisting tax did not constitute "preemption" and the state could enforce its own taxing schemes. The majority thereby dramatically altered a fundamental principle that had existed for years in Indian law—that a state's effort to tax reservation-based activities is invalid unless Congress has expressly authorized the activity. Instead, Justice John Paul Stevens asserted that "more recently such taxes have been upheld unless expressly or impliedly prohibited by Congress."[196] This ruling dictated a significant shift in what the courts would allow regarding state power vis-à-vis tribes. The presumption of state authority in Indian country unless specifically prohibited by Congress is in striking contrast to the preemption test. As Blackmun noted in dissent, "Under the majority's approach, there is no pre-emption unless the States are *entirely* excluded from a sphere of activity and provide no services to the Indians or to the lessees they seek to tax"[197] (emphasis original).

In another case decided in the same term, *Brendale v. Confederated Tribes and Bands of the Yakima Indian Nation*,[198] the Supreme Court, in a vociferously divided opinion, held that the State of Washington had the power to zone non-Indian land within the exterior boundaries of an Indian reservation. The Yakima tribe, conversely, could only enforce its zoning laws on non-Indian landowners within the reservation if the landowner was engaged in "demonstrably serious" activity that threatened to "imperil the political integrity, economic security or the health and welfare of the tribe."[199] "This standard," claimed Justice White, would give the tribe sufficient protection "while at the same time avoiding undue interference with state sovereignty and providing the certainty needed by property owners."[200] *Brendale*, with its presumption of state authority in Indian country, is a clear departure from past understandings of the tribal-state relationship. Interestingly, it involves the same tribe and the same subsidiary issue of state authority in Indian Country as the case we are about to consider—*County of Yakima v. Yakima Indian Nation*. The latter case, however, directly involves the application of state power over Indian landowners inside a reservation.

HISTORICAL BACKGROUND

The Confederated Tribes and Bands of the Yakima Indian Nation have inhabited parts of the area now known as Washington State for more than 12,000 years. Their diplomatic relations with the United States, however, were not confirmed until they entered into a treaty with the United States on June 9, 1855.[201] Primarily a land cession agreement (the Yakima ceded over ten million acres to the federal government), the treaty also established a 1.3-million-acre reservation out of the remaining tribal lands which were "set apart" and demarcated for the "exclusive use and benefit of said confederated tribes and bands of Indians. . . ." No whites, save for Bureau of Indian Affairs officials, were allowed on the reservation "without permission of the tribe." Besides the establishment of a permanently recognized homeland, the treaty, by its very negotiation, confirmed the sovereign status of the Yakima Nation. The Confederated Tribes, in compensation for their ceded lands, much of central Washington, received monetary and material compensation and also secured explicit recognition of their fishing rights. The fishing rights issue would later prove a most contentious point between the Indians and non-Indian settlers, businesses, and governments.

Washington joined the United States as a constituent state in 1889, and in so doing was required to give both the federal government and the tribes in the area assurance that it would not interfere with the rights of Indians. Article 26 of the Washington State Constitution declared the following:

> That the people inhabiting this state do agree and declare that they forever disclaim all right and title to the unappropriated public lands lying within the boundaries of this state, and to all lands lying within said limits owned or held by any Indian or Indian tribes; and that until the title there too shall have been extinguished by the United States, the same shall be and remain subject to the disposition of the United States, *and said Indian land shall remain under the absolute jurisdiction and control of the Congress of the United States . . . ; Provided, That nothing in this ordinance shall preclude the state from taxing as other lands are taxed any lands owned or held by any Indian who has severed his tribal relations, and has obtained from the United States or from any person a title thereto by patented or other grant,* save and except such lands as have been or may be granted to any Indian or Indians under any act of Congress containing a provision exempting the lands thus granted from taxation, which exemption shall continue so long and to such extent as such act of Congress may prescribe.[202] (emphasis original)

Two years earlier Congress had enacted the General Allotment Act, which was designed to speed up the individualization and ultimate absorption of American Indians into American society. The President was authorized, "whenever in his opinion any reservation or any part thereof, of such Indians is advantageous for agriculture or grazing purposes . . . to conduct negotiations with tribes for the allotment of their lands and possession of the surplus (unallotted lands left over) to the government for settlement."

Once a reservation had been allotted, and all family heads had received their 160-acre trust patent (eighty acres to single persons over eighteen and adult orphans, and forty acres to those under eighteen years old), the title to the allotment was to be held in trust for twenty-five years by the government and could not be sold by the Indians. This would be ample time, it was thought, to allow the allottees to adjust to a new life-style and be able to manage their own affairs without federal oversight. After the end of the twenty-five-year period, the restrictive trust patent would be lifted and replaced with a fee patent—an ownership deed allowing individual Indians to do whatever they wanted with their lands.[203]

The ultimate goal of the allotment policy was the cultural extinction of tribalism, with the individualized Indians joining the broader American citizenry as self-supporting citizens. These detribalized individuals, even before receiving their fee patent title, were to "have the benefit of and be subject to the laws, both civil and criminal, of the State or Territory in which they reside . . ." since federal citizenship accompanied their trust allotment. As we saw in the discussion of the *Nice* case, the issue of Indian citizenship was widely debated, notwithstanding the clear language of the 1887 law. It was not until the Supreme Court decided *Matter of Heff* in 1905 that the question was, at least temporarily, put to rest. In this case, the Court forcefully held that Indian allottees became American citizens instantly as soon as they accepted their land allotment. In other words, they were enfranchised from the beginning of the twenty-five-year trust period, not at the end of that period.

Congress and the Bureau of Indian Affairs, however, were infuriated at the *Heff* decision, though it seemed to support what they themselves had been advocating since the 1880s—namely, the assimilation of Indians. A year later Congress responded by enacting the Burke Act, introduced by South Dakota Representative Charles Burke.[204] This amendment to the Allotment Act effectively postponed the bestowal of either federal or state citizenship until the end of the twenty-five-year trust period. In addition, it gave the secretary of the interior the authority to prematurely issue fee patents to "competent" allottees when the secretary determined that they were capable of "managing their own affairs."

So-called competent Indians were effectively on their own and were immediately subject to the full array of state laws and regulations. The remaining and derisively labeled "non-competent" Indians were to remain under federal tutelage for the duration of the trust period.

In April 1917, hastening the issuance of fee patents to satisfy both Euro-American land hunger and as a last gasp to "speed up" the Indian assimilative process, Commissioner of Indian Affairs Cato Sells issued his "Declaration of Policy." Sells proclaimed that "[b]roadly speaking, a policy of greater liberalism will henceforth prevail in Indian administration to the end that every Indian, as soon as he has been determined to be as competent to transact his own business as the average white man, shall be given full control of his property and have all his lands and money turned over to him, after which he will no longer be a ward of the Government."[205]

This policy was steeped in the popular eugenics paradigm of the day. Sells indicated as much when he declared:

> While ethnologically a preponderance of white blood has not heretofore been a criterion of competency, nor even now is it always a safe standard, it is almost an axiom that an Indian who has a larger proportion of white blood than Indian partakes more of the characteristics of the former than of the latter. In thought and action, so far as the business world is concerned, he approximates more closely to the white blood ancestry.[206]

In short, Indians with one-half or more white blood were to be "released" from federal supervision with or without Indian consent. Legally, they were no longer recognized as Indians to whom the United States had a trust responsibility. State tax departments, non-Indian land speculators, and other interested parties prepared for a feeding frenzy as the lands of such newly declared "competent" Indians became purchasable and taxable.

As the new policy was implemented, Congress harangued the Bureau of Indian Affairs, arguing that the commissioner of Indian affairs was not issuing fee patents quickly enough. The tribes complained of just the reverse. For example, Indians on the Yakima as well as Umatilla and Flathead reservations "refused to accept fee patents issued under the declaration of policy because they believed the government had no right to issue such patents unless they applied for them."[207]

Such opposition culminated in the congressional law of February 26,

1927,[208] in which the secretary of the interior was authorized to cancel any fee patents which had been issued to individual Indians without their consent, provided the allottee had not already mortgaged or sold any part of the allotment. The remaining land would revert to its preexisting trust and, by extension, non-taxable status. "Therefore," said Felix S. Cohen, "it would appear that the allottees under the General Allotment Act obtained a vested right to tax exemption which cannot be taken . . . without [their] consent."[209] However, if an allottee voluntarily applied for a fee patent and was properly accorded one, "there seems no reason to believe that his lands would not thereby become subject to state taxation."[210]

The General Allotment Act was formally repudiated on June 18, 1934, with the passage of the Indian Reorganization Act (IRA).[211] Section I of the IRA said that "hereafter no land of any Indian reservation, created or set apart by treaty or agreement with the Indians, Act of Congress, Executive order, purchase, or otherwise, shall be allotted in severalty to any Indian." The IRA effectively stopped the action of allotting tribal lands and indefinitely extended the trust period of previously allotted lands. The trust periods were specifically extended on the Yakima reservation by executive orders numbered 3630, 4168, 5746, and 7036.[212]

The damage caused by the allotment policy throughout Indian Country was grossly evident, however. Collectively, tribal lands had been reduced from 138 million acres in 1887 to 52 million acres in 1934. This 86-million-acre loss had transpired in four ways—"38 million acres of surplus land ceded after allotment, 22 million acres of surplus land opened to white settlement, 23 million acres of fee patented land loss, and 3.4 million acres of original and heirship allotments sold."[213] Yakima, along with the Colville Reservation in Washington, the Fort Berthold in North Dakota, the Klamath in Oregon, and the Rosebud in South Dakota, experienced the most allotments of any reservations around the turn of the century.[214]

THE YAKIMA RESERVATION TODAY

The Yakima Reservation had approximately 7,600 enrolled members in 1992. Of the 1.3 million acres within the reservation, 1.04 million (eighty percent) are held in trust by the United States. A majority of this acreage is unallotted timber and range land. The remaining twenty percent, 260,000 acres, is owned in fee-simple by Indians and non-Indians. Less than one percent of the fee land is owned by the tribe or its members.[215]

The Yakima Reservation is divided into a restricted or "closed" area and an "open" area. The "restricted" area comprises some 807,000 acres of mostly forest and range lands. Permanent structures are prohibited in this area. Most Yakima live in the "open" area, mostly on trust land. This acreage is predominately agricultural and is irrigable. The "open" area has four small towns—Toppenish, Wapato, Harrah, and White Swan.[216] In addition, 104 members of the Yakima Nation own 139 fee land parcels. These are generally home sites and average about ten acres each. Thirty-seven of these Indian-owned parcels, held by thirty-one Yakima families, were the point of contention in this case.

PROCEDURAL HISTORY: THE MASKING BEGINS

According to county records, Yakima County has "routinely levied and collected ad valorem taxes" on the fee-patented parcels "for some time."[217] But there was an important difference of opinion and confusion of fact on how long tribal members had been paying these taxes. The county contended that the tribe's members had been paying taxes on the fee lands for "decades."[218]

The Yakima's attorney maintained, to the contrary, that the Indians' "land ownership and fee . . . had developed to an appreciable degree in recent times."[219] This important discrepancy was apparently left unresolved because of the 1988 Federal District Court's granting of summary judgment in favor of the tribe. A summary judgment meant that no information or data were presented to the court as to when members of the tribe began to secure fee title to the lands in question.

Although this critical issue was not factually determined at the district court level, both the Court of Appeals and the Supreme Court accepted the county's version of the taxation history of the Yakima. However, the information presented earlier—from the 1927 law which authorized the secretary of the interior to cancel any fee patents which had been issued without Indian consent, to the 1934 IRA—would tend to support the county's view only insofar as it was lawfully entitled to tax the fee lands of non-Indians in the area.

In 1987, Yakima County instituted foreclosure proceedings on properties throughout the county to which ad valorem[220] and excise taxes[221] were past due. This included the parcels owned by thirty-one Yakima families who were unable or unwilling to pay the county taxes. In November of that year, the Yakima Nation's government, on its own behalf as a landowner of some of the parcels and on behalf of its members, filed an action in the Federal District Court for the Eastern District of Washington to prevent the county from imposing or collecting taxes.

The tribe sought a declaratory judgment and injunctive relief, asserting that the county's imposition and collection of property taxes and efforts to sell the foreclosed land at a tax sale violated federal law. District Judge Allan McDonald began, appropriately enough, with the United States Commerce Clause which, he said, "cloaks the Federal Government" with exclusive authority over Indian matters. And citing the Supreme Court's well-known precedents—*Warren Trading Post, McClanahan, Moe v. Salish*, and *Montana v. Blackfeet*—he noted that the case law generally affirmed that tribes and their members were exempt from state taxation within the exterior boundaries of their reservations.

Judge McDonald did acknowledge that section 6 of the General Allotment Act authorized the state to tax allotted lands after fee patents had been issued. However, he unequivocally stated that the policy was inconsistent with the subsequent IRA of 1934 "which was designed to rehabilitate the tribes by ending allotment and indefinitely extending the federal trust protection over all Indian lands save for the exceptions noted earlier." He added that "similarly, the Supreme Court has repeatedly found that Congress repudiated the policy of the General Allotment Act with the passage of the Indian Reorganization Act." For support he cited *Mattz v. Arnett*[222] and *Moe v. Confederated Salish and Kootenai Tribes*, which had been written by Justice Rehnquist two years earlier in 1976.[223] In fact, McDonald asserted that, standing alone, *Moe*'s reasoning was compelling enough to deny the state tax. In that case, Montana had also tried to rely on section 6 of the Allotment Act and an early Supreme Court case, *Goudy v. Meath*, to justify taxing Indians who had accepted lands in fee simple. Justice Rehnquist, however, had stated for the unanimous *Moe* Court, that Montana's reliance on *Goudy*, and the fact that the General Allotment Act had never been expressly "repealed," were "untenable" arguments. Basically, the *Moe* court was concerned that the "checkerboard jurisdiction" which would result if Montana were found to have jurisdiction would significantly diminish the size of the Flathead reservation. Quoting from *United States v. Mazurie*[224] in the *Moe* ruling, Rehnquist had said this was determined to be "contrary to the intent embodied in the existing federal statutory law of Indian jurisdiction." In *Moe*, Rehnquist had also dismantled Montana's argument that the General Allotment Act had never been repealed. Notwithstanding *Goudy*, said Rehnquist, "the State has referred us to no decisional authority—and we know of none—giving the meaning for what it contends to Section 6 of the General Allotment Act in the face of the many and complex intervening jurisdictional statutes directed at the reach of State law within reservation land. . . ."[225] Rehnquist conclusively stated that "Congress by its more modern legislation has evinced a clear intent to eschew any such 'checkerboard' approach within an existing Indian reservation, and our cases have in turn followed Congress' lead in this area."[226]

McDonald drew heavily from, and was constrained by, Rehnquist's precedential opinion in *Moe*. He was also abiding by congressional policy and Felix S. Cohen's informed articulation of the federal Indian law. He awarded summary judgment for the tribe and its members and extended an injunction prohibiting the imposition or collection of the taxes on fee-patented lands of the Yakima Nation or Yakima individuals "who have not severed tribal relations, within the exterior boundaries of the Yakima Indian reservation."[227]

Importantly, none of the Yakima involved had severed tribal affiliations, the one exception specified under the Washington Constitution that would have allowed the state or its agencies to tax Indians. Nor, apparently, had any individual Yakima voluntarily sought a fee patent, which, if granted by the secretary of the interior, would terminate the trust relationship between the Indians and the federal government. There was, in fact, no evidence that the individual Yakima or the tribe had sought to have the trust relationship terminated. The county's attorney admitted as much in oral testimony before the Supreme Court on November 5, 1990. Jeffery Sullivan, Yakima County's attorney, was asked by a justice: "Now, when did the trust period expire here? Do we know that?" Sullivan responded: "We don't know that. The record in the stipulation would be that all of these lands were patented under title, under this Amendment 6 or Section 6 [of the General Allotment Act]." The justice again asked, "Well, were the patents issued during the trust period or after the trust period? And does the record tell us that?" Sullivan again had to admit: "The record does not tell us that. We submit that it makes no difference whether it was during the trust period or whether it was after the trust period."[228]

It does make a difference, however. If there was no evidence that the trust relationship had expired or been terminated by either individual, tribal, or federal action, how could the county claim it had legitimate authority to tax Indians? This directly contradicts the basic tenet governing the trust relationship regarding Indian property located within a reservation, particularly since the 1934 IRA.

On appeal, while the 9th Circuit Court of Appeals agreed that the county's excise tax was disallowed, it held that the ad valorem property tax was permissible. In the Court's opinion, the property tax was not considered a "demonstrably serious" threat to the political, economic, or health integrity of the tribe despite the checkerboard jurisdiction which would result. The Court arrived at this conclusion—that the actual loss of land was somehow not a threat to a tribe's integrity—by declaring that section 6 of the General Allotment Act had "not been superseded or otherwise rendered void by subsequent statutes."[229] Although openly acknowledging that the IRA "repudiated the allotment policy," the Appeals Court said that notwithstanding this repudiation, section 6 still had "proper legal effect."

The Court of Appeals in essence found that later law—the 1934 IRA and subsequent revolutionary changes in federal policy, from the assimilation of Indians during the period of 1890–1920 to cultural revitalization and land restoration in the 1930s, accompanied by the indefinite extension of trust status on Indian land—had not effectively recloaked Indian allottees' lands with federal protection against state taxation efforts. The curious logic through which they had arrived at this conclusion defies understanding, but their decision constituted a hammering blow to the Yakima Nation, and especially to the Yakima allottees. The 9th Circuit Court remanded the case back to District Judge McDonald to determine in light of *Brendale*'s "demonstrably serious" test, whether the county's ad valorem tax posed such a threat. The Circuit Court did acknowledge that the Yakima Nation had already presented enough evidence showing that the county's taxation scheme would indeed "affect it in a demonstrably serious way"; however, it still insisted that the District Court had not made its decision based on this evidence. Judge McDonald, in essence, was being chided for failing to apply the *Brendale* test, which was developed two years after his decision! McDonald's opinion reflected a clear understanding of exactly what the "effect" would be on the Yakima families if they were to lose their lands under foreclosure proceedings. Both Yakima County and the Yakima Nation filed for a rehearing at the 9th Circuit Court. This was rejected. The county then filed a writ of certiorari to the Supreme Court, fearing that the Yakima Nation would win on remand since it could easily meet the "demonstrably serious" test. The Yakima Nation filed a cross-petition with the High Court arguing that the district court's judgment was correct and should be reinstated.

MASKING WITHIN THE DECISION: THE OPINION

Scalia and an eight-to-one[230] majority, over the objections of the Yakima Nation and the United States as a supporting respondent, cross petitioner, and *amicus curiae*, affirmed the Court of Appeals ruling that the General Allotment Act did indeed permit a county to impose property taxes on fee-patented Indian lands. The majority, however, also affirmed that the county was disallowed from enforcing an excise tax on the sales of such lands.

In the seminal constitutional law decision *McCulloch v. Maryland*,[231] John Marshall had delivered what would become one of his most famous lines: "The power to tax involves the power to destroy." This evocative statement and the attendant arguments Marshall developed were sufficient to preclude the State of Maryland's taxing an operation of the federal government which it had not created by its own constitution and over which it exercised no control. This theory is even more germane to the situation under discussion. The State of Washington's power to tax could certainly lead to the "destruction" of the Yakima Nation since Indian/tribal sovereignty is based not on ideas, or material, or military power, but is rooted in the land that nurtures the people. Thus, an irrefutable argument can be made that to the extent a tribal nation loses land, to that degree it loses its very sovereignty and cultural identity.

Moreover, unlike the symbiotic constitutional relationship between the states and the federal government, tribal nations' authority derives from their original independence. As the Supreme Court said in *The Kansas Indians* in 1867, when that state attempted to tax the treaty-allotted lands of the Shawnee, Miami, and Wea tribes:

> If the tribal organization of the Shawnees is preserved intact, and recognized by the political department of the government as existing, then they are a "people distinct from others," capable of making treaties, separated from the jurisdiction of Kansas, and to be governed exclusively by the government of the Union. If under the control of Congress, from necessity, there can be no divided authority. If they have outlived many things, they have not outlived the protection afforded by the Constitution, treaties and laws of Congress. It may be that they cannot exist much longer as a distinct people in the presence of the civilization of Kansas, "but until they are clothed with the rights and bound to all the duties of citizens," they enjoy the privilege of total immunity from state taxation.[232]

The Supreme Court noted that the conferring of other rights and privileges did not affect the Indians' distinctive situation, which, the Court stated and the Indians understood, could "only be changed by treaty stipulation, or a voluntary abandonment of their tribal organization. As long as the United States recognizes their national character they are under the protection of treaties and the laws of Congress, and their property is withdrawn from the operation of state laws."[233]

This decision had predated the General Allotment Act by twenty years. And while the Allotment Act authorized state taxation of fee-patented lands, this could only occur when certain conditions were met: namely, the individual allottee had voluntarily abandoned the tribe; had received full citizenship privileges; and had asked the Department of the Interior to lift the trust protection which was restored in 1927 and reconfirmed in 1934 in the IRA. Furthermore, Washington State's constitution, like that of Kansas, contained the disclaimer clause which clearly evidences that state's understanding that it could only tax the lands of individual Indians who had "severed" tribal relations and had received a patent or other grant.

A case more directly related to the case at hand is *Choate v. Trapp*.[234] *Choate* involved an explicit federal law, not a mere proviso on a repudiated law, which purportedly lifted previously imposed restrictions against the selling of allotted Indian land. In *Choate*, which according to Felix Cohen implicitly overruled *The Cherokee Tobacco*, the Supreme Court unanimously ruled that the State of Oklahoma's plans to tax the individual allotments of more than 8,000 Choctaw and Chickasaw—explicitly authorized by a 1908 federal law[235] which (1) removed restrictions from the sale or encumbrance of land held by allottees and (2) provided that lands from which restrictions had been removed should be subject to state taxation—were invalid because Congress had previously, in 1897 and 1898, provided that all allotted lands were to remain nontaxable so long as the original allottee held the title. The State of Oklahoma argued that the tax was a legitimate exercise of governmental authority and that Congress had acted, in the later laws, to withdraw its protection of the Indians' tax-exempt status. The Indians, on the other hand, asserted that the 1908 Act was a violation of the contract they had made with the United States, and that their tax-exempt status was a property right which could not be divested without due process of law.[236]

The 8,110 Chickasaw and Choctaw plaintiffs lost in Oklahoma's trial court and then in the State Supreme Court. They appealed to the United States Supreme Court. The critical questions were: Had the Indians ac-

290 AMERICAN INDIAN SOVEREIGNTY AND THE SUPREME COURT

quired vested rights under the Curtis Act of 1898 which were protected by the Fifth Amendment of the Constitution? and What was the validity of the congressional enactment which purportedly subjected the Indian land to state taxation? The Court carefully drew a distinction between "tribal property and private property" and affirmed that "Congress, in consideration of the Indians' relinquishment of all claims to the common property [in the 1897 and 1898 laws], and for other satisfactory reasons" extended vested rights to the tribal individuals.[237] These rights could not be taken without the individual Indians' consent. The right to remove the restriction, said Justice Joseph Lamar, "was in pursuance of the power under which Congress could legislate as to the status of the ward and lengthen or shorten the period of disability. But the provision that the land should be non-taxable was a property right, which Congress undoubtedly had the power to grant. That right [was] fully vested in the Indians and was binding upon Oklahoma."[238]

These passages illustrate the distinctive manner in which tribal sovereignty and the Constitution's Fifth Amendment were applied in this case. As the Court noted: "Under the provisions of the Fifth Amendment there was no more power to deprive him [the Indian] of the exemption than of any other right in the property. . . . After he accepted the patent the Indian could not be heard, either at law or in equity, to assert any claim to the common property. If he is bound [by the agreement], so is the tribe and the Government when the patent is issued."[239] Congress, therefore, could not impair an Indian's vested private property rights, which "are secured and enforced to the same extent and in the same way as other residents or citizens of the United States."[240] And finally, the Indian's private property "is not subject to impairment by legislative action, even while he is, as a member of a tribe and subject to the guardianship of the United States as to his political and personal status."[241]

Justice Antonin Scalia for the majority and the dissenting justices in *Yakima* disregarded this important Supreme Court case. In order to reach the conclusion that the state could tax Indian land, Scalia had to find a way, because of the Commerce Clause's conferral of plenary power in Indian affairs which necessarily extinguishes a state's authority over Indians or Indian property, to locate a specific grant of authority from the Congress to the states that would authorize this intrusion. This he found in the General Allotment Act. He had, moreover, to ignore the doctrine of tribal sovereignty, which is relevant to individual Indians living on fee-patented estates who have the "same rights in the tribe as those whose estates are held in common."[242]

The Masks of "Unmistaken Intent," "County Sovereignty,"
"Implied Repeals," and "Categorical Allowances"

Scalia's main arguments were the following. First, in a threshold assessment, he declared that section 6 of the General Allotment Act, in providing that Indian allottees were to be subject to all civil and criminal state laws, provided the necessary explicit authorization, thereby allowing states to tax Indians. Although this law was amended by the Burke Act of 1906,[243] which precluded state jurisdiction over allottees until the end of the twenty-five-year trust period, a proviso in that act gave the President discretionary authority to expedite state jurisdiction over allottees by the termination of the trust relationship, though only when the individual allottee was deemed "competent and capable." This limited proviso, according to Scalia, entailed "unmistakably clear" congressional intent to allow state taxation of Indian-owned fee-patented lands. Moreover, Scalia maintained that nothing Congress had done subsequently effected an express repeal of the General Allotment Act. Therefore, it remained good law, according to Scalia.

Second, on the subject of state sovereignty, Scalia said that it had gradually eclipsed tribal sovereignty. Dismissing Chief Justice John Marshall's depiction of tribal sovereignty, which Justice Thurgood Marshall in the 1973 *McClanahan* decision had termed "a platonic notion of Indian sovereignty" that had lost its "independent sway,"[244] Scalia noted that "this Court's more recent cases have recognized the rights of States, absent a congressional prohibition, to exercise criminal (and, implicitly, civil) jurisdiction over non-Indians located on reservation lands."[245]

Third, the Washington State Constitution, which expressly disallowed state taxation of fee-patented Indian lands, except of those Indians who had terminated their tribal affiliations, did, however, according to Scalia, contain a clause which allowed the taxation of certain Indian land. The pertinent clause reads:

> *Provided, That nothing in this ordinance shall preclude the state from taxing as other lands are taxed any lands owned or held by any Indian who has severed his tribal relations, and has obtained from the United States or from any person a title thereto by patent or other grant,* save and except such lands as have been or may be granted to any Indian or Indians under any act of congress containing a provision exempting the lands thus granted from taxation, which exemption shall continue so long and to such an extent as such acts of congress may prescribe.[246] (emphasis original)

Scalia agreed with the Court of Appeals that under this language, the Indian lands not covered by the quoted proviso were not exempted from taxation but merely committed to "the absolute jurisdiction and control of [Congress]. . . . If Congress has permitted taxation, the provision is not violated."[247]

Fourth, Scalia, citing the misnamed "cardinal rule" that says repeals by implication are not favored by the judicial branch, distanced the Court from the *Moe* decision wherein the Rehnquist-led unanimous Court had said that the IRA and other statutes repudiated the jurisdictional force of the Allotment Act. Scalia, instead, insisted that the Yakima Nation and the United States as amici had misunderstood *Moe* and had a "misperception of the structure of the General Allotment Act."[248] The "misunderstanding" arose, said Scalia, because the government and the Indians wrongly thought that *Moe* had held that section 6 of the General Allotment Act had been repealed by implication. And since *Moe* had not mentioned "implied repeal," and because of this abstract theory of the "cardinal rule," they had misstated the *Moe* case.

The so-called misperception of the Allotment Act arose, according to Scalia, because while the Yakima focused on section 6 of the Act as the culprit, it was actually section 5 which was of "central significance."[249] This section dealt with the "alienability of the allotted lands." In other words, after the trust period had expired, the allotted lands could be sold or encumbered, which meant that they also became subject to "assessment and forced sale for taxes."[250] But Scalia then admitted, in conflict with his earlier denouncement of "implied repeals," that section 5 of the General Allotment Act only "implied" that patented allotments were subject to real estate taxes.

Fifth, Scalia rejected the Yakima Nation's political argument that state taxation of Indian land was wholly contrary to the announced federal Indian policy of self-determination and self-governance which has been Congress's official orientation—both in policy announcement and in statutory enactment—beginning with the 1934 IRA and restated in Richard Nixon's 1970 Self-Determination policy, which has been followed by every administration thereafter. In Scalia's words, "this seems to us a great exaggeration."[251] Rather, he stated that while the inpersonam (against the person) jurisdiction over reservation Indians at issue in *Moe* would be significantly disruptive, "the mere power to assess and collect a tax on certain real estate is not as disruptive."[252] Furthermore, even if the tribe's objections were valid, they were told—as were the Indians in *Smith* and in most of the decisions we have reviewed—

that their complaints would have to be taken to Congress since justices could not "pick and choose" among congressional laws. Thus, Scalia held that if the Yakima believed that the objectives of the IRA were obstructed by what Scalia called "the clearly retained remnant of an earlier policy," they would have to go to Congress for relief.[253] From this statement it is easy to see that one of the Court's earlier "cardinal rules," first expressed in *The Cherokee Tobacco*, the so-called last-in-time rule wherein the Court held that a later statute must overrule an earlier explicit treaty, had now been turned on its head.

After having announced these five major rationales, Scalia moved to address the two specific taxes: the excise tax and the property tax. Scalia declared that the state could not impose an excise tax on the Yakima. In order to deny the state's right to tax the "proceeds of the land," when it had just allowed the state to tax the "land itself," Scalia proceeded to engage in a fascinating discourse on shielding the Indians from the excise tax: "It is quite reasonable to say, in other words, that though the object of the *sale* here is land, that does not make land the object of the *tax*, and hence does not invoke the Burke Act proviso [emphasis original]."[254] And then, in a brief flash of insight that one can only wish might have held sway for the entire case, Scalia said, "[w]hen we are faced with these two possible constructions, our choice between them must be dictated by a principle deeply rooted in this Court's Indian jurisprudence: 'statutes are to be construed liberally in favor of the Indians, with ambiguous provisions interpreted to their benefit.'"[255]

Why Scalia was so eager to follow the liberal construction "principle" for this tax on cigarette sales and certain personal property items such as automobiles but refused to even consider it for the more destructive ad valorem "property" tax, which, as specified in the General Allotment and the Burke acts, flows exclusively from ownership of real estate on the anual date of assessment, and of which nonpayment can lead to foreclosure on Indian holdings, is hard to understand. His following the "liberal construction" principle here, but not in his reading of the Yakima treaty, the Washington State Constitution, the General Allotment Act, the Burke Act, the IRA, and the policies of Indian self-determination, is equally hard to fathom. Perhaps the Court felt that the excise tax, which in Scalia's definition was a "tax upon the Indians' activity of selling the land," was undesirable because the ultimate and unspoken goal of the Court was to encourage Indians to sell their allotments, and it believed that the excise tax might be constraining the Indians from making such a sale. This would fit the Court's contemporary stance, which seems to have aimed at revitalizing the assimilation process that slowed when the allotment and termination policies were abandoned.

Returning to the ad valorem tax, Scalia held that it was prima facie valid. Scalia distinguished the Court's recent *Brendale* case on the grounds that that decision involved the Yakima's wish to expand their inherent power to zone, whereas the pending case involved the tribe's "asserted restriction of a State's congressionally conferred powers."[256] There had, indeed, been historic conferral. First, the state's constitutional disclaimer acknowledged that the state would not seek to tax Indian lands; second, the IRA had forcibly repudiated allotment proceedings and in the process had reestablished federal trust restrictions aimed at keeping the states at arm's length from both tribal and individual Indian property.

More importantly, Scalia turned yet another Supreme Court rule on its head—the per se rule, discussed under the *Cabazon* case. This involved the well-established categorical prohibition of state taxation of Indians in Indian country. Scalia disingenuously asserted that while the categorical prohibitions have most often been applied in state taxation cases, "we think it also applies to produce categorical allowance of State taxation when it has in fact been authorized by Congress."[257] Scalia was somehow able to assert that Congress could categorically prohibit and categorically allow state taxation simultaneously, overlooking that one emphatically denies the other. Since Scalia had "categorically" ejected the prohibition of state taxation and had inserted his opposite categorical enunciation, it was unnecessary to consider either a balancing test or even to use the *Brendale* "demonstrably serious" test. Such categorical pronouncements preclude such activities.

In closing, and over the objections of the Yakima, who contended that it was not clear whether the foreclosed parcels had been patented under the General Allotment Act or might, in fact, have been patented under some other statute, Scalia brushed past this salient point and simply remanded the case to have this issue answered.

JUSTICE BLACKMUN'S DISSENT

In two powerful statements, Justice Harry Blackmun challenged the majority's arguably implausible opinion:

> I have wandered the maze of Indian statutes and case law tracing back
> 100 years. Unlike the Court, however, I am unable to find an "unmistakably clear" intent of Congress to allow the States to tax Indian-owned fee-patented lands.[258]

I am mystified how this Court, sifting through the wreckage of the Dawes Act, found any "clearly retained remnant," . . . justifying further erosions—through tax foreclosure actions as in this case—to the land holdings of the Indian people.[259]

Blackmun asserted that the Court, in its application of the "unmistakably clear" intent, was wrong on three counts. First, he described how Scalia had drawn this unmistakable intent from the 1906 Burke Act proviso, which, by its very description, applied only to prematurely patented lands—that is, to allottees who were unilaterally declared "competent" by the Indian affairs commissioner and the secretary of the interior. All the other patented lands, which remained in the hands of allegedly "noncompetent allottees" under the Burke Act, were not subject to state taxation. This is important because, as Scalia noted in his conclusion, it was not even clear that the Yakima families had secured their patents under the General Allotment Act, which the Burke Act had amended. If they had secured allotments through other statutes, then, legally, this proviso would not apply to them.

Furthermore, as Blackmun stated, and as Scalia himself had conceded, the proviso had itself been "orphaned" and thus had no force of law because "its antecedent principal clause"—section 6 of the Allotment Act—was no longer operative. In addition to the later congressional repudiation of the Burke Act under the IRA, the Supreme Court's *Matter of Heff* decision was also overruled by the Supreme Court in *United States v. Nice*. *Nice* effectively locked tribal citizens into the dual status of being American citizens while remaining Indians under federal trusteeship.

Second, Blackmun was unconvinced that it was "strange," as Scalia had put it, for allotted land to be alienable and yet not taxable. He observed, "To impute to Congress an intent to tax Indian land, because the Court thinks it 'strange' not to do so" ignores the more recognized and accepted presumption that "States have no power to regulate the affairs of Indians on a reservation."[260] Pushing Scalia's notion of "strangeness," Blackmun observed, "I find it stranger still to presume that Congress intends States to tax—and, as in this case, foreclose upon—Indian-owned reservation lands."[261] Here is where reliance on *Choate* would have proven beneficial for Blackmun's argument. Scalia's presumption conflicts with Congress's disavowal of the assimilation policies in 1934, which had prompted the General Allotment Act in the first place.[262]

Third, Blackmun attacked the majority for misapprehending federal preemption of the taxation field. He said that the majority's refusal to consider intervening statutes (e.g., the 1934 IRA, and the 1975 Indian Self-Determination Act) because they did not explicitly "repeal" the Dawes and Burke Act, was astounding. These policies and much of the case law effected a dramatic reversal in federal Indian policy and should have factored heavily against the Court's ruling that Congress intended state taxation of Indian-owned land.[263] Besides, said Blackmun, "a repeal—whether express or implied—need not be shown to preclude the States from taxing Indian lands."[264] The more pertinent question was whether Congress had already preempted state law, "not whether it has repealed its own law."[265] Under this principle, and drawing upon a number of Supreme Court opinions, Blackmun found that federal Indian policy and interests, in conjunction with the sovereignty of the Yakima Nation, precluded state laws.

Blackmun seemed bewildered, almost disheartened, by the callous attitude of the majority toward the tribe's efforts to become more self-reliant. Such a long-pursued goal, he believed, would become more difficult, if not impossible, to achieve with state intrusion now being allowed on such an intimate level. What Blackmun was most concerned about was the attitude exemplified by Scalia's statement that the tribe's arguments for continued tax exemptions, which would enable the tribe and its people to continue their development towards self-determination, were merely "a great exaggeration." Blackmun was keenly aware of what was at stake and remained unconvinced by Scalia's statement that "mere" property taxes would be less disruptive of tribal integrity than cigarette sales taxes or personal property taxes. "I cannot," said Blackmun, "agree that paying a few more pennies for cigarettes . . . is more a threat to tribal integrity and self-determination than foreclosing upon and seizing tribal lands."[266]

In closing, Blackmun targeted Scalia's contention that if the Yakima were dissatisfied, all they had to do was lobby Congress. Blackmun poignantly observed that "I am less confident than my colleagues that the 31 Yakima Indian families likely to be rendered landless and homeless by today's decision are well-positioned to lobby for change in the vast corridors of Congress."[267]

Removing the Masks CHAPTER 7

In this punctuated ride through judicial history, I have, as carefully and methodically as possible, studied the literal language of what I have come to consider the most important and byzantine Supreme Court decisions over a period of nearly two hundred years. In this, I have critically appraised each case as to its internal logic, its applicability to the actual historical situation, and to those larger historical/political/legal facts which distinguish the indigenous/federal/state relationship. What has emerged in my final analysis is the realization that justices of the Supreme Court, both individually and collectively, have engaged in the manufacturing, redefining, and burying of "principles," "doctrines," and legal "tests" to excuse and legitimize constitutional, treaty, and civil rights violations of tribal nations and, in some cases, of individual Indians.

As the previous chapters have demonstrated, the Supreme Court, from its earliest years to its most recent rulings, has utilized the rule of law in a unique manner—sometimes as legitimator, sometimes as initiator, sometimes as imperial instigator, sometimes as all three—when it has addressed the issues of tribal national sovereignty and individual Indian rights. The Supreme Court has performed its assorted and sundry tasks in a manner that can be characterized as "lawful" but one, as the fifteen cases have shown, that has had little or nothing to do with "justice." As Colton once said, "in civil jurisprudence it too often happens that there is so much law that there is no room for justice; and the claimant expires of wrong in the midst of right, as mariners die of thirst in the midst of water." [1]

This quotation is even more apt when used as a description of federal Indian law cases. Where the Supreme Court is found exercising the "rule of law," the question that must immediately be raised is "whose rule is it?" Tribal nations, existing as separate and originally independent sovereigns, maintain and govern themselves by their own bodies of laws, regulations, and moral principles. However, in the fifteen cases studied, it was the United States Supreme Court, not a tribal or international court, that was the center for dispute resolution when conflicts arose between the tribal nations and the federal government. In a few cases tribes exercised their right to file suit on their own behalf in an effort to compel the federal government to fulfill its obligations for treaty or statutorily created arrangements (e.g., *Shoshone*, *Sioux Nation*), with mixed results. However, in cases like *Johnson*, *Rogers*, and *Nice*, where no tribes or individual Indians were seeking redress, and in cases like *Cherokee Tobacco*, *Kagama*, *Race Horse*, and *Smith*, where individual Indians, not tribal nations, were involved, rulings were problematic when *tribes* also became directly affected by the Court's decisions.

Although the question of why there is so little "justice" in the presence of so much "law" is a difficult one to answer definitively, the explanation rests at least partially in the fact that indigenous values, laws, and morals are given little consideration by the Supreme Court. Thurman Arnold asserts that "the Supreme Court is the greatest unifying symbol in American government—a place where the ideal of a government of fundamental principles is best exemplified." The Supreme Court has a power that is supposed to prevent governmental action which is prejudicial, arbitrary, or capricious; however the experience of tribal nations too often has been that the Supreme Court has only sustained and legitimated the political and policy directives of the federal government. Over time, these directives have become focused in favor of the expropriation of tribal land, the utter denial or gross diminution of tribal sovereignty, the disavowal of treaty rights, the rejection of aboriginal property title, and the forced assimilation of Indians. These negating actions have come despite federal recognition of tribal nationhood via hundreds of treaties, agreements, and statutes; the existence of the trust relationship; the enactment of numerous policy directives which have unmistakably acknowledged tribal sovereignty; and the enfranchisement of individual Indians through various treaties and laws.

EXPOSING THE JUDICIAL MASKS

David Kairys, an eminent critical legal theorist, identified in his powerful critique of the Rehnquist Court, *With Liberty and Justice for Some* (1993), a number of techniques used in various opinions issued by the conservative Rehnquist court to further the "conservative revolution" with its commitment to "judicial restraint, strict construction of constitutional and statutory language, a return to democracy, and the rule of law, and legal rather than political decision making."[2] These opinions have covered such issues as freedom of expression, participation in the political process, religion, equality, privacy, and due process.

After his analysis of over thirty Supreme Court opinions, Kairys concluded his study by identifying and discussing the distinctive set of "techniques," "doctrines," and other judicial "mechanisms" used by the conservative Court which have caused considerable problems for individuals and groups seeking redress in the areas listed above. I introduce them because they are significant and relevant to the body of law that the Supreme Court has created and continues to emulate with regard to tribes and Indian issues.

First, the conservatives of the High Court, according to Kairys, have developed, without any constitutional basis, a number of new doctrines which effectively infringe on civil rights and liberties. These doctrines have been presented by the justices as if they were essential or eternal verities. For example, the "public forum" doctrine restricts free speech rights. The "harmless error" doctrine has been expanded in the criminal trial process by the classification of constitutional violations as "structural" or "trial" errors. The most substantial of these doctrines, in Kairys's opinion, is the so-called purpose doctrine. This doctrine "excuses and legitimates all manner of constitutional violations unless a victim can prove that the government has acted maliciously and the government cannot suggest an alternative, plausibly benevolent purpose."[3] The purpose doctrine is closely related to the "incidental effects" doctrine which was one of the principle arguments used in both *Lyng* and *Smith*.

A summary review of additional legal doctrines which have served to mask justice for tribal nations and individual Indians in the cases I have discussed would include the "discovery" and "conquest" doctrines (*Johnson, Rogers, Kagama, Tee-Hit-Ton*); the rule of "plenary power" (*Rogers, Kagama, Lone Wolf, Sioux Nation*); and the "political question doctrine" (*Rogers, Cherokee Tobacco, Lone Wolf*). Others include the doctrine of "geographical incorporation" (*Rogers, Kagama, Cherokee Tobacco, Oliphant*); the principle of tribal and individual Indian "dependency-wardship" (*Kagama, Lone Wolf, Nice, Oliphant*); the doctrine of "good faith" (*Lone Wolf, Sioux Nation*); the doctrine of "affirmative delegation" (*Nice, Oliphant*); and the doctrine of "implicit divestiture" (*Oliphant*).

Second, Kairys noted that conservatives "selectively use and abuse precedent and history" as they strive to justify the changes they are making. The fifteen cases examined in this study fully corroborate his statement. In total, this is probably the most damning conclusion we can draw from the Court's decisions in these opinions. We can see that the Court's abuse of history begins in the 1823 *Johnson* ruling, which held that tribes had been both "discovered" and "conquered," is reaffirmed in the 1845 *Rogers* decision which declared that the Cherokee were living on "allotted" lands, and continues in *Oliphant's* very selective use of precedent and reactionary history to deny tribes the right to try non-Indians.

Third, the conservatives, according to Kairys, often take a selected term or phrase, "deprive it of meaning and context, and claim that it supports the opposite of what it clearly meant originally."[4] As an example, Kairys discussed the phrase "from time immemorial," which was first used by the Court in the 1939 *Hague v. Congress of Industrial Organizations.*[5] The labor unions' right to distribute literature on the streets and in parks was challenged by a Jersey City politician, Frank Hague, who had banned the unions from distributing their leaflets. The CIO sued Hague, and the case wound its way to the Supreme Court, which held that the title of streets and parks had been held immemorially in trust for the public's use. Chief Justice William Rehnquist, however, in a 1992 case, *International Society of Krishna Consciousness v. Lee,*[6] appropriated the phrase "time immemorial" and redefined it in such a way as to uphold an airport's ban of leafleting that had been contested by a Hare Krishna group who wished to distribute literature and solicit funds for their religious work. Rehnquist maintained that the government had not allowed speech in (since there had not been) airports "from time immemorial," therefore public air terminals could not be considered "public forums" for purposes of religious expression. The Chief Justice had dramatically redefined the phrases "time immemorial" and "public forum" to constrict what had originally been expansive notions of free speech in public places.

In our fifteen cases, evidence of this type of semantic exercise can be found in *Rogers* where, for instance, Chief Justice Roger Taney defined "geographical incorporation" to deprive the Cherokee Nation of sovereignty over its own territory and citizens by asserting that the crime had been committed in the territory of the United States. In *Kagama* the Court lifted John Marshall's "wardship" analogy likening the relationship between tribes and the United States to that of ward to guardian and redefined it ("Indians are the wards of the nation . . . ") to virtually deprive Indian tribes of an important sovereign right. Finally, in *Race Horse*, the Court methodically defined such treaty phrases as "unoccupied lands" to negate the hunting rights of the tribes.

Fourth, Kairys stated that conservative justices have adopted, with virtually no explanation, "selectively narrow and broad interpretations of constitutional language, statutes, and decisions."[7] The Court did this on several occasions in *Race Horse* (treaty interpretation), *Nice* (statutory construction and prior decision), *Shoshone* (treaty construction), *Tee-Hit-Ton* (statutory construction), *Oliphant* (treaty and statutory interpretation), and finally in *Lyng* (statute) and *Smith* (statute and prior decision). Indian cases should be recognized as unique because of the pre- and extraconstitutional standing of tribes; however, in *Kagama*, the Court intentionally avoided a reliance on past statutes or the U.S. Constitution and simply manufactured a new power—plenary power based on the federal government's ownership of land.

Fifth, a favorite technique of conservatives, Kairys points out, is to use exaggerated and invented appeals to "necessity, emergency, fear, and prejudice to justify denial of fundamental constitutional rights."[8] The *Employment Division v. Smith* case in 1990 can be used to support this statement. Justice Antonin Scalia determined that if Smith and Black were allowed to use peyote, it would only add tinder to the already massive "drug" problem in the United States. As some of our other cases show, the use of fear and paranoia has been a favorite judicial tactic to reduce or suppress and sometimes to eliminate tribal or individual Indian rights. For example, in *Rogers*, Taney asserted that if the federal government did not exercise criminal jurisdiction, white fugitives from justice would use Indian Country as a refuge. In *Cherokee Tobacco*, there was an emphasis on the potential threat to the tax revenue base of the federal government if whites were allowed to slip into Cherokee country to purchase nontaxed tobacco products.

In *Kagama*, the bizarre notion was raised by the federal government's attorneys, though not explicitly used by the Court, that unless the government assumed jurisdiction over major crimes in Indian Country, the Indians might eventually exterminate themselves, thus leaving the United States with no one over whom to exercise plenary power. In *Lone Wolf*, there was the so-called national emergency that, if tribal lands were not quickly subdivided, Indians might perish. In *Tee-Hit-Ton*, there was the fear that the Alaska Native claims were holding up the economic development of the United States, and that unless the State of Alaska was immediately developed, the Russians might stream into the area. In *Oliphant*, Rehnquist used a racist fear that whites would have no guarantee of civil rights protections if they were tried in Indian courts, notwithstanding the existence of the Indian Civil Rights Act. And finally, in *Lyng*,

O'Connor used the extraordinary argument that tribes were trying to wrest away control over lands "owned" by the United States.

Finally, Kairys maintains that conservative justices in a picky and inconsistent way "apply the principles of legal decision making and methodology" that were, at one time, the target of their most effective criticisms of liberals (e.g., judicial activism) in the political arena. For example, in *Race Horse*, the justices, who often espoused judicial restraint and deference to the political branches, openly violated the "political question" rule to read their own intent into a treaty and a law. In *Kagama*, when the Court could find no constitutional authorization for the extension of federal criminal jurisdiction over Indian-on-Indian crimes occurring within a reservation, the justices simply invented their own rationale. And in *Lyng* and *Smith*, the Supreme Court erected a set of justifications to deny Indian religious liberties when Congress and federal policy were staunchly in favor of Indian religious freedom.

Several other semantic techniques can be discerned from the cases I have analyzed which have also led directly to violations of tribal/individual Indian rights. The most important isolated factor allowing for this violation is the presence or absence of *congressional power* (i.e., whether or not Congress has the right to enact various laws without tribal consent, or federal supremacy when challenged by states or private interests). When the Supreme Court, or a lower court, perceives that a tribe or an individual Indian is directly challenging federal sovereignty or a particular federal policy, it generally will side with the political branches, particularly when constitutional provisions such as the Commerce, Treaty, or Property clause are being tested. This should not be surprising, since the Court is an integral part of the ruling alliance of the three branches, which necessarily excludes the participation of tribal nations because of their extraconstitutional standing. The Court, in short, functions predominantly as a legitimator of congressional and executive actions (e.g., *Kagama, Lone Wolf, Nice, Shoshone, Lyng*).

In some cases, the Court may generate, of its own volition, an implied *congressional intent* if it will serve the Court's perception of what it believes is in the affected party's (whether the tribe, the Indian, or the government) interest. Most often, what the Court considers to be in the tribe's interest is not what the tribe itself desires (e.g., *Cherokee Tobacco, Southern Kansas Railway, Race Horse, Nice*).

At times, the Court contrives a scenario in which it pits one law or treaty provision against another and then "chooses" the one most likely to effect whatever political ends it is striving to accomplish. This approach was used in *Rogers* (federal law v. treaty), *The Cherokee Tobacco* (treaty provision v. law), and *Race Horse* (treaty provision v. statute). In each case, the tribal treaty right was defeated by the application of other laws which in their conception had nothing to do with tribes, individual Indians, or their treaty rights. Often, the Court links this adversarial tactic with a manufactured intent, as in *The Cherokee Tobacco*, where the treaty right of tax exemption was defeated by the general revenue law enacted by Congress, although the revenue law did not explicitly apply to Indian territory. In those situations, tribal nations, and sometimes individual Indians, invariably lose.

Finally, an important tool in its manipulation of "intent" and adversarial or competing laws and treaty provisions is the Court's willingness and its rhetorical ability to *retroactively* generate an interpretation of historical events that contradicts the actual occurrence. For instance, in *Johnson*, Marshall retroactively read discovery and conquest principles into the history of the relations between the tribes and the United States. In *The Cherokee Tobacco*, the Court retroactively invented a congressional intent for its reading of the revenue law that had been nonexistent at the actual time of the law's enactment.

In *Kagama*, the Court retroactively asserted that individual Indians were, and had *always been*, wards of the United States. In *Race Horse*, the Court retroactively read an intent into Wyoming's enabling legislation that had not been there in the creation of the state. And in *Lone Wolf*, the Court spoke as if the Congress had wielded plenary power over tribes since the beginning of the Republic, a grossly inaccurate supposition. In sum, the Court used retrohistory to erode the rights of individual Indians in *Nice* and, most recently, in *Oliphant* and *Yakima*, where it went so far as to resurrect a repudiated policy, allotment, and a dead law, the Burke Act's proviso.

IS AN UNMASKING POSSIBLE?

Petra Shattuck and Jill Norgren in their 1991 study, *Partial Justice*, argue that there is a two-tiered structure to federal Indian law[9] which, they assert, "explains the paradox of decisions that allow tribes . . . to seek enforcement of hundred-year-old promises in court but that will not bar Congress from changing its promise ex post facto; that narrowly interpret congressional legislation asserting federal power over internal tribal affairs but confirm at the same time that Congress is free to extend its authority as far as it pleases; that sanction the extinguishment of Indian title at will but demand compensation." [10]

The upper tier of Shattuck and Norgren's system involves the Supreme Court's articulation of principles which describe the exceptional nature of the tribal-federal relationship. This relationship is exceptional because it is exempt from ordinary constitutional standards and procedures. The reification of the doctrines of plenary congressional power, the political question, and judicial deference meant that Indian affairs operated in an extraconstitutional framework. Simultaneously, the development and transmogrification of the "trust" theory gave the United States virtually unlimited authority over tribal national sovereignty, their political rights, and their properties.

On the lower tier, the Court occasionally imposes a set of legal "standards of regularity, calculability, and due process consistent with liberal principles of formal legal rationality." [11] On this level, the administration and enforcement of federal policies are subject to strict judicial scrutiny. Hence, canons of treaty and statutory interpretation (e.g., treaties and laws should be interpreted as Indians would understand them, etc.); insistence that congressional abrogation of treaties be based on explicit statements; and certain constitutional safeguards of individual Indian property rights, etc., have been developed and have produced a number of hard-fought legal victories for tribes or individual Indians.

Of great significance from the Indian perspective, however, is that judicial decisions on the second tier, which impose legal principles of fairness and due process in how the federal government carries out its policies for tribes, "can never breach the larger framework—the first tier—of the unlimited power of the federal government over Indians." [12]

Several of the Supreme Court's and lower federal courts' [13] most recent Indian law decisions provide substantial evidence which tends to support this two-tiered theory of federal Indian law. Regarding the second tier, on May 17, 1993, in *Oklahoma Tax Commission v. Sac and Fox Nation*, the Court unanimously upheld tribal sovereign immunity and voided the state's tax laws aimed at tribal members. "Absent explicit congressional direction to the contrary," said O'Connor, "it must be presumed that a State does not have jurisdiction to tax tribal members who live and work in Indian Country."

Similarly, on June 14, 1995, in *Oklahoma Tax Commission v. Chickasaw Nation*, [14] the Supreme Court held that the state was disallowed from imposing its motor fuels excise tax on fuel sold by tribal businesses in Indian country; but that the state was authorized to impose its income tax on the wages of tribal members who resided outside of Indian country.

In contrast the Supreme Court recently rendered additional first-tier cases that do not bode well for the continuation of tribal treaty rights or for retained tribal sovereignty. In the 1993 case *South Dakota v. Bourland*, one of six diminishment decisions,[15] Justice Clarence Thomas said that the 1868 treaty rights of the Cheyenne River Sioux had been "implicitly" abrogated and that they had lost the power to regulate non-Indian hunting and fishing on Indian lands when Congress enacted a law which called for a taking of over 104,420 acres of Cheyenne River Sioux tribal trust land for the construction of the Oahe dam. Although neither of the congressional acts which took the land and set compensation expressly ended tribal jurisdictional authority over the land, Justice Thomas, in his first Indian law opinion, "presumed no tribal jurisdiction, paid no apparent heed to treaty rights, seemed untroubled by the fact that no individual non-Indian property rights were involved, and scarcely mentioned the canon of construction that requires treaty ambiguities to be construed in favor of Indians."[16] "Congress," said Justice Thomas, "has the power to abrogate Indians' treaty rights . . . though we *usually* [emphasis mine] insist that Congress clearly express its interest to do so."

And, in the 1994 case *Department of Taxation and Finance of New York v. Milhelm Attea & Brothers*[17] the Supreme Court gave states a significant boost in their efforts to prevent non-Indian state citizens from avoiding cigarette taxes by shopping on nearby Indian reservations. The Court unanimously reinstated New York State regulations which limited wholesalers to providing Indian retailers with only enough untaxed cigarettes to supply that reservation's residents. Justice John Paul Stevens, writing for the Court, said the state regulations "do not unduly interfere with Indian trading," even though evidence suggests that the lucrative tribal business in cigarettes will undoubtedly be affected.

Finally, on March 27, 1996, in yet another tier-one decision, the Supreme Court in *Seminole Tribe of Florida v. Florida* (No. 94-12), held in a case with important intergovernmental and economic implications that notwithstanding Congress's clear intent to abrogate the states' sovereign immunity in the Indian Gaming Regulatory Act (IGRA),[18] the Eleventh Amendment to the Constitution prevents Congress from authorizing suits by Indian tribes against states. Although four justices (John Paul Stevens, David Souter, Ruth Ginsburg, and Stephen Breyer) thought this decision was "fundamentally mistaken" and "profoundly misguided," the majority opinion, written by Chief Justice Rehnquist, maintained that the Eleventh Amendment prohibited Congress from enabling the State of Florida to be sued in federal court.

Justice Stevens, who concurred with Souter's dissent, nevertheless authored a separate dissenting opinion. He said that "the shocking character of the majority's affront to a coequal branch of our Government merits additional comment," and proceeded to chide the majority for rendering a broad opinion which prevents "Congress from providing a federal forum for a broad range of actions against States, from those sounding in copyright and patent law, to those concerning bankruptcy, environmental law, and the regulation of our vast national economy."

Shattuck and Norgren's theory fits in very well with the Supreme Court decisions here grouped under the headings of civilizing/paternalistic and nationalist/federalist; however, it cannot explain the third set of cases, which I referred to as constitutional/treaty decisions in Chapter 1 but did not include in this study. The constitutional/treaty consciousness generally produces opinions which affirm tribal sovereignty by perpetuating, and sometimes enhancing, tribal treaty rights, and by recognizing the federal government's legal and moral obligations to tribal nations.

Accompanying this legal consciousness are masks which reflect the Court's genuine, if sometimes stilted, efforts to comprehend and shield tribal rights from private, state, and even federal infringement by recognizing what Sidney Harring termed the "pluralist legal tradition in the United States"—the notion that tribal nations are the original sovereigns in the United States and are not beholden to the U.S. Constitution or the states for their existence.[19] Shattuck and Norgren would most likely posit that these favorable rulings should be grouped under tier two, but I think they represent critical, if abbreviated, moments when the Court genuinely struggles to find a way to acknowledge the extraconstitutional standing of tribes.

The foundational case of such judicial acknowledgment is, of course, *Worcester v. Georgia* (1832), which forcefully construed tribal nations as inherent sovereigns largely independent of state law. Several other important cases contain express language recognizing the distinctive culture and separate political character of tribal existence, which cannot be modified except by mutual treaty stipulations or the tribes' voluntary abandonment of their political organization. In *The Kansas Indians* (1866), the Court noted that "the conduct of Indians is not to be measured by the same standard which we apply to the conduct of other people."[20] In *Ex parte Crow Dog* (1883) the Court unanimously recognized tribal sovereignty and declared that the federal courts lacked criminal jurisdiction over Indian-on-Indian criminal offenses. Said Justice Stanley Matthews,

> It is a case where, against an express exception in the law itself, that law, by argument and inference only, is sought to be extended over aliens and strangers; over the members of a community separated by race, by tradition, by the instincts of a free though savage life, from the authority and power which seeks to impose upon them the restraints of an external and unknown code, and to subject them to the responsibilities of civil conduct, according to rules and penalties of which they could have no previous warning; *which judges them by a standard made by others and not for them*, which takes no account of the conditions which should except them from its exactions, and makes no allowance for their inability to understand it.[21] (emphasis mine)

In *Talton v. Mayes* (1896), another criminal law case involving an intratribal dispute, the question was whether the U.S. Constitution's Fifth Amendment grand jury provision applied to tribal nations. Justice Edward White stated for a unanimous court that the key to this decision depended upon an understanding of where Cherokee powers originated. If Cherokee powers of self-government were considered as "federal powers created by and springing from the Constitution of the United States" then they were controlled by the Fifth Amendment. On the other hand, if Cherokee sovereignty was original, then the tribe's criminal proceedings were not subject to the U.S. Constitution.

The Court gave an in-depth analysis of Cherokee treaty law, applicable federal statutory law, and Cherokee legislative history, concluding that "as the powers of local self government enjoyed by the Cherokee nation existed *prior to the Constitution, they are not operated upon by the Fifth Amendment* [emphasis mine], which, as we have said, had for its sole object to control the powers conferred by the Constitution on the National Government."[22]

In *United States v. Winans* (1905), involving the off-reservation, but treaty-recognized, fishing rights of Yakima Indians, the Court enunciated the reserved rights doctrine. "In other words," said the Court, "the treaty was not a grant of rights to the Indians, but a grant of rights from them—a reservation of those not granted."[23]

And in a 1982 tax decision, *Merrion v. Jicarilla Apache Tribe*, the Supreme Court laid out a clear understanding of the distinctive nature of tribal sovereignty. The Supreme Court held that the tribe had the inherent power to impose a severance tax on petitioners' mining activities as part of its power to govern and to pay for the costs of self-government. Justice Thurgood Marshall's comments on the nature of tribal sovereignty bear repeating:

> To state that Indian sovereignty is different than that of Federal, State or local Governments, . . . does not justify ignoring the principles announced by this Court for determining whether a sovereign has waived its taxing authority in cases involving city, state, and federal taxes imposed under similar circumstances. Each of these governments has different attributes of sovereignty, which also may derive from different sources. These differences, however, do not alter the principles for determining whether any of these governments has waived a sovereign power through contract, and we perceive no principled reason for holding that the different attributes of Indian sovereignty require different treatment in this regard. *Without regard to its source, sovereign power, even when unexercised, is an enduring presence that governs all contracts subject to the sovereign's jurisdiction, and will remain intact unless surrendered in unmistakable terms.*[24] (emphasis mine)

These are important cases in which the Supreme Court wrestled with itself and American law and found a way to recognize the validity of tribal sovereignty, treaty rights, and tribal systems of governance although the Court's interpretation sometimes clashed with powerful private, state, and, on occasion, federal political policy goals. "Tribes teach us," said Milner Ball, "that the non-Indian system is not the only American way, that the dominant structures are contingent, an invention that can be reinvented. . . . By not recognizing and accepting the different Indian reality, we [non-Indians] deny ourselves its gifts and a wider horizon."[25]

I believe, therefore, that it is an oversimplification to say as James E. Falkowski has done, that "Indian law is race law."[26] There is, however, ample evidence to support his historically accurate statement that from the earliest period of contact between indigenous people and "western" peoples, there were "two systems of law—one applying to 'civilized' peoples, and the other applying to the so-called 'backward' races."[27] Without doubt, over the past hundred years or so, the dynamics of cross-cultural and cross-political relations have served only to complicate the relationship between tribal nations and the United States government. This is evident in the diversity of legal masks created and adroitly wielded by the Supreme Court and federal lawyers, and in the dramatic ways that the Court's legal consciousness—nationalist/federal-ist or civilizing/paternalistic—has manifested itself through the use of masks to erase, reduce, or belittle tribal rights, thus precluding the attainment of justice.

Federal Indian law, if we may try to pin down that ill-defined entity, includes a potpourri of western and indigenous actors, historical and current events, ad hoc federal Indian policies and tribal responses, myriad regulations on all levels, and an inconsistent assortment of case law, also on multiple levels. For the Indians, the wash of history has been a tidal flat with an ebb and flow of conflicting interpretations; and, in effect, the historical past serves both to haunt and to enliven the contemporary field of tribal-federal-state relations. Ghosts from this past convey paternalistic, sometimes racist, attitudes and policies on the part of non-Indians; the outmoded, though still accepted, theory of Social Darwinism; persistent challenges to the national government's exclusive power to regulate governmental affairs with tribal nations; and threats to national security by other nation-states intent on colonizing North America. Their aura, on the other hand, illuminates the democratic ideals and principles (both tribal and American-derived) of consent; concern for justice and humanity; and tolerance of cultural and social diversity.

In this long-awaited era of close scrutiny of indigenous peoples worldwide, the developed nations of the globe have a moral and legal obligation to begin the process of rectifying many of the persistent disparities in political/legal/cultural/ and economic power that still dominate indigenous/nonindigenous relations. To begin, the United States, but especially the Supreme Court, can disavow the use of plenary (read: virtually absolute) power and repudiate the despised, outmoded, and always inaccurate doctrine of discovery. As one commentator has observed: "Tribes offer the majority an important insight. Injustice is not peripheral or aberrational. It is built into the legal system. To recognize the validity of the insight would help to save us from idolatry. Tribes clarify for us how one of our great achievements—the constitutional legal system—is a fallen institution." [28]

Furthermore, the Court can facilitate vastly improved intergovernmental relations by reminding both Congress and the president of the political and moral principles—especially that of *consent*—outlined in the Northwest Ordinance of 1787, which said in pertinent part that "the utmost good faith shall always be observed towards the Indians. . . ." Until these and other developments become reality, tribal peoples will remain locked in a grossly inequitable, politically dependent relationship sanctioned and legitimated by the United States Supreme Court, whose opinions handcraft—and are themselves covered by—legal masks and forms of consciousness that reflect the values, traditions, and institutions of the nontribal sector and, correspondingly, have tremendous difficulty coping with tribal values, traditions, and institutions.

Cases Cited

The list includes some short forms used in the text and gives cross references to their full case names. Only those short forms that would not lead the reader easily to the full case name have been so referenced.

Alaska Pacific Fisheries v. United States, 248 U.S. 591 (1916)
Bailey. See *U.S. v. Bailey*.
Barnette. See *West Virginia State Board of Education v. Barnette*.
Bear Lodge Multiple Use Association v. Babbitt, 2:96-CV-63 (1996)
Beecher v. Wetherby, 95 U.S. 517 (1877)
Black v. Employment Division, 721 P.2d 451 (1986)
Bowen v. Roy, 476 U.S. 693 (1986)
Brendale v. Confederated Tribes and Bands of the Yakima Indian Nation, 492 U.S. 408 (1989)
Buster v. Wright, 135 F. 947 (8th Cir.) (1905)
California v. Cabazon Band of Mission Indians, 480 U.S. 202 (1987)
Cantwell v. Connecticut, 310 U.S. 296 (1939)
Cherokee Nation. See *Cherokee Nation v. Georgia*.
Cherokee Nation v. Georgia, 30 U.S. (5 Pet.) 1 (1831)
Cherokee Nation v. Hitchcock, 187 U.S. 294 (1902)
Cherokee Nation v. Southern Kansas Railway Company, 33 Fed. Rep. 900 (1888)
Cherokee Nation v. Southern Kansas Railway Company, 135 U.S. 641 (1890)
Cherokee Tobacco, The, 78 U.S. (11 Wall.) 616 (1871)
Chinese Exclusion Cases, The, 130 U.S. 581 (1889)
Choate v. Trapp, 224 U.S. 665 (1912)
Choctaw Nation v. United States, 119 U.S. 1 (1886)
Civil Rights Cases, The, 109 U.S. 3 (1883)
Confederated Tribes and Bands of the Yakima Nation v. County of Yakima, 903 F.2d 1207 (1990)
Cotton Petroleum Corporation v. New Mexico, 490 U.S. 163 (1989)
County of Yakima v. Confederated Tribes and Bands of the Yakima Indian Nation, 112 S. Ct. 683 (1992)
Crow Dog, Ex parte, 109 U.S. 556 (1883)
Crow Tribe of Indians and Thomas L. Ten Bear v. Repsis, 73 F.3d 982 (1995)
DeCoteau v. District County Court, 420 U.S. 425 (1975)
Delaware Tribal Business Committee v. Weeks, 430 U.S. 73 (1977)

Mackey v. Coxe, 59 U.S. (18 How.) 100 (1856)
Marbury v. Madison, 5 U.S. 137 (1803)
Mashunkashey v. Mashunkashey, 134 P.2d 976 (1942)
Matter of Heff, 197 U.S. 488 (1905)
Mattz v. Arnett, 412 U.S. 481 (1973)
Mayfield, In re, 141 U.S. 107 (1891)
McBratney. See *U.S. v. McBratney*.
McClanahan v. Arizona State Tax Commission, 411 U.S. 164 (1973)
McCulloch v. Maryland, 17 U.S. 316 (1819)
Meehan. See *Jones v. Meehan*.
Merrion v. Jicarilla Apache Tribe, 455 U.S. 130 (1982)
Miller v. United States, 159 F.2d 997 (1947)
Missouri, Kansas and Texas Railway Co. v. Roberts, 152 U.S. 114 (1894)
Mitchel v. United States, 34 U.S. (9 Pet.) 711 (1835)
Moe v. Confederated Salish and Kootenai Tribes of the Flathead Indian Reservation, 425 U.S. 463 (1976)
Montana v. Blackfeet Tribe, 471 U.S. 759 (1985)
Morton v. Mancari, 417 U.S. 535 (1974)
Native American Church v. Navajo Tribal Council, 272 F.2d 131 (1959)
New Jersey v. Wilson, 11 U.S. (7 Cranch) 164 (1812)
Nice. See *U.S. v. Nice*.
Nofire v. United States, 164 U.S. 657 (1897)
Northwest Indian Cemetery Protective Association v. Peterson, 795 F.2d 688 (1986)
Northwestern Bands of Shoshone Indians v. United States, 95 Ct. Cl. 642 (1942)
Northwestern Bands of Shoshone Indians v. United States, 100 Ct. Cl. 455 (1944)
Northwestern Bands of Shoshone Indians v. United States, 324 U.S. 335 (1945)
Oklahoma Tax Commission v. Chickasaw Nation, 115 S. Ct. 2214 (1995)
Oklahoma Tax Commission v. Sac and Fox Nation, 113 S. Ct. 1985 (1993)
Oliphant. See *Oliphant v. Suquamish Indian Tribe*.
Oliphant v. Schlie, 544 F.2d 1007 (1976)
Oliphant v. Suquamish Indian Tribe, 435 U.S. 191 (1978)
Otoe and Missouria Tribes of Indians v. United States, 131 Ct. Cl. 593 (1955)
Parks v. Ross, 60 U.S. (11 How.) 730 (1850)
Passamaquoddy. See *Joint Tribal Council of the Passamaquoddy Tribe v. Morton*, 528 F.2d 370 (1975).
People v. Woody, 61 Cal.2d 716 (1964)
Perrin v. United States, 232 U.S. 478 (1914)
Peyote Way Church of God Inc. v. Thornburgh, 922 F.2d 1210 (5th Cir.) (1991)
Plessy v. Ferguson, 163 U.S. 537 (1896)
Quiver. See *U.S. v. Quiver*.
Race Horse. See *Ward v. Race Horse*, 163 U.S. 504 (1896).
Reynolds v. United States, 98 U.S. 145 (1879)
Rogers. See *U.S. v. Rogers*.
Rosebud Sioux Tribe v. Kneip, 430 U.S. 584 (1977)
Ross. See *Parks v. Ross*.

Roy. See Bowen v. Roy.

Sah Quah, In re, 31 Fed. 327 (1886)

Santa Clara Pueblo v. Martinez, 436 U.S. 49 (1978)

Seminole Tribe of Florida v. Florida, 134 L. Ed. 252 (1996)

Seufert Brothers Company v. United States, 249 U.S. 194 (1919)

Seymour v. Superintendent, 368 U.S. 351 (1962)

Sherbert v. Verner, 374 U.S. 398 (1963)

Shoshone. See Northwestern Bands of Shoshone Indians v. U.S. (1945).

Shoshone Indians v. United States, 85 Ct. Cl. 331 (1937)

Shoshone Tribe of Indians v. United States, 299 U.S. 476 (1937)

Sioux Nation. See U.S. v. Sioux Nation of Indians, 448 U.S. 371 (1980).

Sioux Tribe of Indians v. United States, 146 F. Supp. 229 (1956)

Sioux Tribe of Indians v. United States, 64 F. Supp. 303 (1946)

Sioux Tribe of Indians v. United States, 97 Ct. Cl. 613 (1942)

Sizemore v. Brady, 235 U.S. 441 (1914)

Slaughter House Cases, The, 83 U.S. (16 Wall.) 36 (1873)

Smith. See Employment Division, Department of Human Resources v. Smith
    (1988).

Smith II. See Employment Division, Department of Human Resources v. Smith
    (1990).

Smith v. Employment Division, 721 P.2d 445 (1986)

Smith v. Employment Division, 763 P.2d 146 (1988)

Solem v. Bartlett, 465 U.S. 463 (1984)

South Dakota v. Bourland, 113 S. Ct. 2309 (1993)

South Dakota v. U.S. Department of the Interior, 69 F.3d 878 (1995)

Southern Kansas Railway. See Cherokee Nation v. Southern Kansas Railway (1890).

Spalding v. Chandler, 160 U.S. 394 (1896)

Standing Bear v. Crook, 25 F. Cas. 14,891 (1879)

Standley v. Roberts, 59 Fed. 836 (1894)

Talton v. Mayes, 163 U.S. 376 (1896)

Taylor v. Morton, 23 F. Cas. 784 (C.C.D. Mass., 1855)

Tee-Hit-Ton Indians v. United States, 348 U.S. 273 (1955)

Thomas v. Review Board, Indiana Employment Security Division, 450 U.S. 707
    (1981)

Three Affiliated Tribes of Fort Berthold Reservation v. United States, 390 F.2d 686
    (Ct. Cl., 1968)

Three Tribes. See Three Affiliated Tribes of Fort Berthold Reservation v. United
    States.

Tiger v. Western Investment Company, 221 U.S. 286 (1911)

Tillamooks. See U.S. v. Tillamooks.

Twining v. New Jersey, 211 U.S. 78 (1908)

United States ex. rel. Hualpai Indians v. Santa Fe Pacific Railroad, 314 U.S. 339
    (1941)

United States v. Alcea Band of Tillamooks, 341 U.S. 48 (1951)

United States v. Bailey, F. Cas. 14,495 (C.C. Tenn.) (1834)

United States v. Berry, 2 McCrary 58 (1880)

United States v. Board of Commissioners, 145 F.2d 329 (1944)

United States v. Boyll, 724 F. Supp. 1333 (1991)

United States v. Celestine, 215 U.S. 278 (1909)

United States v. Choctaw Nation, 179 U.S. 494 (1900)

United States v. Clapox, 35 Fed. 575 (D.C. Ore. 1888)

United States v. Cook, 86 (19 Wall.) 591 (1874)

United States v. Joseph, 94 U.S. 616 (1876)

United States v. Kagama, 118 U.S. 375 (1886)

United States v. Lee, 455 U.S. 252 (1982)

United States v. McBratney, 104 U.S. 621 (1881)

United States v. Mazurie, 419 U.S. 544 (1975)

United States v. Mille Lac Band of Chippewas, 229 U.S. 498 (1913)

United States v. Nice, 241 U.S. 591 (1916)

United States v. Pelican, 232 U.S. 442 (1914)

United States v. Quiver, 241 U.S. 602 (1916)

United States v. Rickert, 188 U.S. 432 (1903)

United States v. Rogers, 45 U.S. (4 How.) 567 (1846)

United States v. Sandoval, 231 U.S. 28 (1913)

United States v. Shoshone Tribe, 304 U.S. 111 (1938)

United States v. Sioux Nation of Indians, 518 F.2d 1298 (1975)

United States v. Sioux Nation of Indians, 448 U.S. 371 (1980)

United States v. Sutton, 215 U.S. 291 (1909)

United States v. Thomas, 151 U.S. 577 (1894)

United States v. Tillamooks, 329 U.S. 40 (1946)

United States v. Ward, 28 F. Cas. 397 (1863)

United States v. Washington, 384 F. Supp. 343 (1974)

United States v. Wheeler, 435 U.S. 313 (1978)

United States v. Winans, 198 U.S. 371 (1905)

Ward. See *U.S. v. Ward.*

Ward v. Race Horse, 70 Fed. 598 (1895)

Ward v. Race Horse, 163 U.S. 504 (1896)

Warren Trading Post Co. v. Arizona State Tax Commission, 380 U.S. 685 (1965)

Wau-Pe-Man-Qua v. Aldrich, 28 Fed. 489 (1886)

West Virginia State Board of Education v. Barnette, 319 U.S. 624 (1943)

Wheeler. See *U.S. v. Wheeler.*

White Mountain Apache Tribe v. Bracker, 448 U.S. 136 (1980)

Williams v. Lee, 358 U.S. 217 (1959)

Wisconsin v. Yoder, 406 U.S. 205 (1972)

Worcester v. Georgia, 31 U.S. (6 Pet.) 515 (1832)

Yakima. See *Confederated Tribes and Bands of the Yakima Nation v. County of Yakima.*

Yick Wo v. Hopkins, 118 U.S. 220 (1886)

Yoder. See *Wisconsin v. Yoder.*

APPENDIX B

Supreme Court Justices Authoring the Fifteen Opinions Analyzed

Name	Opinion(s) authored	Nominated by
John Marshall (Chief Justice)	*Johnson v. McIntosh* (1823)	John Adams
Roger B. Taney (Chief Justice)	*U.S. v. Rogers* (1846)	Andrew Jackson
Noah H. Swayne	*The Cherokee Tobacco* (1871)	Abraham Lincoln
Samuel F. Miller	*U.S. v. Kagama* (1886)	Abraham Lincoln
Edward D. White	*Ward v. Racehorse* (1896); *Lone Wolf v. Hitchcock* (1903)	William H. Taft
John M. Harlan	*Cherokee Nation v. Southern Kansas Railway* (1890)	Rutherford B. Hayes
Willis Van Devanter	*U.S. v. Nice* (1916)	William H. Taft
Stanley F. Reed	*Northwestern Band of Shoshone v. U.S.* (1945); *Tee-Hit-Ton v. U.S.* (1955)	Franklin Roosevelt
William H. Rehnquist (Chief Justice)	*Oliphant v. Suquamish* (1978)	Richard Nixon
Harry A. Blackmun	*U.S. v. Sioux Nation* (1980)	Richard Nixon
Sandra Day O'Connor	*Lyng v. Northwest Indian Cemetery Association* (1988)	Ronald Reagan
Antonin Scalia	*Employment Division v. Smith* (1990); *County of Yakima v. Yakima* (1992)	Ronald Reagan

SOURCES: Leon Friedman and Fred L. Israel (eds.), *The Justices of the United States Supreme Court, 1789–1969: Their Lives and Major Opinions* (New York: R. R. Bowker Company, 1969, 1978 supplement); Elder Witt, *Congressional Quarterly's Guide to the U.S. Supreme Court,* 2d ed. (Washington, D.C.: Congressional Quarterly, Inc., 1990):

State from which appointed	Party affiliation	Position held before appointment	Years served
Virginia	Federalist	U.S. Secretary of State	1801–1835
Maryland	Democrat	Lawyer (private practice)	1836–1864
Ohio	Republican	Lawyer (private practice)	1862–1881
Iowa	Republican	Lawyer (private practice)	1862–1890
Louisiana	Democrat	U.S. Senator	1894–1910
Kentucky	Republican	Lawyer (private practice)	1877–1911
Wyoming	Republican	U.S. Court of Appeals (8th Circuit)	1911–1937
Kentucky	Democrat	U.S. Solicitor General	1938–1957
Arizona	Republican	U.S. Attorney General	1972–
Arizona	Republican Democrat	U.S. Court of Appeals (8th Circuit)	1970–1994
Arizona	Republican	Arizona State Court of Appeals	1981–
Virginia	Republican	U.S. Court of Appeals for the District of Columbia	1986–

860–880; Lawrence Baum, *The Supreme Court*, 4th ed. (Washington, D.C.: Congressional Quarterly, Inc., 1992): 56; Henry J. Abraham, *Justices and Presidents: A Political History of Appointments to the Supreme Court*, 3d ed. (New York: Oxford University Press, 1992): Appendix D.

Notes

PREFACE

1. As quoted in Commissioner of Indian Affairs Luke Lea's *Annual Report* (1851), 274.

2. *The Kansas Indians*, 72 U.S. 737 (5 Wall.) 737 (1866), 758.

3. As quoted in William W. Story, ed., *Life and Letters of Joseph Story* (Boston: Little & Brown, 1851), 624.

4. Thurman W. Arnold, *The Folklore of Capitalism* (New Haven: Yale University Press, 1937), 63.

5. Ibid., 62.

6. Thurman W. Arnold, *The Symbols of Government* (New Haven: Yale University Press, 1935), 35.

7. See, for example, Ken Peak and Jack Spencer, "Crime in Indian Country: Another Trail of Tears," *Journal of Criminal Justice* 15 (1987): 485–494; Donald E. Green, "American Indian Criminality: What Do We Really Know," in Donald E. Green and Thomas V. Tonnesen, eds., *American Indians: Social Justice and Public Policy* (Madison: University of Wisconsin Press, 1991): 223–270; and Laurence French, ed., *Indians and Criminal Justice* (Totowa, N.J.: Allanheld, Osmun & Co., 1982).

CHAPTER 1

1. See especially "Indian Law and the Reach of History," *Journal of Contemporary Law* 4 (1977–78): 1–13; "Revision and Reversion" in Calvin Martin, ed., *The American Indian and the Problem of History* (New York: Oxford University Press, 1987), 84–90; and "Laws Founded in Justice and Humanity: Reflections on the Content and Character of Federal Indian Law," *Arizona Law Review* 31 (1989): 203–223.

2. Deloria, "Reach of History," 1.

3. Ibid.

4. Thurman W. Arnold, *The Symbols of Government* (New Haven: Yale University Press, 1935), 36.

5. Ibid., 31.

6. Ibid., 32.

7. Ibid., 33.

8. See especially Felix S. Cohen, *Handbook of Federal Indian Law* (Washington: Government Printing Office, 1942; reprint ed., Albuquerque: University of New Mexico Press, 1972); Charles F. Wilkinson, *American Indians, Time, and the Law: Native Societies in a Modern Constitutional Democracy* (New Haven: Yale University Press, 1987); and Julie Wrend and Clay Smith, eds., *American Indian Law Deskbook* (Niwot, Colo.: University Press of Colorado, 1993).

9. David Kairys, *With Liberty and Justice for Some: A Critique of the Conservative Supreme Court* (New York: The New Press, 1993), 195.

10. Tribes, I argue, have an extraconstitutional status because of their preexisting, original sovereignty; because they were existing sovereigns, they were not parties to the U.S. Constitution or state constitutions. As the Supreme Court said in *Talton v. Mayes*, 163 U.S. 376 (1896), tribal rights of self-government were not delegated by Congress and were thus not powers arising from or created by the federal Constitution. The U.S. Bill of Rights, therefore, does not apply to the acts of tribal governments. An important act was passed in 1968, however, the Indian Civil Rights Act of 1968 (82 St. 77), which for the first time imposed a substantial body of U.S. constitutional law onto tribal courts. This was a major intrusion on tribal sovereignty, although the Indian Civil Rights Act has several important exceptions that differentiate it from the U.S. Bill of Rights. See Vine Deloria Jr. and Clifford M. Lytle's *American Indians, American Justice* (Austin: University of Texas Press, 1983), 126−130, which compares and contrasts the two sets of rights.

Furthermore, the persistence of Indian treaty rights and the fact that Congress and the tribes have never cooperated in any action that would lead to a constitutional amendment incorporating tribes into the American political system give additional proof of the ongoing extraconstitutional status of tribal nations.

11. Arnold, *The Symbols of Government*, 195.

12. The field of Critical Legal Studies was officially born in 1977 at a conference at the University of Wisconsin at Madison. Its membership is quite eclectic and represents a diverse array of scholars and professionals including disgruntled liberals and radical feminists. The main target of Critical Legal Theorists (CRITS) has been to challenge the alleged contrast between politics and the law. They argue that the two are interconnected. For a good overview of the field see the following anthologies: Allen C. Hutchinson, ed., *Critical Legal Studies* (Totowa, N.J.: Rowman & Littlefield Publishers, 1989) and David Kairys, ed., *The Politics of Law: A Progressive Critique* (New York: Pantheon Books, 1982).

13. John T. Noonan Jr., *Persons and Masks of the Law* (New York: Farrar, Straus, and Giroux, 1976).

14. See especially Kairys, ed., *The Politics of Law*, for a good cross-section of essays that lay out the premises of this theoretical approach to the law.

15. Duncan Kennedy, "Toward an Historical Understanding of Legal Consciousness: The Case of Classical Legal Thought in America, 1850−1940," in Stephen Spitzer, ed., *Research in Law and Sociology* (Greenwich, Conn.: JAI Press, 1980), 4.

16. Ibid., 23.

17. Ibid., 6.

18. Robert W. Gordon, "Legal Thought and Legal Practice in the Age of American Enterprise: 1870–1920," in Gerald L. Geison, ed., *Professions and Professional Ideologies in America* (Chapel Hill, N.C.: University of North Carolina, 1983), 72.

19. Elizabeth Mensch, "The History of Mainstream Legal Thought," in David Kairys, ed., *The Politics of Law*, 18–39.

20. Kennedy, "Toward an Historical," 4.

21. Kennedy, "Toward an Historical," 5.

22. Noonan, 1976.

23. Ibid., 20.

24. Ibid., 21.

25. See especially Nancy Carol Carter, "Race and Power Politics as Aspects of Federal Guardianship Over American Indians: Land-Related Cases, 1887–1924," *American Indian Law Review* 4 (1976): 197–248; David E. Wilkins, "The Cloaking of Justice: The Supreme Court's Role in the Application of Western Law to America's Indigenous Peoples," *Wicazo Sa Review* 10 (Spring 1994): 1–13.

26. Noonan, *Persons and Masks*, 25.

27. Ibid.

28. Ibid., 24.

29. See especially *Lyng v. Northwest Indian Cemetery Protective Association,* 485 U.S. 439 (1988); *Cotton Petroleum Corporation v. New Mexico,* 490 U.S. 163 (1989); *Brendale v. Confederated Tribes and Bands of Yakima,* 492 U.S. 408 (1989); *Employment Division v. Smith,* 494 U.S. 872 (1990); *Duro v. Reina,* 110 S. Ct. 2053 (1990); *County of Yakima v. Yakima Nation,* 112 S. Ct. 682 (1992); *South Dakota v. Bourland,* 113 S. Ct. 2309 (1993); and *Department of Taxation v. Attea,* 62 U.S.L.W. 4482 (1994).

30. See, e.g., David E. Wilkins, "Reconsidering the Tribal-State Compact Process," *Policy Studies Journal* 22 (1994): 474–488; Frank Pommersheim, "Tribal-State Relations: Hope for the Future?" *South Dakota Law Review* 36 (1991): 239–276; K. Gover et al., "Tribal-State Dispute Resolution: Recent Attempts," *South Dakota Law Review* 36 (1991): 277–298; Daniel L. Rotenberg, "American States and Indian Tribes: Power Conflicts in the Supreme Court," *Dickinson Law Review* 92 (1987): 81–103; and Glenn A. Phelps, "Representation Without Taxation: Citizenship and Suffrage in Indian Country," *American Indian Quarterly* 9 (1985): 135–148.

31. I am deeply indebted to Prof. Michael Green of the State University of New York-Oneonta for his critical reading of an earlier draft of this chapter and for his assistance in the reformulation of this discussion of different types of legal consciousness and their integral relationship to judicial "masks."

32. Joel B. Grossman and Richard S. Wells, *Constitutional Law and Judicial Policy Making,* 3d ed. (New York: Longman Press, 1988), 11.

33. U.S. Commissioner of Indian Affairs, *Annual Report* (1883), 11.

34. 35 Fed. 575 (1888), 577.

35. Ibid., 579.

36. Francis P. Prucha, *The Indians in American Society: From the Revolutionary War to the Present* (Berkeley: University of California Press, 1988). See especially his chapter entitled "Paternalism."

37. Judicial evidence of separate treatment for the Five Civilized Tribes is available as early as 1832. In the *Worcester* case, Chief Justice John Marshall noted that these tribes were better neighbors than "wild-savage" tribes. And the Pueblo were recognized by the Supreme Court in 1877 (*United States v. Joseph*, 94 U.S. 614) as being much more "civilized" than the "wild" Navajo and Apache tribes. In fact, Commissioner of Indian Affairs T. J. Morgan said in 1891 that Indians in the New Mexican Territory could be classed in two camps: "(a) The civilized Pueblo and Mission Indians," who were "noted for their intelligence, virtue, sobriety, and industry, and [were] Indians only in race and as to a few of their customs; and (b) the wild, nomadic, or savage tribes, not farther advanced in civilization than the hunter state, whose only means of subsistence were the chase and depredations not infrequently committed upon the property of their more civilized and industrious neighbors" (U.S. Department of the Interior, Commissioner of Indian Affairs, *Annual Report*, House Executive Document No. 1, 52d Cong., 1st sess., 28–29).

However, by 1913 Pueblo status was reconfigured by the Supreme Court in *U.S. v. Sandoval* (231 U.S. 28). While a sizable body of statutory and judicial law, including *Joseph*, had held that the Pueblo were not to be federally recognized as Indians for purposes of Indian-related legislation, by 1913 the number of whites inhabiting Pueblo territory had increased dramatically, and federal policy was now focused on coercive assimilation of all Indians. A general guardian/wardship relationship was then declared to exist in which tribal people were viewed as utterly dependent groups in need of constant federal tutelage to protect them from unscrupulous whites and from their own vices.

Thus, the Supreme Court now held that rather than being civilized, sober, and industrious, the Pueblo had become "primitive," "inferior," and "dependent" on the U.S. government. In deferring to congressional power designed to protect the Pueblo from whites selling liquor, the Court went to extraordinary lengths to illustrate its belief that although the Pueblo remained "industrially superior" to other tribes, they were still "easy victims to the evils and debasing influence of intoxicants because of their Indian lineage, isolated and communal life, primitive customs and limited civilization" (p. 47).

38. Prucha, *The Indians*, 10–11.

39. James N. Danziger, *Understanding the Political World: An Introduction to Political Science* (New York: Longman Press, 1991), 222.

40. Boston: Beacon Press, 1966.

41. These are (1) the successful bourgeois revolution which commercializes and modernizes the countryside and assimilates aristocracy and peasantry into the modern economy and democratic policy (Britain, France, and the United States); (2) the conservative revolution, in which the bourgeois revolution is either aborted or never takes place, and where industrialization is carried out from

"above" by a coalition of aristocratic/bourgeois elements in which the bourgeois component is the junior partner (Germany and Japan); and (3) the Communist revolution, in which the middle and urban classes are too weak to constitute even a junior partner in the modernization process and in which a multitudinous and alienated peasantry provide the main destructive revolutionary force that overthrows the old order and then become its primary victims (the former Soviet Union and China).

42. See especially Moore's Chapter 3, "The Last American Civil War: The Last Capitalist Revolution," which is his rich and detailed case study of the American model.

43. Samuel P. Huntington and Jorge I. Dominguez, "Political Development," in Fred I. Greenstein and Nelson W. Polsby, eds., *Macropolitical Theory*, vol. 3 of the *Handbook of Political Science* (Reading, Mass.: Addison-Wesley Publishing Co., 1975), 1–114.

44. Ibid., 66.

45. Ibid.

46. Vincent N. Parillo, *Strangers to These Shores: Race and Ethnic Relations in the United States*, 3d ed. (New York: Macmillan Publishing Co., 1990). See especially Chapter 7, entitled "Native Americans."

47. Robert A. Williams Jr., *The American Indian in Western Legal Thought: The Discourses of Conquest* (New York: Oxford University Press, 1990), 6.

48. For example, several early treaties with the Cherokee and Delaware Tribes contained provisions that would have allowed those tribes political representation in the U.S. Congress. Article 6 of the 1778 Delaware Treaty said, "And it is further agreed on between the contracting parties should it for the future be found conducive for the mutual interest of both parties to invite any other tribes who have been friends to the interest of the United States, to join the present confederation, *and to form a state whereof the Delaware nation shall be the head, and have a representation in Congress. . . .*" [emphasis mine].

49. Vine Deloria Jr., Response to Thomas Biolsi's article, "Bringing the Law Back In," *Current Anthropology* 36 (Aug.–Oct. 1995): 560.

50. Milner Ball, "Constitution, Court, Indian Tribes," *American Bar Foundation Research Journal* 1 (Winter 1987): 21.

51. Ibid., 6.

52. Ibid., 7.

CHAPTER 2

1. See especially Stephen Cornell and Joseph P. Kalt, eds., *What Can Tribes Do? Strategies and Institutions in American Indian Economic Development* (Los Angeles: American Indian Studies Center, 1992).

2. See Vincent N. Parillo, *Strangers to These Shores: Race and Ethnic Relations in the United States*, 3d ed. (New York: Macmillan Publishing Company, 1990,

18–19), who says that all minority groups share the following traits: they are a subordinate group with less control or power than members of a dominant or majority group; they have racial or cultural characteristics that distinguish them from the majority group; their membership is generally ascribed, that is, determined by birth; they have a sense of group solidarity; and they share common experiences of unequal or discriminatory treatment.

3. See especially U.S. Government, American Indian Policy Review Commission, *Final Report* (Washington: Government Printing Office, 1977), 83–94; and Sharon O'Brien, *American Indian Tribal Governments* (Norman, Okla.: University of Oklahoma Press, 1989), 291.

4. See especially Frances Svensson, "Liberal Democracy and Group Rights: The Legacy of Individualism and Its Impact on American Indian Tribes," *Political Studies* 27 (Sept. 1979): 421–439.

5. *Standing Bear v. Crook*, 25 F. Cas. 14,891 (1879); and see Nell Jessup Newton, "Federal Power Over Indians: Its Sources, Scope and Limitations," *University of Pennsylvania Law Review* 132 (1984): 287.

6. Joyotpaul Chaudhuri, "American Indian Policy: An Overview," in Vine Deloria Jr., ed., *American Indian Policy in the Twentieth Century* (Norman, Okla.: Oklahoma Press, 1985), 22.

7. Ibid., 23. See, for example, the foundational cases of *Johnson v. McIntosh* (1823); *Cherokee Nation v. Georgia* (1831); *Worcester v. Georgia* (1832); and *Mitchel v. United States* (1835) for conflicting accounts of how tribal sovereignty has been dealt with by the Supreme Court. Of course, a majority of the cases we examine employ very restrictive definitions of tribal sovereignty or refuse to acknowledge its existence at all; while other cases follow the classic lead of the *Worcester* decision and support the notion that tribes were "distinct peoples, divided into separate nations, independent of each other, and of the rest of the world, having institutions of their own, and governing themselves by their own laws."

8. See the Solicitor's Opinion, "Powers of Indian Tribes," October 25, 1934, 55 I.D. 14, in vol. I, *Opinions of the Solicitor* (Washington: Department of the Interior, 1974), 445–477.

9. Vine Deloria Jr., "Self-Determination and the Concept of Sovereignty," in Roxanne Dunbar Ortiz, ed., *Economic Development in American Indian Reservations* (Albuquerque: University of New Mexico Press, 1979), 27.

10. Gerald R. Alfred, *Heeding the Voices of Our Ancestors: Kahnawake Mohawk Politics and the Rise of Native Nationalism* (New York: Oxford University Press, 1995), 102–03.

11. Lucy Cohen, ed., *The Legal Conscience: Selected Papers of Felix S. Cohen* (New Haven: Yale University Press, 1960), 255.

12. Tribal nations are sovereign since they predate the United States and since their rights were not defined under the federal Constitution. Thus, the U.S. Bill of Rights does not apply to the acts of tribal governments, and limits on state and federal power delineated in the Constitution cannot constrain tribal governing powers. Tribes, for instance, may legally discriminate against non-Indians and nonmember Indians in voting solely on the basis of race (Indian

Civil Rights Act, 82 St. 77, 1968); the Fifth Amendment right to indictment by grand jury does not apply to prosecutions in tribal courts (*Talton v. Mayes*, 163 U.S. 376 (1896); and as separate governments tribes enjoy sovereign immunity (*Santa Clara Pueblo v. Martinez*, 436 U.S. 49, 56 (1978).

13. See especially Joseph C. Burke, "The Cherokee Cases: A Study in Law, Politics, and Morality," *Stanford Law Review* 21 (1969): 500–531; and Jill C. Norgren, *The Cherokee Cases: The Confrontation of Law and Politics* (New York: McGraw Hill, Inc., 1996).

14. *Cherokee Nation v. Georgia*, 30 U.S. (5 Pet.) 1, 55 (1831).

15. Vine Deloria Jr. has forcefully made this argument on several occasions. But see Felix S. Cohen's *Handbook of Federal Indian Law* (1972 edition, 91) where he asserts, with limited proof, that Congress's power over tribes, in addition to the treaty-making power, is "much broader" than its power over commerce "between states." On the previous page, however, Cohen more accurately states that "Congress has no constitutional power over Indians except what is conferred by the Commerce Clause and other clauses of the Constitution."

16. U.S. House, Committee on Indian Affairs, *Report on Regulating the Indian Department*, House Report No. 474, 23d Cong., 1st sess. (1834), 19.

17. 112 U.S. 94, 100 (1884); and see Felix S. Cohen, *Handbook of Federal Indian Law*, 173.

18. Cohen, *Handbook*, 90.

19. Felix S. Cohen, "Erosion of Indian Rights, 1950–1953," *Yale Law Journal* 62 (1953): 352.

20. Petra T. Shattuck and Jill Norgren, *Partial Justice: Federal Indian Law in a Liberal Constitutional System* (Providence, R.I.: Berg Publishers, 1991), 13.

21. 43 St. 253.

22. U.S. Commissioner of Indian Affairs, *Annual Report* (Washington: Government Printing Office, 1905), 60.

23. 241 U.S. 591, 598 (1916).

24. See especially Milner Ball's article, "Constitution, Court, Indian Tribes," *American Bar Foundation Research Journal* 1 (1987): 1–139.

25. Vine Deloria Jr., "The Distinctive Status of Indian Rights," in Peter Iverson, ed., *The Plains Indians of the Twentieth Century* (Norman, Okla.: University of Oklahoma Press, 1985), 237–248.

26. Rachel San Kronowitz et al., "Toward Consent and Cooperation: Reconsidering the Political Status of Indian Nations," *Harvard Civil Rights-Civil Liberties Law Review* 22 (1987): 507–602.

27. David Engdahl, "State and Federal Power over Federal Property," *Arizona Law Review* 18 (1976): 363.

28. Ibid.

29. 82 St. 77.

30. Engdahl, 363.

31. 48 St. 985.

32. *Morton v. Mancari*, 417 U.S. 535 (1974).

33. Washington State's Constitution, art. XXVI, contains an example of one

such disclaimer. See in my Chapter 6 the discussion of the *Yakima* decision for details of this state's clause.

34. Newton, "Federal Power," 196 n. 3.

35. From the earliest Supreme Court sanction of unlimited congressional power—*United States v. Kagama* (1886)—to the Court's first acknowledgment of limits to such authority—*Perrin v. United States* (1914)—plenary power was explicitly cited by the Court in nearly a dozen cases. See David E. Wilkins, "The U.S. Supreme Court's Explication of 'Federal Plenary Power': An Analysis of Case Law Affecting Tribal Sovereignty, 1886–1914," *American Indian Quarterly* 18, no. 3 (Summer 1994): 349–368.

36. *Mashunkashey v. Mashunkashey*, 134 P.2d 976 (1942).

37. George F. Canfield, "The Legal Position of the Indian," *American Law Review* (January 1881): 26–27.

38. See especially David E. Stannard, *The Conquest of the New World: American Holocaust* (New York: Oxford University Press, 1992).

39. See *Fletcher v. Peck*, 10 U.S. (6 Cranch.) 87 (1810); *New Jersey v. Wilson*, 11 U.S. (7 Cranch.) 164 (1812); *Johnson v. McIntosh*, 21 U.S. (8 Wheat.) 543 (1823); *Cherokee Nation v. Georgia*, 30 U.S. (5 Pet.) 1 (1831); *Worcester v. Georgia*, 31 U.S. (6 Pet.) 515 (1832); and *Mitchel v. United States*, 34 U.S. (9 Pet.) 711 (1835).

40. Because of their importance, these cases, especially the so-called Cherokee cases—*Cherokee Nation* and *Worcester*—have been written about by virtually every scholar who has pursued this area of study. The *Mitchel* decision had until recently received scant scholastic attention, but see David E. Wilkins, "*Johnson v. M'Intosh* Revisited: Through the Eyes of *Mitchel v. United States*," *American Indian Law Review* 19, no. 1 (Summer 1994): 159–181.

41. *Johnson*, 572.

42. See *The American State Papers: Public Lands* (Washington: Gales & Seaton, 1832–1861). This eight-volume collection of primary executive and legislative documents dealing with land issues has many reports and other documents which affirm the individual's title to lands purchased from Indian tribes when the transaction was properly executed.

43. Ibid., vol. I (1832), 93.

44. See ibid., vol. II, *Public Lands*, Illinois & Wabash Land Companies, No. 177, 11th Cong., 3d sess., 1810 (1834), 108.

45. *Johnson*, 572.

46. Robert A. Williams Jr., *The American Indian*, 231.

47. Vine Deloria Jr. and Clifford M. Lytle, *American Indians* (p. 4), show that Marshall's characterization of the "doctrine of discovery" was really a corrupted version of the discovery principle first discussed in 1532 by Francisco de Vittoria, a prominent Spanish theologian who had been approached by the King of Spain with a query about what rights, if any, indigenous peoples had that were to be respected by European colonists.

48. See especially Williams, *The American Indian*; and Franke Wilmer, *The Indigenous Voice in World Politics* (Newbury Park, Cal.: Sage Publications, 1993), 1.

49. See Milner Ball, "Constitution, Court," 23–29; and Felix S. Cohen,

"Original Indian Title," *Minnesota Law Review* 32 (1947): 47, who asserts that "the dismissal of the plaintiffs' complaint in this case was not based upon any defect in the Indians' title, but solely upon the invalidity of the Indian deed through which the white plaintiffs claimed title."

50. Howard R. Berman, "The Concept of Aboriginal Rights in the Early History of the United States," *Buffalo Law Review* 27 (1978): 637–667.

51. Deloria and Lytle, *American Indians*, 26–27.

52. *Johnson*, 573.

53. Ibid., 587.

54. Ibid., 574.

55. Ibid., 588.

56. Ibid., 591.

57. Ibid., 603.

58. Ibid., 588.

59. Ibid.

60. Ibid., 591.

61. Ibid.

62. Berman, "The Concept," 655. But see also the informative note in Milner Ball's "Constitution, Court," 58 n. 132, which is a splendid analysis of Marshall's equivocation on the doctrine of conquest.

63. *Johnson*, 591.

64. Ibid., 593.

65. Ibid., 594.

66. Cohen, "Original Indian Title," 48.

67. Deloria and Lytle, *American Indians*, 26.

68. Williams, *The American Indian*, 317.

69. See Wilkins, "*Johnson v. M'Intosh* Revisited."

70. U.S. Commissioner of Indian Affairs, *Annual Report* (Washington: USCIA, Government Printing Office, 1864), 147.

71. 4 St. 411.

72. U.S. Commissioner of Indian Affairs, *Annual Report* (Washington: USCIA, Government Printing Office, 1831), 172.

73. Ibid.

74. U.S. House, Committee of the Whole House, *A Report on Establishing Trading Houses with Indian Tribes*, House Report No. 59, 1st Cong., 1st sess. (January 22, 1818), 3.

75. G. Edward White, *History of the Supreme Court of the United States: The Marshall Court and Cultural Change, 1815–1835* (New York: Oxford University Press, 1991), 705.

76. 4 St. 729.

77. 3 St. 383.

78. U.S. *Congressional Globe*, April 13, 1846, 666.

79. U.S. *Congressional Globe*, July 28, 1846, 1147.

80. Ibid. See also U.S. Senate, Committee on Indian Affairs, Memorial of John Ross. Document No. 331. May 4, 1846, 5.

81. Ibid., Memorial of John Ross, 6.

82. Ibid., 8.

83. U.S. Senate, Memorial of John Ross, 6.

84. 7 St. 478. This treaty and many others may be found in Charles J. Kappler, comp., *Indian Affairs: Law and Treaties*, vol. 2 (Washington: Government Printing Office, 1903).

85. 45 U.S. (4. How.) 568 (1846).

86. These facts are from the written transcript of the United States Supreme Court *Records and Briefs*, pt. 1, vol. 1, December 1845 to December 1846, reel 10. These are microfilm reports of the legal documents—transcripts, legal briefs, certiorari documents, amicus curiae briefs, and so forth—accompanying the case. For some cases, the amount of documentation was slight; for others, it was voluminous, especially those of the later twentieth century. These are outstanding sources of original documentation, particularly the attorneys' briefs.

87. *Johnson v. McIntosh*, 21 U.S. (8 Wheat.) 543, 593 (1823).

88. John P. Frank, *Justice Daniel Dissenting: A Biography of Peter V. Daniel, 1784–1860* (Cambridge: Harvard University Press, 1964), 283.

89. This was a common practice: when uncertainty or serious division of opinion arose on questions before a lower federal court, the presiding judges could send the disputed questions up to the Supreme Court for their answer. Today the procedure is called "writ of certification."

90. Frank, *Justice Daniel*, quoting from the *Arkansas State Gazette*, 283.

91. Ibid., 284.

92. Ibid.

93. 45 U.S. (4 How.) 567, 574 (1846).

94. 45 U.S. (4 How.) 567, 569.

95. Ibid., 570.

96. It figures prominently in *United States v. Wheeler*, 435 U.S. 313 (1975), and in a case I will discuss later, *Oliphant v. Suquamish Indian Tribe*, 435 U.S. 191 (1978). See Milner Ball's article "Constitution, Court" (22–42) for an excellent discussion on the origin of the notion of incorporation and a good analysis of the case law that involves the concept.

97. 45 U.S. (4 How.) 567, 571.

98. David O'Brien, *Storm Center: The Supreme Court in American Politics*, 3d ed. (New York: W. W. Norton & Company, 1993), 203.

99. 19 How. 393 (1853).

100. 45 U.S. (4 How.) 567, 571–572.

101. 7 St. 478 (Kappler, 1903, 327).

102. 7 St. 478 (Kappler, 1903, 326).

103. 7 St. 478 (Kappler, 1903, 327).

104. See discussion in Chapter 1 on this dynamic and pivotal concept.

105. 45 U.S. (4 How.) 567, 572.

106. Ibid.

107. See especially Robert T. Coulter, "The Denial of Legal Remedies to Indian Nations Under United States Law," *American Indian Journal* 3 (1977):

5–11; Newton, "Federal Power," 235–236; and Petra T. Shattuck and Jill Norgren, *Partial Justice: Federal Indian Law in a Liberal Constitutional System* (New York: Oxford University Press, 1991).

108. 448 U.S. 371 (1980).

109. See especially Karl J. Kramer, "The Most Dangerous Branch: An Institutional Approach to Understanding the Role of the Judiciary in American Indian Jurisdictional Determinations," *Wisconsin Law Review* 5–6 (1986): 989–1038.

110. Shattuck and Norgren, *Partial Justice*, 123.

111. Lewis Henkin, "Is There a 'Political Question' Doctrine?" *Yale Law Journal* 85 (Apr. 1976): 598.

112. Robert T. Coulter, "Legal Remedies Denied to Indian Nation Under U.S. Law," *Civil Rights Digest* 10 (1978): 32.

113. Newton, "Federal Power," 236.

114. 45 U.S. (4 How.) 567, 572 (1846).

115. Ibid., 572–573.

116. Ibid., 573.

117. Ibid.

118. Ibid.

119. 60 U.S. (11 How.) 730 (1850).

120. Ibid., 735–736.

121. 60 U.S. (19 How.) 393 (1857).

122. Ibid., 404–405.

123. U.S. Senate. Committee on the Judiciary. Extending the U.S. Criminal Laws Over Indian Territory, Senate Report No. 461, 29th Cong., 1st sess. (July 28, 1846).

124. Ibid., 2.

125. Ibid.

126. Ibid.

127. Ibid.

128. Ibid.

129. Frederick Jackson Turner, "The Problems of the West," *The Atlantic Monthly* 78 (Sept. 1896): 295.

130. Ibid.

131. Ibid., 296.

132. A large number of tribes inhabiting Indian Territory had signed treaties with the Confederate States of America. See James M. Matthews, ed., *The Statutes at Large of the Provisional Government of the Confederate States of America*, reprint ed. (Indian Rocks Beach, Fla.: D & S Publishers, Inc., 1970), 289–411, which contains copies of these interesting treaties.

133. 15 St. 17, 18.

134. 16 St. 13, 40.

135. See Fred L. Israel, ed., *The State of the Union Messages of the Presidents, 1790–1966.* 3 vols. See vol. 2, 1199.

136. Ibid., 1199–2000.

137. U.S. Senate, Committee on the Pacific Railroad, Report on the Pacific Railroad, Report No. 219, 40th Cong., 3d sess. (1869), 15.

138. Ibid.

139. A good contemporary discussion on the history and legal ramifications of the effort to stop Indian treatymaking is found in George William Rice's "Indian Rights: 25 U.S.C. Sec. 71: The End of Indian Sovereignty or a Self-Limitation of Contractual Ability," *American Indian Law Review* 5 (1977): 239–253. Rice supports Cohen's well-reasoned argument that the end of treatymaking did not destroy or weaken tribal political status, per se. The essence of treatymaking, in Cohen's words "was destined . . . to be continued for many decades" in the form of agreements (1972 ed., 67).

140. U.S. Commissioner of Indian Affairs, *Annual Report* (Washington: USCIA, Government Printing Office, 1866), 15.

141. U.S. Commissioner of Indian Affairs, *Annual Report* (1869), 448.

142. U.S. Commissioner of Indian Affairs, *Annual Report* (1871), 1154.

143. U.S. Commissioner of Indian Affairs, *Annual Report* (1811).

144. U.S. Commissioner of Indian Affairs, *Annual Report* (1872), 471.

145. Vine Deloria Jr., "Congress in Its Wisdom: The Course of Indian Legislation," in Sandra L. Cadwalader and Vine Deloria Jr., eds., *The Aggressions of Civilization* (Philadelphia: Temple University Press, 1984), 107.

146. Vine Deloria Jr., "Beyond the Pale: American Indians and the Constitution," in Jules Lobel, ed., *A Less Than Perfect Union* (New York: Monthly Review Press, 1988), 255.

147. The "et cetera" reads as follows (78 U.S. 616 [1871]): "forty-four one-fourth-pounds papers tobacco, four thousand five hundred pounds leaf tobacco, three thousand pounds tobacco in lump, three hundred empty boxes and caddies, six stoves and pipes, two drums for stove, three hammers, one hatchet, one can sweet oil, two cropping brooms, four hundred and sixteen pounds liquorice, four hundred and eighty-two pounds sugar, five pounds sealing wax, wrappers for smoking tobacco, brass for stencils, seventy stencil brands, two pitchforks, one ash-bucket, shovel, and poker, one hundred and twenty-seven packages tobacco, one hydraulic press, one hydraulic pump, six retainers, one large platform scale, one p[ai]r small platform scales, one p[ai]r lever scales, four small rollers, twelve sets moulds, eight screw presses, four leavers, thirteen segment caddy blocks, eighteen segment caddy bands, one large hydraulic wrench, eight small wrenches, twenty-one iron bars for track, one retainer for track, lot finishing irons, lot mould tin, one weight, one liquorice kettle, shovel and poker, one hydraulic leaver, one press and fixtures for manufacturing tobacco, one large tub seive, one common seive, twenty-one sinkers, two factory buildings used as a tobacco factory, and out-houses connected therewith."

148. Ibid.

149. 78 U.S. 616, 618.

150. Ibid., 619.

151. Ibid., 620.

152. Ibid.

153. Ibid.

154. Robert K. Heimann, "The Cherokee Tobacco Case," *The Chronicles of Oklahoma* 41 (1967): 319.

155. Ibid.

156. 78 U.S. 616, 620.

157. Ibid.

158. Ibid., 621.

159. Ibid.

160. Ibid., 622.

161. Cohen, *Handbook of Federal Indian Law*, reprint ed. (Albuquerque: University of New Mexico Press, 1972), 265.

162. 78 U.S. 616, 622.

163. U.S. Supreme Court, *Records & Briefs*, "Brief for Plaintiffs in error, Boudinot and Garland" (1871), 16.

164. 78 U.S. 616, 622.

165. Ibid., 623.

166. U.S. Supreme Court, *Records & Briefs*, "Brief for Plaintiffs" (1871), 14.

167. Ibid., 62–63.

168. In 1883 the Court of Claims awarded him $3,272.25. He had petitioned for $175,000.

CHAPTER 3

1. Russel L. Barsh and James Y. Henderson, *The Road: Indian Tribes and Political Liberty* (Berkeley: University of California Press, 1980), 85.

2. 23 St. 385.

3. 24 St. 388.

4. 26 St. 794.

5. 30 St. 497.

6. 24 St. 182.

7. W. G. Rice, "The Position of the American Indian in the Law of the United States," *Journal of Comparative Legislation and International Law* 16 (1934): 95.

8. Ibid.

9. George F. Canfield, "The Legal Position of the Indian," *American Law Review* (January 1881): 27.

10. 27 St. 645 (1893).

11. U.S. House, Committee on Indian Affairs, *Report on the Curtis Bill — Laws for the Indian Territory*, House Report No. 593, 55th Cong., 2d sess. (1898), 2.

12. 30 St. 497 (1898).

13. Angie Debo, *And Still the Waters Run: The Betrayal of the Five Civilized Tribes*, Norman, Okla.: University of Oklahoma Press, 1989, pp. ix–x).

14. Francis P. Prucha, *American Indian Policy in the Formative Years* (Lincoln: University of Nebraska Press, 1962), 211.

15. U.S. Commissioner of Indian Affairs, *Annual Report* (1856), 557.

16. U.S. Commissioner of Indian Affairs, *Annual Report* (1866), 17.

17. U.S. Board of Indian Commissioners, *Annual Report* (1871), 432.

18. 23 St. 362, 385 (1885).

19. U.S. Supreme Court, *Records & Briefs*, "Brief of Joseph Redding," 8.

20. Ibid., 14.

21. Ibid., 17. In the brief, the term "Courts" is handwritten in the margin as a replacement for the typed word "Government."

22. Interestingly, Garland was one of the attorneys representing Elias Boudinot and Stand Watie in *The Cherokee Tobacco*. In that case Garland had argued vigorously that the Cherokees should be *exempt* from the 1868 Revenue law.

23. U.S. Supreme Court, *Records & Briefs*, "Brief of A. H. Garland," 10.

24. Ibid., 10.

25. Ibid., 11.

26. Ibid., 24.

27. Ibid., 27.

28. 118 U.S. 375, 376.

29. 23 St. 362, 385 (1885).

30. U.S. *Congressional Record* (1885), 935.

31. 118 U.S. 375, 377.

32. Ibid.

33. Ibid., 378.

34. Ibid.

35. Ibid., 379.

36. Ibid., 378–379.

37. F. Cas. 14,495 (C.C. Tenn., 1834).

38. Ibid., 940.

39. Ibid., 939.

40. Ibid., 938.

41. Ibid.

42. Ibid.

43. Ibid., 940.

44. Ibid., 939.

45. Ibid.

46. 118 U.S. 375, 379.

47. F. Cas. 14,495 (C.C. Tenn., 1834), 939.

48. 118 U.S. 375, 379.

49. Ibid.

50. Ibid., 380.

51. Ibid., 383–384.

52. Ibid., 384.

53. Ibid., 384–385.

54. Daniel L. Rotenberg, "American Indian Tribal Death—A Centennial Remembrance," *University of Miami Law Review* 41 (Dec. 1986): 87.

55. Vine Deloria Jr., "Beyond the Pale: American Indians and the Constitu-

tion," in Jules Lobel, ed., *A Less Than Perfect Union* (New York: Monthly Review Press, 1988), 261.

56. Nell Jessup Newton, "Federal Power Over Indians: Its Sources, Scope, and Limitation," *University of Pennsylvania Law Review* 132 (1984): 215.

57. Deloria and Lytle, *American Indians*, 171.

58. 31 Fed. 327, 329 (1886).

59. U.S. Commissioner of Indian Affairs, *Annual Report* (1888), LXXXIX.

60. Vine Deloria Jr., "The Distinctive Status of Indian Rights," in Peter Iverson, ed., *The Plains Indians of the Twentieth Century* (Norman, Okla.: University of Oklahoma Press, 1985), 240.

61. Ibid.

62. 24 St. 388 (1887).

63. "Theodore Roosevelt's First Annual Message, December 3, 1901," in Fred L. Israel, ed., *The State of the Union Messages of the Presidents, 1790–1966.* 3 vols. (New York: Chelsea House, 1966), vol. 2, 2047.

64. Janet A. McDonnell, *The Dispossession of the American Indian, 1887–1934* (Bloomington, Ind.: Indiana University Press, 1991), 10.

65. U.S. Commissioner of Indian Affairs, *Annual Report* (1872), 469.

66. "Grover Cleveland's Annual Message, 1886," in J. D. Richardson, ed., *Compilation of the Messages and Papers of the Presidents, 1789–1897* (Washington: Government Printing Office, 1886), 473.

67. Ibid.

68. 30 St. 990–992.

69. 23 St. 73.

70. 135 U.S. 641, 643.

71. U.S. Supreme Court, *Records & Briefs*, "Transcript of Record," 2.

72. Ibid.

73. Ibid., 3.

74. 135 U.S. 641, 646.

75. Ibid., 646–647.

76. Ibid., 647.

77. U.S. Supreme Court, *Records & Briefs*, "Transcript of Record," 14.

78. Ibid., 15.

79. Angie Debo says that Judge Parker, "who presided over the Fort Smith court from 1875 to 1896, established a record of 172 sentenced to death and 88 actually hanged, nearly all of whom were Indian Territory 'bad men'" (*And Still the Waters Run*, 19).

80. U.S. Supreme Court, *Records & Briefs*, "Transcript of Record," 22.

81. 33 Fed. Rep., 900, 904 (1888).

82. Ibid., 908.

83. 135 U.S. 641, 651.

84. Ibid., 651–652.

85. Ibid., 652.

86. 31 U.S. (6 Pet.) 515, 582 (1832).

87. 5 Wall. 737 (1867).

88. 175 U.S. 1, 11 (1899).

89. 135 U.S. 641, 653.

90. U.S. Supreme Court, *Records & Briefs*, "Brief for the Appellant Statement," 2.

91. Ibid.

92. Ibid., 16–17.

93. Ibid., 19–20.

94. Ibid., 20.

95. 135 U.S. 641, 653.

96. Ibid.

97. Ibid., 654.

98. Ibid.

99. Ibid., 655–656.

100. Ibid., 656–657.

101. Ibid., 657.

102. Ibid.

103. Ibid.

104. Cohen, *Handbook of Federal Indian Law*, 287–288.

105. U.S. House, Committee of the Whole House, *Protection of American Bison and Other Animals*, House Report No. 1876, 51st Cong., 1st sess. (1890), 1.

106. Theoretically, *trusteeship* is a relationship which limits the property rights of the trustee and makes the trustee the servant of the trust *beneficiary*—in this case, the Shoshone-Bannock Tribe. See especially Felix S. Cohen's excellent article, "Indian Wardship: the Twilight of a Myth," in Lucy Cohen, ed., *The Legal Conscience: Selected Papers of Felix S. Cohen* (New Haven: Yale University Press, 1960), 328–334, in which the author contrasts the very different *legal* meanings of *trustee-beneficiary* (the actual relationship between tribes and the United States) and *guardian-wardship* (the perceived relationship between the two).

107. 15 St. 673.

108. 163 U.S. 504, 506.

109. U.S. Commissioner of Indian Affairs, *Annual Report* (1894), 67.

110. Ibid.

111. U.S. Commissioner of Indian Affairs, *Annual Report* (1895), 62.

112. U.S. Commissioner of Indian Affairs, *Annual Report* (1894), 67.

113. Ibid.

114. U.S. Commissioner of Indian Affairs, *Annual Report* (1895), 60; and U.S. Board of Indian Commissioners, *Annual Report* (1896), 991.

115. U.S. Commissioner of Indian Affairs, *Annual Report* (1895), 67.

116. Ibid., 70.

117. Ibid., 73.

118. Ibid., 80.

119. U.S. Commissioner of Indian Affairs, *Annual Report* (1896), 57.

120. Ibid., 58.

121. Ibid., 58–59.

122. Ibid.

123. Ibid.

124. 70 Fed. 598 (1895).

125. Ibid.

126. Ibid., 606.

127. Ibid., 608–609.

128. Ibid., 608.

129. Ibid., 613.

130. U.S. Commissioner of Indian Affairs, *Annual Report* (1896), 60.

131. Ibid.

132. U.S. *Congressional Record* (1896), 1290–1291. This bill was not enacted. Nevertheless, I believe its introduction points to collusion between the Bureau of Indian Affairs, motivated by paternalism and assimilation, and the state's political representatives and administrative officers, motivated by their desire for unquestioned jurisdictional authority over all the land in the state. Additional evidence is found in a House Report in which the Committee on Indian Affairs predicted that the Indians, armed with their district court victory, would "naturally be arrogant and insolent in their intercourse with the settlers" (see U.S. House, Committee of the Whole House, "Rights of Certain Indians to Hunt on Unoccupied Public Domain," Report No. 206, 54th Cong., 1st sess. [January 3, 1896], 1–2).

133. 163 U.S. 504, 505.

134. Ibid., 507.

135. Ibid., 506.

136. Ibid., 507–508.

137. Ibid., 508.

138. Ibid., 509.

139. Ibid.

140. Ibid.

141. Ibid.

142. Ibid., 510.

143. Ibid.

144. Ibid., 515.

145. Ibid., 516.

146. The concept of dual federalism arose after the Civil War. According to this theory, which was prominent from the 1890s to the later 1930s, the states and the national government have separate spheres of authority, and each is considered supreme in its own sphere. The state's sphere is protected by the Tenth Amendment to the Constitution, which says, "The powers not delegated to the United States by the Constitution, nor prohibited by it to the States, are reserved to the States, respectively, or to the People." For more analysis of dual federalism and its other variants, see Deil Wright, *Understanding Intergovernmental Relations*, 2d ed. (Monterey, Cal.: Brooks/Cole Publishing Co., 1982), 185.

147. 163 U.S. 504, 509 (1896).

148. Ibid., 511.

149. Ibid., 512–513.

150. Ibid., 514.

151. 2 McCrary 58 (1880).

152. Ibid., 66.

153. Ibid., 67.

154. Ibid., 69.

155. Ibid.

156. 163 U.S. 504, 514.

157. Ibid., 516.

158. Ibid., 517.

159. Ibid.

160. Ibid., 518.

161. 5 Wall. 787 (1867).

162. 163 U.S. 504, 520.

163. Ibid.

164. For more in-depth analysis of this important decision, including other opinions which have criticized *Ward*'s logic, see David E. Wilkins, "Indian Treaty Rights: Sacred Entitlements or 'Temporary Privileges?'" *American Indian Culture and Research Journal* 20, no. 1 (1996): 87–129; and Brian Czech, "*Ward v. Race Horse*—Supreme Court as Obviator?," *Journal of the West* 35, no. 3 (July 1996): 61–79.

165. See the 1995 10th Circuit Court of Appeals case, *Crow Tribe of Indians and Thomas L. Ten Bear v. Repsis*, 73 F.3d 982 (filed Dec. 26, 1995), which dramatically resuscitated each of the key holdings of the *Ward* ruling. Judge Barrett found *Ward* to be "compelling, well-reasoned, and persuasive" (p. 21). The Supreme Court, on May 28, 1996, chose not to review the case, thereby affirming the 10th Circuit's opinion.

166. See especially *Worcester* (1832), *The Kansas Indians* (1867), and *United States v. Berry* (1880).

167. George Kennan, "Have Reservation Indians Any Vested Rights?" *The Outlook* 70 (Mar. 29, 1902): 765; and see Kennan's "A New Statement from Mr. Kennan," *The Outlook* 70 (Apr. 19, 1902): 956–958.

168. 19 App. 315.

169. Ibid., 332.

170. See especially *Taylor v. Morton*, 23 F. Cas. 784 (C.C.D. Mass., 1855); and *The Chinese Exclusion Cases*, 130 U.S. 581, 600 (1889). In federal Indian law, see *The Cherokee Tobacco*, 78 U.S. (11 Wall.) 616 (1871). But even in *The Cherokee Tobacco*, the Court did not "go to the title of property or of personal protection, or decide anything more than to subject all persons, citizens or otherwise, within our national boundaries to the uniform duties and penalties of the revenue laws" (U.S. House Committee on Indian Affairs, "Investigation of Indian Frauds," Report No. 98, 42d Cong., 3d sess. [1873], 10). "The United States," the report continued, "has not willfully, forcibly violated any treaty made with the Indians, and the doctrine has never had either its legislative, executive, or judicial sanction, that it could, touching their rights of person or of property" (Ibid.). The only exception to this rule, and the only time an Indian treaty has been formally

abrogated, was the extinguishment of the Eastern Sioux treaty rights in 1862 as a consequence of a battle between the Sioux and some whites (see the abrogating legislation at 12 St. 512, 528).

171. Anonymous comment, "Federal Plenary Power in Indian Affairs After *Weeks* and *Sioux Nation*," *University of Pennsylvania Law Review* 131 (1982): 245.

172. Charles Kappler, comp., *Indian Affairs: Laws and Treaties*, vol. 2 (Washington: Government Printing Office, 1903), 754–759.

173. Ibid., 755.

174. Ibid., 758.

175. 25 St. 980.

176. U.S. Senate. Committee on Indian Affairs. "Memorial of Kiowa, Comanche, and Apache Tribes," Miscellaneous Document No. 102, 53d Cong., 2d sess. (1894), 1.

177. Ibid.

178. 187 U.S. 553, 557 (1903). For a good analysis of this decision, see Blue Clark, *Lone Wolf v. Hitchcock: Treaty Rights and Indian Law at the End of the Nineteenth Century* (Lincoln: University of Nebraska Press, 1994).

179. Ibid.

180. U.S. Senate, Committee on Indian Affairs, *Memorial from Kiowa, Comanche, and Apache Indian Tribes: Letter from the Secretary of Interior*, Senate Document No. 76, 56th Cong., 1st sess. (1900), 1–2.

181. Ibid., 6–7.

182. Ibid.

183. Ibid., 4–5.

184. U.S. House, Committee on Indian Affairs. *Agreement with Indians of Fort Hall Reservation*, House Report No. 419, 56th Cong., 1st sess. (1900), 6.

185. U.S. *Congressional Record* (April 2, 1900), 3659.

186. 31 St. 672. Ann Laquer Estin in "Lone Wolf v. Hitchcock: The Long Shadow," in Sandra L. Cadwalader and Vine Deloria Jr., eds., *The Aggressions of Civilization: Federal Indian Policy Since the 1880s* (Philadelphia: Temple University Press, 1994), describes the legislative strategies used to get the Jerome agreement enacted.

187. 187 U.S. 553, 562–563.

188. 19 App. 315, 332.

189. U.S. Supreme Court, *Records & Briefs*, "Brief and Argument for Appellant," 9.

190. Ibid., 16.

191. Ibid., 24.

192. Ibid., 26.

193. Ibid., 29.

194. Ibid., 31.

195. Ibid.

196. Ibid., 34–40.

197. Ibid., 41.

198. Ibid., 42.

199. Ibid., 79.
200. Ibid.
201. U.S. Supreme Court, *Records & Briefs*, "Brief for Appellees," 15–16.
202. Ibid., 19.
203. Ibid., 93.
204. U.S. Supreme Court, *Records & Briefs*, "Reply Brief of Appellants in Opposition to Motion to Dismiss Appeal," 40.
205. 187 U.S. 553, 564.
206. Ibid., 565.
207. Ibid.
208. Ibid.
209. Ibid.
210. 187 U.S. 553, 566.
211. Ibid., 568.
212. Anonymous comment, "Federal Plenary Power," 265 n. 190.
213. U.S. *Congressional Record* (1903), 2028.
214. Ibid.
215. Russel L. Barsh and James Y. Henderson, *The Road: Indian Tribes and Political Liberty* (Berkeley: University of California Press, 1980), 95.

CHAPTER 4

1. Felix S. Cohen, "Indian Claims," in Lucy Cohen, ed., *The Legal Conscience: Selected Papers of Felix S. Cohen* (New Haven: Yale University Press, 1960), 265.
2. 48 St. 985 (1934).
3. Francis P. Prucha, *The Indians in American Society: From the Revolutionary War to the Present* (Berkeley: University of California Press, 1985), 56.
4. See especially Kenneth R. Philp, ed., *Indian Self-Rule: First-Hand Accounts of Indian-White Relations from Roosevelt to Reagan* (Salt Lake City: Howe Brothers, 1986).
5. Vine Deloria Jr. and Clifford M. Lytle, *The Nations Within: The Past and Future of American Indian Sovereignty* (New York: Pantheon Books, 1984), 188.
6. 24 St. 388 (1887).
7. Jill Martin, "'Neither Fish, Flesh, Fowl, nor Good Red Herring': The Citizenship Status of American Indians, 1830–1924," *Journal of the West* 24 (July 1990): 79.
8. 112 U.S. 94, 99 (1884).
9. U.S. *Congressional Record* (Washington: Government Printing Office, 1897), 899.
10. 110 Fed. 942, 947–948 (1901).
11. Ibid., 948.
12. Ibid., 950.
13. Judith N. Shklar, *American Citizenship: The Quest for Inclusion* (Cambridge, Mass.: Harvard University Press, 1991), 1.

14. 197 U.S. 488, 508 (1905).

15. Ibid., 509.

16. U.S. Commissioner of Indian Affairs, *Annual Report* (1906), 28.

17. 34 St. 182 (1906).

18. Ibid., 182–183.

19. See especially *United States v. Celestine*, 215 U.S. 278 (1909); *Dick v. United States*, 208 U.S. 340 (1908); *United States v. Sutton*, 215 U.S. 291 (1909); *Tiger v. Western Investment Company*, 221 U.S. 286 (1911); and *Hallowell v. United States*, 221 U.S. 317 (1911).

20. 241 U.S. 591, 595 (1916).

21. 25 St. 888 (1889).

22. U.S. Supreme Court, *Records & Briefs*, "Transcript of the Case," 4.

23. 241 U.S. 591, 595.

24. "Theodore Roosevelt's Fifth Annual Message, December 5, 1905," in Fred L. Israel, ed., *The State of the Union Messages of the Presidents, 1790–1966.* 3 v. (New York: Chelsea House, 1966), v. 2, 2185.

25. U.S. Commissioner of Indian Affairs, *Annual Report* (1905), 25.

26. 241 U.S. 591, 592 (1916).

27. U.S. Supreme Court, *Records & Briefs*, "Brief of the United States," 10.

28. Ibid.

29. Ibid., 21.

30. Ibid., 22.

31. Ibid., 47.

32. Felix S. Cohen, *Handbook of Federal Indian Law*, reprint ed. (Albuquerque: University of New Mexico Press, 1972), 153.

33. Henry J. Abraham, *Justices and Presidents: A Political History of Appointments to the Supreme Court* (New York: Oxford University Press, 1992), 172–173.

34. Ibid., 173.

35. 188 U.S. 432, 437 (1903).

36. Ibid.

37. See especially *United States v. Mille Lac Band of Chippewas*, 229 U.S. 498 (1913); *United States v. Sandoval*, 231 U.S. 28 (1913); *Perrin v. United States*, 232 U.S. 478 (1914); *Sizemore v. Brady*, 235 U.S. 441 (1914); *United States v. Nice*, 241 U.S. 591 (1916); *Alaska Pacific Fisheries v. United States*, 248 U.S. 78 (1918); and *La Motte v. United States*, 254 U.S. 570 (1921).

38. *United States v. Quiver*, 241 U.S. 602, 605–606 (1916).

39. Ibid., 605.

40. See *Elk v. Wilkins*, 112 U.S. 94, 100 (1884) and *Ex parte Crow Dog*, 109 U.S. 556, 572 (1883).

41. Francis P. Prucha, *The Great Father: The United States Government and the American Indians*, abr. ed. (Lincoln: University of Nebraska Press, 1986), 267.

42. Ibid.

43. 241 U.S. 591, 595.

44. Ibid.

45. Ibid., 596.

46. Janet A. McDonnell, *The Dispossession of the American Indian, 1887–1934* (Bloomington, Ind.: Indiana University Press, 1991), 2–3.

47. Frederick E. Hoxie, *A Final Promise: The Campaign to Assimilate the Indians, 1880–1920* (New York: Cambridge University Press, 1989), 213.

48. 241 U.S. 591, 597.

49. Ibid., 598.

50. See especially *The Slaughter House Cases*, 16 Wall. 36 (1873); and *Twining v. New Jersey*, 211 U.S. 78 (1908).

51. 241 U.S. 591, 599.

52. Ibid.

53. Ibid., 600.

54. Ibid.

55. Ibid.

56. Jay M. Shafritz, *The Dictionary of American Government and Politics* (Chicago: Dorsey Press, 1988), 366.

57. 241 U.S. 591, 598.

58. Ibid., 601.

59. Ibid.

60. U.S. Commissioner of Indian Affairs, *Annual Report* (1917), 65.

61. 41 St. 350 (1921).

62. 43 St. 253 (1924).

63. 41 St. 350 (1921).

64. 43 St. 253 (1924).

65. Hoxie, *A Final Promise*, 214.

66. *U.S. v. Nice*, 241 U.S. 599 (1916).

67. Sharon O'Brien, *American Indian Tribal Governments* (Norman: University of Oklahoma Press, 1989), 84.

68. U.S. *Congressional Globe* (Washington, 1863), 308.

69. Cohen, "Indian Claims," 270.

70. Shattuck and Norgren, *Partial Justice*, 143.

71. Charles Wilkinson's comments in Kenneth Philp, *Indian Self-Rule*, 151.

72. Nancy O. Lurie, "The Indian Claims Commission," *Annals of the American Academy of Political and Social Science* 436 (1978): 98.

73. U.S. Supreme Court, *Records & Briefs*, "Petition for Writ of Certiorari of the Northwestern Shoshone Tribe," 4–5.

74. U.S. Supreme Court, *Records & Briefs*, "Brief for the Petitioner," 3.

75. Deloria, "The Western Shoshones," 17.

76. U.S. Commissioner of Indian Affairs, *Annual Report* (1851), in Wilcomb Washburn, ed., *The American Indian and the United States* (Westport, Conn.: Greenwood Press, 1979), 58.

77. U.S. Commissioner of Indian Affairs, *Annual Report* (1861), in Wilcomb Washburn, ed., *The American Indian*, 78.

78. Deloria, "The Western Shoshones," 17–18.

79. 12 St. 512, 529 (1862).

80. U.S. Supreme Court, *Records & Briefs*, "Petition for Writ of Certiorari," 7.

81. 324 U.S. 335, 341 (1945).

82. U.S. Supreme Court, *Records & Briefs*, "Petition for Writ of Certiorari," 8–9.

83. 18 St. 685 (1863).

84. 18 St. 663 (1863).

85. 18 St. 689 (1865).

86. 13 St. 681 (1863).

87. 13 St. 663 (1863).

88. 324 U.S. 335, 343.

89. U.S. Supreme Court, *Records & Briefs*, "Brief for Petitioners," 14.

90. 13 St. 432 (1865) and 15 St. 17 (1867).

91. 15 St. 673 (1868).

92. 324 U.S. 335, 346.

93. U.S. Supreme Court, *Records & Briefs*, "Brief for Petitioners," 16–17.

94. Ibid., 17.

95. 45 St. 1407.

96. 95 Ct. Cl. 642 (1942).

97. Ibid., 690 (1942).

98. Deloria, "Western Shoshone," 20.

99. U.S. Supreme Court, *Records & Briefs*, "Brief for Petitioners," 20.

100. Ibid., 21.

101. U.S. Supreme Court, *Records & Briefs*, "Brief for the United States in Opposition," 18.

102. 323 U.S. 214.

103. Ibid., 233.

104. Ibid., 242. For a contemporaneous discussion of this "New Deal" Court, see *The New Republic* 112 (June 18, 1945): 833.

105. 324 U.S. 335, 337.

106. Ibid., 338.

107. *U.S. v. Winans*, 198 U.S. 371 (1905), which dealt with fishing rights, held that tribes retained all rights, including the taking of fish, not specifically ceded away in a treaty with the federal government. As Justice McKenna put it: ". . . the treaty was not a grant of rights to the Indians, but a grant of rights from them—a reservation of those not granted" (p. 381). Over the years, the reserved rights doctrine has also been applied to water, land, other natural resources, jurisdictional matters, etc.

108. 299 U.S. 476, 496 (1937).

109. 15 St. 673.

110. *United States ex. rel. Hualpai Indians v. Santa Fe Pacific Railroad*, 314 U.S. 339 (1941).

111. 299 U.S. 476, 496 as quoted in 324 U.S. 335, 338.

112. 324 U.S. 335, 338–339.

113. Cohen, "Indian Claims," 267.

114. Ibid., 270.

115. Ibid.

116. 324 U.S. 335, 339.

117. Ibid.

118. Ibid., 339–340.

119. Ibid., 340.

120. See Charles Chibitty et al., *Indian Treaties* (Washington: Institute for the Development of Indian Law, 1977).

121. 324 U.S. 335, 341.

122. Ibid.

123. Ibid., 348.

124. Milner S. Ball, "Constitution, Court, Indian Tribes," *American Bar Foundation Research Journal* 1 (1987): 21.

125. 324 U.S. 335, 346.

126. Ibid., 346–347.

127. Ibid., 348.

128. Cohen, "Indian Claims," 267.

129. 324 U.S. 335, 349.

130. See *United States v. Winans*, 198 U.S. 371 (1905).

131. 324 U.S. 335, 350.

132. 299 U.S. 476, 485.

133. 304 U.S. 111, 113.

134. 95 Ct. Cl. 331, 335.

135. 145 F.2d 329.

136. 324 U.S. 335, 350.

137. Ibid.

138. Ibid.

139. Ibid., 351.

140. See especially *Worcester v. Georgia*, 6 Pet. 515 (1832); *The Kansas Indians*, 5 Wall. 737 (1866); *Wau-Pe-Man-Qua v. Aldrich*, 28 Fed. 489 (1886); *Jones v. Meehan*, 175 U.S. 1 (1899); *United States v. Winans*, 198 U.S. 371 (1905); and *Seufert Brothers Company v. United States*, 249 U.S. 194 (1919).

141. See, e.g., *Ward v. Race Horse*, 163 U.S. 504 (1986); and *The Cherokee Tobacco*, 11 Wall. 616 (1871).

142. 324 U.S. 335, 353.

143. Reference for the 1929 act is 45 St. 1407. See *Northwestern Bands of Shoshone Indians v. United States*, 95 Ct. Cl. 642 (1942).

144. Ibid., 354.

145. Ibid.

146. Ibid., 354–355.

147. Cohen, "Indian Claims," 265.

148. Ibid.

149. 324 U.S. 335, 355.

150. Ibid.

151. Ibid.

152. Ibid., 356.

153. Ibid.

154. Ibid.

155. 6 Pet. 515, 561.

156. 324 U.S. 335, 357.

157. Ibid.

158. Ibid., 358.

159. Ibid., 359.

160. Ibid., 360.

161. Ibid.

162. Ibid., 361.

163. Ibid., 362.

164. Ibid.

165. Ibid., 363.

166. Ibid., 364–365.

167. Ibid., 365.

168. Ibid., 367.

169. Ibid., 369.

170. Ibid.

171. Lawrence Baum, *The Supreme Court,* 4th ed. (Washington: Congressional Quarterly Press, 1992), 129.

172. United States, *Congressional Record* (March 14, 1945), A1185.

173. Ibid.

174. U.S. Supreme Court, *Records & Briefs,* "Petition for Rehearing," 1.

175. Ibid., 3.

176. U.S. Supreme Court, *Records & Briefs,* "Memorandum as Amicus Curiae," 2, 3.

177. Ibid., 3.

178. U.S. Supreme Court, *Records & Briefs,* "Brief as Amicus Curiae by the National Congress of American Indians in Support of the Petition for Rehearing," 6.

179. U.S. Supreme Court, *Records & Briefs,* "Petition for Rehearing: Brief of Other Counsel," 21.

180. U.S. Commissioner of Indian Affairs, *Annual Report* (1950), 343.

181. Ibid., 342.

182. 67 St. B132 (1953).

183. Ibid.

184. 67 St. 588 (1953).

185. John Collier, "The Unfinished Indian Wars," *The Nation* 184 (May 1957): 458.

186. U.S., *Public Papers of the Presidents of the United States: Dwight D. Eisenhower* (Washington: Government Printing Office, 1953), 166.

187. John R. Wunder, *Retained by the People: A History of American Indians and the Bill of Rights* (New York: Oxford University Press, 1994), 111.

188. Nancy O. Lurie, "The Indian Claims Commission Act," *Annals of the American Academy of Political and Social Sciences* 311 (1957): 56.

189. Philp, ed., *Indian Self-Rule,* 154.

190. U.S. Supreme Court, *Records & Briefs*, "Petition for Certiorari," 1.

191. 23 St. 24 (1884).

192. 26 St. 1095, 1101 (1891).

193. 31 St. 321 (1900).

194. U.S. Supreme Court, *Records & Briefs*, "Petition for Certiorari," 2.

195. 49 St. 1250 (1936).

196. Angie Debo, *A History of the Indians of the United States* (Norman: University of Oklahoma Press, 1989), 387.

197. Ibid.

198. U.S. House, Committee on Agriculture, *Authorizing Secretary of Agriculture to sell Timber Within Tongass National Forest*, House Report No. 873, 80th Cong., 1st sess. (1947), 1.

199. Ibid., 2.

200. Ibid.

201. Ibid., 3.

202. 61 St. 920 (1947).

203. Felix S. Cohen, "Alaska's Nuremberg Laws: Congress Sanctions Racial Discrimination," *Commentary* 6 (Aug. 1948): 136–143.

204. Ibid., 136.

205. 61 St. 920 (1947).

206. U.S. Supreme Court, *Records & Briefs*, "Petition for Writ of Certiorari to the United States Court of Claims by James Craig Peacock, Counsel for Petitioning Tee-Hit-Ton Indians."

207. 128 Ct. Cl. 82, 99.

208. Ibid., 85.

209. Ibid., 87.

210. "Petition for Writ" (J. C. Peacock), 10.

211. Ibid.

212. Ibid., 11.

213. U.S. Supreme Court, *Records & Briefs*, "Memorandum for the United States," 9–10.

214. U.S. Supreme Court, *Records & Briefs*, "Brief of the Attorney General of Idaho, Amicus Curiae," 2.

215. Ibid.

216. U.S. Supreme Court, *Records & Briefs*, "Brief on behalf of the State of New Mexico as Amicus Curiae," 3.

217. 348 U.S. 272–274.

218. Cohen, *Handbook of Federal Indian Law*, 404.

219. Ibid.

220. 49 St. 1250 (1936).

221. 348 U.S. 275–276 (1955).

222. Ibid., 272, 277.

223. Ibid.

224. Ibid.

225. Ibid., 278.

226. Ibid., 279.

227. Ibid.

228. U.S., *Public Papers of the President, Harry Truman* (Washington: Government Printing Office, 1962), 414.

229. See especially *Worcester v. Georgia*, 131 U.S. (6 Pet.) 515 (1832) and *Mitchel v. United States*, 34 U.S. (9 Pet.) 711 (1835).

230. 348 U.S. 272, 281.

231. Ibid., 281–282.

232. 329 U.S. 40 (1946).

233. Ibid., 47.

234. Ibid.

235. Ibid.

236. Ibid., 52–53 n. 30.

237. Felix S. Cohen, "Original Indian Title," in Lucy Cohen, ed., *The Legal Conscience: Selected Papers of Felix S. Cohen* (New Haven: Yale University Press, 1960), 301.

238. Ibid., 303.

239. 329 U.S. 40, 58 (1946).

240. 337 U.S. 86 (1949).

241. Ibid., 106 n. 28.

242. 348 U.S. 272, 283 n. 16.

243. Ibid., n. 17.

244. Ibid., 285.

245. Ibid., 287.

246. Ibid.

247. Ibid., 288 n. 20.

248. Ibid., 289.

249. Ibid., 288–289.

250. Ibid., 289–290.

251. Ibid., 290.

252. Ibid., 290–291.

253. Wunder, *Retained by the People*, 117.

254. 348 U.S. 272, 292.

255. Ibid., 294.

256. Nell Jessup Newton, "At the Whim of the Sovereign: Aboriginal Title Reconsidered," *Hastings Law Journal* 31 (July 1980): 1216–1217.

257. Lurie, "The Indian Claims Commission" (1957), 64–65.

258. 131 Ct. Cl. 593.

259. Wunder, *Retained by the People*, 117.

260. U.S. Supreme Court, *Records & Briefs*, "Petition for Rehearing," by James C. Peacock, Counsel for Tee-Hit-Ton Band, 1.

261. 85 St. 688. ANCSA was one of the most complex laws ever enacted by Congress in an effort to address tribal and national interests where they intersected and overlapped. Under the act, private native corporations were established to receive title to 44 million acres of land; village corporations gained title

ation to the Alaskan natives for extinguishment of all aboriginal claims. For readings about some of the difficulties Alaskan natives have encountered in securing their rights under the law, see Gary C. Anders, "The Alaska Native Experience with the Alaska Native Claims Settlement Act," in P. A. Olson, ed., *The Struggle for the Land* (Lincoln: University of Nebraska Press, 1990), 127–145.

CHAPTER 5

1. See Alvin M. Josephy, *Red Power: The American Indian Fight for Freedom* (New York: American Heritage Press, 1971); Vine Deloria Jr., "The Next Three Years: A Time for Change," *The Indian Historian* 7 (Winter 1974): 25–27, 53; and Emma R. Gross, *Contemporary Federal Indian Policy Toward American Indians* (Westport, Conn.: Greenwood Press, 1989).

2. See especially Richard Nixon's "Special Message on Indian Affairs," July 8, 1970, in U.S., *Public Papers of the Presidents of the United States: Richard Nixon, 1970* (Washington: Government Printing Office), 564–567, 575–576.

3. See especially the act which returned the Blue Lake Lands to Taos Pueblo, 1970 (84 St. 1437); Alaska Native Claims Settlement Act 1971 (85 St. 688); Indian Education Act 1972 (86 St. 335); Restoration of the Menominee Tribe 1973 (87 St. 700); Indian Financing Act 1974 (88 St. 77); Indian Self-Determination and Education Assistance Act 1975 (88 St. 2203); Act Establishing the American Indian Policy Review Commission 1975 (88 St. 1910); Indian Health Care Improvement Act 1976 (90 St. 1400); and American Indian Religious Freedom Resolution 1978 (92 St. 469).

4. See especially *United States v. Washington*, 384 F. Supp. 343 (1974), which involved Indian fishing rights; *Morton v. Mancari*, 417 U.S. 541 (1974), which involved Indian preference regulations; and *Passamaquoddy Tribe v. Morton*, 388 F. Supp. 654 (1975), which involved tribal recognition and Indian land claims.

5. Petra Shattuck and Jill Norgren, "Indian Rights: The Cost of Justice," *The Nation* 227 (July 22–29, 1978): 71.

6. Emma R. Gross, *Contemporary Federal Policy Toward American Indians* (Westport, Conn.: Greenwood Press, 1989), 87.

7. Russel L. Barsh and James Y. Henderson, *The Road* (Berkeley: University of California Press, 1980), 290.

8. Richard Jones, "American Indian Policy: Background, Nature, History, Current Issues, Future Trends," U.S., Congressional Research Service Report for Congress No. 87-227 (Washington: Library of Congress, 1987), 32.

9. Ibid.

10. 88 St. 2203 (1975).

11. Ibid., 2204.

12. Deloria & Lytle, *American Indians*, 23.

13. 88 St. 1910 (1975).

14. Prucha, *The Great Father*, 383.

15. Deloria & Lytle, *American Indians*, 24.

16. U.S. Congress, *Final Report: American Indian Policy Review Commission* (Washington: Government Printing Office, 1977), 571.

17. Ibid., 573.

18. Ibid., 585.

19. 544 F.2d 1007 (1976).

20. U.S. Congress, *Final Report*, 587.

21. Ibid.

22. Ibid.

23. Suquamish population in 1994 had risen sharply to approximately 780 enrolled members. See "Suquamish," in Mary B. Davis, ed., *Native America in the Twentieth Century: An Encyclopedia* (New York: Garland Publishing, Inc., 1994), 620.

24. 435 U.S. 191, 193 n. 1.

25. 12 St. 927 (1855).

26. U.S. Supreme Court, *Records & Briefs*, "Brief for Petitioners," 12.

27. U.S. Supreme Court, *Records & Briefs*, "Brief of Respondents to Petition for Writ of Certiorari," 8.

28. U.S. Supreme Court, *Records & Briefs*, "Petition for Certiorari—Appendix," 30.

29. Ibid., 50.

30. Ibid., 52.

31. Belgarde's appeal to the 9th Circuit Court was still pending when his case was accepted by the Supreme Court for review.

32. 544 F.2d 1007 (1976).

33. Ibid., 1009.

34. Ibid.

35. Ibid., n. 1.

36. Ibid.

37. Ibid., 1009.

38. 12 St. 927.

39. 33 St. 1078.

40. 544 F.2d 1007, 1013.

41. U.S. Supreme Court, *Records & Briefs*, "Petition for a Writ of Certiorari," 3.

42. U.S. Supreme Court, *Records & Briefs*, "Brief of Respondents in Opposition to Petition for a Writ of Certiorari," 6.

43. Ibid.

44. Ibid., 5.

45. In the mid-1970s, the Supreme Court began to print the oral arguments used by the contending lawyers before the bench. (See, for example, U.S., *The Complete Oral Arguments of the Supreme Court of the United States: A Retrospective 1969 Term Through 1979 Term* (Frederick, Md.: University Publications of

America, Inc.) This is valuable because it details the oral arguments used by the attorneys, as well as the bantering back and forth between the justices and the attorneys. Typically, one hour is allotted for argument in a case, divided equally between the two sides. Unfortunately, the justices making the queries are usually not identified by name.

46. U.S. *The Complete Oral* (1979 term), 36.

47. Ibid., 36–37.

48. Ibid., 63–64.

49. Ibid., 66.

50. Ibid., 43.

51. Ibid., 45.

52. Ibid., 46–47.

53. Ibid., 13–14.

54. Ibid.

55. Sue Davis, "Rehnquist & State Courts: Federalism Revisited," *The Western Political Quarterly* 45 (1992): 773.

56. These phrases were coined by Paula Arledge and Anne M. McCulloch in a paper, "Indian Cases and the Modern Supreme Court: Problems in Consistent Interpretation in Extra-Constitutional Cases," presented at the Annual Meeting of the American Political Science Association, Atlanta, November 8–10, 1990 (p. 20).

57. 435 U.S. 191, 195–196 (1978).

58. Rehnquist seems, however, to have a somewhat different view of what might be termed "internal sovereignty," especially as it relates to intratribal matters and affairs. In a few rare cases, Rehnquist has affirmed a tribe's right to exercise elements of sovereignty when the demographics are such that tribal members vastly outnumber nontribal inhabitants of Indian Country and the tribe is flexing a power that has been delegated to them by the federal government. See his opinion for the Court in *U.S. v. Mazurie*, 419 U.S. 544 (1975), for a clear example.

59. United States, Department of the Interior, *Opinions of the Solicitor*, vol. 1, "Powers of Indian Tribes," 55 I.D. 14 (1934) (Washington: Government Printing Office, 1974), 445–477.

60. Ibid., 447.

61. Ibid.

62. Deloria & Lytle, *The Nations Within*, 158.

63. U.S., *Opinions of the Solicitor*, "Powers of Indian Tribes," 445.

64. Ibid., 471.

65. Ibid., 472.

66. Ibid., 475–476.

67. 82 St. 73, 77.

68. See, e.g., Donald L. Burnette Jr., "An Historical Analysis of the 1968 'Indian Civil Rights Act,'" *Harvard Journal of Legislation* 9 (May 1972): 557–626; and Ralph W. Johnson and E. Susan Crystal, "Indians and Equal Protection," *Washington Law Review* 54 (June 1979): 587–631.

69. 435 U.S. 191, 195–196 n. 6.

70. U.S. House, Committee on Indian Affairs, *Regulating the Indian Department*, House Report No. 474, 23d Cong., 1st sess. (1834), 18.

71. 7 St. 333 (1830).

72. 435 U.S. 191, 197.

73. Ibid., 197–198.

74. Russel L. Barsh and James Youngblood Henderson, "The Betrayal: *Oliphant v. Suquamish Indian Tribe* and the Hunting of the Snark," *Minnesota Law Review* 63 (1979): 617.

75. Ibid., 617–618.

76. Ibid.

77. 435 U.S. 191, 199 n. 8.

78. Barsh & Henderson, "The Betrayal," 620.

79. Ibid.

80. 14 F. Cas. 353 (1878).

81. 112 U.S. 94, 108 (1884).

82. 435 U.S. 191, 201 n. 11.

83. Ibid.

84. Ibid., 201.

85. Robert A. Trennert Jr., *Alternative to Extinction* (Philadelphia: Temple University Press, 1975).

86. 435 U.S. 191, 201.

87. Ibid., 202.

88. Ibid., n. 13.

89. Ibid.

90. U.S. House, *Regulating the Indian Department* (1834), 13.

91. Ibid.

92. 435 U.S. 191, 203.

93. Ibid., 204.

94. Ibid., 206.

95. See especially Felix Cohen's "Introduction" in *Handbook of Federal Indian Law* (1972 reprint ed.), and see Charles F. Wilkinson's "Introduction" and Chapter I in *American Indians, Time, and the Law: Native Societies in a Modern Constitutional Democracy* (New York: Yale University Press, 1987).

96. 435 U.S. 191, 206.

97. Ibid.

98. 12 St. 927, article 9.

99. 435 U.S. 191, 208.

100. Ibid., 207.

101. 544 F.2d 1007, 1010.

102. 435 U.S. 191, 208.

103. Ibid.

104. 411 U.S. 164 (1973).

105. 435 U.S. 191, 208.

106. 544 F.2d 1007, 1009.

107. 435 U.S. 191, 209.

108. Ibid., 210

109. Ibid.

110. Barsh & Henderson, "The Betrayal," 634.

111. 109 U.S. 556 (1883).

112. See especially Sidney L. Harring, *Crow Dog's Case: American Indian Sovereignty, Tribal Law, and United States Law in the Nineteenth Century* (New York: Cambridge University Press, 1994), for a historical treatment of this important decision.

113. 109 U.S. 556, 571 (1883).

114. 435 U.S. 191, 211.

115. Ibid., 211–212.

116. Ibid.

117. 435 U.S. 313 (1978).

118. 436 U.S. 49 (1978).

119. A *lesser included offense* is one "composed of some, but not all, of the elements of the greater crime, and which does not have any element not included in the greater offense." *Black's Law Dictionary*, 5th ed. (St. Paul, Minn.: West Publishing Co., 1979).

120. 435 U.S. 313, 322 (1978).

121. Ibid., 323.

122. Wilkinson, *American Indians, Time, and the Law*, 61.

123. Ibid., 49

124. U.S. *Congressional Record* (1978), 18480.

125. *Joint Tribal Council of the Passamaquoddy Tribe et al. v. Morton et al.*, 528 F.2d 370 (1975).

126. Christopher Vecsey, "Introduction: The Issues Underlying Iroquois Land Claims," in Christopher Vecsey and William A. Starna, eds., *Iroquois Land Claims* (Syracuse, N.Y.: Syracuse University Press, 1988), 3.

127. 94 St. 1785 (1980).

128. *New York Times*, July 1, 1980, 1.

129. Vine Deloria Jr., "Reflections on the Black Hills Claim," *Wicazo Sa Review* 4 (Spring 1988): 33.

130. 15 St. 17 (1867).

131. U.S. House, *Report of the Indian Peace Commission*, Executive Document No. 97, 40th Cong., 2d sess. (January 7, 1868), 15–17, reprinted in Francis P. Prucha, ed., *Documents of United States Indian Policy*, 2d ed. (Lincoln: University of Nebraska Press, 1990), 106.

132. Ibid.

133. 15 St. 635.

134. Frank Pommersheim, "The Black Hills Case: On the Cusp of History," *Wicazo Sa Review* 4 (Spring 1988): 19.

135. U.S. *Congressional Record* (January 25, 1978), 836.

136. Ibid.

137. Ibid.

138. Vine Deloria Jr., "The United States Has No Jurisdiction in Sioux Territory," in Roxanne D. Ortiz, ed., *The Great Sioux Nation: Sitting in Judgment on America* (Berkeley: Moon Books, 1977), 142.

139. 19 St. 254 (1877).

140. Pommersheim, "The Black Hills Case," 19.

141. Deloria, "Indian Treaties: A Hundred Years Later," *Race Relations Reporter* (March 1974): 31.

142. See Thomas Biolsi, *Organizing the Lakota: The Political Economy of the New Deal on the Pine Ridge and Rosebud Reservations* (Tucson, Ariz.: University of Arizona Press, 1992).

143. Ibid., 47.

144. 41 St. 738 (1920).

145. The bands were Rosebud, Pine Ridge, Cheyenne River, Lower Brule, and Crow Creek of South Dakota, Standing Rock of North and South Dakota, Santee of Nebraska, and Sioux of Fort Peck Reservation of Montana.

146. See E. B. Smith, comp., *Indian Tribal Claims: Decided in the Court of Claims of the United States, Briefed and Compiled to June 30, 1947,* vol. 2 (Washington: University Publications of America, 1976), 282–373, which details each of the separate twenty-four petitions that appeared before the Court of Claims. The nature of these claims included the alleged failure of the United States to furnish educational facilities to Sioux children under Article 7 of the 1868 Treaty (C-531–1); the value of clothing alleged to be due and not furnished under Article 10 of the 1868 Treaty (C-531–2); the value of rations guaranteed to Sioux Indians by Article 10 of the 1868 Treaty (C-531–4); compensation for alleged failure of the United States to deliver cows and oxen for distribution to families and individuals who selected tracts of land and commenced farming (C-531–5); and the Black Hills case itself, which eclipsed in value all the other claims combined (C-531–7).

And see the discussion of Ralph Case and his efforts on behalf of the Sioux in Edward Lazarus's *Black Hills/White Justice: The Sioux Nation Versus the United States, 1775 to the Present* (New York: Harper Collins Publishers, 1991), Chapter 7, "The Black Hills Claim."

147. Lazarus, *Black Hills/White Justice,* 157.

148. This occurred in C-531–11, C-531–18, C-531–19, C-531–21, C-531–23, and C-531–24. For example, in C-531–18, involving the Rosebud Sioux Indians, the Indians alleged illegal disbursements from their funds in the amount of $560,210.60. The Court's judgment was for $547,347.60, but when "gratuitous offsets" (the total of sums paid to Indian tribes which were not mandated by law) by the government on behalf of the Indians were tallied, it was determined that the offsets totaled $547,347.60. In effect, the tribe's net judgment was $0.00.

The Court of Claims and the Indian Claims Commission had authority to deduct any money or property "given to, or funds expended gratuitously for, the benefit of the plaintiff tribe if the [Indian Claims] Commission found that the nature of the tribe's claim and the entire course of dealings between the United

States and the tribe warranted the offset." The Court of Claims, however, authorized more offsets against judgments than the Indian Claims Commission. See *Felix S. Cohen's Handbook of Federal Indian Law* (Charlottesville, Va.: Michie, Bobbs-Merrill, 1982), 571–572.

149. *Sioux Tribe of Indians v. United States*, 97 Ct. Cl. 613 (1942), cert. denied 318 U.S. 789 (1943).

150. The following is a chronology of the litigation that ensued in the wake of the 1942 case: *Sioux Tribe v. United States*, 105 Ct. Cl. 658 (1946); *Sioux Tribe v. United States*, 2 Ind. Cl. Comm. 646 (1954); *Sioux Tribe v. United States*, 146 F. Supp. 229 (1956); *Sioux Tribe v. United States*, 161 Ct. Cl. 413, F.2d 378 (1963); *Sioux Tribe of Indians v. United States*, 182 Ct. Cl. 912 (1968); *Sioux Nation v. United States*, 23 Ind. Cl. Comm. 358 (1970); *Sioux Nation v. United States*, 24 Ind. Cl. Comm. 98 (1970); *Sioux Nation v. United States*, 33 Ind. Cl. Comm. 151 (1974); *Sioux Tribe v. United States*, 205 Ct. Cl. 148, 500 F.2d 458 (1974); *United States v. Sioux Nation*, 207 Ct. Cl., 518 F.2d 1298 (1975); cert. denied, 423 U.S. 1016 (1975); *Sioux Tribe v. United States*, 38 Ind. Cl. Comm. 469 (1976); and *Sioux Nation v. United States*, 601 F.2d 1157 (1979).

151. *Sioux Tribe v. United States*, 2 Ind. Cl. Comm. 646 (1954).

152. U.S. Supreme Court, *Records and Briefs*, "Respondents' Brief—Brief for the Sioux Nation," 20 n. 16.

153. *Sioux Tribe of Indians v. United States*, 146 F. Supp. 229 (1956).

154. U.S. Supreme Court, *Records and Briefs*, "Respondents' Brief—Brief for the Sioux Nation," 21.

155. Ibid., 24 25.

156. Res judicata dictates that a final judgment already rendered by a court of competent jurisdiction on the merits is conclusive as to the rights of the parties and thereby bars any subsequent actions involving the same claim or course of action. (See *Black's Law Dictionary*.)

157. 88 St. 1499 (1974).

158. U.S. Senate, Committee on Interior and Insular Affairs, "Authorize Appropriations for Indian Claims Commission." Senate Report No. 93-863, 93d Cong., 2d sess. (1974), 5.

159. *United States v. Sioux Nation of Indians*, 518 F.2d 1298 (207 Ct. Cl. 234) (1975).

160. 423 U.S. 1016 (1975). It had first denied certiorari on April 19, 1943.

161. 92 St. 153 (1978).

162. 299 U.S. 476 (1937).

163. 448 U.S. 371, 408 (1980).

164. 182 Ct. Cl. 543 (1968).

165. Ibid., 553.

166. Vine Deloria Jr., "Beyond the Pale: American Indians and the Constitution," in Jules Lobel, ed., *A Less Than Perfect Union* (New York: Monthly Review Press, 1988), 266.

167. 448 U.S. 371, 409 (1980).

168. Louis F. Claiborne, "Oral Arguments" before the Supreme Court,

March 25, 1980, reprinted in *The Complete Oral Arguments of the Supreme Court of the United States, 1979 Term* (Frederick, Md.: University Publications of America, Inc., 1979), 46.

169. Ibid.

170. Arthur Lazarus Jr., "Oral Arguments" before the Supreme Court, March 25, 1980, reprinted in *The Complete Oral Arguments of the Supreme Court of the United States, 1979 Term* (Frederick, Md.: University Publications of America, Inc., 1979), 35.

171. Ibid., 39.

172. 448 U.S. 371, 409 n. 26 (1980).

173. Deloria, "Reflections on the Black Hills Case," 265.

174. 430 U.S. 73 (1977).

175. 448 U.S. 371, 413 (1980).

176. Ibid., 414–415.

177. Ibid., 415.

178. Ibid., 417 n. 30.

179. 448 U.S. 371, 421 n. 32 (1980).

180. Ibid.

181. Ibid., 435.

182. Ibid.

183. Ibid.

184. Ibid.

185. Ibid., 436–437.

186. Ibid., 437.

187. 518 F.2d 1298, 1302 (1975).

188. According to Fergus M. Bordewich, *Killing the White Man's Indian: Reinventing Native Americans at the End of the Twentieth Century* (New York: Doubleday, 1996), 230.

189. See especially Roxanne D. Ortiz, ed., *The Great Sioux Nation* (1977); Peter Matthiessen, *In the Spirit of Crazy Horse* (New York: Penguin Books, 1983); Pommersheim, "The Black Hills Case" (1988); and Deloria, "Reflections on the Black Hills Claim" (1988). See also Pommersheim, "Making all the Difference: Native Testimony and the Black Hills (a review essay)," *North Dakota Law Review* 69 (1993), 337–359, which is a critical review of Edward Lazarus's *Black Hills/White Justice: The Sioux Nation Versus the United States, 1775 to the Present* (1991) and two other books.

CHAPTER 6

1. 102 St. 2285, 2296 (1988); as amended in 105 St. 1278 (1991).

2. Indian Self-Determination Act Amendments of 1994, 108 St. 4250, 4270. This law declared that "it is the policy of this title [Title II—Self-Governance] to permanently establish and implement tribal self-governance" (p. 4271),

which is designed, among other things, "to enable the United States to maintain and improve its unique and continuing relationship with, and responsibility to, Indian tribes, . . . to ensure the continuation of the trust responsibility of the United States to Indian tribes and Indian individuals, . . . [and] to permit an orderly transition from Federal domination of programs and services to provide Indian tribes with meaningful authority to plan, conduct, redesign, and administer programs, services, functions, and activities that meet the needs of the individual tribal communities. . . ." (Ibid.)

3. 101 St. 386 (1987).

4. 1 St. 50 (1789).

5. 101 St. 386 (1987).

6. 1 St. 50, 52 (1789).

7. U.S. Senate, *Final Report and Legislative Recommendations: A Report of the Special Committee on Investigations of the Select Committee on Indian Affairs*, Senate Report No. 101–216, 101st Cong., 1st sess. (1989). Forty-two similar congressional investigations of corruption and mismanagement preceded the 1989 investigation.

8. Robert Dahl, "Decision-Making in a Democracy: The Supreme Court as a National Policy-Maker," *Journal of Public Law* 6 (1957): 293.

9. 485 U.S. 660, 672 (1988).

10. 102 St. 130 (1988).

11. As quoted in Francis P. Prucha, ed., *Documents of United States Indian Policy*, 2d ed. (Lincoln: University of Nebraska Press, 1990), 240–241.

12. Alaska Native Claims Settlement Act, 101 St. 1788; Indian Housing Act, 102 St. 676; Education Amendments Act, 102 St. 1603; Indian Financing Act, 102 St. 1763; Indian Self-Determination Act Amendments, 102 St. 2285; Indian Reorganization Act Amendments, 102 St. 2938; Navajo & Hopi Indian Relocation and Amendments Act, 102 St. 3929; and Indian Health Care Act Amendments, 102 St. 4784.

13. Land taken into trust for Pechanga Band of Luiseno Mission Indians, 102 St. 897; Land Claim of Coushatta Tribe of Louisiana, 102 St. 1097; Reservation for Confederated Tribe of Grande Ronde Community of Oregon, 102 St. 1594; and Quinault Reservation Expansion Act, 102 St. 3327.

14. See the Lac Vieux Band of Lake Superior Chippewa Indians Act, 102 St. 1577.

15. See Economic Development Plan for the Northwestern Shoshone, 102 St. 1575.

16. See Indian Gaming Regulatory Act, 102 St. 2647.

17. See Colorado Ute Indian Water Rights Settlement Act, 102 St. 973.

18. 103 St. 1336 (1989).

19. 104 St. 473 (1990).

20. 104 St. 883 (1990).

21. 104 St. 1292 (1990).

22. 104 St. 3048 (1990).

23. 105 St. 646 (1991).

24. See especially Francis P. Prucha, *American Indian Policy in Crisis: Christian Reformers and the Indian, 1865–1900* (Norman: University of Oklahoma Press, 1976), and his study *The Churches and the Indian Schools: 1888–1912* (Lincoln: University of Nebraska Press, 1979); and Jill E. Martin, "Constitutional Rights and Indian Rites: An Uneasy Balance," *Western Legal History* 3 (1990): 245–269.

25. See Prucha, *American Indian Policy* (1976).

26. Ibid., 57, quoting "Address of the Catholic Clergy. . . ."

27. 24 St. 388 (1887).

28. 43 St. 253 (1924).

29. Vine Deloria Jr., "The Distinctive Status of Indian Rights," in Peter Iverson, ed., *The Plains Indians of the Twentieth Century* (Norman: University of Oklahoma Press, 1985), 245.

30. 92 St. 469 (1978).

31. Deloria, "The Distinctive Status," 247.

32. Wilcomb Washburn, "Indian Policy Since the 1880s," in Sandra L. Cadwalader and Vine Deloria Jr., eds., *The Aggressions of Civilization* (Philadelphia: Temple University Press, 1984), 53.

33. U.S. *Congressional Record* (1978), 2144.

34. *Lyng v. Northwest Indian Cemetery Protective Association*, 485 U.S. 439, 458 (1988).

35. Letter from Thomas L. McKenney, head of the newly established Bureau of Indian Affairs, to Captain George Gray, an Indian agent, dated January 16, 1826. Source: *American State Papers: Documents, Legislative and Executive, of the Congress of the United States*, vol. 2, *Indian Affairs* (Washington: Gales & Seaton, 1834), 707.

36. *Cantwell v. Connecticut*, 310 U.S. 296, 303 (1939).

37. See, e.g., *Sherbert v. Verner*, 374 U.S. 398, 403, 406–409 (1963); and *Wisconsin v. Yoder*, 406 U.S. 205 (1972). "These cases established that the Court will balance the secular interest asserted by the government against the claim of religious liberty asserted by the person affected and only if the governmental interest is compelling and if no alternative forms of regulation would serve that interest is the claimant to be required to yield." Source: U.S. Senate, Document No. 99-16, *The Constitution of the United States of America: Analysis and Interpretation*. 99th Cong., 1st sess. (Washington: Government Printing Office, 1987), 991. [Note: this document was prepared by Johnny H. Killian, ed. of the Congressional Research Service.]

38. Deloria & Lytle, *American Indians, American Justice*, 231.

39. U.S. Supreme Court, *Records and Briefs*, "Brief for the Indian Respondents in Opposition," 2.

40. Ibid.

41. U.S. Supreme Court, *Records and Briefs*, "Brief for the Indian Respondents," 5.

42. Ibid., 6–7.

43. U.S. Supreme Court, *Records and Briefs*, "Brief for the Petitioners," 5.

44. *Lyng*, 485 U.S. 439, 462, Brennan dissent (1988).

45. U.S. Supreme Court, *Records and Briefs*, "Brief for the Indian Respondents," 9.

46. 92 St. 469 (1978).

47. U.S., Federal Agencies Task Force, *American Indian Religious Freedom Act Report*, P.L. 95-341 (August 1979), Appendix A.

48. 485 U.S. 439, 442 (1988).

49. Ibid.

50. U.S., *American Indian Religious Freedom Act Report*," 27.

51. 485 U.S. 439, 443 (1988).

52. Ibid.

53. Ibid.

54. *California v. Block* and *Northwest Indian Cemetery Protective Association v. Peterson*. Vine Deloria Jr. has raised an interesting question regarding exactly who instituted the suit—the Indians or the other groups. "The question is interesting in this respect: if the Indians initiated the suit, their theory of the spiritual value of the lands should have been the primary argument; if not, the secular perspective of the other plaintiffs may have determined the arguments that were used." ("Trouble in High Places," 276.)

55. 485 U.S. 439, 443 (1988).

56. *Northwest Indian Cemetery Protective Association v. Peterson*, 565 F. Supp. 586 (1983).

57. Deloria, "Trouble in High Places," 276.

58. 98 St. 1619 (1984).

59. U.S. House, Committee on Interior and Insular Affairs, *California Wilderness Act of 1983*, House Report No. 98-40, 98th Cong., 1st sess. (1983).

60. Deloria, "Trouble in High Places," 282.

61. *Northwest Indian Cemetery Protective Association v. Peterson*, 795 F.2d 688 (1986).

62. 485 U.S. 439, 445 (1988).

63. Ibid.

64. Ibid., 446.

65. Ibid.

66. Ibid., 447.

67. Ibid., 451–452.

68. 374 U.S. 398, 412 (1963).

69. 485 U.S. 439, 451 (1988).

70. 476 U.S. 693 (1986).

71. Ibid., 696 (1986).

72. 485 U.S. 439, 449 (1988).

73. Ibid., 470 (1988).

74. Ibid., 470–471 (1988).

75. Ibid., 471–472 (1988).

76. Ibid., 450 (1988).

77. Ibid., 465 (1988).

78. Ibid.
79. Ibid., 468 (1988).
80. Ibid., 469 (1988).
81. Ibid., 451 (1988).
82. Ibid., 475–476 (1988).
83. Ibid., 452–453 (1988).
84. Ibid., 476 (1988).
85. Ibid., 454 (1988).
86. Ibid., 455.
87. Ibid., 471 (1988).
88. Ibid., 452 (1988).
89. Ibid., 460 (1988).
90. Ibid., 460–461 (1988).
91. On May 24, 1996, President Clinton issued an executive order to promote accommodation of access to sites considered holy by Indian religious practitioners and to provide additional security for the physical integrity of these sacred sites. However, less than a month later, a federal district court in *Bear Lodge Multiple Use Association v. Babbitt* undermined these same religious rights when it ruled that the National Park Service could not "voluntarily" ban rock climbers during the month of June to accommodate the religious rights of several tribes whose members hold ceremonies at Devils Tower, Wyoming, a sacred site to the Indians, as well as a national monument. The federal government's ambivalent attitude toward the religious rights of indigenous peoples continues.
92. Deloria, "Trouble in High Places," 285.
93. U.S., "Oral Arguments" before the Supreme Court, November 30, 1987, in *The Complete Oral Arguments of the Supreme Court of the United States, 1987 Term* (Frederick, Md.: University Publications of America, 1987), 17.
94. Ibid., 25.
95. Ibid.
96. David Kairys, *With Liberty and Justice for Some: A Critique of the Conservative Supreme Court* (New York: The New Press, 1993), 106.
97. Testimony of Vine Deloria Jr., U.S. Congress, Senate, *Hearing Before the Select Committee on Indian Affairs*, 102d Cong., 2d sess., S. Hearing 102–698 (March 7, 1992), 76.
98. Steve Pavlik, "The U.S. Supreme Court Decision on Peyote in *Employment Division v. Smith*: A Case Study in the Suppression of Native American Religious Freedom," *Wicazo Sa Review* 8 (Fall 1992): 38.
99. *Code of Federal Regulations*, volume 21, chapter 11, section 1307.31 (1990), 82. At least one federal court ruling, *Peyote Way Church of God v. Thornburgh* (922 F.2d 1210 [5th Cir.] 1991), has held that the use of peyote and membership in the NAC is limited to Indians who have at least 25% blood quantum and who belong to federally recognized tribes. But see *U.S. v. Boyll* (724 F. Supp. 1333, 1991), a federal district court decision for the district of New Mexico, which held that peyote use could not be restricted to Indians.

100. See especially *People v. Woody*, 61 Cal. 2d 716 (1964); Welton LaBarre, *The Peyote Cult*, 4th ed. (New York: Schocken Books, 1975); and Omer C. Stewart, *Peyote: A History* (Norman: University of Oklahoma Press, 1987).

101. 707 P.2d 1274 (1985).

102. 721 P.2d 445 (1986).

103. 374 U.S. 398 (1963).

104. 450 U.S. 707 (1981).

105. 721 P.2d 445, 449 (1986).

106. 108 S. Ct. 1444 (1988).

107. Ibid., 1452.

108. Ibid., 1454–1455.

109. Ibid., 1455.

110. 763 P.2d 146, 148 (1988).

111. 108 S. Ct. 1445 (1988).

112. *Equal Employment Opportunity Commission v. ADAPT*, Civ. No. C85-6139-E (D.Or.).

113. U.S. Supreme Court, *Records and Briefs*, "Brief in Opposition to Petition for Writ of Certiorari," Craig J. Dorsay, Respondent's Counsel, 2.

114. Ibid.

115. Richard A. Brisbin Jr., "Justice Antonin Scalia, Constitutional Discourse, and the Legalistic State," *The Western Political Quarterly* 44 (December 1991): 1005–1038.

116. W. John Moore, "Great Right Hope," *National Journal* 24 (1992), 1659.

117. 110 S. Ct. 1595, 1616 n. 2 (1990).

118. Ibid., 1599.

119. Ibid., 1600.

120. Ibid., 1608.

121. Ibid.

122. Ibid.

123. Ibid., 1602.

124. Ibid., 1609.

125. 98 U.S. 145 (1878).

126. *People v. Woody*, 394 P.2d 813, 820 (1964).

127. Ibid.

128. 374 U.S. 398 (1963).

129. 110 S. Ct. 1595, 1608 (1990).

130. Ibid., 1609.

131. Ibid., 1602.

132. Ibid.

133. 455 U.S. 252 (1982).

134. 401 U.S. 437 (1971).

135. 476 U.S. 693 (1986).

136. 475 U.S. 503 (1986).

137. 110 S. Ct. 1595, 1603 (1990).

138. Ibid.

139. Ibid., 1610.

140. Ibid., 1611.

141. Ibid., 1603.

142. Ibid.

143. Ibid., 1615–1616.

144. Ibid., 1604.

145. Ibid., 1612.

146. Ibid., 1620–1621.

147. Ibid., 1621.

148. Ibid., 1604.

149. Ibid., 1621.

150. Ibid., 1605.

151. Ibid., 1612–1613.

152. Ibid., 1616.

153. Ibid., 1606.

154. Ibid., 1613.

155. Ibid.

156. Ibid., 1614.

157. Ibid., 1616.

158. Ibid., 1618 n. 4.

159. Felix S. Cohen, "Indian Self-Government," in Lucy Cohen, ed., *The Legal Conscience: Selected Papers of Felix S. Cohen* (New Haven: Yale University Press, 1960), 314.

160. Linda Greenhouse, "Court Is Urged to Rehear Case on Ritual Drug," *The New York Times*, May 11, 1990: 16.

161. For example, the Association on American Indian Affairs, the Native American Rights Fund, the National Congress of American Indians, and various "green" groups.

162. 105 St. 646 (1991).

163. 107 St. 1488 (1993).

164. See S. 1021, "Native American Free Exercise of Religion Act of 1993," in Senate Hearing, 103–347, Hearing Before the Committee on Indian Affairs, 103d Cong., 1st sess., September 10, 1993 (Washington: Government Printing Office, 1994), 4–52.

165. 108 St. 3125.

166. U.S. *Congressional Record* (May 25, 1993), 56456.

167. Cohen, *Handbook of Federal Indian Law*, 1992 ed., 117.

168. 24 St. 388 (1887).

169. 45 St. 1185 (1929).

170. 30 St. 717 (1898).

171. 67 St. 588 (1953).

172. 24 F. Cas. 937 (1834).

173. 28 F. Cas. 397 (1863).

174. 104 U.S. 621 (1882).

175. Wilkinson, *American Indians, Time, and the Law*, 88.

176. Ibid.

177. Cohen, *Handbook of Federal Indian Law*, 1992 ed., 116.

178. 358 U.S. 217 (1959).

179. 380 U.S. 685 (1965).

180. 411 U.S. 164 (1973).

181. 31 U.S. (6 Pet.) 515 (1832).

182. 358 U.S. 217, 220 (1959).

183. Ibid., 219.

184. 380 U.S. 685, 690 (1965).

185. 411 U.S. 164 (1973).

186. 448 U.S. 136 (1980).

187. Ibid., 142.

188. Ibid., 143.

189. Ibid.

190. Ibid.

191. 480 U.S. 202 (1987).

192. 471 U.S. 759 (1985).

193. Ibid., 765.

194. 480 U.S. 202, 215 n. 17.

195. 490 U.S. 163 (1989).

196. Ibid., 173.

197. 490 U.S. 163, 204.

198. 109 S. Ct. 2994 (1989).

199. Ibid., 3008.

200. Ibid.

201. 12 St. 951 (1855).

202. Washington State Constitution, Article XXVI, Provision 2. *West's Revised Code of Washington Annotated: Constitution of the State of Washington* (St. Paul, Minn.: West Publishing, 1988).

203. See McDonnell, *The Dispossession of the American Indian*, 2.

204. 34 St. 182 (1906).

205. U.S. Commissioner of Indian Affairs, *Annual Report* (1918), 3.

206. Ibid.

207. McDonnell, *The Dispossession of the American Indian*, 108.

208. 44 St. 1247 (1927).

209. Cohen, *Handbook of Federal Indian Law*, 1972 ed., 259.

210. Ibid.

211. 48 St. 984 (1934).

212. U.S. Supreme Court, *Records & Briefs*, "Cross-Petition for a Writ of Certiorari," R. Wayne Bjur, Attorney for Respondent/Cross-Petitioner (Confederated Tribes and Bands of the Yakima Nation), 6 n. 4.

213. McDonnell, *The Dispossession of the American Indian*, 121.

214. Ibid., 8.

215. U.S. Supreme Court, *Records & Briefs*, "Cross-Petition for a Writ of Certiorari," R. Wayne Bjur, 7.

216. Ibid., 8.

217. 112 S. Ct. 683, 687 (1992).

218. U.S. Supreme Court, *Records & Briefs*, "Brief of Petitioners/Cross-Respondents, County of Yakima and Dale A. Gray, Yakima County Treasurer," Jeffrey C. Sullivan, 4.

219. U.S. Supreme Court, *Records & Briefs*, "Brief of Respondents/Cross-Petitioner, Confederated Tribes and Bands of the Yakima Indian Nation," R. Wayne Bjur, 9 n. 5.

220. An ad valorem tax is a tax on the value of property.

221. An excise tax is a tax on the manufacture, sale, or consumption of commodities or upon licenses to pursue certain occupations or upon corporate privileges.

222. 412 U.S. 481 (1973).

223. 425 U.S. 463 (1976).

224. 419 U.S. 544 (1975).

225. 425 U.S. 463, 479 (1976).

226. Ibid.

227. U.S. Supreme Court, *Records & Briefs, Confederated Tribes and Bands of the Yakima Nation v. County of Yakima*, Appendix D, United States District Court for the Eastern District of Washington, No. C-87–654–AAM (1988): 39a.

228. U.S. *Official Transcript Proceedings Before the Supreme Court of the United States* (Washington: Alderson Reporting Company, 1992), 8.

229. 903 F.2d 1207, 1215 (1990).

230. Blackmun's was the lone dissent. Thurgood Marshall retired in 1991. He was replaced by Clarence Thomas, a conservative jurist, who had been narrowly confirmed by the Senate, 52–48. William Brennan, another liberal retiree, had been replaced in 1990 by a virtually unknown moderate-conservative, David Souter.

231. 17 U.S. 316 (1819).

232. 72 U.S. (5 Wall.) 737, 755–756 (1867).

233. Ibid., 757.

234. 224 U.S. 665 (1912).

235. 35 St. 312 (1908).

236. Grant Foreman, "The U.S. Courts and the Indian," *The Overland Monthly* 61 (1913): 578.

237. 224 U.S. 665, 673 (1912).

238. Ibid., 673.

239. Ibid., 674.

240. Ibid., 677.

241. Ibid.

242. 72 U.S. (5 Wall.) 737, 756 (1867).

243. 34 St. 187 (1906).

244. Justice Thurgood Marshall used this phrase in *McClanahan v. Arizona State Tax Commission*, 411 U.S. 164 (1973).

245. 112 S. Ct. 683, 688.

246. Ibid., 688 – 689 n. 2.
247. Ibid., 689 n. 2
248. Ibid., 690.
249. Ibid., 691.
250. Ibid.
251. Ibid., 693.
252. Ibid.
253. Ibid.
254. Ibid., 693.
255. Ibid.
256. Ibid., 692 – 693.
257. Ibid., 693.
258. Ibid., 694.
259. Ibid., 698.
260. Ibid., 696.
261. Ibid.
262. Ibid.
263. Ibid., 695.
264. Ibid., 696.
265. Ibid.
266. Ibid., 698.
267. Ibid.

CHAPTER 7

1. As quoted in Ephraim London, ed., *The World of Law: The Law in Literature*, vol. 1 (New York: Simon & Schuster, 1960), xviii.

2. David Kairys, *With Liberty and Justice for Some: A Critique of the Conservative Supreme Court* (New York: The New Press, 1993), 182.

3. Ibid., 183.
4. Ibid., 187.
5. 307 U.S. 496 (1939).
6. 112 S. Ct. 2701 (1992).
7. Ibid., 188.
8. Ibid.

9. Petra T. Shattuck and Jill Norgren, *Partial Justice: Federal Indian Law in a Liberal Constitutional System* (Providence, R.I.: Berg Publishers, 1991), 190.

10. Ibid., 194.
11. Ibid., 191.
12. Ibid.

13. In 1995, two federal appellate court decisions were handed down which indicate that conservative ideology is now the dominant paradigm of judges at that level. On November 7, 1995, the Court of Appeals for the 8th Circuit in

South Dakota v. United States Department of Interior (64 USLW 2316) held, in a remarkable opinion which places in doubt the status of all Indian land acquired by the government and placed in trust, that the section of the Indian Reorganization Act of 1934 which had authorized the Secretary of the Interior to acquire land in trust for Indians was actually an unconstitutionally delegated legislative power.

A month later, on December 26, 1995, the 10th Circuit Court of Appeals in an equally troubling decision, *Crow Tribe of Indians and Thomas L. Ten Bear v. Repsis* (73 F.3d 982), resurrected the repudiated doctrines of *Ward v. Race Horse* and held that *Race Horse* was "compelling, well-reasoned, and persuasive." Thus, the State of Wyoming's Game and Fish Commission had jurisdiction over Crow Indians even though they were exercising treaty-specific hunting rights.

14. 132 L. Ed.2d 400.

15. In diminishment cases, the Supreme Court has sought to answer the question whether allotment-era laws which opened reservations to non-Indian settlement worked to "diminish" the size of the reservation to encompass only the lands allotted to individual tribal members; or, on the other hand, whether the reservation boundary was left intact and simply allowed non-Indians to homestead within the reservation. For a good discussion of this important issue, see Robert Laurence, "The Unseemly Nature of Reservation by Judicial, as Opposed to Legislative, Fiat and the Ironic Role of the Indian Civil Rights Act in Limiting Both," *North Dakota Law Review* 71 (1995): 392–413; and see the responses to Laurence's piece in the ensuing pages by James A. Grijalva, Alex Tallchief Skibine, Frank Pommersheim, and others.

The "diminishment" cases are: *Seymour v. Superintendent*, 368 U.S. 351 (1962); *Mattz v. Arnett*, 412 U.S. 481 (1973); *DeCoteau v. District County Court*, 420 U.S. 425 (1975); *Rosebud Sioux Tribe v. Kneip*, 430 U.S. 584 (1977); *Solem v. Bartlett*, 465 U.S. 463 (1984); and *Hagen v. Utah*, 114 S. Ct. 968 (1994).

16. Pommersheim, *Braid of Feathers*, 152.

17. 62 USLW 4482.

18. 102 St. 2475 (1988). This act imposed upon those states which sponsor Class III gaming (e.g., slot machines, casino games, banking card games, dog racing, and lotteries) a duty to negotiate in good faith a tribal-state compact with those resident Indian tribes who also wanted to pursue Class III gaming ventures. It also authorized a tribe to bring suit in federal court against a state in order to force performance of that duty in the event the state chose not to negotiate in good faith.

19. Sidney L. Harring, *Crow Dog's Case: American Indian Sovereignty, Tribal Law, and United States Law in the Nineteenth Century* (New York: Cambridge University Press, 1994), 12.

20. 72 U.S. (5 Wall.) 737, 758 (1866).

21. 109 U.S. 556, 571 (1883).

22. 163 U.S. 376, 384 (1896).

23. 198 U.S. 371, 381 (1905).

24. 455 U.S. 130, 148 (1982).

25. Ball, "Constitution, Court, Indian Tribe," *American Bar Foundation Research Journal* 1 (Winter 1987): 138.

26. James E. Falkowski, *Indian Law/Race Law: A Five-Hundred-Year History* (New York: Praeger Publishers, 1992), 2.

27. Ibid., 2.

28. Ball, "Constitution," 137–138.

Glossary

Ad inconvenienti: Legal term meaning 'from inconvenience.' Describes an argument founded upon the hardship of the case and the inconvenience or disastrous consequences to which a course of reasoning would lead.

Aboriginal title (also known as Indian title or Indian right of occupancy): Broadly defined, this refers to ownership of the lands inhabited by a tribe based on immemorial rights arising long before contact with Euro-Americans. Under federal Indian law, there is contrary precedent on the actual status of aboriginally held Indian lands, with some decisions referring to Indian title as a "mere" right of occupancy and other cases describing it as a "sacred" right of occupancy. All federal case law does agree that while aboriginal Indian title involves the tribes' holding an exclusive right of occupancy (a possessory interest), it does not involve the ultimate fee, which is said to reside in the United States, unless Congress has given title to the tribe or the land has been purchased outright by the tribe.

Ad valorem tax: A tax imposed on the value of property; a tax of a fixed proportion of the value of the property to be charged. The most common ad valorem tax is that imposed by states, counties, and cities on real estate.

Adversarial method: System of fact-finding used in American trials in which each side is represented by an attorney who acts as an advocate.

Affirm: In appellate court, to reach a decision that agrees with the result reached in a case by the lower court.

Affirmative delegation: Legal doctrine that tribes possess only those powers of self-governance specifically mentioned in treaties or which Congress has positively granted to them via statute.

Allotment policy (also known as General Allotment or the Dawes Act): Federal Indian policy initiated in 1887 (ended in 1934 with the enactment of the Indian Reorganization Act) designed to break up tribal governments, abolish Indian reservations by the allotment of communally held reservation lands to individual Indians for private ownership, and force Indians to assimilate into Euro-American cultural society.

Amicus curiae: Legal term meaning 'friend of the court'; a person not a party to litigation who volunteers or is invited by the court to give an opinion on a case.

Appellate court: A court having jurisdiction of appeal and review; a court to which causes are removable by appeal, certiorari, error, or report.

Assimilation: The biological, cultural, social, and psychological fusion of distinct groups to create a new, ethnically homogenized society.

Balancing test: A process of judicial decision making in which a court weighs the relative merits of the rights of the individual against the interests of the government.

Brief: A written argument of law and fact submitted to a court by an attorney representing a party having an interest in a lawsuit.

Bureau of Indian Affairs (BIA): A federal agency established in 1824 and moved to the Department of the Interior in 1849. Originally, BIA personnel served as a diplomatic corps responsible for overseeing trade and other relations with Indian tribes. By the 1860s, however, it had evolved into the lead colonizing agent for the federal government and dominated virtually every aspect of tribal life within reservations. Today, the BIA is more involved in advocating programs focused on tribal educational, social, economic, and cultural self-determination.

Burden of proof: The need to establish a claim or allegation; in a criminal case, the state has the burden of proof.

Canons of construction: The system of basic rules and maxims which are recognized as governing the construction or interpretation of written instruments. In federal Indian law, for example, treaties, agreements, and laws are to be construed in a manner favorable to Indian tribes or their members. See also *Treaty.*

Categorical allowance: Legal mask which holds that state governments, despite evidence to the contrary, have been authorized by Congress to tax Indians in certain situations.

Certification, writ of: A procedure whereby a lower court requests that a superior court rule on specified legal questions so that the lower court may correctly apply the law.

Certiorari, writ of: A writ issued from the Supreme Court, at its discretion and at the request of a petitioner, to order a lower court to send the record of a case to the Court for its review. There is a requirement that four Supreme Court justices agree to hear a case before it can be considered by the Supreme Court.

Circuit court of appeal: An intermediate level appellate court in the federal system having jurisdiction over a particular region.

Civil law: The body of law dealing with the private rights of individuals (e.g., negligence, contracts, property), as contrasted with criminal law.

Clan: A division of a tribe tracing descent from a common ancestor. Typically, a clan shares a common identity, level of organization, and property base.

Collateral estoppel: A legal rule that prohibits an already settled issue's being retried in another form.

Commerce clause: The provision of the federal Constitution, Article I, section 8, clause 3, which gives Congress exclusive powers over interstate commerce. It states that "The Congress shall have the power to . . . regulate Commerce with foreign Nations, and among the several States, and with the Indian Tribes."

This clause is one of the two bases (the other being the Treaty Clause) considered sufficient to empower the federal government to deal with Indian tribes.

Communal land ownership: A system of community ownership rather than individual possession.

Compelling state interest: One which the state is forced or obliged to protect. Term used to uphold state action in the face of attack grounded on Equal Protection or First Amendment rights because of serious need for such state action. See also *Strict scrutiny test.*

Concurring opinion: An opinion by a justice that agrees with the result reached by the majority in a case but disagrees with the Court's rationale for its decision.

Conquest, doctrine of: Legal doctrine under international law which entails the acquisition of territory by a victorious state from a defeated state in warfare. The state acquiring by conquest is regarded as the successor to the rights and duties previously applicable to the territory.

Consent: A concurrence of wills. Consent always implies freedom of judgment, deliberation, and freely given acquiescence in what is considered desirable. Consent is a material element in the political relationship between tribal nations and the U.S. established in the 1787 Northwest Ordinance, which said that "the utmost good faith shall always be observed toward the Indians, their lands and their property shall never be taken from them without their consent. . . ." The political principle of consent holds that the U.S. may validly take political or legal actions towards tribal rights or resources only with the express consent of the tribe or tribes involved.

Consent decree: A regulatory agency procedure to induce voluntary compliance with its policies. A consent order usually takes the form of a formal agreement whereby an organization or industry agrees to stop a practice in exchange for the agency's cessation of legal action against it.

Criminal law: Law governing the relationship between individuals and society. It deals with the enforcement of laws and the punishment of those who, by violating laws, commit crimes.

Declaratory judgment: A court rule determining a legal right or interpretation of the law but not imposing any relief or remedy.

Demonstrably serious: Legal test which holds that states can exercise jurisdiction over fee land within a reservation unless the tribe can prove that the impact of the state action will be "demonstrably serious" and will imperil the political integrity, economic security, or the health and welfare of the tribal members.

Demurrer: A motion to dismiss a lawsuit in which the defendant admits to the facts alleged by the plaintiff but contends that those facts are insufficient to justify a legal cause of action.

Dependency status: Legal mask which unilaterally reduced tribes from a status as independent nations to a position of subservient dependency in their relation to the U.S. government. See also *Guardianship/wardship.*

Dichotomization of federal Indian law: Theory that tribal nations cannot expect any consistent political relationship with the federal government because of the conflicting goals, policy orientations, and legal perspectives wielded by the three branches of the federal government and the states (e.g., whether tribes are delegated sovereigns or inherent sovereigns; whether tribes are included in general congressional acts or are excluded from the force of those measures; whether tribes are incorporated in the U.S. constitutional framework or remain largely extraconstitutional polities in their relationship to the federal government.

Discovery, doctrine of: This doctrine was first fully articulated in U.S. law in the seminal Supreme Court case *Johnson v. McIntosh* in 1823. The Court held that European explorers' "discovery" of land occupied by Indian tribes gave the discovering European nation (and the U.S. as successor) "an exclusive right to extinguish the Indian titles of occupancy, either by purchase or conquest." This meant that the "discovering" nation had preempted other European powers' involvement with the tribes in a particular geographic area. More importantly, as interpreted by western policymakers and legal scholars, this doctrine effectively excluded Indian tribes from direct participation as national entities in the process of international community development.

Dissenting opinion: A formal written opinion by a justice who disagrees with the result reached by the majority.

Domestic-dependent nation: Phrase coined by Chief Justice John Marshall in the 1831 case *Cherokee Nation v. Georgia* to describe the status of tribal nations vis-à-vis their relationship to the federal government. The Court concluded that tribes lacked foreign national status because of their geographic proximity in the United States, were not states within the meaning of the U.S. Constitution, but still had a significant degree of internal autonomy as "domestic-dependent nations."

Due process: Government procedures that follow principles of essential fairness. The Fifth and Fourteenth amendments guarantee persons that they will not be deprived of life, liberty, or property by the government until fair and usual procedures have been followed.

Equal footing: Doctrine which holds that states newly admitted into the Union are on an equal footing with the original states in all respects. Every new state is entitled to exercise all the powers of government which belong to the original states. This condition of equality applies primarily to political standing and sovereignty rather than to economic or property rights.

Equity: Law based on principles of fairness rather than strictly applied statutes.

Error, writ of: An order issued by an appeals court commanding a lower court to send up the full record of a case so that it may be reviewed for error.

Establishment clause: That provision of the First Amendment to the U.S. Constitution which provides that "Congress shall make no law respecting an establishment of religion, or prohibiting the free exercise thereof. . . ." This language prohibits a state or the federal government from creating a church, or enacting laws which aid one, or all, religions, or giving preference to one religion, or forcing belief or disbelief in any religion.

Ex parte: A hearing in which only one party to a dispute is present.

Excise tax: A tax on the manufacture, sale, or consumption of a product. It embraces every form of tax burdens not laid directly upon persons or property.

Exclusion: Theory that congressional laws do not apply to tribal nations unless Congress expressly writes them into the legislative measure. See *Inclusion*.

Exclusive powers: Powers reserved for either the federal government, state government, or tribal government, but not exercised by all three.

Extraconstitutional: Outside the constitutional framework. Tribes were preexisting and original sovereigns and did not participate in the creation of the U.S. Constitution which focused on the establishment of the federal government and the relationship between the central government and the constituent states. Thus, tribal sovereign rights do not arise from and are not protected by the provisions of the Constitution. The Indian Civil Rights Act of 1968 modified the relationship slightly because portions of the Constitution's first ten amendments, for the first time, were made applicable to tribal governments in their treatment of persons under tribal jurisdiction.

Federalism, dual: A nineteenth-century concept that the functions and responsibilities of the federal and state governments were theoretically distinguished and functionally separate from each other.

Federally recognized tribes: Indian tribes recognized by the federal government as self-governing entities with whom the U.S. maintains a government-to-government political relationship. This relationship may be established by treaty or agreement recognition, congressional legislation, executive order action, judicial ruling, or by the secretary of the interior's decision. Recognized tribes are eligible for special services and benefits designated solely for such tribes (e.g., Bureau of Indian Affairs educational and law-enforcement assistance, Indian Health Service care), but they also benefit by and are subject to the federal government's trust doctrine and plenary power.

Fee-simple ownership: An estate in land of which the inheritor has unqualified ownership and sole power of disposition.

Five Civilized Tribes: A term coined by whites for the remarkable social, educational, economic, and political progress made by the Cherokee, Choctaw, Chickasaw, Seminole, and Creek Indians after their coerced removal from the Southeast to lands west of the Mississippi during the Indian Removal era of the 1830s and 1840s.

Free Exercise Clause: The First Amendment to the U.S. Constitution, which provides that "Congress shall make no law respecting an establishment of religion, or prohibiting the free exercise thereof." See also *Establishment clause*.

Geographic incorporation: Legal doctrine that tribes, by residing within what are considered the territorial boundaries of the U.S., are subject to the political jurisdiction of the federal government.

Good faith: Legal doctrine first articulated in the Northwest Ordinance of 1787 which expressly states that the federal government shall always observe "the utmost good faith towards the Indian tribes. . . ." Good faith is a state of mind denoting honesty of purpose, freedom from intention to defraud, and, generally speaking, means being faithful to one's duty or obligation. According to the federal courts, an act is done in good faith if done honestly, even though negligently.

Guardianship/wardship: The legally specious characterization of the political relationship between tribes and the federal government, now largely defunct, often attributed to Chief Justice John Marshall in his 1831 ruling in *Cherokee Nation v. Georgia,* where he asserted that Indian tribes were not foreign nations but were "domestic-dependent nations" whose relationship to the United States "resembled that of a ward to a guardian." As the federal government's allotment and assimilation campaign mushroomed in the 1880s, Marshall's analogy of Indian wardship to federal guardians became reified in the minds of federal policymakers and Bureau of Indian Affairs officials, who popularized the phrase and relied on it to justify any number of federal activities (e.g., suppression of Indian religious freedom, forced allotment of Indian lands, unilateral abrogation of Indian treaty rights) designed to hasten the assimilation of Indian people into mainstream American society. Despite the federal government's reliance on the phrase, Indian wardship and federal guardianship remained an illusion which was unsupported by legal authority or tribal consent.

Harmless error: Legal doctrine that minor or harmless errors during a trial do not require reversal of the judgment by an appellate court. An error is considered "harmless" if reviewing court, after viewing the entire record, determines that no substantial rights of the defendant were affected and that the error did not influence or only slightly influenced the verdict.

Implicit divestiture: Legal doctrine that tribes, by becoming subject to the dominant sovereignty of the U.S. via geographic incorporation, implicitly surrendered or were divested of certain sovereign powers, for example, criminal jurisdiction over non-Indians. According to this doctrine, unless a tribe has been affirmatively delegated governing powers via express treaty (or agreement) provisions or explicit congressional enactments, then it is assumed that those non-specified powers have been "impliedly" lost to the tribes. See also *Affirmative delegation.*

Implied repeal: The superseding of an existing law, rule, or treaty provision without an express directive to that effect.

Incidental effect: Legal test which holds that if, for example, prohibiting the exercise of religion is not the object of the law but merely the incidental effect of a generally applicable and otherwise valid provision, then the First Amendment has not been offended.

Inclusion: Theory that congressional laws apply to tribal nations unless Congress explicitly states in the measure that tribes are to be excluded from the act's provisions. See *Exclusion.*

Indian Civil Rights Act: A congressional law passed in 1968, the ICRA was the first legislation to impose many of the provisions of the U.S. Bill of Rights on the actions of tribal governments vis-à-vis reservation residents; set out a model code for courts of Indian offenses; and required states to secure tribal consent before assuming legal jurisdiction in Indian Country.

Indian Claims Commission: Congress established this commission in 1946 in an effort to resolve the hundreds of accumulated claims tribes had against the federal government, frequently stemming from the federal government's failure to fulfill prior treaty or agreement terms. Designed as a commission but working more as an adversarial judicial body, the commission awarded over $800 million on nearly 300 claims before it was terminated by Congress in 1978. A number of unresolved tribal claims were passed on to the U.S. Court of Claims.

Indian Country: Broadly, it is country within which Indian laws and customs and federal laws relating to Indians are generally applicable. But it is also defined as all the land under the supervision and protection of the United States government that has been set aside primarily for the use of Indians. This includes all Indian reservations and any other areas (e.g., all other Indian communities, including the various pueblos and Indian lands in Oklahoma, and individual Indian allotments which are still held in trust by the federal government) under federal jurisdiction and designated for Indian use. And according to some courts, it also includes privately held non-Indian lands within the boundaries of Indian reservations, rights-of-way (including federal and state highways), and any additional lands tribes may have acquired.

Indian removal: Federal policy enacted in 1830 and lasting into the 1850s which authorized the president to negotiate with a majority of eastern (and other) tribes for their relocation to lands west of the Mississippi River.

Indian Reorganization Act: Commonly known as the Wheeler-Howard Act, this 1934 congressional measure is considered by most knowledgeable sources to be the most important piece of Indian legislation enacted in the twentieth century. Largely the brainchild of Commissioner of Indian Affairs John Collier, the IRA provided, for those tribes that adopted it, an end to the devastating allotment policy, for the purchase of new lands to offset some of those lost through allotment, a measure of economic restoration, cultural regeneration, and the opportunity for tribes to adopt constitutionally based governments.

Indian self-determination policy: While the federal government had turned towards Indian self-determination in the 1960s, the policy was officially inaugurated by President Richard Nixon in 1970 and by Congress in 1975 through the Indian Self-Determination and Education Assistance Act. As Nixon proclaimed: "Both as a matter of justice and as a matter of enlightened social policy, we must begin to act on the basis of what the Indians themselves have long been telling us. The time has come to break decisively with the past and to create the conditions for a new era in which the Indian future is determined by Indian acts and Indian decisions." To ensure tribal input into decision making, Congress directed the secretaries of the appropriate agencies, upon the request of any Indian tribe, to enter into contracts with tribes to design, carry out, and evaluate programs and services previously provided by the federal government.

Indian Territory: Lands west of the Mississippi River, principally present-day

Oklahoma and Kansas. This area eventually became the home of many relocated eastern and other tribes, including the Five Civilized Tribes.

Indigenous: The United Nations Working Group on Indigenous Populations defines indigenous populations as those "composed of the existing descendants of peoples who inhabited the present territory of a country wholly or partially at the time when persons of a different culture or ethnic origin arrived there from other parts of the world, overcame them, and by conquest, settlement or other means, reduced them to a nondominant or colonial situation; who today live more in conformity with their particular social, economic and cultural customs and traditions than with the institutions of the country of which they now form a part, under a State structure which incorporates mainly the national, social and cultural characteristics of other segments of the population which are predominant."[1]

In extenso: Legal term meaning at length, in full, verbatim.

Infringement: Legal doctrine which holds that in litigation between Indians and non-Indians arising out of conduct on an Indian reservation, resolution of conflicts between the jurisdiction of state and tribal courts has depended, absent a governing act of Congress, on whether the state action infringed on the right of reservation Indians to make their own laws and be ruled by them. In other words, the courts have placed restrictions on the exercise of state jurisdiction if the state's actions interfere or infringe on the tribal right of self-government.

In personam: Legal term meaning against the person; involving the person. Action seeking judgment against a person involving his personal rights and based on jurisdiction of his person, as distinguished from a judgment against property.

Judicial activism: A philosophy that courts should not be reluctant to review and, if necessary, strike down legislative and executive actions.

Judicial deference: Judicial philosophy which motivates justices to acquiesce to decisions made by the political department of government. See also *Political question.*

Judicial restraint: A philosophy that courts should defer to the political branches whenever possible.

Judicial review: The power of a court to determine the constitutionality of legislative and executive actions and to declare them null and void if found to be in violation of the Constitution. Courts also review the judgments of lower courts at times in order to determine the legality and appropriateness of decisions.

Jurisdiction: The authority of a court to hear a case or controversy and to enforce its rulings.

Last-in-time: Legal rule which holds that if there is a conflict between a treaty provision and an act of Congress (or between two acts of Congress), the one latest in time prevails.

Majority opinion: An opinion in a case that is subscribed to by a majority of the justices who participated in the decision.

Manifest destiny: Nineteenth-century belief in the inevitability of the continued territorial expansion of U.S. boundaries westward to the Pacific Ocean and beyond. The notion of "manifest destiny" was frequently used by American expansionists to justify physical relocations of tribal nations as well as the annexations of Texas, Oregon, California, and other territories.

Merits of case: Legal phrase meaning the essential issues; the substantive rights presented by an action.

Moot: Unsettled or undecided. Describes a question presented in a lawsuit that cannot be answered by a court either because the issue has resolved itself or because conditions have so changed that the court is unable to grant the requested relief.

Motion: An application, normally incidental to an action, made to a court or judge for the purpose of obtaining an order or rule directing something to be done in favor of the applicant.

Nation: A social group which shares a common ideology, common institutions and customs, a sense of homogeneity, and a belief in a common ancestry. A prerequisite of nationhood is an awareness or belief that one's own group is unique in a most vital sense; therefore, the essence of a nation is not tangible but psychological, a matter of attitude rather than of fact. A nation may comprise part of a state, be coterminous with a state, or extend beyond the borders of a single state.

Native American Church: A religious organization, formally organized in 1918, by Indians whose beliefs include the sacramental use of the peyote cactus.

Original jurisdiction: The authority of a court to try a case and to decide it, as opposed to appellate jurisdiction. The Supreme Court has original jurisdiction under Article III of the Constitution.

Per curiam: Legal term describing an action taken by the court as a whole. A per curiam opinion is an opinion of the court in which the judges or justices are all of one mind and the question involved is so clear that the opinion is not elaborated by an extended discussion of the supporting reasons.

Per se rule: From the Latin expression meaning 'by itself' or 'in itself,' refers to Congress's ability to exercise exclusive plenary authority. In federal Indian law a rule promulgated in some courts to the effect that while Congress may authorize a state to tax a tribe or its members, "[i]t has not done so often, and the Court consistently has held that it will find the Indians' exemption from state taxes lifted only when Congress has made its intention to do so unmistakably clear."

Petitioner: A party seeking relief in court. When a writ of certiorari is granted by the Supreme Court, the party seeking review is called the petitioner, and the party responding is called the respondent.

Plenary power: Complete in all aspects or essentials. However, in federal Indian policy and law, this term has three distinct meanings: a) exclusive—Congress, under the Commerce Clause is vested with sole authority to regulate the federal government's affairs with Indian tribes; b) preemptive—Congress may enact legislation which effectively precludes state government's acting in Indian related matters; c) unlimited or absolute—this judicially created definition maintains that the federal government has virtually boundless governmental authority and jurisdiction over Indian tribes, their lands, and their resources.

Plurality opinion: An opinion announcing the decision of the Supreme Court, but having the support of less than a majority of the justices.

Political question: A question that courts refuse to decide because it is deemed to be essentially political in nature or because its determination would involve an intrusion on the powers of the legislative or executive branch.

Preemption: A doctrine under which an area of authority previously left to the states is, by act of Congress, brought into the exclusive jurisdiction of the federal government.

Prima facie: Legal term meaning 'at first sight.' In reference to evidence, adequate as it appears, not requiring more. Describes a fact presumed to be true unless disproved by evidence to the contrary.

Property clause: The provision of the federal Constitution, Article IV, section 3, clause 2, which declares that "[t]he Congress shall have power to dispose of and make all needful rules and regulations respecting the territory or other property belonging to the United States. . . ." While the Constitution is silent as to the methods of disposing of federal property, congressional authority is considered comprehensive over all public lands. Thus, no state can tax public lands of the U.S., nor can state legislation interfere with the power of Congress under this clause.

Public forum doctrine: Legal doctrine involving the range of places and contexts in which the constitutional right of free speech has been contested. The Supreme Court's analysis in recent cases has started with a determination of whether certain spaces are "public forums." A public forum, according to the Supreme Court, is government property that has either (1) traditionally been available for public expression and has as a principal purpose the free exchange of ideas (traditional public forum); or (2) been specifically designated by the government as a public forum (designated public forum). If the spaces in question are not adjudged to be public forums, the infringement on speech, even if it is the most protected speech, is not strictly scrutinized; any "reasonable" restriction is constitutionally permissible.

Purpose doctrine: Term coined by the Critical Legal theorist David Kairys, which, he suggests, has allowed the Rehnquist Court to legitimate a number of constitutional violations unless a victim can prove that the government has acted maliciously and the government cannot suggest an alternative, plausibly benevolent purpose. Kairys says the purpose doctrine is synonymous with the incidental effects test and other judicial techniques which have worked to constrict individual constitutional rights in the areas of free speech, free exercise of religion, and due process.

Res judicata: Legal term meaning 'the thing has been decided.' The principle that an existing final judgment rendered upon the merits, without fraud or collusion, by a court of competent jurisdiction, is conclusive of rights, questions, and facts in issue, as to the parties and their privies.

Respondent: The party against whom a legal action is filed.

Reserved rights doctrine: Judicially crafted concept which holds that tribal nations retain all rights (that is, to self-government, cultural expression, lands, water, hunting, fishing, etc.) which have not been expressly granted away in treaties or agreements.

Separation of church and state: Legal doctrine outlined in the First Amendment to the U.S. Constitution, which reflects the philosophy that church and state should be separated. As concerns interference with the free exercise of religion and establishment of religion, the Supreme Court has confirmed that the separation must be complete and unequivocal. Nevertheless, while the First Amendment was intended to erect a wall of separation between church and state, the amendment does not say that in every and all respects there shall be a separation of church and state. Total separation is not regarded as possible in an absolute sense, according to a Senate publication on the subject, and some relationship between government and religious organizations is believed to be inevitable.[2]

Separation of powers: Constitutional doctrine mandating the equal division of powers between the executive, legislative, and judicial branches. The separation is a fundamental characteristic not only of the federal government, but also of state governments and some tribal governments. Under this doctrine, one branch is not permitted to encroach on the domain or exercise of another.

Solicitor general: Justice Department official whose office represents the federal government in all litigation before the U.S. Supreme Court.

Sovereignty: A western concept, both complex and contested, central to modern political thought. Its importance is bound up with specifying the essential character of the territorial state. Implicit in the discussions about the term since Bodin, Machiavelli, and Hobbes is the conviction that the state is the ultimate arbiter of its own fate in relation to the outside world. Each state is "sovereign" in international society, a law unto itself. However, absolute sovereignty no longer exists for any modern state because of international interdependence and the interpenetration of domestic and international politics, the mobility and globalization of capital and information, and the rising influence of transnational social movements and organizations. Sovereignty in modern times more accurately connotes legal competence; the power of a culturally and territorially distinctive group of people to develop institutional arrangements that both protect and limit personal freedoms by social control.

Standing; standing to sue: The right of parties to bring legal actions because they are directly affected by the legal issues raised.

Strict scrutiny test: A measure which is found to affect adversely a fundamental right (e.g., free exercise of religion or speech) will be subject to this test, which requires the state to establish that it has compelling interest which justifies the law and that distinctions created by law are necessary to further some governmental purpose.

Sui juris: Legal term meaning 'the only one of its kind.'

Supremacy clause: Article VI, clause 2, which declares the federal Constitution and laws "to be the Supreme Law of the Land," provides to the federal government powers that cannot be exercised by the states and that the states must heed.

Termination policy: Federal Indian policy from approximately 1953 to the mid-1960s which legislatively severed federal benefits and support services to certain tribes, bands, and California rancherias and forced the dissolution of their reservations. This policy was exemplified by House Concurrent Resolution No. 108 in 1953, the infamous "termination resolution"; Public Law 83-280, which conferred upon several designated states full criminal and some civil jurisdiction over Indian reservations within those states and consented to the assumption of such jurisdiction by any other state that chose to accept it; and relocation—a federal policy focused on the relocation of Indians from rural and reservation areas to urban areas.

Test: A criterion or set of criteria used by courts to determine whether certain legal thresholds have been met or constitutional provisions violated.

Treaty: A formal agreement, compact, or contract between two or more sovereign nations that creates legal rights and duties for the contracting parties. A treaty is not only a law but also a contract between two nations and must, if possible, be so construed as to give full force and effect to all its parts. Treaties can be bilateral (involving only two nations) or multilateral and deal with single or multiple issues. Indian treaties are of the same dignity as international treaties, but because of the unique political (trust) relationship which unfolded between tribes and the United States, the federal courts have created several so-called canons of construction which are designed to protect Indian rights. These serve to distinguish Indian treaties from those the United States negotiates with foreign nations: (1) A cardinal rule in the interpretation of Indian treaties is that ambiguities in treaty language are to be resolved in favor of the Indians; (2) Since the wording in treaties was designed to be understood by the Indians, who often could not read and were not skilled in the technical language often used in treaties, doubtful clauses are to be resolved in a nontechnical way as the Indians would have understood the language; and (3) Treaties are to be liberally construed to favor Indians. These three legal doctrines have been enforced inconsistently by the courts, the Congress, and the executive branch; for example, the courts have also ruled repeatedly that Congress in exercising its plenary power may unilaterally abrogate Indian treaty provisions without tribal consent.

Treaty clause: The provision of the U.S. Constitution, Article II, section 2, which gives to the president the power "by and with the consent of the Senate, to make treaties, provided two thirds of the Senators present concur."

Tribal sovereignty: The spiritual, moral, and dynamic cultural force within a given tribal community empowering the group toward political, economic, and, most importantly, cultural integrity; as well as maturity in the group's relationships with its own members, with other peoples and their governments, and with the environment.

Tribe: A community or combination of communities all of which occupy a common territory, share a political ideology, and are related by kinship, traditions, and language.

Trust doctrine: One of the unique foundational concepts underlying the political-moral relationship between the United States government and American Indian nations. The trust doctrine, also known as the trust relationship, has historical roots in several sources: in treaties and agreements with individual tribes; in the international law doctrine of trusteeship first broached in papal bulls and related documents during the time of European nations' first encounters with indigenous societies when the European states assumed a protective role vis-à-vis these societies and their territories; and in constitutional clauses, executive orders and policies, and statutory and case law. Broadly defined, the trust doctrine is the unique legal and moral duty of the federal government to assist Indian tribes in the protection of their lands, resources, and cultural heritage. The federal government, many courts have maintained, is to be held to the highest standards of good faith and honesty in its dealing with Indian peoples and their rights, resources, and funds. Nevertheless, since the trust doctrine is not explicitly constitutionally based, it is not enforceable against Congress, although it has occasionally proven a potent source of rights against the executive branch. Importantly, the trust doctrine, which is also referred to as a trustee-beneficiary relationship (with the federal government serving as the trustee and the tribes as the beneficiary) is not synonymous with the so-called guardian-ward relationship which was said to exist between the U.S. and tribes from the 1860s to the 1930s.

Unmistakable intent: Evidence gleaned by the court (e.g., express statutory language, legislative documents, etc.) that unequivocally shows what Congress intended to do by enacting a particular statute. If the court finds what it considers "unmistakable intent," the disputed legislation (or provision thereof) is upheld as constitutional.

Wardship: See *Guardianship.*

Writ: A written order or an oral command issuing from a court that commands the recipient to perform or not perform acts specified in the order.

NOTES

1. U.N. Economic and Social Council Commission on Human Rights, *Preliminary Report on the Problem of Discrimination Against Indigenous Populations,* as quoted in Franke Wilmer, *The Indigenous Voice in World Politics* (Newbury Park, Calif.: Sage, 1993).

2. Johnny H. Killian, ed., *The Constitution of the United States: Analysis and Interpretation* (Washington, D.C.: Government Printing Office, 1987), 970. (Senate Document No. 99-16, 99th Cong., 1st Sess., rev. and annot. version of 1964 federal publication).

References

GOVERNMENT DOCUMENTS

Israel, Fred L., ed. *The State of the Union Messages of the Presidents, 1790–1966.* 3 vols. New York: Chelsea House, 1966.

Richardson, J. D., ed. *Compilation of the Messages and Papers of the Presidents, 1789–1897.* 10 vols. Washington: Government Printing Office, 1907.

U.S. *American Indian Religious Freedom Report*, P.L. 95-34. Washington: Federal Agencies Task Force, 1979.

U.S. *American State Papers*, vols. I–V. Washington: Gales and Seaton, 1833–1861.

U.S. Commission on Civil Rights. *Indian Tribes: A Continuing Quest for Survival.* Washington: Government Printing Office, 1981.

U.S. Congress. House. *A Report on Establishing Trading Houses with Indian Tribes.* H. Doc. 59, 15th Cong., 1st sess. (1818).

———. House. *Report on Regulating the Indian Department.* H. Rept. 474, 23d Cong., 1st sess. (1834).

———. House. *Report of the Indian Peace Commission.* Exec. Doc. 97, 40th Cong., 2d sess. (1868).

———. House. *Elias Boudinot and Cherokee Tobacco Factory.* H. Rept. 52, 41st Cong., 2d sess. (1870).

———. House. *Memorial of Elias C. Boudinot.* Misc. Doc. 4, 43d Cong., 1st sess. (1873).

———. House. *On E. C. Boudinot-Cherokee Tobacco Case.* H. Rept. 920, 45th Cong., 2d sess. (1878).

———. House. *Elias C. Boudinot Can Sue in Court of Claims.* H. Rept. 120, 46th Cong., 2d sess. (1880).

———. House. *Protection of American Bison and Other Animals.* H. Rept. 1876, 51st Cong., 1st sess. (1890).

———. House. *Report on the Curtis Bill Laws for the Indian Territory.* H. Rept. 593, 55th Cong., 2d sess. (1898).

———. House. *Railroad Companies in Indian Territory.* H. Rept. 826, 55th Cong., 2d sess. (1898).

———. House. *Memorial from Kiowa, Comanche, and Apache Tribes Against Agreement.* H. Doc. 333, 56th Cong., 1st sess. (1900).

———. House. *Agreement with Indians of Fort Hall Reservation*, H. Rept. 419, 56th Cong., 1st sess. (1900).

————. House. *Issuing or Withholding Rations from Indians.* H. Doc. 391, 57th Cong., 1st sess. (1902).

————. House. H. Rept. 873, 80th Cong., 1st sess. (1947).

————. House. H. Rept. 98-110, 98th Cong., 1st sess. (1983).

U.S. Congress. Senate. *Memorial of John Ross and Others.* S. Doc. 331, 29th Cong., 1st sess. (1846).

————. Senate. *Extending the U.S. Criminal Laws over Indian Territory.* S. Rept. 461, 29th Cong., 1st sess. (1846).

————. Senate. *Report on Pacific Railroad.* S. Rept. 219, 40th Cong., 3d sess. (1869).

————. Senate. *Memorial of Kiowa, Comanche, and Apache Tribes.* Misc. Doc. 102, 53d Cong., 2d sess. (1894).

————. Senate. *Kiowa, Comanche, and Apache Indian Reservation: Letter from the Secretary of Interior.* S. Doc. 77, 55th Cong., 3d sess. (1899).

————. Senate. *Number of Adult Male Indians Belonging to the Kiowa, Comanche, and Apache Tribes in October, 1892.* S. Doc. 84, 55th Cong., 3d sess. (1899).

————. Senate. *Quantity, Nature, and Character of the Lands of the Kiowa, Comanche, and Apache Reservation.* S. Doc. 75, 56th Cong., 1st sess. (1900).

————. Senate. *Memorial from Kiowa, Comanche, and Apache Indian Tribes: Letter from the Secretary of Interior.* S. Doc. 76, 56th Cong., 1st sess. (1900).

————. Senate. *Agreement with the Kiowa, Comanche, and Apache Tribes.* S. Doc. 170, 56th Cong., 1st sess. (1900).

————. Senate. *Indian Affairs: Laws and Treaties.* 2 vols. Charles J. Kappler, ed., S. Doc. 452, 57th Cong., 1st sess. (1903).

————. Senate. S. Rept. 93-863, 93d Cong., 2d sess. (1974).

————. Senate. *Final Report. A Report of the Special Committee on Investigations of the Select Committee on Indian Affairs.* S. Rept. 101-216, 101st Cong., 1st sess. (1989).

————. Senate. Select Committee on Indian Affairs, *Testimony of Vine Deloria Jr.,* 102d Cong., 2d sess. (1992).

U.S. Congress. Special Report. *American Indian Policy Review Commission: Final Report.* Washington: Government Printing Office (1977).

U.S. Congress. *The New American State Papers: Indian Affairs.* Wilmington, Del.: Scholarly Resources, 1972.

U.S. *Congressional Globe.* 1834, 1846, 1863, 1870.

U.S. *Congressional Record.* 1874, 1885, 1896–1897, 1900, 1903, 1945, 1978, 1993.

U.S. Congressional Research Service. *American Indian Policy: Background, Nature, History, Current Issues, Future Trends,* by Richard S. Jones. Washington: Government Printing Office, 1987.

U.S. Department of the Interior. *Commissioner of Indian Affairs: Annual Report* for the years 1851, 1861, 1864, 1866, 1869, 1872,1875, 1884, 1888, 1894–1896, 1900, 1905–1906, 1913, 1950.

————. *Solicitor's Opinions.* Washington: Department of the Interior, 1934.

————. Supreme Court. *The Complete Oral Arguments of the Supreme Court of the*

United States. Frederick, Md.: University Publications of America, Inc., 1979–1980, 1988, 1990, 1992.

————. Supreme Court. *Records and Briefs.* Microfilm reprints.

Weekly Compilation of Presidential Documents. Washington: Government Printing Office, 1994.

West's Revised Code of Washington Annotated: Constitution of the State of Washington. St. Paul, Minn.: West Publishing, 1988.

ARTICLES AND BOOKS

Abraham, Henry J. *Justices and Presidents: A Political History of Appointments to the Supreme Court.* New York: Oxford University Press, 1992.

Agresto, John. *The Supreme Court and Constitutional Democracy.* Ithaca: Cornell University Press, 1984.

Anders, Gary C. "The Alaska Native Experience with the Alaska Native Claims Settlement Co.," in P. A. Olson, ed., *The Struggle for the Land.* Lincoln: University of Nebraska Press, 1990.

Arledge, Paula, and Anne M. McCulloch. "Indian Cases and the Modern Supreme Court: Problems in Consistent Interpretation in Extra-Constitutional Cases." Paper delivered at the Annual Meeting of the American Political Science Association, Atlanta: November 8–10, 1990.

Arnold, Thurman W. *The Folklore of Capitalism.* New Haven: Yale University Press, 1937.

————. *The Symbols of Government.* New Haven: Yale University Press, 1935.

Ball, Milner S. "Constitution, Court, Indian Tribes." *American Bar Foundation Research Journal* 1 (1987): 1–139.

Barsh, Russel L. "Law and Legislation," in Duane Champagne, ed., *The Native North American Almanac.* Detroit: Gale Research Inc. 1994, 449–471.

Barsh, Russel L., and James Youngblood Henderson. "The Betrayal: *Oliphant v. Suquamish Indian Tribe* and the Hunting of the Snark." *Minnesota Law Review* 63 (1979): 609–640.

————. *The Road: Indian Tribes and Political Liberty.* Berkeley: University of California Press, 1980.

Baum, Lawrence. *The Supreme Court,* 4th ed. Washington: Congressional Quarterly Press, 1992.

Beck, Peggy V., and Anna L. Walters. *The Sacred: Ways of Knowledge, Source of Life.* Tsaile, Ariz.: Navajo Community College Press, 1977.

Berkhofer, Robert F. Jr. *The White Man's Indian: Images of the American Indian from Columbus to the Present.* New York: Alfred Knopf, Inc., 1978.

Berman, Howard R. "The Concept of Aboriginal Rights in the Early History of the United States." *Buffalo Law Review* 27 (1978): 637–667.

Biolsi, Thomas. *Organizing the Lakota: The Political Economy of the New Deal on the Pine Ridge and Rosebud Reservations.* Tucson: University of Arizona Press, 1992.

Black's Law Dictionary, 5th ed. St. Paul, Minn.: West Publishing Company, 1979.

Brisbin, Richard A. Jr. "Justice Antonin Scalia, Constitutional Discourse, and the Legalistic State." *The Western Political Quarterly* 44 (December 1991): 1005–1038.

Burke, Joseph C. "The Cherokee Cases: A Study in Law, Politics, and Morality." *Stanford Law Review* 21 (February 1969): 500–531.

Burt, Larry W. *Tribalism in Crisis: Federal Indian Policy, 1953–1961.* Albuquerque: University of New Mexico Press, 1982.

Cadwalader, Sandra L., and Vine Deloria Jr. *The Aggressions of Civilization.* Philadelphia: Temple University Press, 1984.

Canfield, George F. "The Legal Position of the Indian." *American Law Review* (January 1881): 21–37.

Carter, Nancy Carol. "Race and Power Politics as Aspects of Federal Guardianship over American Indians: Land-Related Cases, 1887–1924." *American Indian Law Review* 4 (1976): 197–248.

Chibitty, Charles, Kirke Kickingbird, and Lynn Kickingbird. *Indian Treaties.* Washington: Institute for the Development of Indian Law, 1977.

Clark, Blue. *Lone Wolf v. Hitchcock: Treaty Rights and Indian Law at the End of the Nineteenth Century.* Lincoln: University of Nebraska Press, 1994.

Cohen, Felix S. "Alaska's Nuremberg Laws: Congress Sanctions Racial Discrimination." *Commentary* 6 (August 1948): 136–143.

————. "The Erosion of Indian Rights, 1950–1953: A Case Study in Bureaucracy." *Yale Law Journal* 62 (1953): 348–390.

————. *Handbook of Federal Indian Law.* Washington: Government Printing Office, 1942; reprint ed., Albuquerque, N. Mex.: University of New Mexico Press, 1972.

————. *Felix S. Cohen's Handbook of Federal Indian Law.* Rennard Strickland et al., eds. Charlottesville, Va.: Michie, Bobbs-Merrill, 1982.

————. "Indian Claims," in Lucy Cohen, ed., *The Legal Conscience: Selected Papers of Felix S. Cohen.* New Haven: Yale University Press, 1960, 264–272.

————. "Indian Self-Government," in Lucy Cohen, ed., *The Legal Conscience: Selected Papers of Felix S. Cohen.* New Haven: Yale University Press, 1960, 305–314.

————. "Indian Wardship: The Twilight of a Myth," in Lucy Cohen, ed., *The Legal Conscience: Selected Papers of Felix S. Cohen.* New Haven: Yale University Press, 1960, 328–334.

————. "Original Indian Title," in Lucy Cohen, ed., *The Legal Conscience: Selected Papers of Felix S. Cohen.* New Haven: Yale University Press, 1960, 273–304.

————. *The Legal Conscience: Selected Papers of Felix S. Cohen.* Lucy Cohen, ed. New Haven: Yale University Press, 1960.

Colbert, Thomas B. "The 'Death Knell of the Nation,'" in John W. Johnson, ed., *Historic U.S. Supreme Court Cases, 1690–1990: An Encyclopedia.* New York: Garland Publishing Co., 1992, 418–421.

Collier, John. "The Unfinished Indian Wars." *The Nation* 184 (May 1957): 458–459.

Cornell, Stephen. *The Return of the Native: American Indian Political Resurgence.* New York: Oxford University Press, 1988.

Cornell, Stephen, and Joseph P. Kalt, eds. *What Can Tribes Do? Strategies and Institutions in American Indian Economic Development.* Los Angeles: American Indian Studies Center, 1992.

Coulter, Robert T. "The Denial of Legal Remedies to Indian Nations Under U.S. Law." *American Indian Journal* 3 (September 1977): 5–11.

———. "Lack of Redress." *Civil Rights Digest* 10 (Spring 1978): 30–37.

———, and Steven M. Tullberg. "Indian Land Rights," in Sandra L. Cadwalader and Vine Deloria Jr., eds., *The Aggressions of Civilization.* Philadelphia: Temple University Press, 1984, 185–213.

Czech, Brian. "*Ward v. Race Horse*—Supreme Court as Obviator?" *Journal of the West* 35, no. 3 (July 1996): 61–79.

Dahl, Robert A. "Decision-Making in a Democracy: The Supreme Court as a National Policy-Maker." *Journal of Public Law* 6 (1957): 279–295.

Danziger, James N. *Understanding the Political World: An Introduction to Political Science.* New York: Longman Press, 1991.

Davis, Sue. "Rehnquist & State Courts: Federalism Revisited." *The Western Political Quarterly* 45 (1992): 773–782.

Debo, Angie. *A History of the Indians of the United States.* Norman: University of Oklahoma Press, 1970.

———. *And Still the Waters Run: The Betrayal of the Five Civilized Tribes.* Princeton: Princeton University Press, 1940; reprinted 1973.

Deloria, Vine, Jr. *Custer Died for Your Sins: An Indian Manifesto.* New York: Macmillan, 1969. Repr. Norman: University of Oklahoma Press, 1988.

———. *Behind the Trail of Broken Treaties: An Indian Declaration of Independence.* New York: Delacorte Press, 1974. Repr. Austin: University of Texas Press, 1985.

———, ed. *American Indian Policy in the Twentieth Century.* Norman: University of Oklahoma Press, 1985.

———. "Beyond the Pale: American Indians and the Constitution," in Jules Lobel, ed., *A Less Than Perfect Union.* New York: Monthly Review Press, 1988, 249–266.

———. "Congress in Its Wisdom: The Course of Indian Legislation," in Sandra L. Cadwalader and Vine Deloria Jr., eds., *The Aggressions of Civilization.* Philadelphia: Temple University Press, 1984, 106–130.

———. "The Distinctive Status of Indian Rights," in Peter Iverson, ed., *The Plains Indians of the Twentieth Century.* Norman: University of Oklahoma Press, 1985, 237–248.

———. *God is Red: A Native View of Religion,* rev. ed. Golden, Colo.: Fulcrum Publishing, 1994.

———. "Indian Law and the Reach of History." *Journal of Contemporary Law* 4 (1977–1978): 1–13.

————. "Indian Treaties: A Hundred Years Later." *Race Relations Reporter* (March 1974): 29–32.

————. "Laws Founded in Justice and Humanity: Reflections on the Content and Character of Federal Indian Law." *Arizona Law Review* 31 (1989): 203–223.

————. "The Next Three Years: A Time for Change." *The Indian Historian* 7 (Winter 1974): 25–27, 53.

————. "Reflections on the Black Hills Claim." *Wicazo Sa Review* 4 (Spring 1988): 33–38.

————. "Revision and Reversion," in Calvin Martin, ed., *The American Indian and the Problem of History*. New York: Oxford University Press, 1987, 84–90.

————. "Trouble in High Places: Erosion of American Indian Rights to Religious Freedom in the United States," in M. Annette Jaimes, ed., *The State of Native America: Genocide, Colonization, and Resistance*. Boston: South End Press, 1992, 267–290.

————. "The United States Has No Jurisdiction in Sioux Territory," in Roxanne D. Ortiz, ed., *The Great Sioux Nation: Sitting in Judgment on America*. Berkeley: Moon Books, 1977, 141–146.

————. "The Western Shoshones." *American Indian Journal* 2 (January 1976): 16–20.

————. "Worshipping the Golden Calf: Freedom of Religion in Scalia's America." *New World Outlook* (September–October 1991): 22–24.

————, and Clifford M. Lytle. *American Indians, American Justice*. Austin: University of Texas Press, 1983.

————, and Clifford M. Lytle. *The Nations Within: The Past and Future of American Indian Sovereignty*. New York: Pantheon Books, 1984.

Echo-hawk, Walter. "Loopholes in Religious Liberty: The Need for a Federal Law to Protect Freedom of Worship for Native People." *Native American Rights Fund Legal Review* (Summer 1991): 7–12.

Engdahl, David E. "State and Federal Power over Federal Property." *Arizona Law Review* 18 (1976): 283–384.

Estin, Ann Laquer. "*Lone Wolf v. Hitchcock:* The Long Shadow," in Sandra L. Cadwalader and Vine Deloria Jr., eds., *The Aggressions of Civilization: Federal Indian Policy Since the 1880s*. Philadelphia: Temple University Press, 1984.

"Federal Plenary Power in Indian Affairs After *Weeks* and *Sioux Nation*." *University of Pennsylvania Law Review* 131 (1982): 235–270.

Foreman, Grant. "The U.S. Courts and the Indian." *The Overland Monthly* 61 (June 1913): 573–579.

————. *Indian Removal: The Emigration of the Five Civilized Tribes of Indians*. Norman: University of Oklahoma Press, 1932.

————. *The Last Trek of the Indians*. Chicago: University of Chicago Press, 1946.

Frank, John P. *Justice Daniel Dissenting: A Biography of Peter V. Daniel, 1784–1860*. Cambridge: Harvard University Press, 1964.

French, Laurence, ed. *Indians and Criminal Justice*. Totowa, N.J.: Allanheld, Osmun & Co., 1982.

Gordon, Robert W. "Legal Thought and Legal Practice in the Age of American
Enterprise: 1870–1920," in Gerald L. Geison, ed., *Profession and Professional
Ideologies in America*. Chapel Hill: University of North Carolina Press, 1983,
70–110.

Green, Donald E. "American Indian Criminality: What Do We Really Know?"
in Donald E. Green and Thomas V. Tonnesen, eds., *American Indians: Social
Justice and Public Policy*. Madison: University of Wisconsin Press, 1991.

Greenhouse, Linda. "Court Is Urged to Rehear Case on Ritual Drug." *The New
York Times* (May 11, 1990): 16.

Gross, Emma R. *Contemporary Federal Policy Toward American Indians*. Westport,
Conn.: Greenwood Press, 1989.

Grossman, Joel B., and Richard S. Wells. *Constitutional Law and Judicial Policy
Making*, 3d ed. New York: Longman Press, 1988.

Hall, Gilbert L. *The Federal Indian Trust Relationship*, 2d ed. Washington: Institute for the Development of Indian Law, 1981.

Harring, Sidney L. *Crow Dog's Case: American Indian Sovereignty, Tribal Law, and
United States Law in the Nineteenth Century*. New York: Cambridge University
Press, 1994.

Heimann, Robert K. "The Cherokee Tobacco Case." *The Chronicles of Oklahoma*
41 (1967): 299–322.

Henkin, Lewis. "Is There a 'Political Question' Doctrine?" *Yale Law Journal* 85
(April 1976): 597–625.

Hoxie, Frederick E. *A Final Promise: The Campaign to Assimilate the Indians,
1880–1920*. New York: Cambridge University Press, 1984.

Huntington, Samuel P., and Jorge I. Dominguez. "Political Development," in
Fred I. Greenstein and Nelson W. Polsby, eds., *Macropolitical Theory*, vol. 3
of *Handbook of Political Science*. Reading, Mass.: Addison-Wesley Publishing
Co., 1975, 1–114.

Hurtado, Albert L., and Peter Iverson, eds. *Major Problems in American History:
Documents and Essays*. Lexington, Mass.: D. C. Heath, 1994.

Hutchinson, Allen C., ed. *Critical Legal Studies*. Totowa, N.J.: Rowman & Littlefield, 1989.

Josephy, Alvin M., Jr., ed. *Red Power: The American Indians' Fight for Freedom*.
New York: American Heritage Press, 1971.

Kairys, David. *The Politics of Law: A Progressive Critique*. New York: Pantheon
Books, 1982.

———, ed. *With Liberty and Justice for Some: A Critique of the Conservative Supreme Court*. New York: The New Press, 1993.

Kappler, Charles J., comp. *Indian Affairs: Laws and Treaties*. 2 vols. Washington:
Government Printing Office, 1903.

Kelly, Lawrence C. *The Assault on Assimilation: John Collier and the Origins of Indian Policy Reform*. Albuquerque: University of New Mexico Press, 1983.

Kennan, George. "Have Reservation Indians Any Vested Rights?" *The Outlook* 70 (March 29, 1902): 759–765.

———. "A New Statement from Mr. Kennan." *The Outlook* 70 (April 19, 1902): 956–958.

Kennedy, Duncan. *Toward an Historical Understanding of Legal Consciousness: The Case of Classical Legal Thought in America, 1850–1940.* Research in Law and Sociology 3, Stephen Spitzer, ed. Greenwich, Conn.: JAI Press, 1980.

Kramer, Karl J. "The Most Dangerous Branch: An Institutional Approach to Understanding the Role of the Judiciary in American Indian Jurisdictional Determinations." *Wisconsin Law Review* 5–6 (1986): 989–1038.

Kronowitz, Rachel San, Joanne Lichtman, Stephen P. McSloy, and Matthew G. Olsen. "Toward Consent and Cooperation: Reconsidering the Political Status of Indian Nations." *Harvard Civil Rights-Civil Liberties Law Review* 22 (Spring 1987): 507–622.

LaBarre, Welton. *The Peyote Cult,* 4th ed. New York: Schocken Books, 1975.

Lurie, Nancy O. "Epilogue," in Imre Sutton, ed., *Irredeemable America: The Indians' Estate and Land Claims.* Albuquerque, N. Mex.: University of New Mexico Press, 1985, 363–382.

———. "The Indian Claims Commission." *Annals of the American Academy of Political and Social Science* 436 (1978): 97–110.

Martin, Calvin, ed. *The American Indian and the Problem of History.* New York: Oxford University Press, 1987.

Martin, Jill. "Constitutional Rights and Indian Rites: An Uneasy Balance." *Western Legal History* 3 (1990): 245–269.

———. "'Neither Fish, Flesh, Fowl, nor Good Red Herring': The Citizenship Status of American Indians, 1830–1924." *Journal of the West* 24 (July 1990): 75–87.

Matthew, James, ed. *The Statutes at Large of the Provisional Government of the Confederate Tribes of America.* Indian Rocks Beach, Fla.: D&S Publishers, 1970.

McDonnell, Janet A. *The Dispossession of the American Indian, 1887–1934.* Bloomington, Ind.: Indiana University Press, 1991.

McNickle, D'Arcy. *Native American Tribalism: Indian Survivals and Renewals.* New York: Oxford University Press, 1973.

Medcalf, Linda. *Law and Identity: Lawyers, Native Americans, and Legal Practice.* Beverly Hills: Sage Publications, 1978.

Mensch, Elizabeth. "The History of Mainstream Legal Thought," in David Kairys, ed., *The Politics of Law.* New York: Pantheon Books, 1982, 18–39.

Moore, Barrington. *The Social Origins of Dictatorship and Democracy.* Boston: Beacon Press, 1966.

Moore, W. John. "Great Right Hope." *National Journal* 24 (1992): 1659.

Nagel, Joane. *American Indian Ethnic Renewal: Red Power and the Resurgence of Identity and Culture.* New York: Oxford University Press, 1996.

Newton, Nell Jessup. "At the Whim of the Sovereign: Aboriginal Title Reconsidered." *Hastings Law Journal* 31 (July 1980): 1215–1285.

———. "Federal Power over Indians: Its Sources, Scope, and Limitations." *University of Pennsylvania Law Review* 132 (1984): 195–288.

———. "Introduction." *Arizona Law Review* 31 (1989): 193–202.

———. "Let a Thousand Policy-Flowers Bloom: Making Indian Policy in the Twenty-First Century." *Arkansas Law Review* 46 (1993): 25–75.

Noonan, John T., Jr. *Persons and Masks of the Law.* New York: Farrar, Straus & Giroux, 1976.

Norgren, Jill. *The Cherokee Cases: The Confrontation of Law and Politics.* New York: McGraw Hill, 1996.

———, and Petra T. Shattuck. "Limits of Legal Action: The Cherokee Cases." *American Indian Culture and Research Journal* 2 (1978): 14–25.

O'Brien, David. *Storm Center: The Supreme Court in American Politics,* 3d ed. New York: W. W. Norton & Company, 1993.

O'Brien, Sharon. *American Indian Tribal Governments.* Norman: University of Oklahoma Press, 1989.

"105 Million Award to Sioux Is Upheld," *New York Times,* July 1, 1980, 1.

Ortiz, Roxanne D. *The Great Sioux Nation: Sitting in Judgment on America.* Berkeley: Moon Books, 1977.

Otis, D. S. *The Dawes Act and the Allotment of Indian Lands.* Norman: University of Oklahoma Press, 1973.

Parillo, Vincent N. *Strangers to These Shores: Race and Ethnic Relations in the United States,* 3d ed. New York: Macmillan Publishing Co., 1990.

Pavlik, Steve. "The U.S. Supreme Court Decision on Peyote in Employment Division v. Smith: A Case Study in the Suppression of Native American Religious Freedom." *Wicazo Sa Review* 8 (Fall 1992): 30–38.

Peak, Ken, and Jack Spencer, "Crime in Indian Country: Another Trail of Tears." *Journal of Criminal Justice* 15 (1987): 485–494.

Pearce, Roy Harvey. *Savagism and Civilization: A Study of the Indian and the American Mind.* Baltimore: The Johns Hopkins Press, 1953.

Peroff, Nicholas C. *Menominee Drums: Tribal Termination and Restoration, 1954–1974.* Norman: University of Oklahoma Press, 1982.

Philp, Kenneth R., ed. *Indian Self-Rule: First-Hand Accounts of Indian-White Relations from Roosevelt to Reagan.* Salt Lake City: Howe Brothers, 1986.

Pommersheim, Frank. "The Black Hills Case: On the Cusp of History." *Wicazo Sa Review* 4 (Spring 1988): 18–25.

———. *Braid of Feathers: American Indian Law and Contemporary Tribal Life.* Berkeley: University of California Press, 1995.

———. "Making all the Difference: Native Testimony and the Black Hills: A review essay." *North Dakota Law Review* 69 (1993): 337–359.

———. "Tribal-State Relations: Hope for the Future?" *South Dakota Law Review* 36 (1991): 239–276.

Prucha, Francis P. *American Indian Policy in Crisis: Christian Reformers and the Indian, 1865–1900.* Norman: University of Oklahoma Press, 1976.

———. *American Indian Policy in the Formative Years.* Lincoln: University of Nebraska Press, 1962.

————. *The Churches and the Indian Schools: 1888–1912.* Lincoln: University of Nebraska Press, 1979.

————, ed. *Documents of United States Indian Policy,* 2d ed. Lincoln: University of Nebraska Press, 1990.

————. *The Great Father: The United States Government and the American Indian.* 2 vols. Lincoln: University of Nebraska Press, 1984; abr. ed. Lincoln: University of Nebraska Press, 1986.

————. *The Indians in American Society: From the Revolutionary War to the Present.* Berkeley: University of California Press, 1985.

Rice, George William. "Indian Rights: 25 U.S.C. Sec.71: The End of Indian Sovereignty or a Self-Limitation of Contractual Ability?" *American Indian Law Review* 5 (1977): 239–253.

Rice, W. G., Jr. "The Position of the American Indian in the Law of the United States." *Journal of Comparative Legislation and International Law* 16 (1934): 78–95.

Rotenberg, Daniel L. "American Indian Tribal Death: A Centennial Remembrance." *University of Miami Law Review* 41 (December 1986): 409–423.

Shafritz, Jay M. *The Dictionary of American Government and Politics.* Chicago: Dorsey Press, 1988.

Shattuck, Petra T., and Jill Norgren. "Indian Rights: The Cost of Justice." *The Nation* 227 (July 22–29, 1978): 70–72.

————. *Partial Justice: Federal Indian Law in a Liberal Constitutional System.* New York: Oxford University Press, 1991.

————. "Political Use of the Legal Process by Black and American Indian Minorities." *Howard Law Journal* 22 (1979): 1–26.

Shklar, Judith N. *American Citizenship: The Quest for Inclusion.* Cambridge, Mass.: Harvard University Press, 1991.

Snipp, C. Matthew. *American Indians: The First of This Land.* New York: Russell Sage Foundation, 1991.

Stannard, David E. *The Conquest of the New World: American Holocaust.* New York: Oxford University Press, 1992.

Stewart, Omer C. *Peyote: A History.* Norman: University of Oklahoma Press, 1987.

Story, William W., ed. *Life and Letters of Joseph Story.* Boston: Little & Brown, 1851.

Strickland, Rennard. *Fire and the Spirits: Cherokee Law from Clan to Court.* Norman: University of Oklahoma Press, 1982.

Svensson, Frances. "Liberal Democracy and Group Rights: The Legacy of Individualism and Its Impact on American Indian Tribes." *Political Studies* 27 (September 1979): 421–439.

Trennert, Robert A., Jr. *Alternative to Extinction.* Philadelphia: Temple University Press, 1975.

Turner, Frederick Jackson. "The Problems of the West." *The Atlantic Monthly* 78 (September 1896): 289–297.

Tyler, Samuel L. *A History of Indian Policy.* Washington: Government Printing Office, 1973.

Vecsey, Christopher. "Introduction: The Issues Underlying Iroquois Land Claims," in Christopher Vecsey and William A. Starna, eds., *Iroquois Land Claims.* Syracuse, N.Y.: Syracuse University Press, 1988, 1–16.

Washburn, Wilcomb E. *The American Indian and the United States.* 4 vols. Westport, Conn.: Greenwood Press, 1973.

———. *The Assault on Indian Tribalism: The General Allotment Law Dawes Act of 1887.* Philadelphia: J. B. Lippincott, 1975.

———. "Indian Policy Since the 1880s," in Sandra L. Cadwalader and Vine Deloria Jr., eds., *The Aggressions of Civilization.* Philadelphia: Temple University Press, 1984, 45–57.

White, G. Edward. *History of the Supreme Court of the United States: The Marshall Court and Cultural Change, 1815–1835.* New York: Oxford University Press, 1991.

Wilkins, David E. "The Cloaking of Justice: The Supreme Court's Role in the Application of Western Law to America's Indigenous Peoples." *Wicazo Sa Review* 10 (Spring 1994): 1–13.

———. "*Johnson v. M'Intosh* Revisited: Through the Eyes of *Mitchel v. United States.*" *American Indian Law Review* 19 (Summer 1994): 1–23.

Wilkinson, Charles F. *American Indians, Time, and the Law: Native Societies in a Modern Constitutional Democracy.* New Haven: Yale University Press, 1987.

Williams, Robert A., Jr. *The American Indian in Western Legal Thought: The Discourses of Conquest.* New York: Oxford University Press, 1990.

Wilmer, Franke. *The Indigenous Voice in World Politics.* Newbury Park, Cal.: Sage Publications, 1993.

Wrend, Julie, and Clay Smith, eds. *American Indian Law Deskbook.* Niwot, Colo.: University Press of Colorado, 1993.

Wunder, John R. *Retained by the People: A History of American Indians and the Bill of Rights.* New York: Oxford University Press, 1994.

Index